KV-638-505

Constellation Caliban
Figurations of a Character

Edited by
Nadia Lie & Theo D'haen

.1121388
LIBRARY
ACC. No.
01017706
DEPT.
CLASS No.
822.33 G4 LIE
WITHDRAWN
UNIVERSITY
COLLEGE CHESTER

Rodopi
Amsterdam - Atlanta, GA
1997

Coverdesign: Hendrik van Delft
Illustration: Woodcut after Pieter Breughel (fragment)

ISBN: 90-420-0244-1 (bound)
ISBN: 90-420-0238-7 (paper)
© Editions Rodopi B.V., Amsterdam - Atlanta, GA 1997
Printed in The Netherlands

Accession no.
01017706

University of **HESTER CAMPUS**
Chester LIBRARY
01244 513301

This book is to be returned on or before the last date stamped below. Overdue charges will be incurred by the late return of books.

CANCELLED

2 APR 2008

1 2 MAY 2008

Series Editors
C.C. Barfoot and Theo D'haen

For I am all the subjects that you have

(Caliban in W. Shakespeare, *The Tempest*, I.ii)

Table of Contents

Preface

In "Calibán," an essay published in the early 1970s, the Cuban critic Roberto Fernández Retamar launched an appeal to consider literature and history not just from the point of view of Prospero, but also from that of Caliban. Twenty years on, Fernández Retamar's appeal was echoed in an essay, "Culture," by the American "New Historian" Stephen Greenblatt. Greenblatt wants to take in not only "the power of Prospero" but likewise "the accents of Caliban." The subsequent publication of two major studies wholly devoted to Caliban – Alden T. Vaughan and Virginia Mason Vaughan's 1991 *Shakespeare's Caliban: A Cultural History* and the 1992 *Caliban*-volume in the Chelsea House *Major Literary Characters* series – bears out the degree to which literary and cultural studies have taken these appeals seriously. In fact, a whole new discipline seems to have emerged: "Calibanology."

The present volume does not aim to simply add yet another chapter to Calibanology, or the history of "Caliban's eventful odyssey from Shakespeare's time to the present" (Vaughan and Vaughan 1991: ix). True, some authors dealt with in our volume's various contributions here for the first time receive serious attention, at least in English, as far as their involvement with Caliban is concerned: Ponce, Zweig, Guéhenno, Williams. Yet, rather than narrowly focus upon Shakespeare's character itself, we preferred to see Caliban as a cultural icon conveniently allowing for the most varied kinds of research and reflection. Some contributors adhere more strictly to the established terms of the Caliban-debate. Barbara Baert, for instance, pays attention to the iconological precedents of Shakespeare's Caliban, while Kristine Vanden Berghe discusses Aníbal Ponce's representation of the same character, as Maarten van Delden does for José Enrique Rodó. Other contributors start from a discussion of Caliban and then move to wider reflections of a sociological nature, as does Koenraad Geldof, or to a discussion of hermeneutics, as we find Ortwin de Graef doing. Some contributions, such as that of Dirk Delabastita for instance, are of a more general theoretical nature. Others, such as those of Herman Servotte and Hedwig Schwall, stick to close-reading. Still others approach the subject from a predominantly contextual point of view. Such is the case with Philipsen and Verbeeck. A number of the essays here gathered look at specific Caliban-adaptations in terms of their relationship to paradigmatic — often generically so — ways of writing. In this respect, A. James Arnold is concerned with "roots-thinking," Chantal Zabus and Theo D'haen deal with "postmodernist" and "counter-postmodernist" rewritings, and Youngs is interested in science-fiction and the literature of travel. Nadia Lie relates Caliban to postcolonialism, while Paul Franssen and Jürgen Pieters situate him with regard to New Historicism.

Regardless of their diversity, though, a common social discourse underlies all contributions to the present volume. This is a discourse that pays attention to the way in which cultures keep redrawing the boundaries obtaining between centers and margins, between the Self and the Other, but also between writer and critic, between the researcher and his or her object. This is the same discourse that led Harold Bloom to exclaim, not without some irritation, that at present we live "in the Age of Caliban" rather than in "the time of Ariel or of Prospero" (1992: 1). It is this discourse, too, that makes for numerous carry-overs between the various contributions. D'haen and Zabus discuss similar phenomena of rewriting, but obviously differ as to the degree of uniformity with which the center rewrites the margin. Arnold's views on roots-thinking shed a different light on Lie's Retamar. Pieters' dynamic view of the relationship between Prospero and Caliban likewise resonates in Servotte's Auden interpretation. Charles Darwin's ideas are important for De Graef's Browning, but also for Maarten van Delden's Rodó. In a final move, Cedric Barfoot rewrites the social discourse subtending our common enterprise as a poem, completing the circle that initially led us from the creative work of art to scholarly reflection, and which now takes us back into the creative realm. We have chosen not to explicitate this ongoing cross-fertilisation by way of cumbrous footnotes or cross-references. Neither do we feel like steering the reader's interpretation by any specific thematic ordering. We think that the part objective, part arbitrary ordering principle of sheer chronology leaves our reader maximum freedom to continually re-configure the present volume in function of his or her own topical needs or desires.

All together, then, the present volume can be seen as an illustration of an alternative mode of writing cultural history, a mode that perhaps most closely approximates Walter Benjamin's concept of "constellation." Benjamin uses the image of the constellation to clarify his own idea of history as retrospective construction. Though the signs of the zodiac do not really exist, we do "see" them from our particular observational point of view. According to Benjamin, this is analogous to true historical knowledge: what we are concerned with is not the reconstruction of things as they really were, but rather a configuration of past and present that allows for genuine insight. In a similar way, the present volume assembles different figurations of Caliban, in the hope that this will lead to one or more flashes of insight. In other words, we do not aim for a "cultural history" along genealogical reception history lines, but rather for a "constellation Caliban" which might – and would – look differently when observed from another angle, or when a different selection of stars were made, but which is not therefore any less "true".

We would like to thank the following colleagues, all of whom have in one way or another substantially aided us in bringing this project to a successful conclusion: the Staff and Librarians of the Royal institute of Anthropology in Leiden, and particularly Gert Oostindie of the Department of Caribbean Studies for arranging a visiting fellowship which enabled one of the editors to carry out preliminary research crucial to our project, the Staff of the Computer Department of the Faculty of Letters of Leuven University, and particularly Frederik Truyen, without whom camera-ready copy would forever have remained beyond us, Ortwin de Graef, who volunteered a number of valuable suggestions as to the conception and ordering of the present volume, and last but not least all our co-authors, who generously and enthusiastically devoted some of their valuable research time to this project, and who have patiently awaited its publication.

The editors

Caliban's Afterlife

Reading Shakespearean Readings

Dirk Delabastita

The relative brevity of *The Tempest* (little more than half the length of *Hamlet*) has not stopped it from becoming a notoriously problematic play that has engendered a plethora of critical, poetic, theatrical, and other responses. This large body of readings or rewritings of Shakespeare's play turns out to bring the character of Caliban into focus as one of its central interpretive cruxes. Since Frank Kermode's influential Arden edition of the play it has become customary to locate him at, or near "the core of the play" (Kermode 1988 [1954]: xxiv), while as early as 1817 William Hazlitt could make the confident claim that "the character of Caliban is generally thought (and justly so) to be one of the author's masterpieces" (quoted from Palmer 1968: 68).

Unlike most other essays in this volume, the present contribution does not set out to investigate one specific retelling of, or sequel to Caliban's story. My aim is rather to present a few general remarks about the nature and limitations of our interpretation of *The Tempest* in general and Caliban in particular by focusing on a number of salient characteristics of the rich critical and artistic traditions which have clustered around the play. More precisely, I intend to look into a number of interpretive and discursive strategies that have typically been used to enable and justify certain readings of Caliban, hoping that this exercise will also result in a few practical suggestions towards optimizing the systematic and comparative study of such readings. So my analysis is situated on the meta-level insofar as it does not deal, in the first place, with Caliban as such (Shakespeare's or anybody else's). Most examples will be culled from the critical tradition, but it is hoped that the validity of my remarks extends to the various more 'creative' or 'artistic' responses to the play.

The basic storyline of Shakespeare's play is misleadingly straightforward. It tells of a man (Prospero) first so absorbed in his study of the magic arts that he allows his ducal power to be taken from him, and then employing the acquired knowledge to take his dukedom back again from the usurpers. The overall dramatic structure is circular, magic (now fully mastered) being used to recover what had been lost through magic (not yet mastered) in the first place.[1] Once political control is again in Prospero's hands, the expert knowledge whose acquisition had cost its forced surrender is promptly discarded: it is significantly *not* handed down to the next generation. In fact, for all the 'nurture' she received from her father, Miranda – a child when she was banished with Prospero but now a queen-to-be as Ferdinand's prospective wife – seems ill equipped for her future role on the slippery stage of Italian court politics. Her astounding naiveté in the face of moral degradation and cunning policy ("O brave new world") reminds one of the blindness with which Prospero had stumbled into political self-destruction somewhat less than a generation ago. The play's spatial symbolism (*Italy* → *island* → *Italy*) underscores the circularity of the plot: Prospero's misgovernment is paid for by a nearly fatal ordeal at sea, which eventually lands him and his daughter on Caliban's island; another sea-ordeal, this time masterminded by Prospero

---

[1] Jan Kott is among the relatively few critics to insist on the plot's circular quality (1967: 238). E.E. Stoll, on the contrary, is one of those who would contest my presentation: he believes that Shakespeare construes Prospero's downfall as "wholly owing to the machinations of Antonio" (1969: 31). However, not by any stretch of the imagination can one reconcile this assertion of Prospero's innocence with the evidence provided by the play (e.g. lines I.ii.88ff). The present essay is mainly concerned with the way in which interpretations are bound to exploit the vagueness and ambiguities inherent in the play, but this example goes to show that there are, as one would expect, forms of manipulation which are not somehow justified by either text or context.

and intended for his enemies, heralds the change of fortune which will take them back to Italy and restore legitimate political order.

The above plot synopsis is of course grossly incomplete. For example, if the plot's circular movement seems to bring the main players back to square one, there is no denying that much has happened along the way in terms of both power and knowledge, with most characters acting out one or more roles in a very involved power-game and in the process finding out about their true natures, or even transforming their nature. Time takes its toll and forces the circular movement into a cyclic pattern: a new generation, personified by Miranda and Ferdinand, wakes up to their budding sexuality and is preparing a new future, while an older generation of men are having to take stock of their lives or face the consequences of their past actions. Sexuality ties in with this theme of knowledge and self-discovery, but it also has a power-related dimension: "Thou didst prevent me; I had peopled else/ This isle with Calibans" (I.ii.352-53). These and other complications combine with the play's extreme economy of expression to produce "probably the most enigmatic and the most fascinating of Shakespeare's plays" (Delbaere-Garant 1985: 293).

Interpreting Caliban: Intertextuality between History and Anachronism

One way to crack the code of the play is to look into its intertextual dimension in the hope that a knowledge of Shakespeare's sources will somehow reveal a shortcut to the play's meanings and/or the writer's intentions. After all, the classic move of reducing meaning to origin enables the identification of Caliban's alleged source to provide a reassuring symbolical grasp of the character by making his name transparent and matching it by an historically and psychologically consistent substance. Numerous critics have in this way tried to unearth the sources and analogues that Shakespeare may have drawn on consciously or unconsciously in fashioning the fantastic character of Caliban: "of individual characters in *The Tempest*, Caliban and Ariel have understandably provoked the most energetic search for possible prototypes" (Righter 1968: 56). This task has proved far from easy:

> The dramatist's possible sources in history, literature,
> folklore, pageantry, iconography, and allegory are
> immense, and the range of suggested prototypes and
> influences is almost endless.
> (Vaughan & Vaughan 1991: 273-74)

Moreover, owing to the circumstance that *The Tempest* is traditionally
held to be Shakespeare's last play, his earlier work and the other romances
in particular lend themselves to being viewed as a mine of possible
influences too. As E.M.W. Tillyard put it, the play "gains much in lucidity
when supported by the others" (1938: 49).[2] However, besides the sheer
multitude of possible influences, there are three more difficulties which
beset the source criticism variety of Caliban interpretation.

First, Caliban was probably not a replica of some single influence or
model that had come Shakespeare's way, but must have been forged out of
a wide variety of historical and fictional materials. This fact is entirely in
keeping with what we know about Shakespeare's eclectic methods of
composition and it has been widely acknowledged. It is, however, usually
understood as an incentive to step up the search for more, as yet unspotted
sources and all too rarely as a reminder that concepts such as 'influence' or
'model' are really in need of further clarification and should be used with
due caution. In fact, as my second and third points will suggest, alternative
concepts of intertextuality have been advanced, adding extra dimensions to
the question of Caliban's sources and yielding totally different interpretive
results.

A second complicating factor is, indeed, that the traditional notions of
'source' or 'influence' may well be far too reductive. Thus, it has been
argued that texts derive their meaning from the multiple relations they
entertain with an endless variety of other texts to which they are
intimately connected – often contrary to all appearances – by virtue of
their belonging to the same discursive network. This notion, which goes
back to Michel Foucault, designates a field of textual practices defined by a

---

[2] This approach is exemplified e.g. by G. Wilson Knight (1968). See also the rather
superficial discussion by Vaughan & Vaughan in their otherwise admirable book
(1991: 83-85).

common agreement about what is thinkable and sayable in certain communicative situations in a speech community. The overall function of such a discursive network is to reflect and uphold the ideology of its participants. Any text can in this way be seen as a kind of space where such 'fields' or 'discourses' manifest themselves, often meeting and intersecting. Even a 'traditional' critic like Philip Brockbank has no difficulty recognizing the play's multiple voices:

> In relation to its immediate sources it touches the colonizing enterprise of Shakespeare's England. In relation to one strain of dramatic tradition it is a morality, about the cure of evil and the forgiveness of sin; in relation to another, it is a pastoral entertainment, fit to celebrate the fertility and order of nature; and it owes to the masque its felicitous handling of illusion, spell, and rite. In relation to Shakespeare's own art, it seems to recollect much that has gone before, and to shadow forth [...]·the playwright's role in the theatres of fantasy and reality. (Brockbank 1966: 184)

The notion of discourse has wider implications than the well-known genre classifications alluded to by Brockbank, but the citation nevertheless makes it clear that for those who adopt this way of thinking the notion of intertextuality goes way beyond the spotting of individual sources. Such a reading of *The Tempest* is advocated by Barker and Hulme (1985: 196):

> Intertextuality, or con-textualization, differs most importantly from source criticism when it establishes the necessity of reading *The Tempest* alongside congruent texts, irrespective of Shakespeare's putative knowledge of them, and when it holds that such congruency will become apparent from the constitution of discursive networks to be traced independently of authorial 'intentionality.'

For example, Paul Brown (1985) attempts a contextual or intertextual interpretation of *The Tempest* and finds that Caliban's status as a 'savage' derives largely from a body of colonialist discourse which reflects

Elizabethan-Jacobean concerns with civility/incivility, order/disorder, and control/masterlessness not only in the newly discovered and charmingly exotic American territories, but, much more surprisingly, also in the troublesome Irish province closer to home. In a similar vein, Terence Hawkes suggests that the roots of the Prospero-Caliban relationship find "their true nourishment in the ancient home-grown European relationships of master and servant, landlord and tenant" (Hawkes 1986: 3) and cannot be divorced from the discursive field of the enclosure movement which was in full swing in Shakespeare's very own Warwickshire during the period of the play's composition.

If intertextuality operates so imperceptibly and so much beyond the individual writer's conscious control as it seems to have done in the cases just referred to, one wonders how its effect on text production and interpretation could ever be bridled by anybody. One pressing problem that follows from this is whether the later reader or rewriter of *The Tempest*, including the historian of Caliban interpretations, can avoid inscribing the 'original' Shakespearean text in the discursive networks *of his/her own period*. In more traditional terms, are later readings/rewritings of Caliban doomed to be anachronistic? This is a third problem that needs looking into.

Indeed, if it is reasonable to assume that sources or models are chronologically and logically prior to the texts that undergo the influence, several intertextually based readings of Caliban strike one as having a distinct anachronistic ring. For example, Caliban has been perceived as an image of Darwin's missing link, as the Freudian Id, as a noble savage, as an omen of the African slave-trade, and so on. One feels tempted to argue that Shakespearean scholars can in all safety dismiss such readings insofar as they do not intend, or do not manage, to elucidate the Shakespearean *Tempest*, but merely appropriate Shakespeare's early-seventeenth century text to explore or articulate the individual sensibility of the latter-day rewriter or the more collective preoccupations of his or her culture. Caliban then becomes a mere emblem of the interpreter's own situation.[3]

---

[3] It is somewhat surprising (at first sight) and therefore all the more symptomatic (on further reflection) that an anachronistic slant may prove hard to avoid even in the attempts of 'New Historicists' like Barker & Hulme (1985), Brown (1985),

However, an overhasty rejection of anachronistic readings of Caliban risks missing one important point. Such readings are based on some perceived *analogy* between Shakespeare's and the later rewriter's respective universes (cf. Jan Kott's 'Shakespeare our Contemporary') and this in turn presupposes an interpretation of the original which, while perhaps being selective, may well have historical pertinence. This point is also made by Stephen Orgel in his discussion of the 1970 Jonathan Miller production of *The Tempest* at the Mermaid, where the author points out that the historical analogy (in this case, with modern colonialism) need certainly not be an impediment to a clear-sighted perception of the complexity of Shakespeare's play (Orgel 1987: 83, 85). Such cross-historical analogies which unfold the play's prophetic quality in a retrospective manner could be justified by invoking some allegedly universal archetype or *condition humaine*, but they can also – perhaps more fruitfully – be understood in the historical terms of some specific configuration of socio-economic, political, linguistic, etc. factors common to Shakespeare's situation and that of his later audience.

At any rate, the wide range of intertextually determined readings of Caliban presses home the age-old hermeneutic difficulty of distinguishing between an historical understanding of a text and the text's appropriation for the sake of self-expression and self-understanding. Some would say that these two kinds of reading are legitimate in their own right, but fulfil essentially different functions in society and accordingly belong to different fields of cultural production. A well-established distinction allots the strictly historical position to 'academic' or 'scholarly' criticism, whereas the various 'artistic' responses are given licence to adapt the historical text to esthetic or other ends which are quite extrinsic to the reality of early Jacobean England. But this distinction merely rephrases the original problem without solving it. After all, as the well-known argument

---

Hawkes (1986), and others to correct the New Critical blindness to history and politics. Witness the argument of Meredith Anne Skura that this recent criticism "not only flattens the text into the mold of colonialist discourse and eliminates what is characteristically "Shakespearean" in order to foreground what is 'colonialist,' but it is also – paradoxically – in danger of taking the play further from the particular historical situation in England in 1611 even as it brings it closer to what we mean by 'colonialism' today" (quoted from Bloom 1992: 224).

goes, it is precisely in their pretence of 'objectivity' that scholarly critics
may most clearly show their involvement in contemporary ideology and
politics. Conversely, one may recall the example of W.H. Auden's poetic
meditations in *The Sea and the Mirror*, to which several 'academic' critics
writing on *The Tempest* in the wake of Frank Kermode (1988: lxii) have
ascribed full critical authority. In other words, if one may be tempted to
go along with Anne Righter's view that *The Tempest* is "an extra-ordinarily
obliging work of art" which has tended to encourage criticism of the kind
that is "illuminating in itself, as a structure of ideas, without shedding
much light on its ostensible object" (Righter 1968: 22), one will also feel
that the author's all too confident division between the criticism that
merely illuminates itself and that which illuminates its object calls for
qualification. Interestingly enough, in the references section of her edition,
she argues that "the best criticism of *The Tempest* [...] tends to take the
form of derivative creation by other dramatists or poets" and again
Auden's *The Sea and the Mirror* is singled out as being "particularly
valuable for its insights into the play" (53).

Interpreting Caliban: a Maze of Intratextual Relationships

The Tempest is like an acoustic chamber where other texts and discourses
can be heard reverberating, perhaps also texts originating from the later
reader's culture. But the play also generates its own internal echoes (Kott
1967: 245; Brower 1968: 153; Palmer 1968: 16; etc.) and a study of these
places Caliban back where Shakespeare originally gave him the spark of
life, that is, in the narrative and dramatic structures of the play. The
specialists of narratology and of the semiotics of theatre and drama have
emphasized the need to view characters as the cumulative effect of a
multitude of textual relationships. Along the same lines, H.C. Sherwood
has argued that it is wiser

> in discussing the significance of Caliban, or any other
> Shakespearean character for that matter, to ask in what
> ways this figure serves the design of the play as a whole
> and to recognize that to extract him from his dramatic
> environment, as though he had an independent existence,

may lead to a distorted view of him.
(Sherwood 1973: 62-63)

Thus, if the master-slave relationship and the dynamic of repression, submission, and rebellion are crucial to the character of Caliban, it goes without saying that the constitution of Caliban will be affected – indirectly but nonetheless substantially – by the other characters in Caliban's habitat who find themselves trapped or enthroned in comparable power relations. To give a classic example, whatever one makes of it, the play clearly prompts a comparison between the subplot of Caliban's (and Stephano's and Trinculo's) conspiracy against Prospero and that of Antonio and Sebastian against Alonso.

A second example of a suggested analogy I could quote here is one which has found fewer adherents in the critical tradition: Prospero's efforts to recover the dukedom which is legitimately his from the usurper Antonio are mirrored by Caliban's attempts to recover his native island from its usurper, Prospero. In our present age of political correctness this view looks perfectly acceptable to many – which is indeed why some (e.g. Clark 1986: 51) now find it necessary to challenge it – but generations of critics have simply ignored this possible reading, in the best of cases making a grudging admission that there may be a kind of moral justice in the fact that at the end of the play Caliban is again the master of his island. To be fair to those critics, it needs pointing out that Prospero's version of the story of his settlement on the island remains "systematically silent about Prospero's own act of usurpation: a silence which is curious, given his otherwise voluble preoccupation with the theme of legitimacy" (Barker & Hulme 1985: 200). But then, one is left wondering why the critics in question have so confidently trusted Prospero's version to be authoritative and representative of Shakespeare's views. Can these readers be accused of symbolical complicity in Prospero's colonialist policies?

As this second example may suggest, 'intrinsic' readings looking for a definition of Caliban in the play's analogies and internal patterning are not without problems either. For a start, the maze of differential relationships connecting characters and situations in *The Tempest* happens to be so dense and elaborate that the hope of an exhaustive description must remain a chimera. All the same, if the objective of a complete inventory is abandoned, this will be at the cost of risking interpretive bias and distortion. Another snag is that there is no foolproof criterion for knowing when difference underscores similarity, and when similarity serves to highlight difference. The best example of this kind of dilemma may be that of Caliban's mother, Sycorax, and her very ambivalent relationship with Prospero. There are several striking biographical similarities between the two: both are or were magician, master of Ariel, parent of a child of the opposite sex, and ruler of the island after having been exiled from home. Interestingly, most critics have either ignored these shared traits or made them subservient to whatever is seen to differentiate the characters. Thus, Frank Kermode sums up their relationship in terms of the simple opposition between Sycorax's black magic and Prospero's white magic, Caliban's deformity being the result of his mother's evil magic and communion with the devil (Kermode 1988: xl-xli). In several more recent readings, however, any differences are backgrounded to show the similarities to advantage:

> On the surface, Prospero and Sycorax are antitheses; even posthumously, they are inveterate enemies. But as the play progresses, the similarities between the two sorcerors grow increasingly marked. [...] And late in the play, the identification of the two in Shakespeare's mind becomes strikingly manifest: Prospero, celebrating and renouncing his magic in a great set piece, does so with a speech of Ovid's Medea (5.1.33 ff.). (Orgel 1987: 20)

The issue is not, clearly, whether the differences outnumber the similarities or the other way round, but rather which traits are regarded as mere *accidentals* (cf. Stephen Orgel's "on the surface") and which ones as *essentials* ("identification [...] in Shakespeare's mind"). Decisions are made in a weighing exercise, not a counting contest. If the differences are construed as accidentals, they will either be ignored or be made to paradoxically accentuate the similarities, and vice versa. This explains why in the following example the comparison of Caliban and Ariel can be driven to its somewhat unexpected conclusion without offending our sense of logic:

> Unlike and contrasted as they are, they have, as the simple denizens of earth and air, some traits in common: an aversion to labor and a longing for liberty; a primitive sense of humor and a fondness for tricks and pranks; a childish pleasure in tastes and sounds, sights and lights; a spontaneous and unsophisticated love of nature; and (deeper within them) a fear of a higher power, on the one hand, and a craving for affection and approbation, on the other. *Thus the contrast between them is heightened.*
> (Stoll 1969: 27; emphasis added)

The heart of the matter is of course that our very perception of similarities and dissimilarities rests on an interpretive act and is therefore bound to be selective insofar as it requires a standard or *tertium comparationis* which cannot but reflect the interpreter's and his/her culture's frame of reference.

A clear example of these difficulties is found in an early, but still worthwile specimen of 'intrinsic' interpretation, viz. Allan H. Gilbert's article "*The Tempest*: Parallelism in Characters and Situations" from 1915. The author presents an array of analogies between characters and dramatic situations and then proceeds to argue that these constitute a "daring and effective [...] device for the clear presentation of character" (73) and are important "in bringing out some of the truths embodied in the drama" (72). Very much to the satisfaction of the writer's sense of artistic decorum and moral justice, all analogies perceived by Gilbert indeed point in the same direction to converge in the revelation of the play's ultimate truth.[4] Needless to say, Gilbert's parallelisms of character have been selected to exclude any 'discordant' analogies and in this way achieve the sought-for harmony. The above-mentioned analogy which points to Prospero as the

---

[4] Reuben Brower produces different results with a similar reading method: "So viewed, Shakespeare's analogies may perhaps seem too much like exploding nebulae in an expanding though hardly ordered universe. But Shakespeare does not 'multiply variety in a wilderness of mirrors'; he makes use of a few fairly constant analogies that can be traced through expressions sometimes the same and sometimes extraordinarily varied. And the recurrent analogies (or continuities) are linked through a key metaphor into a single metaphorical design." (Brower 1968: 154)

usurper of the island is predictably one of those symmetries to be swept under the carpet.

Moreover, the satisfying convergence of all analogies perceived by Gilbert depends entirely on the writer's moralistic axiom: "The parallels of the play emphasize the contrasts of the characters in virtue while bringing out their truth to type" (74). This produces a clear bias in the recognition of similarities and dissimilarities. Thus, the fact that the notions of power and domination are only faintly present in Gilbert's *tertium comparationis* inevitably shapes his understanding of what he appears to view as the play's most powerful contrapuntal effect, i.e. the contrast between Miranda and Caliban. Against a background of accidental likenesses ("Both have been brought up on the island without knowledge of the ways of the world, and both have been pupils of Prospero," 71), the fundamental difference between the two must lie in the "devilish nature of Caliban, appealed to only by stripes" and incapable of taking "impress of virtue" (71). Many would believe that the actual circumstances of Prospero's educative project with Caliban go some way towards explaining its failure. After all, perhaps one cannot expect much goodwill or smooth progress from one "which first was [his] own King" (I.ii.344) and now finds himself reduced to a pupil by a newcomer who not only takes possession of the island but also imposes new ways of thinking expressed in an alien tongue. Gilbert's moralistic slant typically precludes such 'political' considerations from becoming part of the equation: his reading is geared to demonstrate that the play vindicates the existence of a certain moral order ("the best of civilized wisdom [...] the perfect natural life," 74) exemplified by Miranda ("this Eve of an enchanted paradise"). Significantly, then, the mechanism of 'closure' ('occlusion', 'erasure') seems to be at work in a reading which purports to embrace all the text's dramatic and narrative possibilities.

In spite of the difficulties just discussed, the study of the complex play of difference and similarity in terms of character and plot opens up interesting critical avenues. Especially for those investigating the critical, theatrical, etc. afterlife of Caliban, it seems particularly helpful to be aware of possible similarities and contrasts overtly or more latently present in the play, but perhaps ignored by the later rewriter. Every version of Caliban can in this way be read as a selection from a wide range of possible Calibans which are to a greater or smaller extent compatible with the complex plot structure of Shakespeare's play. This plot structure would have to be conceived of as a network of possibilities afforded by Shakespeare's text. As Stephen Orgel has put it:

> [All] interpretations are essentially arbitrary, and Shakespearian texts are by nature open, offering the director or critic only a range of possibilities. It is performances and interpretations that are closed, in the sense that they select from and limit the possibilities the text offers in the interests of producing a coherent reading. (Orgel 1987: 12)

Historically speaking, the text of *The Tempest* which has come down to us and which is based on the 1623 First Folio edition has to be regarded as a script and therefore an essentially incomplete text with the superstructure of the performance missing. Every single staging of the play – including the performances by Shakespeare's own troupe – accordingly has the status of an interpretation, too. Quite apart from the question of textual variants, there is no reason to suppose that every early-seventeenth-century performance realized the script's theatrical potential in the same manner. Neither Shakespeare himself nor his contemporary audiences could have been aware of all the potential analogies and ambiguities contained in the text. To claim the contrary would be to underestimate the pervasive power of ideology: ideologies make one think about reality *in terms of* certain pre-established notions so that one lacks the critical distance needed to think *about* those notions. Therefore, while sharing Stephen Orgel's relativistic outlook, I beg to differ with his implicit suggestion that all the contradictions of the play's critical history can be ascribed to, and are magisterially checked by the Bard's authorial control:

> Caliban has been an ineducable brute, a sensitive savage, a European wild man, a New-World native, ugly, attractive, tragic, pathetic, comic, frightening, the rightful owner of the island, a natural slave. The question of correctness is not the issue in these readings; the play will provide at least some evidence for all of them, and its critical history is a good index to the ambivalences and ambiguities of the text. Historical arguments

> claiming to demonstrate that Shakespeare could not have
> intended Prospero to be seen as unattractive or Caliban
> as sympathetic are denying to the Renaissance's greatest
> playwright precisely that complexity of sensibility which
> is what we have come to value most in Shakespearian
> drama, and in Renaissance culture as a whole.
> (Orgel 1987: 11)

Without wanting to take away from Shakespeare's unique sensibility, I
believe we do him too much credit by assuming that he was consistently
on top of his complex material. In a later passage of his introduction to the
play, Orgel gives what is probably a more realistic assessment when
commenting on Peter Brook's 1968 production of *The Tempest*:

> it is designed to bring into the theatre a recognition of
> how powerfully subversive much of the play's energy is,
> how incompletely it controls its ambivalences and
> resolves its conflicts. (Orgel 1987: 87)

An exhaustive or definitive description of this network of the play's
potentialities is surely beyond mine, or anyone's grasp, but the working
hypothesis of its existence has considerable heuristic value. This is what I
would like to demonstrate starting from a simple example. In spite of its
claimed status as a mere descriptive tool, the diagram reproduced below
amounts to a partial interpretation of the play in its own right, and maybe
a debatable one at that. Yet, as a structured field of semantic possibilities it
is certainly helpful in mapping and comparing readings of Caliban, as well
as of the other characters in the play:

	NATURE	CULTURE
COMMUNION	hospitality, generosity fertility, vitality harmony with bountiful nature *life-giving*	moral sensibility proper regulation of passion education *order, self-control*
	chaos, savagery coarseness animal lewdness	*life-taking* corruption ambition
ISOLATION	stupidity	cold calculation

It goes without saying that critics have almost unanimously described Caliban in terms of one, or both, of the two Nature boxes of the diagram, even though in his dealings with Stephano and Trinculo he appears to be vulnerable to 'civilized' vices as well. But the 'semiotic square' permits a more refined comparison of different versions of Caliban by raising the question whether Caliban is trapped in a single category, or is allowed to partake of different ones and/or to undergo a transformation in the course of the play. In terms of narratological analysis this double question can be rephrased as follows: Is Caliban a simple or a complex character, and is he a static or a dynamic character? A key fragment in *The Tempest* inspiring speculation about this second question occurs at the end of the play:

> PROSPERO: [...] Go, sirrah, to my cell;
> Take with you your companions; as you look
> To have my pardon, trim it handsomely.
> CALIBAN: Ay, that I will; and I'll be wise hereafter,
> And seek for grace. What a thrice-double ass
> Was I, to take this drunkard for a god,
> And worship this dull fool! (V.1.291-97)

Few critics would go along with Jan Kott's view that Caliban is the only character in the play to change (Kott 1967: 270), but many have effectively construed the quoted excerpt as evidence that Caliban is, after all, capable of redemption or nurture:

> In renouncing his folly he has advanced in wisdom [...]
> His use of the word *grace* is of particular interest with its
> religious overtones, as though his consciousness is
> stretched to glimpse something of the mercy and
> magnanimity that govern the last scene.
> (Sherwood 1973: 34)

However, if such a conclusion happens to clash with the critic's scheme of
values, the easiest solution is to simply ignore the fragment in question.
Another strategy is to acknowledge the fragment but take a slight view of
its importance. Bonamy Dobrée, for example, is one of those who claim
that Caliban cannot be regenerated:

> True, he says at the end, when ordered to tidy up
> Prospero's bedroom, – "I will be wise hereafter and seek
> for grace" – because he realizes he was a fool to follow a
> god with a bottle. We are not impressed.
> (Dobrée 1969: 51)

Similarly, according to Clifford Leech, "Caliban will 'sue for grace'
because Prospero is more imposing in his ducal robes, as well as evidently
more powerful, than the drunken Stephano in his borrowed finery" (1958:
26). The mid-eighteenth century critic Joseph Warton acknowledges the
passage and its likely or possible implications, but not without taking
Shakespeare to task, however gently, for what he regards as an esthetic
flaw:

> I always lament that our author has not preserved this
> fierce and implacable spirit in Calyban, to the end of the
> play; instead of which, he has, I think, injudiciously put
> into his mouth, words that imply repentance and
> understanding. (Warton 1968 [1753]: 44)

Is Caliban's professed change of heart genuine and does it add to the
substance of the character, or is it just another confirmation of his
unregenerate stupidity and slavishness? The evidence offered by the play is
flimsy and it is the interpreter's emphasis that tips the balance one way or
another.

Interpreting Caliban: Text, Intertextuality, and the Caliban-Watcher

If the construction of a model of possible text-bound readings of Caliban can be said to have a certain heuristic value, this will manifest itself most clearly when one proceeds to *correlate* the range of intrinsic readings with the range of intertextual readings. After all, the clear separation of the 'intrinsic' and 'extrinsic' study of literature which used to determine the make-up of literary studies as a discipline has long been shown to be spurious. Thus, a certain interpretation of the play's plot and characters will invite certain intertextual references and preclude others and, conversely, if *The Tempest* is read in the light of some particular text or discourse, this is likely to favour the appreciation of certain intratextual patterns and to relegate others to the reader's or rewriter's blind spot. The historian of Caliban's manifold re-interpretations can gain much from studying precisely this interdependence.

It seems fair to assume that in every reading act intratextual and intertextual evidence are carefully selected, if not necessarily in a conscious way, and balanced against each other in what is undoubtedly an extremely complicated negotiating process. Critics are often found to generally favour one type of evidence over the other, i.e. textual as opposed to contextual/intertextual. Thus, Barker & Hulme (1985) argue that most traditional criticism is inadequate insofar as it is based on the assumption that "single texts are the ultimate objects of study and the principal units of meaning" (196). They regret that intertextuality, if it is not overlooked altogether, is all too often understood in terms of singular sources that are used to either underpin the critic's overall interpretation by conferring a sense of historical justification on it, or to explain away individual features that cannot otherwise be made to fit the interpretation. E.E. Stoll, for one, is quite adamant that "*The Tempest*, like every other Shakespearean or popular Elizabethan drama, stands like a tub on its own bottom, is a story in its own right and for its own sake" (Stoll 1969: 25). As far as Caliban is concerned, this critical opinion really continues a line of argument stretching all the way back to Dryden which holds that Caliban delivers such extravagance and fascination that he cannot be extracted from the play and reduced to some extraneous model, source, or influence. Indeed, it will be remembered that Dryden mentions Caliban as a "species of himself," explicable in genetic terms only by "the copiousness of

[Shakespeare's] invention" in a way which leads Dryden to use the word 'create' for the first time in a literary sense (Smith 1969: 5). But then, in recent years, as was explained above, new ways of thinking about discourse and intertextuality have arisen, provoking a cross-current against this prevailing emphasis on Caliban's text-based unicity.

The correlation between the intratextual and the intertextual materials that go into an interpretation is one important parameter that determines overall reading strategies, but the complex process of weighing one type against the other can of course also be observed in readings of individual passages. The following example is one of many I could quote to show how this negotiating process is conducted differently by a number of critics and accordingly leads to a radically different outcome. What is at stake here is Caliban's sensitivity to music, expressed most famously in his widely quoted "this isle is full of noises" speech (III.ii.133-41). Interestingly, this speech has been regarded as a measure of Caliban's humanity by some, and as proof of his essential bestiality by others. These contradictory interpretations are of course part of a wider interpretative logic, but my aim is merely to indicate how different kinds of evidence have been resorted to by their respective adherents. To the twentieth-century mind the appreciation of music would count as a higher feeling found essentially in humans, but those wishing to stress Caliban's coarseness or subhuman nature have found a very powerful intertextually based argument in the fact that "the ability to respond to music was then thought to be an attribute to beasts which lacked reason" (Clark 1986: 58), so that Caliban's fondness for the island's music does more to range him with the animal kingdom than to indicate the presence of a higher nature. G. Wilson Knight (1968: 139) makes essentially the same observation, as does Frank Kermode, who refers to Horace's *De Arte Poetica* as a classical analogy for the Elizabethan popular belief in question (1988: xlii).

I found only one case of a critic enlisting intratextual information in order to hold Caliban's susceptibility to music against him, namely the Allan H. Gilbert article from 1915 referred to above. In his comparison of Ferdinand and Caliban the author discovers important differences between their respective comments on the mysterious noises of the island (cf. lines I.ii.390ff for Ferdinand and the above-mentioned speech for Caliban):

> Caliban's speech on the noises of the island is more impressive than that of Ferdinand on the mysterious music of Ariel, partly because that of Ferdinand is more conventional; but this very conventionality makes it more fitting to the character of the prince. Ferdinand talks of *music*, and the savage Caliban contrasts himself with him by speaking of *noises*. (Gilbert 1915: 73; Gilbert's emphasis)

As I will go on to suggest below, the widely accepted fact that the poetry of Caliban's speech is more powerful than that of Ferdinand is often seized on by those wishing to construe the music-charmed Caliban as a man capable of finer human sentiments, but from Gilbert's perspective it is bound to be an embarassment. In the first half of the above quotation he tries to talk himself out of it, but he will of course convince only those who admit to being bored by the conventionality of the language of Hamlet, Hal or any other of Ferdinand's princely likes in Shakespeare. For the rest, Gilbert's argument rests on selective quoting as much as on selective reading. Caliban does not really speak of "noises" only, but of "noises,/ Sounds and sweet airs, that give delight" (III.ii.133-34) and these emanate from such eminently musical sources as "instruments" and "voices." Incidentally, Caliban's phrase "sweet airs" is a literal echo of Ferdinand's speech, while Ferdinand also speaks of "sounds." And if music induces sleep in Caliban, it has a rather similar therapeutic effect on Ferdinand by allaying his passion. In short, the music's effect on the two characters is not all that different and neither is their respective poetic phraseology.

It is generally the critics who somehow stand up for Caliban as a music lover who resort to intratextual analysis. Accordingly, they either ignore the above-mentioned Elizabethan lore about music's effect on lower beings, or they believe that its relevance in the given context is outbalanced by the exquisite lyricism of Caliban's poetic speech, which gives an iconic dimension to the description of the island's sweet airs by being so musical itself. For example, Echeruo (1980: 80) draws attention to the sheer textuality of Caliban's speech by describing it as

> a marvellous evocation of a truly enchanted island. It is
> worth noting that Caliban curses only when he is
> speaking to or about Prospero.

The critic's afterthought in the quotation usefully reminds us that his reading of the passage is part of a larger interpretive design which involves, among other things, raising Caliban above the animal primitivism often attributed to him and showing him to be no less a victim than a perpetrator. The ecstatic poetic vein of Caliban's language is here assumed to dispel any intertextually inspired thoughts of a superficial, purely sensuous response to music such as one might have expected from the most primitive creatures, and it endows Caliban's speech with "a quality that approaches the mystical" (Sherwood 1973: 33). Not surprisingly, critics holding a low opinion of Caliban have been bothered by such possible inferences, and at least one found that "this speech *sometimes seemed to [him]* to be *a little* out of character" (Stoll 1969: 29; emphasis added). As in the Joseph Warton quotation above, the danger of inconsistency in the critic's interpretation is here averted by masking the problematic feature as an unfortunate lapse of artistic control on Shakespeare's part, with the cautious formulation (see the accumulation of hedges in the italicized part!) serving to forestall any possible reproach of critical presumptuousness. Incidentally, Caliban has a habit of speaking in verse in other passages too in contrast to the prose used by his comrades and generally reserved by Shakespeare for less dignified characters. This has not escaped the attention of critics from Schlegel onwards and again certain critics have had to be inventive to explain this away, but their strategies will have to be passed over.

Anyway, the reading of Caliban's speech on the island's sweet airs rests on a selection of 'relevant' evidence, which can either be of an intertextual (contextual, encyclopaedic) nature, or be derived from the text's internal structure. In either case, the selection is not only based on an assessment of the argument's intrinsic merit, but informed by its subservience to a wider interpretive design, which is in its turn likely to be biased by the interpreter's poetics and ideology. Discussing this last point would take us beyond the description of interpretive strategies into the minefield of historical explanation, but attempting that would require a much longer essay.

References

Barker, Francis and Peter Hulme. 1985. "Nymphs and Reapers Heavily Vanish. The Discursive Con-texts of *The Tempest.*" In John Drakakis, ed. *Alternative Shakespeares.* London/New York: Methuen, 191-205.

Bloom, Harold, ed. 1992. *Caliban (Major Literary Characters).* New York/Philadelphia: Chelsea House.

Brockbank, Philip. 1966. "*The Tempest:* Conventions of Art and Empire." In *Later Shakespeare.* Stratford-upon-Avon Studies 8. London: Edward Arnold, 183-202.

Brower, Reuben A. 1968. "The Mirror of Analogy" [1951]. In Palmer 1968: 153-75.

Brown, Paul. 1985. "'This Thing of Darkness I Acknowledge Mine.' *The Tempest* and the Discourse of Colonialism." In Dollimore and Sinfield 1985: 48-71.

Clark, Sandra. 1986. *Shakespeare. The Tempest.* Harmondsworth: Penguin.

Delbaere-Garant, Jeanne. 1985. "Prospero To-day. Magus, Monster or Patriarch." In G. Debusscher and J.P. van Noppen, eds. *Communiquer et traduire. Hommages à Jean Dierickx.* Bruxelles: Editions de l'Université de Bruxelles, 293-302.

Dobrée, Bonamy. 1969. "The Tempest" [1952]. In Smith 1969: 47-59.

Dollimore, Jonathan and Alan Sinfield, eds. 1985. *Political Shakespeare. New Essays in Cultural Materialism.* Manchester: Manchester UP.

Echeruo, Michael J.C., ed. 1980. *William Shakespeare. The Tempest.* London: Longman.

Gilbert, Allan H. 1915. "*The Tempest.* Parallelism in Characters and Situations." *Journal of English and Germanic Philology* 14: 63-74.

Hawkes, Terence. 1986. "Playhouse-Workhouse." In *That Shakespeherian Rag. Essays on a Critical Process.* London/New York: Methuen, 1-26.

Kermode, Frank, ed. 1988. *The Arden Edition of the Works of William Shakespeare. The Tempest* [1954]. London/New York: Routledge.

Knight, G. Wilson. 1968. "The Shakespearian Superman [1947]." In Palmer 1968: 130-52.

Kott, Jan. 1967. *Shakespeare our Contemporary*. Second edition. London: Methuen.

Leech, Clifford. 1958. "The Structure of the Last Plays." In *Shakespeare Survey* 11. Cambridge: Cambridge UP, 19-30.

Orgel, Stephen, ed. 1987. *The Tempest*. Oxford/New York: Oxford UP.

Palmer, David J., ed. 1968. *Shakespeare. The Tempest. A Casebook*. London/Basingstoke: Macmillan.

—, ed. 1971. *Shakespeare's Later Comedies. An Anthology of Modern Criticism*. Harmondsworth: Penguin.

Righter, Anne, ed. 1968. *The Tempest. New Penguin Shakespeare*. Harmondsworth: Penguin.

Sherwood, H.C. 1973. *The Tempest (W. Shakespeare)*. Oxford: Basil Blackwell.

Skura, Meredith Anne. 1989. "The Case of Colonialism in *The Tempest*." In *Shakespeare Quarterly* 40 (1): 42-69. Reprinted in Bloom 1992: 221-48.

Smith, Halleth, ed. 1969. *Twenthieth Century Interpretations of The Tempest. A Collection of Critical Essays*. Englewood Cliffs, N.J.: Prentice-Hall.

Stoll, Elmer Edgar. 1969. "The Tempest" [1940]. In Smith 1969: 25-33.

Tillyard, E.M.W. 1938. *Shakespeare's Last Plays*. London: Chatto and Windus.

Vaughan, Alden T. and Virginia Mason Vaughan. 1991. *Shakespeare's Caliban. A Cultural History*. Cambridge: Cambridge UP.

A Muddy Mirror

Paul Franssen

Along with Shylock the Jew, Shakespeare's Caliban has become a focus of controversy due to political developments in the modern world. [1] Whereas before the present century *The Tempest* was usually read as a timeless allegory of art versus nature, which was often linked to the notion that this play marked Shakespeare's farewell to the stage, most recent interpretations stress the importance of the historical moment of its conception in broader terms, in particular with regard to the early stages of the process of colonization. As a consequence, Caliban has come to be identified as a far from neutral European construction of the racial Other, in particular in the New World. As a result of this paradigm shift, traditional allegorical readings of *The Tempest* in terms of such universal categories as elements, mental faculties, or nature versus civilization have come to seem ahistorical, as they fail to acknowledge the constructedness of such so-called eternal truths, which in the modern view reflect the power relations of early modern society. On the other hand, fashionable interpretations of the play that take into account only its colonial dimension risk overlooking part of the textual evidence, as Meredith Anne Skura (1989) has shown convincingly.

---

[1] I am deeply indebted to my colleague Ton Hoenselaars for his stimulating commentary and practical support during the early stages of writing this essay.

What is needed, therefore, is an approach that harmonizes both the historically specific and the universal aspects of the text. The present essay is no more than a sketch of some elements that might go into such an undertaking, and tries to build on the findings of recent attempts at creating such a fusion, notably the afore-mentioned article by Skura (1989). I will first survey the critical debate of the last few decades, before turning to a discussion of the seemingly deliberate vagueness in the play's text concerning Caliban's provenance and identity. Next, I will show how this indeterminacy is in fact foregrounded by two related universal aspects of the play: the allegorical imagery of elements and microcosm. Both of these can be read as suggesting the constructedness of notions of the Other in general, and of Caliban, the racial or cultural Other, in particular.

Over the last century or so, critical responses to Caliban have almost inevitably been determined by readings of *The Tempest* in the light of the English colonial project. In particular, Caliban has often been seen as the first portrayal of a native American in the English literary canon. As early as 1808, Edmond Malone suggested that some of the so-called Bermuda-pamphlets, which dealt with a spectacular shipwreck, were relevant to *The Tempest* (Kermode 1966: xxvi). Although rival views abounded for much of the nineteenth century, as attested by the survey of Vaughan and Vaughan (1993: 89-117), in the present century the interpretation of *The Tempest* as a whole, and thus also of Caliban, in terms of the colonial experience, particularly with relation to the Caribbean, has become the standard reading. With some qualifications, this seems to be the approach of that most prestigious, and much-maligned, editor of the play, Frank Kermode (1966 [1954]), as well as that of Leo Marx (1981 [1964]). Both see Prospero as an admirable character, the torch-bearer of civilization, who on the whole bears the stamp of authorial approval. Caliban, by contrast, is at least partly the colonial subject, who personifies unredeemed nature, which needs to be tamed by Prospero's art.

More recently, radical critics have seen *The Tempest*, as well as some of its earlier critics and editors, as complicit in the colonial enterprise, and so in need of deconstruction; alternatively, some of them have seen the play as an early example of anti-colonial feeling. This also means that Caliban, who had already replaced Prospero as the thematic centre of the play in Kermode (1966), has become by far the most important character in the play. Roberto Fernández Retamar, for instance, has no hesitations about limiting the setting to the Caribbean and turning Caliban into a symbol of resistance against colonial encroachments (1989: 8-9). Much the same is true for George Lamming (1992). Malcolm Evans has called attention to the journal of Edward Harrison, written during his 1929 visit to British Honduras, in which Harrison identifies Caliban with the oppressed inhabitants of the Caribbean (Evans 1986: 28). Stephen J. Greenblatt, too, has used the play as an example of early contacts between the Old and the New Worlds, concentrating on Caliban's language (1976). Paul Brown looks for aporias in the texture of the play, hoping to show that it "foreground[s] precisely those problems which it works to efface" (1985: 48); those problems are, of course, mainly to do with colonial power relations, or how to keep Caliban in check. On the whole, such approaches to *The Tempest* accept Kermode's premise of Caliban's central importance, while reversing his value judgements. Rather than a noble empire builder bringing the best of Western civilization to a benighted savage, Prospero has come to symbolize the arrogance of British or European cultural and political hegemony (Hulme 1992: 89-134). Conversely, Caliban's role has shifted from the savage that Prospero takes him for to the rebellious victim of western colonial expansion.

Of late, there has been a modest reaction against the nearly exclusive emphasis on the colonial aspects of the play. This has taken a number of forms, mainly a reorientation towards early-modern domestic British politics on the one hand, towards ahistorical psychology on the other. Recent critics who have read the play as at least in part a reflection of internal British politics include Hawkes (1986) and Greenblatt (1988). Skura (1989) goes even further, in arguing convincingly against excessive attention to the colonial context, and substituting a psychological reading which only marginally touches on the colonial. Bernard J. Paris completely disregards the issues of history and geographical setting, and analyses Prospero as a reflection of Shakespeare's own neurotic personality (1989). Even Peter Hulme (1992), while concentrating on the Caribbean context, sees this as only one discourse, which coexists with a Mediterranean element. Jonathan Hart (1996), too, sets out to temper the high seriousness and moral indignation associated with the anti-colonial reading by reconciling this approach with one in terms of the genre of romance, and ends by resurrecting the notion that this play was Shakespeare's farewell to the stage.

This variety of approaches has led to a great confusion over the racial identity of Caliban. He has been taken as an American Indian, but also as a black slave, as an Irishman or Welshman, or as a European "wild man" (Vaughan and Vaughan 1993, *passim*). Yet, this confusion is not entirely due to the wide variety of critical views, but also to inconsistencies within the text itself, which seems to resist attempts at arriving at a unified conception of Caliban. On the surface, there is in fact little textual evidence to connect Prospero's island with the Caribbean or any other part of the New World. The only connection with the Bermudas specifically lies in Ariel's reference to the "still-vexed Bermudas" as a place where he was once sent "at midnight to fetch dew" (I.ii.228-29). If anything, this only proves that Prospero's island is *not* a representation of the Bermudas. Surely, as a spirit Ariel should be as capable of travelling great distances at enormous speed as Puck, who can "put a girdle round about the earth/ In forty minutes" (*MND*, II.i.175-76; Wells and Taylor 1986: 358). Besides, bearing in mind the context, Ariel is trying to impress on Prospero his great services already performed, as a prelude to asking for an early release. For that reason alone, it would make more sense for him to refer to a distant journey he once undertook at Prospero's behest than to a small errand to a neighbouring island. On the other hand, there is a great deal of textual evidence that associates the island with the Old World. Unlike Shakespeare's usual sloppiness, in this late play the geographical indications seem to be quite consistent in placing the island somewhere in the Western Mediterranean. The royal party was travelling back to Naples from the wedding at Tunis, while Prospero came to the island after being put to sea in a leaky boat after his exile from Milan, presumably once again in the Mediterranean. Surely one of the functions of the manifold references to Carthage and Dido throughout II.i is to remind us of Aeneas' voyages throughout this area. Sycorax, Caliban's mother, was a native of Algiers and had been exiled from there, sailors dropping her on this island (I.ii.261-65). This suggests that Caliban himself must be considered as a North-African.

Nevertheless, as Kermode (1966), Hulme (1992), Vaughan and Vaughan (1993), and many others have shown, there are a number of unmistakable allusions to the New World in general, the Caribbean in particular. "Bow-wow," the refrain to Ariel's song "Come unto these yellow sands" (I.ii.381), has been linked with reports of sounds uttered during Indian dances (Kermode 1966: xxxiii). Caliban's god "Setebos" bears the name of a Patagonian deity (Hulme 1992: 107; Vaughan and Vaughan 1993: 38). Caliban's own name is usually explained as an anagram of "Cannibal," a word that was originally linked with the Caribbean in particular (Fernández Retamar 1989: 6; Hulme 1992: 41). Other etymologies have been suggested but are not usually taken seriously; for a survey, see Vaughan and Vaughan (1993: 31-36). Moreover, Trinculo associates Caliban with a "dead Indian" (II.ii.32) and Stephano speaks of "savages and men of Ind" (II.ii.57). In addition, there are resemblances between Prospero's ambiguous relationship with Caliban and the discourse of early-modern colonialism. In particular, Peter Hulme has adduced many parallels, including an intriguing resemblance between Prospero's paradoxical need of Caliban as a provider of food and narratives of early contacts between Europeans and indigenous populations in the New World, in which European technological superiority, consisting mainly in their possession of fire-arms, proved unequal to the task of providing sufficient food. In spite of their seeming omnipotence they had to rely on the natives to give them something to eat (Hulme 1992: 129-30).

As a consequence of the diversity of cultural contexts suggested by the text, Caliban is among the most elusive of Shakespeare's characters. Not only do commentators disagree on whether he should be seen as a European wild man, a Moor, a native American, or an amalgam of all of the above, but even on whether he is human at all; whether he is a complete savage or whether he has some redeeming traits; whether he should be seen as the non-European victim of colonial exploitation or, perhaps, as a member of the English lower orders. Peter Hulme notes that critics are intrigued by Caliban's originality, yet exasperated by the internal inconsistencies in his character, which makes it nearly impossible to visualize him (1992: 107). This problem becomes very acute for those involved with actual productions of *The Tempest*; it is small wonder that Caliban has been played in various non-human costumes, as a fish, dog, lizard, monkey, snake, and tortoise, as well as a racial Other (Suchet 1989: 169).

This sense of Caliban's indeterminacy is not limited to professional critics and theatre makers: to the other characters within the play, Caliban is somewhat of a puzzle, too. Man, monster, fish; perfectible or irredeemable: doubtfully or confidently, they each try to fit him into the straightjacket of their preexistent notions, but this effort inevitably fails. Caliban always seems to defeat their expectations, either by disappointing them or, in fact, by doing better than they had believed possible. Kermode has suggested that Caliban is at the centre of the play's thematic structure, as the "criterion" (1966: li), the yardstick by which several of the other characters are measured; his "function is to illuminate by contrast the world of art, nurture, civility" (xxv). In view of the indeterminacy that surrounds Caliban, - however, this assertion becomes somewhat problematic: if we can ask anything of a criterion, it is that it should be well-defined and unchangeable, which Caliban is not. Instead, as I hope to show in the remainder of this essay, Caliban functions more like a "walking screen for projection," as Skura has put it (1989: 60). Not only for Prospero, but also for several other characters he functions as a dark mirror, in which they see their own desires and anxieties reflected. Greenblatt has spoken of the tendency to turn non-Europeans, in particular American natives, into a "screen onto which Renaissance Europeans, bound by their institutions, project their darkest and yet most compelling fantasies," in other words, the "Freudian id" (1976: 567).

Yet even the metaphor of a projection screen is not entirely satisfactory; in suggesting passivity on the part of Caliban, it smacks of the *tabula rasa* that earlier colonial writers saw in the natives of the New World, while obscuring the tendency not just to interpret but also to treat non-Europeans in accordance with Western preconceptions of what constituted civilization. Greenblatt quotes Peter Martyr, who clearly sees native Americans as passive recipients of our cultural imprint:

> For lyke as rased or vnpaynted tables, are apte to receaue
> what formes soo euer are fyrst drawen theron by the
> hande of the paynter, euen soo these naked and simple
> people, doo soon receaue the customes of owre Religion,

and by conuersation with owre men, shake of theyr
fierce and natiue barbarousnes. (Greenblatt 1976: 562)

Caliban, by contrast, does not shake off his "barbarousnes" at all; rather,
in the longer run, he is impervious to all attempts at projecting visions on
him, and shakes off other characters' attempts at making sense (or a
servant) of him in their own terms.

For a truly fitting and indeed historically defensible metaphor for
Caliban's function, we have to turn to the play itself. "Thou earth,"
Prospero calls his rebellious slave (I.ii.314). We have been informed that
this epithet "hints at darkness or dirt, or, more likely, baseness of
character" (Vaughan and Vaughan 1993: 15). This may be Prospero's
immediate meaning, but the word has farther-reaching implications, which
ultimately cast doubt on Prospero's pronouncements on Caliban in
general. Prospero's exclamation forms part of a pattern of imagery of the
elements, in which Caliban is connected to earth, Ariel, as his name
suggests, to the air. Prospero addresses him as: "thou, which art but air"
(V.i.21). Yet Ariel is also associated with the other lighter elements, such
as water (I.ii.191,301), and especially with the purest of the four to be
found on earth, fire (I.ii.191,199-200). That he also does Prospero's
"business in the veins o' the' earth" (I.ii.255) may seem to associate him
with the earth, too, but this may well refer to the operation of
"subterranean waters" (Kermode 1966: 26; Orgel 1994: 115). Ariel is the
precise opposite of Caliban, and it is small wonder that he would not obey
the "earthy and abhorred commands" of Sycorax, Caliban's mother
(I.ii.273).

The connection of both Ariel and Caliban with the opposing elements,
which goes back at least as far as Schlegel (Kermode 1966: lxxxi), is in line
with contemporary Neoplatonic thinking, which held that of the four
elements earth was the grossest, and the most liable to shake off its form
and regress to the primeval chaos of shapeless matter (Panofsky 1972: 132-
35, and Lewis 1974: 62-63). Neoplatonic theories of the four elements are
an obvious frame of reference for discussions of magic; as Geoffrey
Bullough suggests, one of the sources for Prospero's Art may have been
Greene's *Friar Bacon and Friar Bungay*, which contains an extended
discussion between two magicians, along the lines of "alchemical and neo-
Platonic thought," on the merits of spirits of the earth and spirits of fire,

the former being characterized as "gross" and "dull" (Bullough 1975: 252-53). In a Neoplatonic context, the "grossness" and "dullness" of the earth implies that it resists attempts at imposing a Platonic form on it. This same Platonic image of a shape or mould is used later in the same scene in which Prospero calls Caliban "earth," when Miranda says to him: "Abhorred slave,/ Which any *print* of goodness wilt not take" (I.ii.350; emphasis added). In other words, Caliban is like sand on the beach, which we may mould into a particular pattern, such as a sand castle, as long as it is wet; but as soon as the wind dries it, it will fall apart, or otherwise the waves may come and make our pains their prey. So, too, all attempts at making sense of Caliban by pushing him into a preexistent pattern seem to have a limited validity; a change in situation may put Caliban in a wholly new light and undermine previous assessments.

Morally speaking, the elemental opposition between Ariel and Caliban has ambiguous implications as far as Caliban is concerned. On the one hand, it suggests that he is, as Prospero thinks, natural man, unrefined, and untouched by Platonic forms. His elemental make-up in itself suggests that he is "irrational, almost subhuman" while Ariel is "intuitive, superhuman, yet considerably lower than the angels" (Bullough 1975: 258). In such a reading, of course, Prospero's domination over Caliban is a natural one; and it is in such a context that the elemental imagery is usually seen (Vaughan and Vaughan 1993: 82-83; 116-17). On the other hand, in the Neoplatonic view, shapeless matter is not so much immoral as amoral; it is autonomous, obeying the laws of its innate chaos rather than of form. Though we may prefer the refinement of the higher echelons of creation, the lower are not to be condemned. According to Panofsky, for Neoplatonists,

> even matter with its purely negative character cannot be counted as evil [...]. Yet, owing to this negative character matter can, in fact, must, cause evil, for its nothingness acts as a passive resistance to the *summum bonum*: matter tends to remain shapeless and is apt to cast off the forms which have been forced upon it. (Panofsky 1972: 134)

From a similar perspective, Andrew Marvell was willing, some decades later, to give the body its due in its dialogue with the soul (Margoliouth

1952 [1927]: 20-21), a debate that Christine Rees has compared to "a contest between Ariel and Caliban, with Prospero conspicuous by his absence" (1989: 68). For Rees, the result is a draw, although she admits that Augustine would "have found for the body" as the flesh as such is not sinful (1989: 65); it only becomes sinful in so far as the soul misguides it. This is precisely the point made by the body:

> What but a soul could have the wit
> To build me up for sin so fit?
> (Marvell in Margoliouth 1952: 20, ll.40-41)

In other words, Prospero's right to impose his form on Caliban depends on the degree of his own perfection, how close he is to the *summum bonum*. In so far as he is himself imperfect, imposing a pattern on Caliban will be worse than leaving him in his natural state. For a mere human to try and form another Adam from clay may even be considered an act of Pride. As I will try to demonstrate in the following, the patterns that other characters, not only Prospero, try to impose on Caliban throughout the play are not those of perfection, but reflections of their own imperfections. This is most clearly the case with Prospero, to whom Ariel and Caliban function as extensions of his own personality; but he only acknowledges the Caliban inside himself in the final scene of reconciliation.

It is precisely because Caliban is so shapeless that he invites attempts to fit him into some system or discourse or other; yet ultimately he proves resistant to all of these. This can be illustrated by the reactions to Caliban of Prospero, Miranda, and the Neapolitans. Prospero may treat his servant Caliban with great harshness in the play's present, yet in so far as we may believe his words, originally he had seen him as an object of charity, to be educated and taught his language; in Neoplatonic terms, he had attempted to impose a pattern on what he saw as nearly shapeless matter. Yet Prospero's charity was not necessarily as unselfish as it may seem; he may well have seen this as a chance to make up for his failure of control in Milan, when his absorption in his secret studies had made him neglect his rebellious brother; in other words, he projected his previous experiences and failings on to Caliban. When Caliban refused to be patronized and even tried to rape Miranda, however, Prospero's attitude changed, and in the play's present he even goes out of his way to order Ariel to torture him whenever he is disobedient.

Prospero's version of what happened obviously bears some resemblance to the colonial discourse, as it exhibits the same pattern of initial friendship and subsequent betrayal (Hulme 1992: 130-31), and attributes a lawless sexuality to the natives (Kermode 1966: xxxix; cf. Greenblatt 1976: 567). Yet it should not be overlooked that the text presents Prospero's conception of Caliban as largely a construction of his own subconscious fears and desires: desire for control, fear of insurrection and the loss of his daughter to a man – any man. I will come back to the deeper implications of Prospero's concern with his daughter's virginity later in my argument. As Peter Hulme has argued, Prospero actually seems to provoke Caliban's rebellion, which he knows is doomed to fail, as a conscious attempt at exorcising his memories of Antonio's successful *coup d'état* twelve years earlier (1992: 121-23). This suggests once again that Caliban is defined by Prospero's preconceived ideas about a resemblance between his rebellious brother and his ungrateful servant.

When Prospero's masque has to be interrupted because of the imminent arrival of the conspirators, which he had almost forgotten about, Prospero realizes his own vulnerability, associated with the onset of old age – the winter that the masque had been trying to deny (IV.i.114). Once again, he projects his anxiety on his disobedient servant:

> A devil, a born devil, on whose nature
> Nurture can never stick; on whom my pains,
> Humanely taken, all, all, lost, quite lost;
> And as with age his body uglier grows,
> So his mind cankers. (IV.i.188-92)

This assertion, which Kermode seems to take at face value (1966: lv), has been rightly seen as an example of Prospero's tendency to project his own concerns on Caliban (Orgel 1994: 183n). In so far as the play's internal chronology can be taken seriously, Caliban should be about 24 years old, so still fairly young (Orgel 1994: 28n; Vaughan and Vaughan 1993: 9n).

It is not only to Prospero that Caliban has this function of mirroring his darker side, that which he fears most; even Miranda, very much her father's daughter in this respect, can only see him as the horrible monster that has tried to rape her. She of course has good reason to be angry with him, yet her exceptional harshness towards him contrasts with her mercifulness towards all other characters. Her attitude towards the ship in distress is the proper one expected of a heroine, full of compassion:

> O, I have suffered
> With those that I saw suffer: a brave vessel –
> Who had, no doubt, some noble creature in her –
> Dashed all to pieces! O, the cry did knock
> Against my very heart – poor souls, they perished.
> (I.ii.5-9)

Even when her father tells her of the usurpation and the consequent banishment, which might well have ended in both their deaths, her dominant attitude is one of compassion rather than anger or vengefulness: "Alack, for pity!," "Alack what trouble/Was I then to you!" (I.ii.132, 151-52).

Of all the manifold crimes in the play, it is only Caliban's aggressive male sexuality that seems to rouse her to anger:

> Abhorred slave,
> Which any print of goodness wilt not take,
> Being capable of all ill! (I.ii.350-52)

This speech is so uncharacteristic of Miranda that early editors followed Dryden in transferring it to Prospero instead (Kermode 1966: 32n). Obviously, for Miranda, Caliban is the scapegoat on which she projects all her fears of sexuality, which may have been strengthened by her father's repressiveness which she has internalized. Projecting her anxiety on Caliban, and on Caliban alone, leaves her free to pursue Ferdinand with the panache that we have come to expect from Shakespearean heroines, but that must have been perceived as quite unladylike behaviour in the period. She silently challenges her father's authority by seeing Ferdinand behind his back, when she thinks he is "safe," "hard at study" (III.i.19-21), and she even tells Ferdinand her name, against her father's express command (III.i.36-37). Once her fears of sexuality have been exorcised by projecting them on Caliban, she can indulge in the acceptable face of sexual desire, embodied by Ferdinand. Yet Prospero's treatment of Ferdinand constantly underlines the fundamental similarity between him and Caliban: both are made to do the same degrading work, bearing logs, as a sort of penance for their sexual interest in Miranda. By accepting this work willingly, Ferdinand shows his willingness to chasten his desire, and subjugate it to the demands of marriage (Kermode 1966: lvii). His acceptance of the burden of logs stands in marked contrast to Caliban's unwillingness to work, which is of a piece with his reported attempt to ravish Miranda. It is therefore Ferdinand's willingness to face up to his responsibilities rather than the absence of sexual desire that makes him acceptable to Miranda. So to Miranda, too, Caliban is the threatening Other, on whom she projects her fears.

Trinculo and Stephano have a wholly different perception of Caliban, which reflects the differently constituted desires and fears of their class. Whereas with Miranda and her father, these desires and fears are mainly connected with control and sexuality, Trinculo and Stephano, belonging to the lower orders, are more preoccupied with humbler matters, those associated with both ends of the digestive tract, oral and anal. Just before Trinculo spots Caliban, he sees a thunder cloud, and describes this as a "foul bombard that would shed his liquor" (II.ii.21). This projection of his chief interest in life on the cloud is paradigmatic of his subsequent treatment of Caliban. First he wonders whether Caliban is "a man or a fish." The latter possibility, perhaps, suggests food to him, yet Caliban's smell is proof that he is no longer edible:

> a very ancient and fish-like smell; a kind of not-of-the-
> newest poor-John. (II.ii.25)

From the oral phase, concerned with food and drink, Trinculo now passes to the anal. As Freud has argued, money and excrements are frequently associated, and the putrid smell of Caliban puts Trinculo in mind of the possibility of making a profit out of him by displaying him on fairs, as Englishmen do with dead Indians. Stephano, who arrives a moment later, takes over where Trinculo has left off, and considers selling Caliban to an emperor as a curiosity. When he discovers Trinculo hiding under the "mooncalf," this evokes excremental associations (cf. Skura 1989: 64):

> Thou art very Trinculo indeed! How cam'st thou to be
> the siege of this mooncalf? Can he vent Trinculos?
> (II.ii.101-02)

When they discover that Caliban is not a mindless monster, but a human being of sorts, who much to their surprise even speaks their language, they begin to project new stereotypes on him, turning him into an object of religious conversion. They make him swear by the bottle, and "kiss the book" (II.ii.136), thereby juxtaposing their worship of Bacchus with the Christian religion. Finally, they also turn him into an object of political subjection. At this stage, Caliban indeed is like a colonial subject *to them*, but not necessarily in himself.

By all these constructions, which tell us more of their own minds than of Caliban, Trinculo and Stephano try to make sense of their "monster" ; yet one by one he shakes them off and proves them inadequate. He is not an edible fish, for he smells too much. In fact, he is not a fish at all, for he has arms rather than fins (II.ii.33). He is not a dumb monster that can be sold as a curiosity, for he speaks a civilized language. Trinculo is not his excrement, but has merely been seeking shelter from the storm underneath Caliban's gaberdine. Caliban will not be commanded by his new masters, but in fact manipulates them for his own ends, to assassinate Prospero. Rather than their intellectual inferior, he alone is wise enough to understand that the beautiful clothes laid ready for them as a decoy are "but trash," which will deflect them from their purpose (IV.i.223). Before the end of the play, he has come to the conclusion that his worship of these men as gods was foolish.

When Caliban's party join the others, Sebastian and Antonio are also amazed at his appearance. Their reaction to him is reminiscent of that of the two servants, Trinculo and Stephano, which underlines the underlying similarity between the aristocratic and the demotic rebels:

> SEBASTIAN: Ha,ha!
> What things are these, my lord Antonio?
> Will money buy ' em?
> ANTONIO: Very like. One of them
> Is a plain fish, and no doubt very marketable. (V.i.263-66)

36   *Paul Franssen*

Antonio's identification of Caliban as a "marketable," hence presumably edible, fish, telescopes Stephano's and Trinculo's concerns with food and money, the oral and the anal.

It is not just these first impressions of Caliban that turn out to be inaccurate, however. Also Prospero, who has known him for many years, turns out to be mistaken in his assessment of his servant. Prospero's constructions of Caliban the obedient slave and teachable child are exploded by the latter's attempt to rape Miranda. Next, there is Prospero's accusation that he is an irredeemable savage, on whom nurture will not stick; the mirror image of his brother Antonio. Yet, as has often been remarked, this putative monster has a remarkable sense of beauty, and a rich inner life:

> Be not afeard, the isle is full of noises,
> Sounds, and sweet airs, that give delight and hurt not.
> Sometimes a thousand twangling instruments
> Will hum about mine ears; and sometime voices,
> That if I then had waked after long sleep,
> Will make me sleep again, and then in dreaming
> The clouds methought would open and show riches
> Ready to drop upon me, that when I waked
> I cried to dream again. (III.ii.132-41)

Besides, unlike Antonio, he proves willing to learn from his experiences in the end. He admires Prospero when the latter is dressed in his official garb:

> O Setebos, these be brave spirits indeed.
> How fine my master is! I am afraid
> He will chastise me. (V.i.261-63)

When Prospero tells him to go to his cell, he replies:

> Ay, that I will; and I'll be wise hereafter,
> And seek for grace. What a thrice-double ass
> Was I to take this drunkard for god,
> And worship this dull fool! (V.i.294-97)

In all these ways, attempts at defining Caliban seem to go awry. Here he may seem the obedient servant again, who has learned from his mistakes; but perhaps he is only lying low (cf. Evans 1986: 72).

Caliban even refuses to live up to the implications of his name. If, as Peter Hulme has argued at some length, the name is an anagram of cannibal (1992: 83-84), throughout *The Tempest* Caliban is never shown to be in the least interested in eating human beings (Skura 1989: 51). Just like his name refuses quite to match the word "cannibal," so his behaviour, too, is not what might be expected of a man-eater. Rather, it is Trinculo and Stephano that exhibit latent cannibalistic tendencies when they wonder whether he is a fish, therefore edible.

I started out my argument by pointing out that Prospero compares Caliban with the earth, whereas Ariel is repeatedly associated with the three lighter elements that make up the earth. In Renaissance cosmology, these elements were not just the building blocks of the world, but also of each of its denizens: "I am a little world made cunningly/ Of Elements, and an Angelike spright," as John Donne put it (Gardner 1978: 13). Shakespeare's own Cleopatra declared that she was "fire and air; my other elements/ I give to baser life" (*A & C* 5.2.284-85; Wells and Taylor 1986: 1165). In the light of the Renaissance commonplace of the analogy between the microcosm and the macrocosm, the opposition between Caliban and Ariel gains an extra dimension, which again foregrounds the degree to which Caliban is constructed by Prospero. Consider Prospero's words to Ariel at the turning point of the play, when Prospero (depending on one's reading) either decides to forgive his enemies, or reveals to Ariel what his plans were to begin with:

> Hast thou, which art but air, a touch, a feeling
> Of their afflictions, and shall not myself,
> One of their kind, that relish all as sharply
> Passion as they, be kindlier moved than thou art?
> Though with their high wrongs I am struck to th' quick,
> Yet with my nobler reason 'gainst my fury

> Do I take part. The rarer action is
> In virtue than in vengeance. (V.i.21-28)

Prospero's phrase "with my nobler reason" suggests that to him Ariel is analogous to that reason. If Ariel represents Prospero's "nobler reason," the implication might be that Caliban stands for his "fury," his desire for vengeance, which he has to repress. At that very moment Caliban is in fact carrying out his own plan of vengeance against Prospero. And of course, in this play of mirrorings and repetitions, Caliban's vengeance is comparable to Prospero's in a number of ways. First of all, he is the victim of a usurpation: from his point of view, he had inherited the sovereignty over the island from his mother Sycorax, and this has been stolen from him by Prospero:

> This island's mine by Sycorax my mother,
> Which thou tak'st from me...
> For I am all the subjects that you have,
> Which first was mine own king, and here you sty me
> In this hard rock, whiles you do keep from me
> The rest o' th' island. (I.ii.331-32; 341-44)

This puts him in the same position as Prospero himself, whose legitimate power over Milan had been wrested from his hands by his wicked brother Antonio. Caliban desires to avenge himself on Prospero, and sees his chance at the very moment that Prospero is preoccupied with his own plans of revenge. This suggests that Caliban's base desires are not fundamentally different from Prospero's, and indeed even symbolize them.

In addition, Prospero's words to Ariel also contain another antithesis, between "reason" and "passion": much as he would like to be as dispassionate as Ariel, who is a mere spirit, Prospero here acknowledges that he, too, "relish[es] all as sharply/ Passion as they," that is, as his brother and Alonso. In the context, the "Passion" seems to stand for illegitimate desires rather than mere vengefulness, as it is associated with the King of Naples and Antonio as much as with Prospero himself. Here it might be noted that Caliban, too, has uninhibited desires, not just of vengeance, but also of regaining power over the island; and, more ominously, of raping Miranda. Prospero's protectiveness of Miranda, his obsession with preserving her "virgin-knot" (IV.i.15), has been seen as evidence of repressed incestuous desires (Taylor 1982; Skura 1989: 60). This is precisely what he sees reflected in Caliban, and therefore punishes in the Other on whom he projects his own sinful desires. Even Ferdinand is treated severely, as he, too, embodies the desire of a sexual union with Miranda that, while legitimate in him, is unacceptable in Prospero himself. The point, here, is not that Caliban does not really do or want these things; but that this is all that Prospero can see in him, the reflection of his own wicked tendencies that he feels he must repress.

Up to a point, then, Prospero treats Caliban as a kind of allegorical personification of his id, whereas Ariel is his superego. Throughout the play, Prospero has problems controlling his irrational impulses, just like he finds it hard to keep Caliban in check (Paris 1989: 216-18). As many critics have noted, at the end he speaks some mysterious words about Caliban that also seem to suggest an acceptance of his own shortcomings: "This thing of darkness/ I Acknowledge mine" (V.i.275-76). Here Prospero takes responsibility for even the most refractory of his subjects, who had rebelled against him, as if he was something within Prospero (Skura 1989: 66; Evans 1986: 80). Prospero has to accept the fact that he himself is not just an airy spirit, but also earth, with the base desires for anarchy that go with it. Only if he can do this, if he can acknowledge that this thing of darkness is his, too, will he be able to forgive those others who have been led astray by their passions.

In providing a mirror for other characters in the play, while simultaneously repeatedly disproving the patterns they impose on him, Caliban is similar to another Shakespeare character that is notoriously difficult to pin down, and on whom the other characters in the play, too, project their constructions, in accordance with their own desires and obsessions. Prince Hamlet, too, is variously constructed within the play as the unhappy lover, the man thwarted in his ambitions, the dutiful avenger; and he seems to disappoint all Hamlet-watchers at Elsinore. Caliban is, if anything, an even darker mirror of the human mind, on which illicit sexual desires and sexual anxieties, greed, vengefulness, and hunger are projected. He lacks Hamlet's redeeming grace, the self-questioning that adds even more possible constructs to those imposed by other characters. Yet in his poetry and in his sometimes surprising good sense, Caliban rises above each of the generalizations imposed on him from outside.

The notion that the Other can never be completely known, and that what we regard as knowledge are mere self-serving constructions may be a (post)modern insight, yet one that has universal validity. As I have tried to show, in its elemental imagery combined with the reactions of the various characters to Caliban, *The Tempest* can be used to illustrate this theme; at the very least, it does not resist such a reading. Yet this universal theme has its historically specific implications, too, in that. it shows up the self-serving nature of Western attempts at reading the Other – racial, colonial, or social – in line with our preexistent notions of power, civilization, and morality.

References

Brown, Paul. 1985. "'This Thing of Darkness I Acknowledge Mine.' *The Tempest* and the Discourse of Colonialism." In Dollimore and Sinfield 1985: 48-71.

Bullough, Geoffrey. 1975. *Narrative and Dramatic Sources of Shakespeare.* Vol. VIII. London: Routledge and Kegan Paul.

Dollimore, Jonathan and Alan Sinfield, eds. 1985. *Political Shakespeare. New Essays in Cultural Materialism.* Manchester: Manchester UP.

Evans, Malcolm. 1986. *Signifying Nothing. Truth's True Contents in Shakespeare's Texts.* New York: Harvester/Wheatsheaf.

Fernández Retamar, Roberto. 1989. "Caliban. Notes Toward a Discussion of Culture in Our America" [1971]. In *Caliban and Other Essays.* Tr. Edward Baker. Minneapolis: U of Minnesota P, 3-45.

Gardner, Helen, ed. 1978. *John Donne. The Divine Poems* [1952]. 2nd ed. Oxford: Clarendon.

Greenblatt, Stephen J. 1976. "Learning to Curse. Aspects of Linguistic Colonialism in the Sixteenth Century." In Fredi Chiappelli, ed. *First*

Images of America. The Impact of the New World on the Old. Berkeley: U of California P, 561-80.

—. 1988. "Martial Law in the Land of Cockaigne." In *Shakespearean Negotiations. The Circulation of Social Energy in Renaissance England.* Oxford: Clarendon Press, 129-63.

Hart, Jonathan. 1996. "Redeeming *The Tempest*; Romance and Politics." In: *Cahiers Elisabéthains* 49: 23-38.

Hawkes, Terence. 1986. *That Shakespeherian Rag. Essays on a Critical Process.* London and New York: Methuen.

Hulme, Peter. 1992. *Colonial Encounters. Europe and the Native Caribbean 1492-1797* [1986]. London: Routledge.

Kermode, Frank, ed. 1966. *The Arden Edition of the Works of William Shakespeare. The Tempest* [1954]. London: Methuen.

Lamming, George. 1992. *The Pleasures of Exile* [1960]. Ann Arbor: U of Michigan P.

Lewis, C.S. 1974. *The Discarded Image. An Introduction to Medieval and Renaissance Literature* [1964]. Cambridge: Cambridge UP.

Margoliouth, M. H. ed. 1952. *The Poems and Letters of Andrew Marvell* [1927]. 2nd ed. Vol. 1. Oxford: Clarendon Press.

Marx, Leo. 1981. "Shakespeare's American Fable." In *The Machine in the Garden. Technology and the Pastoral Ideal in America* [1964]. London: Oxford UP, 34-72.

Orgel, Stephen, ed. 1994. *The Tempest.* Oxford and New York: Oxford UP.

Panofsky, Erwin. 1972. *Studies in Iconology. Humanistic Themes in the Art of the Renaissance* [1939]. New York: Harper and Row.

Paris, Bernard J. 1989. "*The Tempest*: Shakespeare's Ideal Solution." In Norman N. Holland, Sidney Homan, and Bernard J. Paris, eds. *Shakespeare's Personality.* Berkeley: U of California P, 206-25.

Rees, Christine. 1989. *The Judgment of Marvell.* London/New York: Pinter Publishers.

Skura, Meredith Anne. 1989. "Discourse and the Individual. The Case of Colonialism in *The Tempest*." *Shakespeare Quarterly* 40: 42-69.

Suchet, David. 1989. "Caliban in *The Tempest*." In Philip Brockbank, ed. *Players of Shakespeare 1* [1985]. Cambridge: Cambridge UP, 167-79.

Taylor, Mark. 1982. *Shakespeare's Darker Purpose. A Question of Incest.* New York: AMS Press.

Vaughan, Alden T., and Virginia Mason Vaughan. 1993. *Shakespeare's Caliban. A Cultural History* [1991]. Cambridge: Cambridge UP.

Wells, Stanley and Gary Taylor, eds. 1986. *The Complete Works of William Shakespeare*. Oxford: Clarendon Press.

Caliban as a Wild-Man

An Iconographical Approach

Barbara Baert

In *The Tempest* we learn little about Caliban's outward appearance, but the few characteristics which Shakespeare does attribute to him seem scarcely those of a human being. The other characters see him as a slave (Prospero: "We'll visit Caliban my slave," I.ii.310), a creeping monster (Stephano: "this is some monster of the isle with four legs," II.ii.66) or a tortoise (Prospero: "Thou Tortoise," I.ii.317); he is thought to stink of fish or possibly to look like a fish (Trinculo: "What have we here? a man or a fish? dead or alive? A fish: he/ smells like a fish; a very ancient and fish-like smell," II.ii.24-26); he is called black and dirty (Prospero: "Filth as thou art," I.ii.347; "Thou Earth," I.ii.316), and so on.

These rather less than elegant qualities of Caliban bear some similarity to those of the so-called "wild-man": a creature driven by instinct who lacks all finer feelings and morals. He behaves almost like an animal: creeps on all fours, lives in a cave and feeds off his natural surroundings. The relationship between Caliban and the wild-man has already been pointed out by A. and V. Vaughan: "Shakespeare and his audience experienced a lifetime of vicarious familarity with this legendary creature. How plausible it would have been for the dramatist to incorporate some wild-man characteristics into a pastoral drama like *The Tempest*" (Vaughan and

Vaughan 1991: 56 f., 70). However, this observation could not immediately allow them to come to terms with the variety of characteristics shown by Caliban. The reasons for this are twofold.

First, Vaughan and Vaughan worked with a narrow and superficial concept of the wild-man. They tried to cast Caliban in the mould of a wild-man without sketching the process of the cultural growth of this concept and without paying due attention to the many social functions which it encompasses. For this reason Caliban's characteristic traits seemed to go beyond those of the traditional wild-man, and the analogy between the two was dismissed as incomplete. Should Vaughan and Vaughan have investigated the genre of the wild-man more comprehensively (in all its variants) and above all in greater detail (with due regard to socio-cultural stratification), it would have been apparent to them that Caliban's complexity does not constitute a 'departure' from the type of the wild-man, but rather that this complexity is precisely essential to the very genre of the wild-man itself.

Second, the Vaughans limited their investigation of the relationship between Caliban and the wild-man to the level of literature. Yet, the most revealing transformations of the wild-man are thematized in the visual arts. The wild-man – and his many derivatives in varying social contexts – is defined primarily by his specific outward appearance (next to his actions), and this can be interpreted more explicitly in pictures. An investigation into the visual constituents of the genre of the wild-man (its 'iconography') provides more source-material, which can thus provide us with a broader outlook on the various socio-cultural ramifications. The aim of my contribution, then, is to further our insight into the genesis, function and context of Shakespeare's 'salvage and deformed slave' (Kermode 1988: 2) by concentrating on the iconography of the wild-man.

The Origins of the Wild-Man

To begin with, the way in which the character of Caliban is rooted in the imagery of the wild-man can be clarified through the exploration of the type's historical context. The wild-man has two sources. The first goes back on descriptions of the world dating from Classical Antiquity.[1] In these, exotic races are classified according to physical abnormalities. "Wild" men and women are here classified as a separate race, not necessarily because of any specific physical abnormality, but rather on the basis of their sub-human, brutish status. In other cases "the wild ones" is a collective name for the strange races of monsters in their entirety. These classical writings on wild-men were transmitted via medieval *compendia* and compilations, usually under the heading of "Marvels of the East." Several of the relevant manuscripts were illustrated. In a wood-cut from an incunable (Augsburg, 1475) of Conrad von Megenberg's *Buch der Natur* (ca. 1350, New York, Pierpont Morgan Library) (fig. 1) there figures a map of the world accompanied by illustrations depicting various of these races with their typical abnormalities (Husband 1980: cat. n.° 3).

The second source of the wild-man lies in the Indo-Germanic past, where, together with nymphs, satyrs, mermaids and mermen, he was said to populate impenetrable forests. The Anglo-Saxon world believed, for instance, in a '*wodewose*' or 'green man' (Bernheimer 1952: 19, 21-48). We know of these proto-christian demigods only in the form in which they surfaced in the twelfth century. This is the period in which Western culture increasingly comes to rely on the written word (Price 1992: 93-117). The mythical element of the idea of the wild-man must by then already have been weakened by the various waves of Christianization that had swept through Europe.

In contrast to the type of wild-man figured in the race-descriptions of Antiquity, the Indo-European wild-man is pictured as hairy (Husband 1980: 7 f.). A wild-man with skin like an animal features in the Luthrell Psalterium (1335-40, East-English, London, British Library, Ms. Add. 42130, fol. 70) (fig. 2) (Husband 1980: 3, fig. 3). But medieval illustrations in copies and transcriptions of the relevant Classical works also favour this animal-like appearance. Thus the wild-man of Classical Antiquity is re-

LIBRARY, UNIVERSITY COLLEGE CHESTER

---

[1] The most important sources are: Pliny, *Historia naturalis*, 77 BC and Solinus, *Collectanea rerum memorabilium*, 5th c. An extensive discussion of these texts can be found in J.B. Friedman (1981).

visualised in terms of Germanic archetypes; this is apparent from a print of Hartmann Schedel's chronicle of the world (Nürnberg, 1493, wood-cut by Michaël Wolgemut and Wilhelm Pleydenwurff. Hamburg, National-museum), in which a wild-woman is included among Plinian monsters (fig. 3) (Husband 1980: 48, cat. 4, fig. 22; Möller 1963: 15-16). In this way, on the level of iconography a fusion occurs between both sources, and the resulting 'wild-man' is reminiscent both of the mythical figures of native pre-Christian culture, and of the exotic and abnormal races banished to the outer limits of Divine Creation.

Characteristics and Functions of the Wild-Man. Approaching Caliban[2]

In the European cultural heritage, the wild-man represents everything that is non-human. The wild-man is the reverse of all that is human. Within the exclusively agrarian-monastic society of the early Middle Ages this dichotomy came down to a division of nature into a natural realm, in which belonged human beings, and a super-natural one, in which figured wild-men. From the twelfth century on, with the progress of urbanization and the related development of a sedentary society, the polarity was no longer located in nature itself, but was extended and transferred to where that which was outside nature, such as human beings, was contrasted with that which was within nature, such as wild-men. This was also the moment in which man's natural environment increasingly came to be demystified. Thus nature, no longer intrinsically dualistic, came to be subsumed in its entirety into the concept of the wild-man.

A still greater alienation with regard to this (non-agrarian) nature develops from the fifteenth century onwards, when the town emerges as a clearly defined socio-cultural phenomenon. The wild-man, who from the twelfth century onwards personified the wildness of nature, though not necessarily in any pejorative sense, now stands for "wildness" and

---

[2] In 1987 P. Vandenbroeck organized an exhibition in the Koninklijk Museum voor Schone Kunsten [Royal Museum of Fine Arts] in Antwerp which focused on the image of 'the Other'. Within this context, a lot of space and attention was given to the wild-man and specifically to his social and cultural functions. The present contribution is partly indebted to the text of the exhibition-catalogue.

"unculturedness." These are exactly the characteristics that had come to be associated with nature in the course of the fifteenth century, as a corollary to the process of civilization involving the aristocracy and the bourgeoisie. These shifts of meaning can be illustrated in a concrete manner.

The *Magnus ludus de homine salvatico* (1208) ("The Great Play of the Wild-Man") is both the earliest documented evidence and the first example of the phenomenon of the wild-man in drama. The play was staged in Padua to celebrate Whitsun. There is another example from Aarau (Switzerland): the *Ludus at virum dictum wildman* from the year 1399 (Bernheimer 1952: 51). These plays served as rites of passage connected with the changing of the seasons (usually from winter to summer), in which the wild-man dies a sacrificial death. A wood-cut (1566, New York, The Metropolitan Museum of Art, Harris Brisbane Dick Fund) after a work by Pieter Breughel probably illustrates just such a rite of passage (fig. 4). Although he gradually loses the magical role he plays in such seasonal rites of passage, his unique relation to nature continues to be the most important characteristic of the wild-man.

From the fifteenth century on, the wild-man is incorporated into didactic literature relating to the three estates (e.g. the ballads of Henri Baude (ca 1430-1496) (Husband 1980: 131)). The estates (peasant, commoner, noble) were complementary conditions of man, ordained by God Himself and thus deemed to be indispensable for maintaining the balance of the Creation (Albrecht 1962: 185). The wild-man, then, is added as a fourth 'estate.' Within this context, he mostly laments the decay of society, and glories in the fact that he himself is in tune with nature.[3] The drawing (fig.

---

[3] Sometimes the wild-man also functions as the embodiment of the Laws of Nature (see a manuscript from the southern Low Countries, ca. 1473-1474 (Brussels, Koninklijke Bibliotheek, Ms. VI 823, fol. 68f.) (Vandenbroeck 187: 21, no. 20). We cannot go further into the matter of the wild-man and late medieval theories about the so-called Golden Age, *aetas aurea*. This "theory of descent" states that in the beginning all things were perfect, but that history suffers from moral "erosion." Often, the wild-man is related to the restoration of the origin of the world. In this context, the wild-man plays a "positive" role (Vandenbroeck 1987: 18-19). A second "positive" role can be found in hagiographical iconography. The early christian penitents and/or hermits signify the *ecclesia primitiva* and thus the state of purity before the Fall; see: Chrysostomos as wild-man in the *Leben der Heiligen* (Lives of Saints) (Part II. *Winterteil* [Winter part]), fol. 188 f. (print by Günther Zainer,

5) showing a wild-man in front of his dwelling-place, a hollow tree, thus illustrates a literary genre; it bears the heading *Ballade d'un home sauvage* ("Ballad of a wild man") (French, ca. 1500, Paris, Bibliothèque Nationale, Ms. fr. 2366, fol. 3v.) (Husband 1980: fig. 1).

Caliban, "the savage" (Miranda: I.ii.357) also has a unique insight into nature; only he knows the fertile areas of the island. Prospero is dependent on this knowledge; he needs this brute as a guide. Without him, he is defenceless in the face of the uncultivated land. Caliban says to Prospero: "and then I lov'd thee,/ and show'd thee all the qualities o' th' isle,/ The fresh springs, brine-pits, barren place and fertile" (I.II.338-340), and earlier Prospero had impressed upon Miranda the fact that: "we cannot miss him: he does make our fire,/ fetch in our wood, and serves in offices/ That profit us" (I. II.313-314). Thus, with his specific talents, the wild-man can complement the human condition, can actually improve it.

The wild-man has still other specific functions. In the towns, the wild-man had become indispensable in parades or religious plays; the wild-man consistently appears in Shrove Tuesday festivals; and courtly culture mirrored itself in him. In the dichotomy obtaining between wild nature and town, between the uncultivated and the cultured, the wild-man became the reservoir for everything that distinguished the Human from the Wild. In this connection, P. Vandenbroeck (1987: 141 ff.) develops the theory of "negative self-definition." By defining the wild-man, one establishes one's own definition of Self through contrast. This self-definition through inversion takes place both on the level of the individual and on the level of the social classes.

From the fourteenth century onwards, then, works of art by and for the nobility, not only show familiarity with the phenomenon in question, but also bear witness to "active" participation in the mechanisms of this negative self-definition. The nobility, seeking its legitimacy as it does in the domains of battle, feudal organisation of agriculture, hunting and love, will thus visualize the wild-man in exactly these contexts (Vandenbroeck 1987: 11).

Augsburg, 1471, New York, Pierpont Morgan Library, PML 27324) (Husband 1980: cat. no. 22, fig. 60).

Representations of conflicts between savages and knights depict the opposition between self-control and unbridled agression, as can be seen on an English gilt perfume chest in the Victoria and Albert Museum in London (fig. 6) (Möller 1963: 48). A hairy wild-man is besieged by hunting hounds in a miniature in the margin of Queen Mary's psalter (1300-1325, London, British Library, Royal ms. 2 B VII, fol. 173) (fig. 7) (Husband 1980: 3, fig. 5). In the realm of love the wild-man stands for bestial lusts as opposed to the nobility's refined culture of courtly love. In the *Taymouth Hours*, (English, 14th c.) a wild-man assaults a lady (London, British Library, Yates Thompson ms. 13) (Bernheimer 1952: fig. 260). Caliban is in a similar fashion accused of having molested Miranda (Prospero: "thou didst seek to violate/ The honour of my child," I.ii.349).

In the context sketched, the wild-man usually appears in the role of victim. In a Swiss tapestry (1450-1475) now in the Nationalmusem in Copenhagen (fig. 8) (Husband 1980: 90; Vandenbroeck 1987: 19) and on a love-chest (a common wedding present) now in the Historisches Museum in Basel (Husband 1980: 91), he is "tamed" and chained by a woman. Caliban too is mastered and detained in his own typical wild-man's dwelling place, the cave (Caliban to Prospero: "and here you sty me/ In this hard rock, whiles you do keep from me/ The rest o' th' island," I.ii.344-46). Moreover, it is not only Prospero that commands him, but also Miranda ("Deservedly confin'd into this rock,/ Who hadst deserv'd more than a prison," I.ii.363-64).

In the meantime, the old, dramatized rite of the wild-man lived on at court also in the form of tournaments, masquerades and royal rituals (Goldsmith 1958: 481-91). A miniature on the opening folio of the *Grands chroniques de France* by Jean Froissart (late fifteenth century) shows a group of frenzied wild-men before Charles VI and his retinue (London, British Library, Harley Ms. 4380) (fig. 9) (Husband 1980: Pl. XII). In 1515, Henry VIII organized a festival during which the appearance of a group of wild-men caused two formerly rival camps of knights to join forces against this common enemy (Vandenbroeck 1987: 9). The event was brought to a close by couples dancing. Here the wild-man is courtly entertainment, yet as such functions also as a catalyst for the nobility's perception of itself.

Masquerades involving wild-men were also organized at the court of the
Stuarts (Vaughan and Vaughan 1991: 80). And in the anti-masquerade the
wild-men were played by actors, who were later joined by the courtiers.
Here the nobility assimilates the wildness in order to define its own
identity. In 1575, Robert Dudley, Lord Leicester, staged a play for Queen
Elizabeth, at the end of which a *Hombre Salvagio, with an Oken plant pluct
up by the roots in hoiiz hande* recites a poem by George Gascoigne, which
makes it clear that the wild-man wishes to become her subject. At the
Elizabethan court, the theme of the wild-man was treated frequently in the
light of (voluntary) political subjection. This fits into the framework of
absolutist policies with regard to Ireland and the colonies (Vaughan and
Vaughan 1991: 65 f.).

It is possible that the stage character of Caliban is an allusion to these
ideological happenings at court. The figure of the wild-man as carniva-
lesque entertainment is balanced by the dramaturgically elaborated
character of Caliban. It is well known that the so-called "higher" artistic
genres exploit and "elevate" popular themes and festival material. In
contrast to the savages in plays by Shakespeare's contemporaries, which
cannot be treated here, Caliban is not murdered. He comes to his senses
and accepts his subordination to Prospero (Caliban: "Ay, that I will; and
I'll be wise hereafter,/ And seek for grace. What a Thrice-double ass/ Was
I, to take this drunkard for a God,/ And worship this dull fool!" V.i.294-
97). It could be significant, moreover, that the play was staged on the
occasion of Elizabeth Stuart's marriage (1612) (Wells and Taylor 1987:
957). As has been demonstrated on the basis of the iconography, the
sexuality of the savage is central, as an inverse phenomenon, to the themes
of courtly love and marriage.

Shakespeare's Caliban and the Formal Hybridity of the "Modern" Wild-Man

As has been indicated, Caliban's morphology is vague and ambiguous. The
main difficulty lies in the fact that attributes referring to his external
appearance can be intended as terms of abuse and humiliation reflecting
the subjective perception of the speaker. "Savage," as Miranda calls him, is,
it is true, a clear reference to the type of the wild-man.

"You earth" (I.ii.316) and "filth" (I.ii.347) are likewise integral parts of the "classic" discourse of the wild-man. Shakespeare does not mention one feature that originally was seen as essential to the type of the wild-man, viz. hairiness, because in Renaissance iconography this had already faded somewhat into the background. Jacob Van Oost the Elder (17th c.) titles his painting of a stocky, bearded, naked man, carrying a hunting bag containing some sort of fowl on his back, "Wild-Man" (Genève, Museum Kilmarnoc) (fig. 10). The hybridity of Caliban's external appearance may thus be rooted in the iconography of the wild-man as it developed between the Middle Ages and modernity.

There is, for instance, Trinculo's striking observation about Caliban: "a man or a fish" (II.ii.24-26), or "being but half a fish and half a monster" (III.ii.28). Now this comparison with a fish can also be connected with the iconography of the wild-man. Mermaids and mermen stem from the same Indo-Germanic mythical past that also the wild-man comes from. They belong, then, to the same semantic field and appear, moreover, to be mutually interchangeable.[4] This is apparent from scenes in which wild-men and sea-monsters fight each other. In a tapestry from Doornik (1515) (Nürnberg, Germanisches Nationalmuseum) a sea-monster forces its way into the territory of the wild-men and abducts a wild-woman (fig. 11). In *Der naturen bloeme* by Jacob van Maerlant (13th c.) – a medieval Dutch counterpart to the classical "Marvels of the East," it is said of the wild-man/woman: "There are people living there [India] who wear no clothes and whose body is covered with rough hair. As soon as anyone approaches them, they dive into the water because they live both on land and in the river" (Hogenelst and van Oostrom 1995: 94). The illustration shows a hairy couple whose lower body is in water. It is even suggested that Caliban actually physically embodies some characteristics of a fish.[5] A French Book of Hours includes a miniature showing a monster which is

---

[4] Originally this concept had a much wider frame of reference, of which the semantic field of 'otherness' was just one nuclear element (Vandenbroeck 1987: 7, 132; see also: Hufeland 1976: 1-18).

[5] The fishy smell is a subjective component. The stench characterizes both the Wild-Man and that which derives from Evil or the Devil (Prospero: "got by the devil himself," I.ii.321; "malice," I.ii.369).

half fish, half wild-man (New Haven, Yale University, Beinecke Library, Ms. 436, fol. 86v) (fig. 12).[6]

All ages have their physical hybrids of human beings and animals. One way in which these entered European art was through the artifacts of Central-Asiatic peoples who settled in Western Europe between the fifth and the eleventh century (Baltrusaitis 1993: passim). Originally, these hybrid figures had a primarily decorative function, and throughout the Middle Ages they feature on parchment manuscripts, populate misericords, adorn manuscript capitals, and serve as gargoyles on Gothic cathedrals (Gaignebet and Lajoux 1985: passim).

Around 1500, these playful monsters gained a new lease of life under the infuence of the grotesque. This form or style of ornamentation, called after the places where it was found initially (*grottos*), became popular after the discovery of some classical examples of the style in the ruins of ancient Rome. Grotesques combined characteristics of plants, animals and human beings. Frequently, the lower body of a grotesque was modelled after a fish. Usually, these grotesques fulfilled a purely formal role. Because of their ancient origins, they were immensely popular in the sixteenth and seventeenth centuries. These drolleries, as they are also known, came to be part of the period's common visual tradition. The character of Caliban, then, was fitted into the idiom of the grotesque in a spontaneous and probably unconscious way.

As to the portrayal of the wild-man, the transition to modernity also made itself felt in new works based on classical texts. The *Meerwunder* by Albrecht Dürer (engraving, ca. 1498, New York, Metropolitan Museum of Art, Isaac D. Fletcher Fund, 19.73.80) is based on Ovid (Lange 1900: 194-204) and shows a man with the tail of a fish, who has abducted a woman (fig. 13) (Husband 1980: 196-198, fig. 131). He carries a tortoise as a shield. Especially the latter detail seems to be related to Caliban: Prospero calls him "tortoise" (I.ii.317).

---

[6] Apparently England had been familiar with the figure of the half savage, half fish for a long time. In the description of a beam of support dating from 1161, an "aquatic monster" is referred to as "hairy" (Bernheimer 1952: 40; see further Druce 1915: 115 f).

Figures

Fig. 1: Wood-cut from the *Buch der Natur* by Conrad von Megenberg (ca. 1350), Augsburg, 1475. New York, Pierpont Morgan Library.

Fig. 2: Miniature from the Luthrell psalter, East English, 1335-40. London, British Library, Ms. Add. 42130, fol. 70.

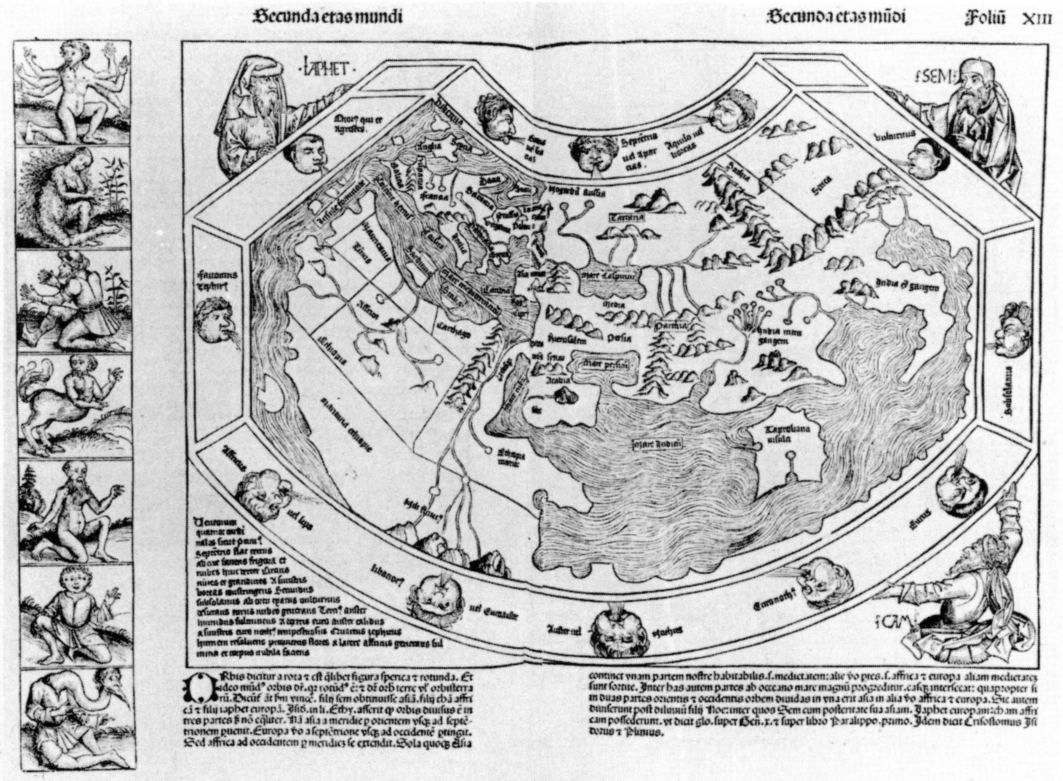

Fig. 3: Wood-cut by Michaël Wolgemut and Wilhelm Pleydenwurff from Hartmann Schedel's *Chronicle of the World*, Nürnberg, 1493. Hamburg, Nationalmuseum.

Fig. 4: Wood-cut after a work of Pieter Breughel, 1566. New York, The Metropolitan Museum of Art, Harris Brisbane Dick Fund.

Fig. 5: Drawing, French, ca. 1500. Paris, Bibliothèque Nationale, Ms. fr. 2366, fol. 3v.

Fig. 6: English gilt
perfume chest,
mid-14th c.
London, Victoria
and Albert
Museum.

Fig. 7: Miniature in the margin of Queen Mary's psalter, 1300-1325. London, British
Library, Royal ms. 2 B VII, fol. 173.

Fig. 8: Swiss tapestry, 1450-1475. Copenhagen, Nationalmuseum.

Fig. 9: *Grands chroniques de France* by Jean Froissart, late 15th c. London, British Library, Harley Ms. 4380, fol. 1.

Fig. 10: Painting by Jacob van Oost the Elder, 17th c, Genève, Museum Kilmarnoc.

Fig. 11: Tapestry from Doornik, 1515. Nürnberg, Germanisches Nationalmuseum.

Fig. 12: Miniature from a French Book of Hours. New Haven, Yale University, Beinecke Library, Ms. 436, fol. 86v.

Fig. 13: Engraving, *Meerwunder*, by Albrecht Dürer, ca. 1498. New York, Metropolitan Museum of Art, Isaac D. Fletcher Fund, 19.73.80.

Fig. 14: Engraving by Jacques de Gheyn, ca. 1600. Antwerp, Prentenkabinet, no. II.G.517.

Fig. 15: Miniature from English manuscript, "Marvels from the East," 11th c. London, British Library, Cotton Ms. Tiberius B.V. vol. 1, fol. 81v.

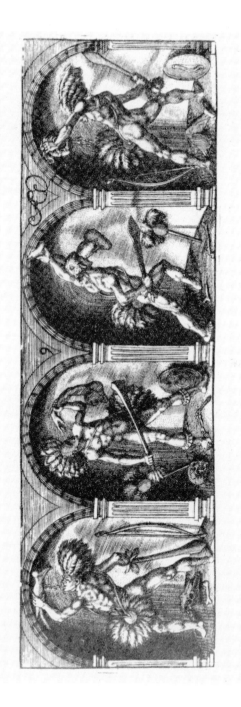

Fig. 16: Engraving of the so called "monogrammist," ca. 1540.

Fig. 17: Painting by Albert Eeckhout, mid-17th c. Copenhagen, Museum of Ethnography.

The return to the Ancients also resulted in a revival of classical descriptions of the world and its races. In 1601, Pliny's *Historia naturalis* was translated into English by Philemon Holland (*History of the World*); only a few years prior, actually, to Shakespeare's *Tempest* (Vaughan and Vaughan 1991: 75). As stated, the savage in the Plinian context was a more general term for the Monstrous (Stephano: "man-monster," III.ii.12). That may have been the reason that the concept of the wild-man became less distinct as time went by. Once the concept had been assigned to the category of the Monstrous, the way was clear for a fragmentation and proliferation of its external features that could scarcely be kept in check; and that is also what happened to Caliban.

Shakespeare's Caliban and the Semantic Plurality of the "Modern" Wild-Man

The modern return to the classical descriptions, in contrast to the medieval inclination to *mirabilia*, had aroused a desire to locate these peoples in real geographic terms. Thus, from the fifteenth and sixteenth century on, the wild-man became integrated into the newly discovered, exotic cultures (Vandenbroeck 1987: 24-39). Because of the flexibility of his internal and external characteristics, the wild-man is the appropiate channel for "grasping" these "Others." Not only did the wild-man function automatically as a "shock-absorber" for the frightening "strangeness," but the exotic Other was also assigned to the concept of the wild-man. Often, this latter mechanism is only semi-conscious and naturally must have the effect of contributing to the higher self-image of the Westerner. Whereas at first the wild-man constituted a socio-cultural metaphor for the self-image of a few classes, this self-definition through opposites now extended to the Western self-image as a whole.

It goes without saying that all this is felt most pressingly in a context in which the "exotic" and the "non-exotic" confront each other: the colonies. In a series of engravings of masked figures (ca. 1600) by Jacques De Gheyn (thus referring in turn to a theatrical [carnivalesque?] reality), a wild-man is represented as the companion of an Indian woman (Antwerp, Prentenkabinet, no. II.G.517.) (fig.. 14) (Vandenbroeck 1987: 35). What they have in common is a costume made of leaves (wild nature).

From the sixteenth century onwards, groups of people who were known to Europe even before the age of exploration, such as Turks and Gypsies, were grafted onto the exotic-geographic conception of the wild-man as well. Because of its great variety, the image of the wild-man becomes strongly eclectic and somewhat destabilized. This is already apparent in Geiler von Kayserberg, a fifteenth-century theologian from Strasburg. His concept of the wild-man is already a five-fold conglomerate (Husband 1980: 12; Bernheimer 1952: 91; Möller 1963: no. 12): the *solitarii* (holy penitents), the *sacchani* (satyrs), the *Hispani* (Gypsies), the *pigini* (Pygmees), and the *diaboli* (devilish wild-men). Caliban too is accused by Prospero of being "got by the devil himself" (I.ii.321).

In the sixteenth century, under the influence of Humanism and colonialism, a new iconographic genre emerges relating to "the four continents." In a series of prints by Adriaen Collaert (ca. 1595, Antwerp, Prentenkabinet, II/G. 203-206) the continent of America bears the following heading: *Europa machte mich der Welt, Gott mir bekandt/ Gold, das sonst Herren macht, liess mich zur Sclavin werden/ Ich bin bey Reichtum arm in meinem eignen Land/weil meine Erde wird geführt auf andre Erden* (Vandenbroeck 1987: 21, note 11).[7] Caliban too deplores his captivity in his own habitat, the cave, and laments the predatory cultivation of the free and native earth in exchange for education (e.g. language) (I.ii.333-47). The phenomenon of the slave even appears to be a motif associated exclusively with America. Perhaps this is a further argument for situating *The Tempest* in this continent after all, rather than in North-Africa for instance (as maintained by Wells and Taylor 1987: 957). The lack of familiarity with strong drink is another stereotype associated with the Indian. Caliban is drunk and blames his condition on some deity: "That's a brave god, and bears celestial liquor:/ I will kneel to him" (II.ii.118-19).

Caliban thus embodies an ambiguity which is typical of the confused state in which the genre of the wild-man found itself around 1500. On the one hand, he incorporates a strong element of the monstrous of the medieval

---

[7] Europe made me known to the world, God to myself. Gold, otherwise a maker of masters, made me a slave. For all my riches I am poor in my own land, because my earth is brought to another earth.

wild-man, albeit one which had in the meantime been furnished by the genre with a hybrid external appearance; on the other hand, he bears witness to the exotic-colonial area of application which the wild-man had acquired by the time of the sixteenth century. The complaint of the colony refers to a more positive point of view; the mechanism of self-definition through opposites plays a less central role here.

Caliban the Cannibal

Although Caliban does not appear to be a man-eater, "Caliban" can be derived etymologically from "cannibal."[8] This name is, by the way, also used as a generic term in the play ("O ho, O ho! Would't had been done!/ Thou didst prevent me; I had peopled else/ This isle with Calibans" (I.ii.351-53)). An eleventh-century English manuscript containing the "Marvels of the East" (London, British Library, Cotton Ms. Tiberius B.V. vol. 1) shows a giant eating a human body (folio 81v) (fig. 15) (Husband 1980: 39). Its back is partly covered with hair, although in the Middle Ages this association is not particularly widespread.

From the sixteenth century onwards, however, Indians are iconographically associated with the consuming of parts of the human body. This is apparent from an engraving by the so-called "monogrammist" dating from about 1540 (fig. 16) (Vandenbroeck 1987: 25) and from a painting by Albert Eeckhout (mid-seventeenth century) of an Indian woman as a cannibal (a foot protrudes from her basket of food) (Copenhagen, Etnographic Museum) (fig. 17) (Vandenbroeck 1987: fig. 38; Dam-Mikkelsen and Lundbaek 1980: 34-44). In neither of these works of art are the figures portrayed as monstrous, but rather in traditional costume and

---

[8] Other hypotheses are: 1. Carib (Caribean), since 1492 "Caribes" and "Canibales" are used interchangeably. 2. Camibia: village in Algeria (mother); 3. Kalebôn: Arabic for "dirty dog"; 4. Kaliban: Gypsy language for "black" (English policies inimical towards Gypsies) (Vaughan and Vaughan 1991: 26). Only rarely is the wild-man given a proper name: he is seldom individualized. Perhaps Bremo, the cannibal from the revised edition of the anonymous *Mucedorus* (1598), staged at the court by Shakespeare's company in 1610, preceded his own personalization of the wild-man (Vaughan and Vaughan 1991: 67 f.).

feathers. It is, therefore, the act of cannibalism itself which points to the "wild," inappropriate and monstrous.

Albert Eeckhout produced his painting for a courtly target audience, apparently with a repressive ideology. Yet, the tide was turning in Europe. The successful English expedition to Virginia in 1606-1607 provoked discussion about whether or not the Indians had civil law (Nash 1972: 55-86). The painter John White, whose paintings show evidence of respect for the native Indians, was a member of the movement which defended the freedom of indigenous peoples (Hulton and Quinn 1964). Eventually, this would lead to the romantic ideal of the unspoilt, innocent savage. The wild-man becomes an exponent of the exotic.

Conclusion

For Vaughan and Vaughan, the intrinsic connection between Caliban and the wild-man was evident, but their argument remained underdeveloped. Iconography, however, allows us to broaden the issue. The intimate relation between drama and picture is contained in the history of the genre of the wild-man itself. The journey leads from magic ritual through popular play to classical theatre, followed closely by the iconography which represents the wild-man in these socio-functional "acts." To a considerable extent, though, the iconographic material goes beyond the literary. In other words, the wild-man appears to have developed, at least to a certain degree, an autonomous visual tradition. In this way it was possible to outline an area in which the typology of Caliban could be anchored, and to find links which would have remained hidden without the study of the non-textual material. His habitat, the cave, and his brutish behaviour and use of language obviously define the wild-man. Yet, to a somewhat lesser extent, the same can be maintained for his status as a slave, his similarity to a fish, and even for one of the etymological explanations of his name. Likewise, the emergence and development of colonialism can be usefully incorporated into the history of the wild-man. In this connection, there are clear pointers in the direction of the (North-American) Indian.

Translated by Maria Sherwood

References

Albrecht, B. 1962. *Stand und Stände. Eine Theologische Untersuchung.* Paderborn: Bonifacius.

Baltrusaitis, J. 1993 (re-print of 1981). *Le moyen âge fantastique.* Paris: Flammarion

Bernheimer, R. 1952. *Wild Men in the Middle Ages. A Study on Art, Sentiment and Demonology.* Cambridge: Harvard UP.

Bruster, D. 1995. "Local Tempest. Shakespeare and the Work of the Early Modern Playhouse." *The Journal of Medieval and Renaissance Studies* 25 (1): 33-53.

Buchner, B. 1975. "The Savage European. A Structural Approach to European Iconography of the American Indian." *Studies in the Anthropology of Visual Communication: Society of the Anthropology of Visual Communication* 2: 80-86.

Bullough, G. 1975. "Romances: *Cymbeline, The Winter's Tale, The Tempest.*" In *Narrative and Dramatic Sources of Shakespeare.* London/New York: Routledge and Kegan Paul.

Dam-Mikkelsen, B. and T. Lundbaek. 1980. *Ethnographic Objects in the Royal Danish Kunstkammer. 1650-1800.* Copenhagen: Etnographic Museum.

Dupley, E. and M. Novak, eds. 1972. *The Wildman within. An Image in Western Thought from the Renaissance to Romanticism.* Pittsburgh: Pittsburgh UP.

Druce, G.C. 1915. "Some Abnormal and Composite Human Forms in English Church Architecture." *Archaeological Journal* 72: 115 a.f.

Friedman, J.B. 1981. *The Monstrous Races in Medieval Art and Thought.* Cambridge: Harvard UP.

Gaignebet, Cl. and J.-D. Lajoux. 1985. *Art profane et religion populaire au Moyen Age.* Paris: Presses Universitaires de France.

Gaines, B. and M. Lofaro. 1976. "What did Caliban Look Like?" *Mississippi Folklore Register Meeting* 10: 175-188.

Goldsmith, R.H. 1958. "The wild-man on the English Stage." *Modern Language Review* 53: 481-91.

Hogenelst, D. and F. van Oostrom. 1995. *Handgeschreven wereld. Nederlandse literatuur en cultuur in de Middeleeuwen.* Amsterdam: Prometheus.

Hufeland, K. 1976. "Das Motiv der Wildheit im mittelhochdeutscher Dichtung." *Zeitschrift für Deutsche Philologie* 95: 1-18.

Hulton, P.H. and M.D. Quinn. 1964. *The American Drawings of John White. 1577-1590.* s.l.

Husband, T. 1980. *The Wild Man. Medieval Myth and Symbolism, (exh. cat.).* New York: Metropolitan Museum of Art.

Kermode, F., ed. 1988. *The Arden Edition of the Works of William Shakespeare. The Tempest* [1954]. London/New York: Routledge.

Lange, K. 1900. "Dürer's Meerwunder." *Zeitschrift für Bildende Kunst* 11: 194-204.

Miner, E. 1972. "The Wild Man Through the Looking Glass." In Dupley and Novak 1972: 87-114.

Möller, L.L. 1963. *Die Wilden Leute des Mittelalters, (exh. cat.).* Hamburg: Museum für Kunst und Gewerbe.

Nash, G.B. 1972. "The Image of the Indian in the Southern Colonial Mind." In Dupley and Novak 1972: 55-86.

Price, B.B. 1992. *Medieval Thought.* Oxford: Blackwell.

Roller, H.U. 1965. "Der Nürnberger Schembartlauf. Studien zum Fest- und Maskenwesen des späten Mittellaters." *Volksleben* 11. Tübingen: Tübinger Vereinigung für Volkskunde.

Thomas, K. 1971. *Religion and The Decline of Magic. Studies in Popular Beliefs in Sixteenth and Seventeenth Century England.* New York: Scribner.

Tinland, F. 1968. *L'homme sauvage. Homo Ferus et Homo Sylvestris.* Paris: Payot.

Vandenbroeck, P. 1989-1990. "Jheronimus Bosch' zogenaamde 'Tuin der Lusten'." In *Jaarboek van het Koninklijk Museum voor Schone Kunsten Antwerpen* 9-210 (I), 9-192 (II).

—. 1987. *Over wilden en narren, boeren en bedelaars. Beeld van de andere, vertoog over het zelf, (exh. cat.).* Antwerp: Koninklijk Museum voor Schone Kunsten.

Vaughan, A.T. and V. Mason Vaughan. 1991. *Shakespeare's Caliban. A Cultural History.* Cambridge: Cambridge UP.

Wanckel, C.O. 1975. *Giants and Wild Men in the Middle Ages.* s.l.. Reginal Essay Price British Archaeological Association.

Wells, S. and G. Taylor, 1987. *The Complete Oxford Shakespeare, vol. 22. Comedies.* Oxford: Clarendon Press.

White, H. 1972. "The Forms of Wildness. Archaeology of an Idea." In Dupley and Novak 1972: 3-38.

Wittkower, R. 1942. "Marvels of the East. A Study in the History of Monsters." *Journal of the Warburg and Courtauld Institutes* 5: 159-97.

Gazing at the Borders of *The Tempest*

Shakespeare, Greenblatt and de Certeau

Jürgen Pieters

> *If it is the task of cultural criticism to decipher the power of Prospero, it is equally its task to hear the accents of Caliban.*
>
> (Stephen Greenblatt, "Culture")

> *Caliban is, therefore, the occasion to which every situation, within the context of* The Tempest, *must be related. No Caliban no Prospero!*
>
> (George Lamming, "A Monster, a Child, a Slave")

There appears to be no play throughout the whole Western canon in which the word "now" features as prominently as in Shakespeare's *The Tempest*. Even though the fact has been acknowledged before (Smith 1969: 4), we still seem a long way off from a sustained analysis as to Shakespeare's predilection for this particular adverb in this particular play. I immediately hasten to add that I do not intend to provide such an analysis in the pages to follow, though I do believe that any attempt to do

so might profitably take as its starting-point one of the many illuminating
analyses to have come out of the critical project which Stephen Greenblatt
towards the beginning of the nineteen-eighties labelled "new historicism"
or "cultural poetics" (Greenblatt 1982). One possible entry into the
problematic sketched above would be the chapter on the works of
Christopher Marlowe in Greenblatt's own *Renaissance Self-Fashioning from
More to Shakespeare* (1980: 193-221). In this particular essay, Greenblatt
shows Marlowe's plays to be firmly rooted within the historical matrix of
Renaissance colonialism, which he believes to be characterized above all
by the "acquisitive energies of English merchants, entrepreneurs, and
adventurers, promoters alike of trading companies and theatrical
companies" (194). Read against this background, Marlowe's writings,
bespeaking a strong fascination with "the idea of physical movement" and
a central concern with the *persona* of "the quintessential alien," turn out to
be, in Greenblatt's view, complex "meditation[s] on the roots of [the]
behavior" shared by most of the Europeans who first set foot on the
distant shores of the New World (194).

In by now largely familiar fashion, Greenblatt's essay starts off from a
resonant historical anecdote, taken from the diaries of the English
merchant John Sarracoll, who in 1586 took part in an expedition financed
by the Earl of Cumberland to the coasts of Western Africa. The particular
excerpt on which Greenblatt focuses concerns the events of November 4th
when Sarracoll and his companions laid anchor off the coasts of Sierra
Leone, where they came upon a walled settlement "of about two hundred
houses" (193). Upon their entering the small town, the English soldiers to
their no small surprise saw the townspeople fleeing in all directions,
leaving the "finely built" houses to the taking of their 'visitors'. The latter,
the merchant acknowledges, stood amazed at what they saw: "We found
their houses and streets so finely and cleanly kept," Sarracoll writes, "that
it was an admiration to us all, for that neither in the houses nor streets was
so much dust to be found as would fill an egg shell" (193). After having
found back their way out of this maze of small yet tidy streets, the English
for no apparent reason set the town on fire. The leavetaking procedures
took less than a quarter of an hour, Saracoll adds, "the houses being
covered with reed and straw" (193).

For no apparent reason. What immediately strikes Greenblatt in Sarracoll's account is indeed the calm and casual manner in which the merchant recalls this sudden act of collective violence, the "moral blankness that rests like thick snow on Sarracoll's sentences" (194), as Greenblatt puts it. Rather than explaining the hidden motives one might suspect to underlie this rash and impulsive deed, Sarracoll emphasizes the velocity with which the fire spread, while simultaneously reminding himself – as if there were no conflict whatsoever between the two recollections – of the admiration he felt upon first seeing the negro-houses. Yet *is* there any real conflict, Greenblatt wonders? Might there not be instead "an aesthetic element in [Sarracoll's] admiration of the town, so finely built, so intricate, so cleanly kept, [which] somehow fuel[s] the destructiveness?" (194)

Part of the answer to the latter question can be found in *Marvelous Possessions. The Wonder of the New World* (1991), a later work of Greenblatt's, in which the new historicist method which in *Renaissance Self-Fashioning* served mainly for the analysis of literary texts, is brilliantly transposed onto the domain of non-literary Renaissance travel-writing. In the final chapter of this book ("The Go-Between"), Greenblatt offers the reader a stimulating analysis of *The Conquest of New Spain* (*Historia Verdadera de la Conquista de la Nueva España*), an-eye-witness account by one Bernal Díaz del Castillo of the three so-called Yucatán voyages that were undertaken by Spanish explorers in the second decade of the sixteenth century. The immediate interest of the *Historia* for our purposes lies in the fact that one of the episodes on which Díaz focuses contains remarkable parallels to Sarracoll's story. As a confidant of Cortés – who led the third Yucatán-voyage of 1519 – Díaz witnessed the conquest of the magnificent City of Mexico, whose marvelous palaces and gardens provoked in the Spanish *conquistadores* the same admiration Sarracoll experienced upon entering the much smaller town of the Sierra Leone "Negroes": "I say again," Díaz is quoted by Greenblatt, "that I stood looking at it and thought that never in the world would there be discovered other lands such as these." And he goes on: "[Of all these wonders that I then beheld] to-day all is overthrown and lost, nothing left standing" (133).

Despite his undoubtedly taking part in the 'overthrow' of the city, Díaz, writing nearly half a century after the events, obviously feels no need to provide any explanation as to the motives underlying the sudden urge of

destruction that overtook Cortés's men. He only keeps repeating that the
original view of the city left both him and his companions speechless:
"Gazing on such wonderful sights," Díaz adds, "we did not know what to
say, or whether what appeared before us was real" (133). Yet if the
taciturnity of the Spaniards lasted longer than that of their English
counterparts on the coasts of Western Africa – as did the ensuing
proceedings – both the outcome and the cause of the events recorded were
by and large identical: initial feelings of wonder and 'admiration' followed,
in a manner that can only be described as the *non-sequitur* of colonialism, by
an outburst of utter destruction.

'Admiration', 'wonder', 'marvels'. The Renaissance discourse of discovery
is replete with these and similar terms, all of which denote a "decisive
emotional and intellectual experience [felt] in the presence of radical
difference" (Greenblatt 1991: 14). As recalled several times throughout
Marvelous Possessions, the literally stupefying feeling of marvel immediately
triggers off in the colonists the need for appropriation, be it conceptual,
linguistic and/or physical. The term which Greenblatt uses to describe the
phenomenon, is "blockage": a cultural-psychological mechanism in which
the object of wonder is decisively marked and excluded as radically other.
Whereas Greenblatt's further analysis provides us with some idea as to the
ambivalent dialectics of the feeling of 'wonder', it is to the work of Michel
de Certeau (an influence Greenblatt has acknowledged whole-heartedly[1])
that we can turn for a particularly apt description of this highly complex

---

[1] De Certeau is more present in *Marvelous Possessions* than in any other work by
Greenblatt. In the introduction to *Learning to Curse* (Greenblatt 1990: 3) he is cited
together with Raymond Williams, Bakhtin, Foucault and Kenneth Burke as one of
the many guides on Greenblatt's intellectual journeys. The name of de Certeau
does not feature in the index to *Renaissance Self-Fashioning*. The earliest mention of
de Certeau in Greenblatt's work appears to be the essay "Loudun and London"
(Greenblatt 1986), which starts off from *La Possession de Loudun* (Certeau 1970).
The same study crops up in *Shakespearean Negotiations* (Greenblatt 1988: 185),
more precisely in a footnote on the subject of exorcism (where it is mentioned as
one of many studies on the subject). It may be interesting to keep in mind that de
Certeau was a visiting lecturer in California from 1978 to 1984.

mechanism. As a consequence of the experience of wonder, de Certeau writes, "[a] part of the world which appeared to be entirely other is brought back to the same by a displacement that throws uncanniness out of skew in order to turn it into an exteriority behind which an interiority, the unique definition of man, can be recognized" (1988: 219).

Even though the point is in no way over-emphasized in Greenblatt, it does seem important (especially in view of de Certeau's definition) to bear in mind that the experience of wonder at first left Díaz and his company speechless. What is witnessed cannot immediately be grasped in the conceptual frame of one's native language: it is something so strange and uncanny that at once it demands to be transformed, renamed and appropriated into familiar categories. Yet, immediately following this appropriative transformation a new threatening possibility arises, viz. that the other – identified, de Certeau recalls, as belonging to the great family of mankind – might turn out to be remarkably and dangerously similar to the self. Thus, whereas at first the feeling of wonder is seen to effect a "crucial break with an other that can only be described, only witnessed, in the language and images of sameness" (Greenblatt 1991: 135), immediately afterwards and in a strangely dialectical manner the same feeling "erect[s] absolute difference at the point of deepest resemblance" (ibid.).

The important thing to understand about Díaz' work, Greenblatt believes, is indeed his repeated insistence on the "radical distinction between Spanish practices and Aztec practices that are disturbingly homologous" (130). It is as if he were afraid to recognize part of the Mexicans' savage and ritual doings as his own. The most obvious instance of his fear is to be found in his account of religious practices he witnessed in a Mexican temple (132). At this point, all the wild stories of human sacrifice and ritual cannibalism Díaz is sure to have known from contemporary travel-books suddenly become threateningly real. Yet, while Díaz obviously feels revolted at what he sees, there is at the same time and somehow conversely a semi-conscious feeling that his own religion, one of the many motives for his embarking on a mission to the New World, actually – albeit symbolically – feeds on very similar practices (134). What Díaz describes at the point when he enters the temple is thus, Greenblatt writes, "not the unimaginably alien [...] but a displaced version of his own system of belief: temple, high altar, cult of holy blood, statues before which offerings are made, 'symbols like crosses'" (134).

Díaz cannot help but feel that what the savages do is uncannily similar to his own practices of worship, yet he will not and cannot tolerate the sense of brotherhood which this similarity somehow logically entails. All implied parallels between the culture of the other and the culture of the self must be warded off in a mysterious movement of psychic defense which results in utter destruction: "for a moment you see yourself confounded with the other," Greenblatt writes, "but then you make the other become an alien object, a thing, that you can destroy or incorporate at will" (135). And that is exactly what the Spanish will do.[2]

While the reasons for this display of massive destruction may have something to do with the Spaniards' genuine fear of being eaten alive by the savages (136), it would be a gross misunderstanding to consider their violent behaviour as an unmediated expression of brute *Wille zur Macht* (cf. Greenblatt 1980: 197). There is infinitely more to what Greenblatt in his essay on Marlowe termed the "acquisitive energies" of Renaissance Europeans, an aggregate of heterogeneous stimuli one might somewhat euphemistically label "the colonialist impulse." Even though the terminology may not in itself do sufficient justice to the complexity of whatever emotional and strategic considerations drove the colonists westward – a complex of often contradictory religious, cultural, ideological and pragmatic elements, as it turns out – it does seem crucial to understand

---

[2] Cf. also *Renaissance Self-Fashioning* in the chapter on the works of Spenser: "Europeans destroyed Indian culture not despite those aspects of it that attracted them but in part at least because of them. The violence of the destruction was regenerative; they found in it a sense of identity, discipline, and holy faith. In tearing down what both appealed to them and sickened them, they strengthened their power to resist dangerous longings, to repress antisocial impulses, to conquer the powerful desire for release." (Greenblatt 1980: 183) Greenblatt's conclusion is in need of some qualification, especially since in the chapter on Marlowe which follows the Spenser-chapter colonialist violence is proven to be counter-productive: instead of strengthening the colonists' sense of identity, it "reinforc[ed] the condition [it was] meant to efface" (198), viz. the feeling of homelessness as a consequence of the growing abstraction of categories of time and place. Colonialism, seen as the drawing of boundaries, the desperate longing for closure, precisely effects what it was set out to destroy: lack of certainty, meaning and identity.

that most of these were related to and to some degree even strengthened their central belief that the universe was characterized above all by unity and order, prime qualities which they believed to be symbolized in the image of the so-called Great Chain of Being. While the 'Chain' was, as A.O. Lovejoy has indicated, of quintessential epistemological and ontological importance during the Middle Ages, at the beginning of the early modern period, while increasingly coming under attack, the explanatory force of the symbolic structure retained considerable strength (Lovejoy 1936). Its impact, as E.M.W. Tillyard has illustrated in his infamous *The Elizabethan World Picture*, was even still such that every new discovery – of which there were plenty at that time – in one way or another had to be fitted into the chain before it could become, as it were, 'real' (Tillyard 1943). Yet whereas Tillyard is convinced that the chain itself warrants smooth continuity between the medieval period and the early Renaissance,[3] most historians nowadays believe that during the period Tillyard is writing about – the reigns of Henry VIII, Elizabeth I and James I – the medieval world-order slowly began to break down, ironically through this large-scale encounter with the Other. These frequent encounters, at home *and* abroad, in the eyes of some Elizabethans exposed the chain as an ideological framework, not a natural given. As Greenblatt puts it towards the end of his essay on Marlowe: "On the distant shores of Africa and America and at home, in their 'rediscovered' classical texts, Renaissance Europeans were daily confronting evidence that their accustomed reality was only one solution, among many others, of perennial human problems. Though they often tried to destroy the alien cultures they encountered, or to absorb them into their ideology, they could not always destroy the testimony of their own consciousness" (Greenblatt 1980: 219). The movement again is paradoxically dialectical: while, as Greenblatt puts it in *Marvelous Possessions*, the belief in one universal order is a fundamental precondition for the mechanism of blockage (1991: 121), the encounter with other cultures at the same time results in growing skepticism as to the exclusiveness of the European world-view and the God-given rather than the ideological nature of the Chain itself.

---

[3] Tillyard believes the transition from the Middle Ages to the early modern period to consist of slight modifications, a 'simplification' as he calls it of a "much more complicated medieval picture" (1943: 2-3; 100).

"[T]o burn a town or kill all of its inhabitants is to make an end and, in so doing, to give life a shape and a certainty that it would otherwise lack," Greenblatt writes *à propos* of Sarracoll's company (197). Yet, ultimately, this outrageously violent behaviour does not do away with the "uncircumscribed hell" the Europeans, like the heroes of Marlowe's plays, carry within.

All of this leads us to the second path onto which, according to Greenblatt, the feeling of wonder can open, one which does not lead, as with Díaz and Sarracoll, from "identification to estrangement" and hence to the urgent need of the "renaming, transformation, and appropriation" of the other, but, the other way round, "to articulations of hidden links between the radically opposed ways of being and hence to some form of acceptance of the other in the self and of the self in the other" (Greenblatt 1991: 135). This, it could be argued, is the path which Prospero has been following when towards the end of *The Tempest* he is finally able to acknowledge Caliban his. Read in this way, Prospero's words are taken to signal a purely mental, intellectual form of appropriation, the understanding that "the thing of darkness" he has been grappling with throughout the play is as much (and even more of) a reference to the stranger within as to the real, physically subjected other. Prospero's oft-quoted line can of course be interpreted differently – as indeed it often has been, as the assertion of his brute power over Caliban rather than as a reflection on his internalization of the other. Yet, the question remains whether the two readings are actually as opposed as they are sometimes made out to be. I am led to this remark by what I believe to be a crucial passage in the introductory chapter to *Renaissance Self-Fashioning*, in which Greenblatt states that the mechanism of 'self-fashioning' – the idea, emerging in the early modern period, that the self is not given as such, but has instead to be formed, 'fashioned' within the constraints imposed by society at large – has to be located "at the point of encounter between an authority and an alien" (Greenblatt 1980: 9): every self needs an authority to which it can submit – the King, the Bible, the State, ... – and an alien – the savage, woman, Satan, ... – over and above which it can position itself and from which it can demand submission. The important thing to grasp, Greenblatt adds, is that the alien, whether as a pure figment of the imagination or as a real live being, is simultaneously interiorised and really 'out there': "If both the authority and the alien are located outside the self, they are at the same time experienced as inward necessities, so that both submission and destruction are always already internalized" (9). The 'thing of darkness', in other words, is as much within as without. Furthermore, in questioning the existence of a definite, clear-cut borderline between self and other, it radically undermines the stable identity of the self, as indeed I hope to make clear with particular reference to *The Tempest*.[4]

The reference to Shakespeare's play immediately casts doubt over Greenblatt's belief – stated in the final chapter of *Marvelous Possessions* – that the path of wonder is a bifurcated one. In Greenblatt's view, the feeling in one direction leads, as with Díaz and Sarracoll, from "identification to estrangement" – from 'brother' to 'other' as Greenblatt puts it, whereas in the second one it follows the opposite path, from "radical alterity [...] to a self-recognition that is also a mode of self-estrangement: you *are* the other and the other is you" (Greenblatt 1991: 135). Greenblatt does not deal extensively with *The Tempest* in *Marvelous Possessions*, yet the evolution which the relationship between Prospero and Caliban undergoes throughout the play does seem to suggest a way out of his problematic dichotomy.[5] Rather than being "sharply opposed," I believe Shakespeare's play may enable one to perceive Greenblatt's separate 'paths' of wonder as two coexistent and possibly consecutive phases of one basic attitude ('wonder', 'colonialism', 'divine providence' or what you will).

Ironically, my reservations regarding Greenblatt's dichotomy spring from his own extensive analysis, earlier in *Marvelous Possessions*, of the well-known

---

[4] Greenblatt's concept of self-fashioning could no doubt also be read along the lines of Slavoj Zizek's Lacanian analysis of the workings of ideology (cf. especially Zizek 1989 and 1991). Fascinating though the prospect seems, it will have to be postponed to a later occasion.

[5] There are two other essays by Greenblatt in which *The Tempest* is treated more exhaustively: "Martial Law in the Land of Cockaigne" (1988: 129-63) and "Learning to Curse: Aspects of Linguistic Colonialism in the Sixteenth Century" (1990: 16-39).

late-medieval travel-book *Mandeville's Travels*. In this work Greenblatt detects the meanderings of the second path of wonder, where the other is not marked as radically different, but becomes a *brother*-ly other. In his analysis Greenblatt emphasizes the fundamental dividedness of the *Travels*: while in the first half Mandeville seems convinced that the various peoples he writes about all in one way or another deviate from the true Christian belief (the other is not only radically different, he is also radically wrong), in the second half there is a "collapse of the other into the same and an ironic transformation of the same into the other" (1991: 43-44). In the first part Mandeville has eyes only for the central Christian *doxa*, whereas in the second one he ultimately and somewhat unexpectedly gives voice to a belief newly arrived at, that his key to the complexity of nature is probably not the only one. "[W]e wot not whom God loves ne whom he hates," Mandeville confesses (45).

Remarkable though this may seem, Greenblatt adds, we should not let ourselves be too easily misled by Mandeville's overt "tolerance," especially since on closer inspection his broad-mindedness might well turn out to be no more than some sort of "theoretical curiosity" (46). Not only does it become increasingly obvious that throughout the book there is one people which is stigmatized as radically other – the Jews (50), it also remains highly questionable whether Mandeville (if such indeed is the name of the author of the *Travels*) has ever left Europe, let alone met the exotic races he writes about (33). Very likely, Greenblatt writes, Mandeville's tolerance *vis-à-vis* the other is a mere "metaphoric embrace," an artificial gesture of *comraderie* which leaves one to wonder "what [would be] its exigency in the real world" (46). What would have been left of Mandeville's tolerance if, like Prospero, he were to spend some real time with his 'antipodes' in a far-away country or on a far-away island? Conversely, Greenblatt's afterthoughts on *Mandeville's Travels* could even lead one to consider Prospero's 'acknowledgment' of Caliban as a similar 'metaphoric embrace', one which, possibly, Prospero engages in only because he already knows that very soon he will be able to set sail to Milan.

All in all, the above remarks might lead us a few steps further on our journey of wonder. One of the valuable suggestions Shakespeare seems to be making in *The Tempest*, is that it might help if, like Greenblatt and de Certeau, we were to regard the self and the other not as stable, fixed entities but as indissolubly interlocked, in a state of constant dialectical interplay, permanently negotiating the borders which divide and bind them together, constantly oscillating in time, from 'brother' to 'other' and backward. In thematizing these and other borders as relationally and ideologically positioned rather than as natural and immutable demarcations, Shakespeare's play is undeniably a product of its age, a time which, as de Certeau and other historians have shown, marks the beginning of the dissolution of the medieval religious cosmos in which all nature – including the limits differentiating one natural category from another – was believed to be God-ordained.[6] From the early modern period on – the era which both de Certeau and Greenblatt take as their field of enquiry – limits, borders and demarcations gradually begin to be seen as human and hence mutable constructs.

One of the artificial limits playfully thematized within *The Tempest* is, of course, the borders of the plot itself. In a path-breaking analysis, Peter Hulme has pointed out that Prospero's limiting of the history of the island to the date of his arrival is altogether not untypical of the practices of colonial historians (Hulme 1986: 123-5). "Here in this island we arriv'd," Prospero says (I.ii.171), convinced of the fact that with these words everything has been said. Paradoxically however, Prospero's silence only strengthens our belief, Hulme believes, that *The Tempest* is a play "where so much of what is crucial has taken place before the curtain rises" and that there is more to the play than Prospero's version of it (Hulme 1986: 114).[7]

---

[6] Cf. Certeau: "Recent works reveal the importance of transformations which took place in Western Europe from the sixteenth to the eigteenth century." (1988: 211) De Certeau's analysis of these transformations can be found in the fourth chapter of *The Writing of History*, "The Formality of Practices: "From Religious Systems to the Ethics of the Enlightenment (the Seventeenth and Eighteenth Centuries)" (1988: 147-205).

[7] It is this belief that seems to separate most 'new historicist' readings of *The Tempest* from those by so-called 'old historicists'. Whereas the latter attune their whole reading of Shakespeare's play to the figure of Prospero, the former are convinced that it is in no way possible to understand Prospero's doings without reference to Caliban. Typical new historicist readings of *The Tempest* would be Barker and Hulme (1985), Brown (1985), Hawkes (1985), Hulme (1986), Cartelli

Prospero's silence, in other words, makes us wonder what his first meeting
with Caliban actually must have been like. Interestingly, Shakespeare's play
contains two mutually exclusive accounts of that first encounter. In the
version of Caliban Prospero is at first seen to behave quite gently to the
native, whom he even teaches a new language. But then Prospero's attitude
changes completely – for no reason at all, Caliban's silence seems to imply –
and he drives Caliban away to the outer rim of the island, robbing him of all
"the qualities o' th'isle." In retort of Caliban's reproaches, Prospero accuses
his slave of having attempted to rape Miranda, an accusation, it must be
noted, which meets with Caliban's awkward silence.

While the blind spots in both Caliban's and Prospero's versions of the 'real
beginning' of the play, might lead one to wonder which of the two accounts
comes closer to the truth, Shakespeare very wisely doesn't bother to solve
the question. What is more important is that both stories – like most stories
of actual colonial encounters – involve a decisive demarcation, in one form
or another, between self and other. Again, I would like to turn to the work
of de Certeau who in a number of his essays has provided us with a most
illuminating reading of the phenomenon. I would like to take as a more
specific point of departure his analysis of Jean de Léry's *Histoire d'un voyage
faict en la terre du Brésil* (1578), the fifth chapter of *The Writing of History*
(Certeau 1988: 209-43). Given the story of his life, de Léry may turn out to
be a more reliable guide on our journey, one who might provide us with a
better understanding of the relationship between Prospero and Caliban than
either Díaz, Mandeville or Sarracoll could (Certeau 1988: 212-13). A young
French "partisan of the Reformation," Jean de Léry sailed from Geneva (his
self-chosen place of exile) to distant Brazil, where he was to join the
expedition of admiral Nicolas Durant de Villegagnon, a former fellow-
student of Calvin, who had departed to the New World to found a
Protestant mission on an island in the Bay of Rio. Very soon however,
"disgusted by the admiral's theological fluctuations," as de Certeau puts it, de
Léry withdraws from the mission and for a period of three months he lives
along the coast with the Tupinambou Indians before finally returning to
Geneva and from thence to his native country.

(1987); typical old historicist ones, apart from Tillyard (1943), can be found aplenty
in Smith (1969).

The full *Histoire* then, with its twenty-two chapters, can be read as the account of De Léry's circular journey, the plot of which, as Janet Whatley (1990: xxxvi) has pointed out, shows a number of striking similarities to that of Shakespeare's play: both protagonists are westerners forced to spend some time in a strange country peopled with strange beings and both after a significant period of time return to their native countries, thus concluding a journey "at the end of [which] the Savage is invented" (Certeau 1988: 213). There are of course important differences between the stories of Prospero and de Léry – the most important one being that the latter at no point seems to intend to turn the Tupinambou into his slaves – yet even the most superficial reading of the *Histoire* shows that in de Léry's mind too the mechanism of cultural 'blockage' is decisively at work.

Lack of space prevents me from a more thorough treatment of de Certeau's reading of de Léry's text, yet there is one central line of thought in his analysis that I would like to pursue: the problematic of writing versus speech, a highly suggestive dichotomy which, as de Certeau points out in his analysis of de Léry's text, can serve as a backdrop against which "the problems that the rising sun of the New World and the twilight of medieval Christianity would reveal to an intelligentsia" (Certeau 1988: 211) become strikingly significant. The dichotomy itself is taken up most explicitly in Shakespeare's play in the second scene of Act Three. In that scene Caliban advises Stephano and Trinculo first to take Prospero's books before they attempt to kill him: "Remember," Caliban says, "First to possess his books, for without them/ He's but a sot, as I am, nor hath not/ One spirit to command: they all do hate him/ As rootedly as I. Burn but his books" (III.ii.89-93). In so many words, Caliban, in defining the basic difference between Prospero and himself as a matter of possessing 'books' (i.e. written authority), sets the stakes for a play which Greenblatt in one of his discussions of *The Tempest* has called "[p]erhaps the profoundest literary exploration [of the] encounter between a lettered and an unlettered culture" (Greenblatt 1990: 23).[8] Caliban's words can easily be taken as a comment on

---

[8] Greenblatt mentions this particular passage in the title-essay of *Learning to Curse* (1991: 16-39). The essay – a very early one – clearly lacks the complexity of the lectures collected in *Marvelous Possessions*. The same remark can be made with reference to another essay in *Learning to Curse*, "Filthy Rites," in which Greenblatt

the new 'scriptural economy' which de Certeau believed to originate in the
rupture between the Middle Ages and the time when Shakespeare was
writing. While up to the sixteenth century, as de Certeau writes, the order of
the universe was guaranteed through reference to the sole Word of God, at
the beginning of the early modern period (roughly coinciding with de Léry's
age) this "religious cosmos [and its Author, jp] already appears to be replaced
by the text" (Certeau 1988: 216-7). This evolution in itself – a consequence of
many factors (the breaking up of the Christian *doxa* into different churches,
the discovery of the New World and of new ways of seeing, ...), all of which
rendered it increasingly difficult to view the world within the traditional
framework of the medieval Chain of Being – resulted in a wholly new status
of writing as such, of which, according to de Certeau, early-Renaissance
travel-books and ethnographical descriptions such as de Léry's give
exemplary evidence (Certeau 1988: 211). Rather than as a transparent
window on the immensity of the natural Empire of God, writing at that
point in time began to function as an instrument producing the Empire of
Man, who is now seen to assume the author-ity previously held by the
Divine Author himself. Writing – and this is something Caliban seems to
understand perfectly – has become an instrument of power, a means to fix
and produce reality.[9] He who possesses writing, possesses reality, possesses
power and civilization, possesses the other and has, as Caliban puts it,
"spirits to command." Caliban's words immediately remind one of the
passage in the *Histoire* in which De Léry recounts the moment when the
Tupinambou for the first time were confronted with the wonder of writing,

---

analyses the encounter between one John G. Bourke, U.S. Army Captain and
amateur ethnographer, and the Mexican Zuñi Indians in 1881. Here Greenblatt
interprets Bourke's 'wonder' as follows: "the very conception that a culture is alien
rests upon the perceived difference of that culture from one's own behavioral
codes, and it is precisely at the points of perceived difference that the individual is
conditioned, as a founding principle of personal and group identity, to experience
disgust" (Greenblatt 1990: 61). Later in the same essay, Greenblatt, somewhat
belatedly when compared to the more complex analyses in *Marvelous Possessions*,
acknowledges that the feeling of disgust "often coexists with understanding and
admiration." All in all, the cultural analyses in *Marvelous Possessions* seem to be at
least one step ahead of Greenblatt's earlier work.

[9] Cf. Ahearne 1995: 52ff and Certeau 1988: 214-15.

which "in their eyes [...] seemed like some kind of sorcery" (Certeau 1988: 214). While to de Léry writing in many ways is still a gift from God, a token of civility which the Indians lack completely, Caliban ironically perceives 'books' for what they really are: fragile materialisations of *a* truth (of a *pouvoir-savoir* as Foucault would have it), not the embodiment of the Word of God, but rather an embodiment of discursive Power itself. To further the irony, one could even say that it is precisely this insight which at some points in the play sets Caliban off from Prospero. The latter still seems to cling to old, 'medieval' conceptions of truth and books: for Prospero books and writing are what they are to de Léry, "a body of truth," a "faithful transmission of the origin" of all there is to know, i.e. the divine Logos. In the eyes of Prospero, knowledge, writing and books are pure, uncontaminated by matters base and political, and this is perfectly reflected in his early dichotomization in I.ii between his 'library' and his 'dukedom': "my library/ Was dukedom large enough," Prospero confesses to Miranda, while somewhat later in the same scene he recounts how Gonzalo, having heard of Prospero's impending exile, "furnished" his master "with volumes that/ I prize above my dukedom." Paradoxically of course, it was precisely his infatuation with his books and his library which led to his exile in the first place. When near the ending of the play Prospero decides to throw his books into the sea, he simultaneously throws off his old conception of (divine) truth and replaces it with a new insight in the Foucauldian power-knowledge Caliban already possessess.

Paradoxically, Caliban seems to have come to this insight precisely through his having taken over, or, more correctly, through his having been forced to take over Prospero's language, i.e. language seen in its broad sense, as defined by George Lamming: "not English, in particular, but speech and concept as a way, a method, a necessary avenue towards areas of the self which could not be reached in any other way" (Lamming 1984: 109). It is this language, Lamming writes, "which makes Caliban aware of possibilities" and confronts him with a part of himself – yet another 'thing of darkness'? – he was not aware of before. If we would have to give the 'way' Lamming refers to a name, it would be the 'path of pragmatism' or of 'purpose'.[10] For, whereas

---

[10] Read in this way Miranda's words to Caliban become heavy with irony: "I pitied thee,/ Took pains to make thee speak, taught thee each hour/ One thing or other:

at the beginning of the play, Caliban is still complaining about the poisoned gift of Language he has received from Prospero ("You taught me language; and my profit on't/ Is, I know how to curse. The red plague rid you/ For learning me you language!" (I.ii.365-7)), it becomes clear from the second scene in the third act on that Caliban has now grown 'wiser'. While upon their first meeting Caliban in all his 'naïve' generosity and bounteous hospitality showed Prospero the riches of his island, he now promises Stephano and Trinculo possession of these same treasures, but only in return for a service they are to do him first. With Prospero's language he seems to have taken over Prospero's strategic reasoning, and it would take (and still will take) several generations to find out where the path of pragmatism ultimately leads to.

A reading like the above not only emphatically undermines Prospero's conviction, stated in IV.i that Caliban is "a born devil, on whose nature Nurture can never stick," it also exposes as a delusion his belief that the 'scriptural economy' of which he himself during his stay on the island has become a prime representative, can completely capture the other. In much the same way as de Léry would eventually come to understand that the interpretative fabric of his learned writing could not fully capture the enigmatic 'fable' of the Tupinambou, so Prospero learns that part of Caliban's alterity – the Certalian 'excess' – will remain forever out of reach and, more threateningly, one step ahead.

Much as was the case with de Léry, then, something of Prospero does not return from the island on which he has spent so significant a part of his life (cf. Certeau 1988: 227). While the thought in itself might lead us to conclude that in *The Tempest* Shakespeare in very subtle ways deconstructs the Certalian categories of writing and speech, some caution seems to be in order: not only does it leave unanswered the question whether Shakespeare's theatre-language (written speech/spoken writing) actually falls under the category of 'writing', it also starts from the premise that as 'writing' it is of a

---

when thou didst not, savage,/ Know thine own meaning, but wouldst gabble like/ A thing most brutish, *I endow'd thy purposes/ With words that made them known*" (I.ii.353-58; emphasis added).

different, 'smarter' nature than the writing of de Léry. The complexities of cultural customs which de Léry fails to see, Shakespeare, in this view, is quick to capture. While de Léry fails to come to the conclusions Prospero arrives at at the end of the play, Shakespeare in all his splendid genius sees through the paradoxical nature of human relationships, knowledge and power. That at least is what we are led to conclude. Tempting though the idea may be, however, it is only one half of the key-dilemma on the new historicist-agenda: is Shakespeare free from all the worldly constraints (epistemological and other) that are imposed upon his lesser talented fellow-beings like de Léry, or – and this is the other half of the dilemma – is he, like them, fundamentally bound by the conventions of his time. The question is much too complex to be dealt with within the bounds of one single essay, but it might, after one more small detour, bring us back to our point of departure. Toward the end of "Martial Law in the Land of Cockaigne," yet another of his discussions of *The Tempest*, Greenblatt arrives at the question underlying most if not all of his work on Shakespearean drama: "What then is the relation between the theater and the surrounding institutions?" (Greenblatt 1988: 158). The ensuing answer immediately makes clear why the question is best asked in a discussion of *The Tempest*: it is precisely this play, Greenblatt writes, which "offers us a model of unresolved and unresolvable doubleness: the island in *The Tempest* seems to be an image of the place of pure fantasy, set apart from surrounding discourses; and it seems to be an image of the place of power, the place in which all individual discourses are organized by the half-invisible ruler," be it a divine one or an earthly one (ibid.). This doubleness itself, I believe, finds its supreme expression in the very adverb Shakespeare seems to have foregrounded in his play: 'now' taken on the one hand as the *hic et nunc* of the illusion of art itself (Greenblatt's place of fantasy) and, on the other hand, 'now' as the ultimate indication that every theatrical 'now' in some way relates to a worldly 'now' outside the walls of the theatre. Whether or not this should lead us to consider Shakespeare's play as a staging of the permanent battle between both 'now's' or, conversely, as a brilliant deconstruction of the dichotomy suggested above is a question better addressed at another occasion. Yet, in whichever direction future investigations might lead us, the voice of Shakespeare, like the 'fabulatory' speech of the Tupinambou, will no doubt continue to exceed the boundaries of our exegetical apparatus.

References

Ahearne, Jeremy. 1995. *Michel de Certeau. Interpretation and its Other.* Cambridge: Polity Press.

Arac, J. and B. Johnson, eds. 1991. *Consequences of Theory. Selected Papers from the English Institute, 1987-1988.* Baltimore and London: The Johns Hopkins UP.

Barker, Francis and Peter Hulme. 1985. "Nymphs and Reapers Heavily Vanish. The Discursive Con-texts of *The Tempest.*" In Drakakis 1985: 191-205.

Brown, Paul. 1985. "'This Thing of Darkness I Acknowledge Mine.' *The Tempest* and the Discourse of Colonialism." In Dollimore and Sinfield 1985: 48-71.

Cartelli, Thomas. 1987. "Prospero in Africa. *The Tempest* as Colonialist Text and Pretext." In Howard and O'Connor 1987: 99-115.

Certeau, Michel de. 1970. *La Possession de Loudun.* Paris: Julliard.

—. 1988. *The Writing of History* [1975]. Translated by Tom Conley. New York: Columbia UP.

—. 1992. *The Mystic Fable, vol.I: The Sixteenth and Seventeenth Centuries* [1987]. Translated by Michael B. Smith. Chicago and London: U of Chicago P.

Dollimore, Jonathan and Alan Sinfield, eds. 1985. *Political Shakespeare. New Essays in Cultural Materialism.* Manchester: Manchester UP.

Drakakis, John, ed. 1985. *Alternative Shakespeares.* London and New York: Methuen.

Greenblatt, Stephen J. 1980. *Renaissance Self-Fashioning from More to Shakespeare.* Chicago and London: The U of Chicago P.

—. 1982. "Introduction" to "The Forms of Power and the Power of Forms in the Renaissance." *Genre* 15 (1-2): 3-6.

—. 1986. "Loudun and London." *Critical Inquiry* 12: 326-46.

—. 1988. *Shakespearean Negotiations. The Circulation of Social Energy in Renaissance England.* Berkeley: U of California P.

—. 1990a. "Culture." In Lentricchia and McLaughlin 1990: 225-32.

—. 1990b. *Learning to Curse. Essays in Early Modern Culture.* New York and London: Routledge.

—. 1991. *Marvelous Possessions. The Wonder of the New World.* Oxford: Clarendon Press.

Hawkes, Terence. 1985. "Swisser-Swatter. Making a Man of English Letters." In Drakakis 1985: 26-46.

Howard, Jean E. and Marion F. O'Connor. 1987. *Shakespeare Reproduced. The Text in History and Ideology.* New York and London: Methuen.

Hulme, Peter. 1986. *Colonial Encounters. Europe and the Native Carribean 1492-1797.* London and New York: Methuen.

Kermode, Frank, ed. 1954. *The Arden Edition of the Works of William Shakespeare. The Tempest.* London: Methuen and Co. Ltd.

Lamming, George. 1984. *The Pleasures of Exile* [1960]. London and New York: Allison and Busby.

Lentricchia, Frank and Thomas McLaughlin. 1990. *Critical Terms for Literary Study.* Chicago and London: U of Chicago P.

Lovejoy, Arthur O. *The Great Chain of Being. A Study of the History of an Idea.* Cambridge, Mass.: Harvard UP.

Pease, Donald. 1991. "Toward a Sociology of Literary Knowledge. Greenblatt, Colonialism, and the New Historicism." In Arac and Johnson 1991: 108-53.

Pieters, Jürgen. 1996. "Van oude dingen, de zaken die voorbijgaan. Het New Historicism en de paradigmawissel in het historisch literatuuronderzoek." *Tijdschrift voor Literatuurwetenschap,* n.°4, 276-88.

Smith, Hallet, ed. 1969. *Twentieth Century Interpretations of The Tempest.* Englewood Cliffs, N.J.: Prentice Hall, Inc.

Tillyard, E.M.W. 1943. *The Elizabethan World Picture.* London: Chatto and Windus.

Whatley, Janet, ed. 1990. *Jean de Léry. History of a Voyage to the Land of Brazil, Otherwise called America.* Berkeley: U of California P.

Zizek, Slavoj. 1989. *The Sublime Object of Ideology.* London: Verso.

—. 1991. *For They Know Not What They Do. Enjoyment as a Political Factor.* London: Verso.

Look Who's Talking

Caliban in Shakespeare, Renan and Guéhenno

Koenraad Geldof

The Jester

There are eras of which it is very difficult to say whether they constitute an end or a beginning. Such are, for instance, the sixteenth and seventeenth centuries, in the course of which many authors came to realise that a certain secular conception of the world was slowly crumbling under the weight of an increasing social, cultural and political complexity. A symbolic universe defined by structures of similarity and in which the hegemony of allegorical interpretation as well as the semantic and normative transitivity of knowledge and practice assured the relative homogeneity of a form of life and thought, is replaced by the innumerable forms of the experience – at times painful and grotesque, at times experimental and innovative – of the same and the other (Foucault 1988: 60ff; Certeau 1988: 71ff; Certeau 1990b: 195ff). A new relationship to the world, the other and the self emerges and, in a considerable number of cases, this results in a curious and variously proportioned mixture of tradition and innovation. Eventful times, unruly times that seem to be certain of one thing only: doubt and uncertainty. Hence the wide-spread sentiment of a state of crisis and the correlative sense of a world in need of reconstruction. Should one mourn that which is passing away or should one sing the glory of the feverish new dawn rising on the horizon? Such is the fundamental ambiguity that traverses numerous texts, literary or not, of the period and locks in mutual opposition – even within their underlying epochal affinity – so many discourses of the sixteenth and seventeenth centuries.

What to make, in this interdiscursive constellation, of Shakespeare's *The Tempest* (1611-12) and of that bizarre character called Caliban? That the piece partakes in the in-between mentioned above is certain. Still, the exact nature of this participation must be specified. *The Tempest*, we may recall, is the last piece written by Shakespeare. It closes an oeuvre and, in many ways, an era. The action takes place on an island whose status is hybrid. On the one hand, it does not quite resemble the magical fairy-islands of medieval literature, even though it retains some of their traits in the events that take place on it; while on the other hand, it is not yet that profane space that will serve, a little later, as the docile and mute ground for the frenetic activities of that cardinal hero of the entrepreneurial myth, Robinson Crusoe. This semi-magical, semi-profane place is profoundly marked by the tension between two conflicting logics of power.[1] According to the first logic, the legitimacy of power follows, as if naturally and spontaneously, from a set of qualities including birth and education. The efficacy of this legitimation – that is to say, the authority this power exerts over those that submit themselves to it – is based on a faith in the omnipotence of power, allegorically represented in the fusion of the natural and the supernatural. If, at the end of the day, Prospero vanquishes Alonso and his allies, this is essentially due to the fact that these latter form part of Prospero's own universe of faith. Yet the victory of the king-magician is only partial and no doubt provisional, since one crucial character remains strangely distant in the scene of the final reconciliation: Antonio, Prospero's brother. Family membership, which is essential for the first form of legitimate power – as is indeed emphasised

---

[1] My remarks on the mutation of the problem of (State) power in the course of the sixteenth and seventeenth centuries are primarily based on Luhmann 1989: 65-148 and Certeau 1990b.

through the imminent, and expedient, marriage of Ferdinand to Miranda, no longer has any role to play here, which is all the more surprising seeing that it already exists. Antonio represents another logic of power. To be sure, he still inhabits the same cultural space as Prospero in the sense that he incarnates the sole threat recognised by traditional legitimate power, i.e. the conspiracy of peers. But this is not all, nor is it even essential. Antonio signals a form of power without faith, a power that is no longer the natural emanation of a social position but is rather the result of a consciously strategic effort at appropriation. He is the most Machiavellian[2] of all the nobles in *The Tempest*, a man without conscience, a cunning strategist ready to kill when necessary (Prospero, on the contrary, only terrifies others in order to consolidate their faith in his omnipotence), and he is moreover one of those singularly unimpressed by the demonstrations of magical power. If need be, he himself invents new magical terrors without believing in them, simply in order to further his cause. As a result of the crucial difference between Prospero and Antonio, and given the inauspicious silence of the latter at the end of the play, the reader will never know whether Prospero's victory is definitive, or whether it is rather the swan song of a type of power soon to be superseded by more prosaic conceptions and practices of power.

Where does Caliban figure in this conflict? Up to a certain point, it is possible to say that he doesn't figure in it at all. To be sure, Caliban has been expropriated by Prospero, he is a creature of nature subjugated by the creature of culture that is Prospero. Still, Caliban is neither a "noble savage" akin to Montaigne's cannibals, nor the kind of *idiot savant* that was another current character of the age. The few affinities some have tried to detect between Caliban and Montaigne's cannibals are, it seems to me, subordinated to the dominant semantic and actantial thrust of the play, that is to say, to the conflict between two logics of power sketched above. From this perspective, Caliban appears as a creature that is not so

---

[2] For the Machiavellian nature of Antonio and his discourse, see Kermode 1994. Contrary to Kermode's suggestions, however, I would attribute a much more substantial weight to the question of political power, and this at the expense of the, to my mind excessive, importance Kermode accords the character of Caliban and the nature-culture opposition.

much natural as it is socially inferior, incapable of rising to the level of Prospero. Even if his education had been a success, he would have needed a marriage to be fully accepted, and this is ruled out from the very start: nobility does not ally itself with commoners. A socially inferior being, then, who is neither particularly clever – he really believes that Trinculo and Stephano are reliable workers, nor driven by some notion or other of taking control: indeed, Caliban is less motivated by any logic of power than by the infra-political logic of vengeance. That is why he wishes to destroy the master and his emblems, the books, rather than replace them with a view to another politics. To the extent that Caliban's resistance to Prospero is predicated on resentment, it is, actantially speaking, far less dangerous than is Antonio's conspiratorial zeal: the latter's relation to Prospero remains uncertain and open, whereas Caliban's coup, burlesque rather than seditious, shamefully misfires and leaves him humbly obedient to his master. The hierarchy between Prospero and Caliban is never threatened. The real risk is situated elsewhere and doubtlessly only becomes truly acute after the act, after the curtain has fallen. In this sense Shakespeare's play is a truly transitional nexus in which an older order triumphs for the last time, though the triumph is already no longer total, and in which a later dispensation timidly announces itself. What can be expected from this point onwards is that Prospero's future will be most precarious.

The Heir

In the meantime, history continues its slow labour of transformation and the still ambivalent in-between of the sixteenth and seventeenth centuries progressively moulds itself into a space where the political, social, economic and cultural contradictions proliferate. The eighteenth and nineteenth centuries are marked by the forcible emergence of two new historical actors about to enter into a bitter battle for power: the "third estate" or bourgeoisie, and the "people." This period witnesses two revolutions whose compatibility will remain undecided well into the twentieth century. The 1789 Revolution redefines the very notion of "legitimate power" in making the citizen both the origin and the destination of political structures. Yet, the interpretation of this event is equivocal from the very beginning: everybody refers to 1789 without there being a genuine consensus as to the exact nature of the revolutionary process. The nineteenth century and the industrial revolution further compound the confusion. In line with the spectacular eruption of capitalist modes of production, the nature of the signifier "people" alters and, little by little, a wholly different notion of revolution begins to circulate. The anonymous mass of "the poor" becomes that of the "proletariat" for whom 1789 is only an insignificant reshuffle in the board of management. To fully transform social reality now means to break, violently if necessary, the political and economic power of the wealthy classes. In such a programme, a simply political revolution no longer suffices: the modern revolution will have to be social and economic.

The nineteenth century, then, is haunted by the idea of History. Attempts are made to divine its direction – progress or decadence, to find out the principle[s] that really make[s] history move – ideas, the forces of economic production, the proletariat, the Party, the people, enlightened minds, etc.[3] Such is, roughly, the politico-social and intellectual stage on which Ernest Renan (1823-92) makes his appearance.[4] The start of his intellectual career is grandiloquent, visionary, optimist, confident. *L'Avenir de la science. Pensées de 1848* inaugurates a long labour of reflection and writing marked from the beginning, it seems, by an unshakeable faith in the progress of human history, in the emancipatory capacities of scientific rationality.

Renan will always remain faithful to his ambitious vocation of knowledge, but the concrete modalities of his philosophy of history are subject to considerable change. This can be clearly seen with the publication of *L'Avenir de la science*, which Renan had previously kept in his drawer as a secret source of inspiration and only presented to the wider public in 1888 under the cover of a preface revealing the evolution of his thought since 1848. On the whole, the preface states that *L'Avenir* is a book of the

---

[3] See also Angenot 1989: 315ff.

[4] The few preliminary remarks on Renan in what follows are primarily inspired by Beaumarchais 1984, Gaulmier 1985, Psichari 1977 and, to a lesser extent, Sirinelli 1992.

author's youth which shares with all such debutant efforts its undeniable weaknesses (cf. Renan 1890: ix). To begin with, philosophy in those remote days suffered from an excessive confidence in the role of humanity as a decisive agent in history. History does retain its sense and direction, but the Renan of 1888 adds that its moving force is perhaps less humanity itself than a kind of historical fatality[5] or evolutionary law which precisely eludes human initiative (cf. Renan 1890: xiii).[6] However this may be, and despite all his doubts, Renan maintains his humanist creed, albeit clearly in a profoundly disenchanted form. Only his confidence in the salvational power of scientific knowledge preserves him from the bleakest pessimism. In its turn, this entails a second substantial revision of the 1848 humanism, which in some of its aspects was a humanism with a social or even egalitarian dimension. In 1888, the progress of the human species no longer depends on the common effort of all, but must be attributed to a very specific class of men, that of the *savants*, the scholars and scientists. From this point onwards, knowledge is the true motor force of human evolution; only great culture, "intensive culture," matters and it develops beyond, next to and, if necessary, *in spite of* the "extensive culture" of the masses. The preface puts this more crudely: "almost all my illusions of 1848 had been shattered, rendered impossible. I saw the fatal necessities of human society; I resigned myself to a state of creation in which a great deal of evil serves as the condition for a small amount of good, where an imperceptible quantity of aroma is extracted from an enormous *caput mortuum* of waste matter" (Renan 1890: ii-iii). What Benjamin would later denounce as the very scandal of "culture" – to wit, that all work of culture is born from a state of barbarism – is dryly assumed here by Renan, who makes it the indispensable condition for scientific, social and cultural progress. This aristocratic "humanism" also explains why Renan no longer recognises the necessity to educate the popular masses. Such a project would be detrimental to the very quality of cultural production: "A layer of water that spreads out has the habit of becoming thinner" (Renan 1890:

---

[5] Cf. Renan 1890: iii, where the author speaks of "fatal necessities of human society."

[6] This passage is reminiscent of what Foucault was to say some decades later concerning the posssibly entirely ephemeral importance of the anthropological paradigm; see Foucault 1988.

viii). In the realm of the education and acculturation of inferior social classes, the virtues to be inculcated are rather those of docility and of respect for the social hierarchy.[7] Such, then, is Renan's attitude towards the "socialist problems" (Renan 1890: i) of the period, that is to say – and Renan's formulation is highly symptomatic, towards the social question whose diverse aspects would acquire a more definite shape in the latter half of the nineteenth century. The fatal price of progress is social inequality. And the sole source of power and salvation is called knowledge.

In this intellectual, moral and political state of mind, Renan publishes, from 1878 onwards, a series of "philosophical dramas," collected in one volume in 1888,[8] the same year that saw the prefaced edition of *L'Avenir de la science*. In the first edition of *Caliban* (1878), the author warns his audience: "Dear reader, please find in the game [*jeu*] that follows the entertainment [*divertissement*] of an ideologue, not a theory; a fantasy of the imagination, not a political thesis" (Renan 1878: ii).[9] Game, entertainment, fantasy – it is as if Renan wants to beg his readers' pardon; the qualifications appear to place what is about to begin among the author's minor, less serious productions. The philosophical drama will only be a brief intermezzo. Yet Renan turns recidivist: further plays follow, and the preface to the 1888 collection clearly shows that the stakes of the philosophical dramas far exceed the level of a simple "divertissement." The sense of the literary intervention is double. First, the philosophical dramas constitute a kind of correction, both epistemological and anthropological, of the human sciences. These latter, as distinct from the exact sciences, are irremediably hybrid: the conceptual element never purely figures *more geometrico* in them, it is always beset

---

[7] This is also one of the essential lessons of *La Réforme intellectuelle et morale* which Renan published in 1871. In this work, he directs his attention to the causes of France's shameful defeat in the 1870 war against Germany. It is primarily this Renan which the Right sought to canonise as one of its *maîtres-à-penser*.

[8] The pieces in question are *Caliban* (sequel to *The Tempest*), *Eau de jouvence* (sequel to *Caliban*), *Le Prêtre de Nemi*, *L'Abesse de Jouarre* (1802) and *Le Jour de l'an 1886: prologue au ciel*.

[9] All translations by Ortwin de Graef.

with a good deal of faith, that is to say, with purely normative and ideological concerns. It is therefore advisable to adapt the enunciative structure of these sciences to their hybrid nature and to conceive them in the manner of dialogues where differing points of view can be performed and brought to interact. Renan puts it as follows: "There are no dialogues on geometry; for geometry is true in an impersonal manner. But everything that involves a shade of faith, of voluntary adherence, of choice, antipathy, sympathy, hatred and love, is best served with an expository form where each opinion is incarnated in one person and comports itself like a living being. These were the reasons that led me, one day, to choose the form of the dialogue to express certain trains of thought" (Renan 18887: ii). We have come a long way from the "divertissement d'idéologue." In addition to this, the term "ideologue" is not really appropriate here, since in these plays each ideological position comes up against its other and the monological is thereby dissolved into an enunciative multiplicity that is thoroughly dialogical. Will the Renan we discover here be different from the author of the preface to *L'Avenir de la science*?

The dialogue is further doubled by a second structural component of the philosophical drama which equally carries an epistemological charge: the action. The plays, in fact, have nothing to do with "the real history, that which happened" (Renan 1888: ii); rather, they pertain to "the ideal history, that which has materially never occurred but has nonetheless come to pass in an ideal sense thousands of times" (Renan 1888: ii). The subject matter will be possible events, either those that could have taken place, or those that may well take place one day. What emerges from this is a laboratory in which the creation of hypothetical situations allows the author to think through certain ideas or convictions to the end.[10] In this respect, the plays also reveal their anthropological purport to the extent that they demonstrate the relativity of all ideas and of human power: the human being is fatally caught in a set of intersubjective and social relations which it does not control, it is master neither of its actions, nor of its thoughts: "Man clearly sees, at this point in time, that he will never know

---

[10] Concomitant to this is Renan's evident refusal of all anecdotism. He only admits a theatre that is "free and without local colour" (Renan 1888: ii).

anything either of the supreme cause of the universe, or of his own destiny. [...] A dramatic action is better suited to draw out these doubts, these twilights, these audacities followed by retrenchments, these comings and goings of thought, than all abstract discussions together" (Renan 1888: iii). It remains to be seen whether the *savant*, the hero of Renan-the-ideologue's discourse, will succeed in resisting the numerous dramatic turns and detours and in firmly establishing his power. What is at stake here is the very possibility of aristocratic humanity. Up to this point, we have only come across one single indication that fully conforms to the world-view proposed in the preface to *L'Avenir de la science*, to wit the double, artistic and social significance Renan attributes to his dramatic output. Let us say, all too swiftly, that Renan aspires to a form of theatre that would live up to the requirements of his aristocratic humanism. Which explains his irritation with contemporary drama: "Such a theatre would evidently have nothing in common with our present theatre, that poor substitute for the coffee-concerts, where foreigners, those from the provinces, the bourgeoisie only look for a way to spend an agreeable evening" (Renan 1888: ii-iii). Given the fact that, according to Renan, books are already distributed through two different channels, one popular, the other reserved for a small elite of "connaisseurs," dramatic art, too, would benefit from a clearer differentiation between the mass audience happy with "honest *entertainment* [*divertissement*]" (Renan 1888: iii; emphasis added) and an "elite audience" that knows how to appreciate the conceptual imagination and can enrich it with its own imagination (see Renan 188: iii).

Does aristocratic art defend and illustrate aristocratic humanity? A reading of *Caliban* and, to a lesser extent, *Eau de jouvence* might give us an answer. As we have seen, at the end of *The Tempest* all appears to return to order and Prospero and his allies prepare themselves for the return journey to Milan. Apparently, the play effects a revolution in the etymological sense of the term (see Arendt 1985: 25-81). Still, the reconciliation between the noble protagonists was not total and, consequently, the return will doubtlessly have been somewhat hazardous. Such is the point of departure for Renan's *Caliban*. A first striking difference from Shakespeare: the number of actors is considerably increased. Among the new characters, there are bourgeois, artists, *savants*, men of the cloth, and, last but not least, the people. The social universe has become more complex and when the conflict between the various parties finally bursts into flame, it is certain that it will not turn into the kind of family quarrel we witnessed in Shakespeare. And conflict there will be. Prospero keeps aloof from public affairs and is concerned only with his science. Meanwhile, everyone is displeased, everyone grumbles. Caliban, for instance, continues his overt mockery of Prospero: "I told him [Prospero] that I would be good, and he was dumb enough to believe me" (Renan 1888: 10). Visibly, he has still not forgiven Prospero for having illegitimately taken possession of his island. He is a rancorous being for whom language is only an instrument of slander and calumny. Yet something fundamental has changed. Caliban's discontent has become more philosophical, more political. He is no longer simply moved by a blind desire for vengeance: Renan has turned him into a social human being and has substituted the island with the city, a metonymical condensation of the social universe. Caliban's discourse targets social inequality, the economic exploitation of the many by the few (Renan 1888: 12). From this point onwards, Prospero is only the name of a contested social order, the name, too, of all the illusions deployed by power to fool the people. As for Caliban, he no longer buys it and he gives Prospero's principal lieutenant, Ariel, a piece of his mind: "When the people will realise that the upper classes have led them by superstition, you'll see what kind of life they will have in store for their old masters. This hell we have been frightened with never existed. These monsters created by Prospero's magic were imaginary; but they tormented me as if they were real. Magic! you just wait and see – soon there won't be any left" (Renan 1888: 17). Such is the discourse of a revolutionary in the modern sense of the term. What is still missing for the moment is a propitious occasion to effectively move on to action. It will not be long in the waiting.

Then there are the members of the upper classes who, it seems, no longer form a homogeneous front defending the same interests. In the face of an imminent popular revolt, the nobility and the aristocrats react differently and Renan makes use of a scene of feasting to allow both to voice their opinions. The noblemen gradually come to realise what Prospero still has not grasped, namely that the era of magical and natural power approaches its end. To control the masses, it is pointless to educate them, as is suggested by Simplicon, a schoolmaster (Renan 1888: 36-37); rather, what is needed are myths, and faith. Yet this latter is poignantly absent, as are the means to re-animate it. Not even the idea of the "nation" can resolve the problem: "The nation, no matter how you conceive of it, will only ever respond to the interests of the few. The many will be sacrificed. How do you convince people to get themselves killed for a cause that will only ever benefit a small number of the privileged?" (Renan 1888: 36). The situation of the nobility is one of deadlock; what remains is either a rather naïve cynicism or a quietist hedonism: "all is vanity, except the joy of the present hour" (Renan 1888: 39), says Orlando, one of the noblemen. Bonaccorso and Bevilacqua, representatives of the bourgeoisie, share the nobility's total disdain for the people, but they distinguish themselves by their greater political realism. From their perspective, the threat of a popular revolution ought not to be trivialised. One should not make too much fun of Caliban and the populace: "As time goes by, Caliban may well have a future" (Renan 1888: 47). The inertia of the nobility is therefore to be strongly condemned, for it renders the situation even more dangerous: "Instead of dancing, we would be better employed arming ourselves" (Renan 1888: 41). In short, the established order is already dying away, more as a result of inner uncertainty and inaction than of exterior pressure. Trinculo, the jester, aptly summarises the dead-end when he sighs: "I have never seen a feast that looked more like a funeral than this one." Or again: "No silliness to come up with, then! O evening of the end of the world!" (Renan 1888: 46). And Prospero? Far away from Milan, in the tranquillity of his Pavian retreat, he pursues his research, the end of which is not to increase the knowledge of life, nor to consolidate his power, but to find a way to die peacefully and without pain (Renan 1888: 69). A *mise en abyme* of the future?

Finally, the hour of revolt has arrived, the people rise and Caliban puts himself at the head of the crowd: he is in command now – contrary to Shakespeare's Caliban, Renan's protagonist moves at the centre of the battle for power, he *is* its centre. Yet on closer inspection, Caliban remains a curious revolutionary. Faced with a people that, incidentally, does not even know him[11] and has trouble understanding his discourse,[12] he plays

---

[11] "A man of the people: This Caliban is full of common sense! Where is he from? What clarity in what he says! He loves the people" (Renan 1888: 58).

the role of the radical and the incorruptible, proclaiming a State without privileges and exhorting the people to destroy all the symbols of the old regime, starting with Prospero's books, the veritable source of the enslavement of the people (Renan 1888: 55-57). The seditious rhetoric seduces the people and soon the newly fashioned revolutionary is canonised by an intellectual: "Every revolution produces its great man. The great man of this one is Caliban, the great citizen Caliban" (Renan 1888: 57). Yet as soon as Caliban has assured himself of the unconditional loyalty of the people, he abandons all revolutionary action and re-styles himself as a genuine statesman: "Citizens, a little silence! Place your interests in our hands. Surveys will be undertaken; commissions will be nominated; all will be given satisfaction. We have come from you, we are for you, we are by you. The sole preoccupation of the government will be the welfare of the people. But citizens, order is necessary. Put down your arms, return to your homes, crown your victory with moderation and the respect of property" (Renan 1888: 63). Even though Caliban's victory is total and Prospero's reign is definitively relegated into the past – he and his spirits are impotent, since nobody believes in their power,[13] the political and social balance is swiftly re-established: the gullible people obey Caliban and, notwithstanding some token resistance on the part of the noblemen, the "owners" discover that the revolution was a highly moderate one, that they will not find it difficult to get along well with the new power, especially as it is astonishingly deferential to their interests.

---

[12] "Caliban: The main thing is that we are exploited./ First man of the people: What did he say?" (Renan 1888: 53)

[13] See Renan 1888: 67-86, and in particular Ariel's discourse, the most important passages of which are the following: "O my master, our art is vanquished; it is impotent against the people. [...] How was it that, through our charms, we could so easily persuade our adversaries on the enchanted island? It was because Alonso and his allies were susceptible to our charms. They were open to them, they believed in them. [...] The people won't have any of this. [...] Magic no longer has a purpose. The revolution is realism. All that is an appearance to the eye, all that is ideal, not substantial, does not exist for the people. [...] The people is positivist. To be susceptible to our terrors, one must believe in them. What is to be done when the people is positivist?" (Renan 1888: 76-78)

Strange to behold: it is not the revolutionary who takes over power in order to change its nature, it is power that transforms the revolutionary. Here is how Caliban expresses himself in a monologue immediately after he has seized the power: "No, I would not have believed that reigning would be so sweet. [...] I was unfair to Prospero; slavery had embittered me. But now as I'm lying here in his bed, I judge him as one judges a colleague. There was good in him, and, in many things, I am disposed to imitate him" (Renan 1888: 64). As regards the people, Caliban's discourse turns into downright cynicism: "What is more odious [...] than this importunate impatience of the people, this train of impossible petitions with which they burden me! What avid longing for joy! what subversive pretensions! [...] Property is the stabiliser of society; I feel a great deal of sympathy for the owners" (Renan 1888: 64-65). In addition, the new leader even goes so far as to protect his old master from the Inquisition which refuses to accept that Prospero, through the device of his "euthanasia"-project, blurs the boundaries between man, God and nature: for the Church, scientific freedom must submit to the law of faith. Truly the incarnation of the secular republican State, Caliban intervenes in favour of Prospero, thereby showing himself a reliable lieutenant of what previously he hated with a passion: science. When the Papal legate tries to convince Caliban that Prospero is nothing but an incorrigible heretic, he alludes to his dark past as a slave. Caliban retorts as follows: "Shut up. Do not remind me of those days... What once was, is no longer. I am the heir of Prospero's rights; I must defend him. Prospero is my protégé. He must be allowed to work in peace, with his philosophers and his artists, under my patronage. His labours shall be the glory of my reign. I will have my part in them. I will exploit him; such is the law of this world" (Renan 1888: 96-97). The old Duke has lost his political sovereignty but, as a citizen, he has gained absolute freedom of research (Renan 1888: 90-91). Prospero's reaction? "Upon my faith, long live Caliban!" (Renan 1888: 91)

After all these turns in *Caliban*, the reader is entitled to ask who exactly has gained what. Let us begin with the indisputable loser, fooled by this story and by History: the people. It believed that it could take possession of the world, but in the end it remained what it had ultimately always been: an indistinct mass used by others in their own interests. In the end, the disillusioned people realise that Caliban is just another master: "And he [Caliban], he announced that he would not resemble the others. [...]

You believe that the world is changing, and it always remains the same"
(Renan 1888: 93). Thus, the power of the few over the innumerable mass
of humans emerges as something of a fatality. Caliban does not leave the
battle victorious either. True, he has passed from slavery to the rank of
master, but his being will henceforward be determined by the structures of
power. The accession to power, it seems, coincides equally fatally with the
negation of the origins of whoever reigns. It would moreover be wrong to
say that Caliban takes precedence over his master, since, in a certain way,
he continues to depend upon him. The splendour of the State is the
business of *savants* and artists, not politicians. By destroying the tutelage
exerted by the nobility and the Church over State and culture, Caliban has
liberated these latter, but the State is presently re-inscribed in an
instrumental relation towards the world's true centre of gravity: the order
of knowledge. Thus, in the long run, Prospero is the one who wins by
losing. The collapse of magical power and knowledge signifies the total
emancipation of human knowledge, represented by the noble race of
savants. Behind the backs of the revolutionaries reigns, in all sovereignty,
the eternal cunning of knowledge which continues, through an
imperturbable and slow continuous progression, to perfect itself, beyond,
thanks to or in spite of all surface ruptures of history. At the end of the
day, Caliban is only an accidental hero, he remains the poor slave he
always was, working for the infinite and eternal development of the Spirit.
Decidedly, if history turns out to be rational, it is because it is thoroughly
cynical. All of this, incidentally, is amply confirmed by the sequel to
Caliban, Eau de jouvence. Prospero and the vicissitudes of power in a
world replete with superstition and religious fanaticism are its only
protagonists. Caliban must content himself with the modest role of
protector of the autonomy of free scientific research from anything that
threatens it in any way. In the preface, Renan affirms that after Caliban's
coup d'Etat, Prospero lost, for the moment, an instance of the sublunary
power that is ultimately his birthright, but that in the meantime Caliban
is better than any other solution (Renan 1888: 107-11). After all, what's
the difference? Seeing that the Spirit can pursue its labour. Even
Prospero's death, at the end of *Eau de jouvence* (Renan 1888: 241-48), is not
really dramatic, since the continuity of his reign, the reign of the Spirit, is
guaranteed by his heir, Caliban, who solemnly proclaims: "Master, thou
shalt be obeyed" (Renan 1888: 247).

The Schizophrenic

In Shakespeare, Caliban was a being in the margin of the story, a walk-on walked over by the powers at play. Renan rendered him more paradoxical. The inferior being is metamorphosed into a social and political human being and he seizes power. Still, far from emancipating himself from the tutelage of Prospero, Caliban continues to serve him. The revolution is therefore not necessarily a catastrophe for the power of knowledge, even though it is the work of popular force. Yet in the first decades of the twentieth century the Renanian scenario is seriously challenged. The Great War, perfecting the technology of death to a previously unknown degree, calls into question the very value of Western civilisation.[14] The aftermath of the war is marked by numerous anti-establishment movements – at once socio-economic, political and cultural – that are so many symptoms of an aged society, suffering itself as a disease and riddled with internal conflicts. The plot is thickened further by that Eastern glow that puzzled and surprised Romain Rolland. The dawn of a new civilisation, the definitive end to social inequality, the ultimate vengeance of the poor... : the Russian Revolution does not fail to intoxicate many Western minds and – crucially – renders any reference to the signifier "revolution" considerably more complicated and ambiguous.[15] Is 1917 the legitimate heir of 1789, a kind of world-scale fulfilment of the ideas of Rousseau and Robespierre, or is it rather an entirely new event whose very sense and extent remain to be thought? Does Russia imitate France or, on the contrary, should France, bourgeois republic that it is, imitate Russia and perfect the process begun two centuries earlier? Such are the questions that divide opinion and give rise to an increasingly sharp line of demarcation between those who think the twentieth-century world according to the ideas of 1789 – the socialists and the radical republicans – and those who find a political and intellectual point of reference in

---

[14] For a concise analysis of this epoch of upheaval, whose importance for the 1920s and '30s is sometimes underestimated, see Furet 1995: 49-78 and Hobsbawm 1994: 21-53.

[15] As regards the discursive confusion surrounding the events of 1917 and their significance for France, see Kriegel 1974: 33ff and, especially, Furet 1995: 17-48.

Moscow – the communists, certain artistic avant-garde groups and the newly styled fellow travellers.

The face of the world has decidedly changed. Caliban and Prospero cannot but be affected by it. In 1928, Jean Guéhenno (1890-1978), *normalien*, future member of the *Académie*, but nowadays largely (and significantly) forgotten,[16] publishes *Caliban parle*, his second book, fragments of which had already been published in *Europe*, a journal founded by Romain Rolland as an international(ist) forum for independent and pacifist intellectuals.[17] The previous year, this self-taught ex-labourer[18] had already

---

[16] In *Dernières lumière, derniers plaisirs*, his intellectual testament, Guéhenno writes: "The true death of authors is the second death, the death into oblivion, the one that arrives ten, twenty years after they have disappeared. [...] Innumerable are they who are not named" (Guéhenno 1977: 208). In a tragical twist of history, Guéhenno has joined the ranks of those that are not or no longer talked about. Even though he is constantly mentioned in the biographies of others and in the many monographs on intellectuals and the history of the 20s and 30s, he still awaits his own biography. In addition, with the exception of some rare, and unpublished, doctoral dissertations (e.g. Librowski 1985) and a few reviews and occasional pieces (e.g. Rioux 1978, Ory 1979), Guéhenno's oeuvre, comprising some twenty books, has almost entirely escaped the attention of critics and historians of twentieth-century French literature and culture. Wrongly. I shall return to this in an essay on the entirety of Guéhenno's writing and thought. In the present pages, I shall primarily restrict myself to the Caliban theme.

[17] For the concrete circumstances of the genesis and publication of *Caliban parle*, see Guéhenno 1957: 92-93 and Rolland 1975: 19 and *passim*. This latter document is extremely revealing in that Rolland, even though he was Guéhenno's intellectual model, seems to have been disappointed by the form of *Caliban parle*: too much literature, not enough social criticism. The same source also mentions Guéhenno's willingness to instantly rewrite this text, which he partly considered a failure (Rolland 1975: 37). This intention is also rehearsed in Guéhenno 1973: 424.

[18] This humble origin recently won Guéhenno the slightly dubious honour of being included in a *Dictionary of proletarian authors* (Maricourt 1994: 98-99). This is somewhat surprising for an author who always looked on ideologico-social labels, be they labels of labour inspiration, with suspicion, and who, in addition, never made a secret of his aversion to all so-called proletarian literature (see a.o. Guéhenno 1962b: 240).

attracted attention with the publication of *L'Evangile éternel*, a half-biographical, half-monographic study on Michelet which, in many ways, reads like an anti-Renan and a veritable hymn to the people (Guéhenno 1962). The volume contains many elements typical of Guéhenno's later work: his hatred of the organic intellectuals of the wealthy classes, a fundamentally ambivalent attitude towards high culture and towards the idea of the radical transformation of this same culture, a love of the people and of ordinary, every-day culture, and, finally, his refusal to dissociate historical, political and social reflections from the autobiographical dimension – Guéhenno is an integral part of the histories he recounts. Where in these late nineteen-twenties should we situate this author, still relatively unknown at the time? The pages in which *Caliban parle* first appeared offer us some indications. *Europe*, we said, was the organ of independent internationalist intellectuals.[19] It was born from the pacifist movement of the Great War, whose undisputed figurehead was the author of *Au-dessus de la mêlée* (1915), Romain Rolland.[20] This movement, as is well known, primarily found its recruits among the small intellectuals (school-teachers from the provinces) and, in ideological terms, oscillated between a republican and a vaguely socialist position, centrally articulated around the mythical figure of Jean Jaurès.[21] The ensuing idealist and humanist discourse stood in a tense, if not overtly hostile, relation to the budding post-war communism. In the increasingly polarised intellectual and ideological climate of the left – should the example of Moscow be followed or not?, the question of the commitment of intellectuals becomes

---

[19] That is to say, those that signed the *Déclaration d'Indépendance de l'Esprit*, published in June 1919 by Rolland in the still socialist *L'Humanité* (see Rolland 1935: 1ff). Among the signatories we find the young Guéhenno (Rolland 1975: Guéhenno's first letter). Topologically speaking, *Europe* belongs to the field of restricted production: it is a journal by intellectuals for intellectuals, which partly explains the ambiguous ideology it would defend.

[20] The most profound study of the various pacificist movements of the left, of their journals, their recruitment, their ideological ramifications, is undoubtedly Prochasson 1993. It covers the period 1900-1938 and my remarks in what follows are largely indebted to it.

[21] See Rolland 1916 and Guéhenno 1979: 13-21, 123-28.

a crucially urgent issue. On the model of the Tours Conference rupture between socialists and communists (Robrieux 1980), two alternatives confront each other on the intellectual scene: the first, represented by Barbusse, that other anti-establishment hero of the Great War, whose best-seller *Feu* had even moved Lenin, amounts to a politics of alliance with the communist cause, albeit that a certain margin of autonomy is retained; while the second consists in defending at all cost the independence of spirit and a universalist humanism that is cultural rather than political.[22] Two distinct journals originated from this conflict: Barbusse's *Clarté* and Rolland's *Europe*.[23] The rise of the fascist or crypto-fascist extreme Right and Stalin's accession to power, which signified, among other things, an intensification of pro-USSR international propaganda, further compounded the confusion. Barbusse leaves *Clarté*, which meanwhile had become a stronghold of Trotskyist resistance, in order to found *Monde*, in 1928, a cultural organ of international communism whose editorial policies, however, harboured a good deal of ideological surprises for the Soviets.[24] Rolland, for his part, progressively develops in the direction of an open and unequivocal commitment in favour of the USSR[25] and *Europe*'s pages are more easily available for the revolutionary cause even though it preserves a space for proper reflection, which leads to a heterogeneous, at times even contradictory but invariably ambivalent, discursive set-up.[26]

---

[22] The key-texts for this rather tragic family quarrel are Barbusse 1921 and Rolland 1935. Guéhenno, and many others with him, always deplored the events of Tours, that is to say, the end of hope in a grand movement of unified *French* socialism; see e.g. Guéhenno 1957: 44.

[23] For a concise description of these two journals, see Bernard 1972: 310-12 and, of course, Prochasson 1993: 178-237.

[24] See Bernard 1972: 312 and Morel 1985: 208ff and *passim*. Barbusse formally supported the French Communist Party in 1925.

[25] See, among others, Rolland 1935 and 1975; and Furet 1995: 320ff.

[26] At certain moments, the same equivocal attitude can be detected in the relations between *Europe* and the movements of the Right; see Prochasson 1993: 217.

Taking the floor in the late twenties, then, is a hazardous business: one always risks being applauded by undesirable, even compromising sympathisers. Still, Caliban does speak. Not mincing his words. A matter, first of all, of settling accounts with Renan: "I have quite often been tempted to correct the portrait it pleased Mr Renan to make of me" (Guéhenno 1962b: xxv). Or again: "I hear you, my master: they have changed my Caliban. Such language coming from me astonishes you, no doubt" (Guéhenno 1962b: xxiii). The point is to smash the conventional image of a primitive, barbarian Caliban. Yet from the outset, Caliban's exercise in self-rehabilitation proves to be equivocal. His aggressiveness towards Renan seems secondary to his other objective: it is necessary, he says, to save Renan from the frankly reactionary interpretation his work has suffered. Renan is not Caliban's enemy – the latter even humbly pays homage to the former (cf. Guéhenno 1962b: xix). The same hesitation between revolt and recognition characterises the relation between Caliban and Prospero. Again, the target of Caliban's philippic is not so much Prospero as it is those who, in one way or another, have cast themselves as so many Prosperos in order to flaunt their supposed superiority over the people, the destitute. It is their use of culture that needs to be condemned, not culture as such (Guéhenno 1962b: 5). Neither Prospero nor Caliban are the true masters of the world – that is the part of the owners of property, those who have money: "If Mr Renan were to return on earth, there would be little to surprise him: it's still the same farce for three characters: the spirit, money, and me. If I name the spirit first, it is purely out of reverence. For his is not the leading part, far from it. Money is the hard taskmaster of both of us" (Guéhenno 1962b: 50). Such is the real social antagonism whose outcome will determine the course of history. In Guéhenno, Caliban and Prospero have become more than just strategical allies, as we shall soon see.

Caliban presents himself as a man of the people, as the mouthpiece of the "humans without history" (Guéhenno 1962b: 7), who, for centuries and centuries, have made and continued to make history even as the official accounts prefer to ignore them.[27] By way of its discourse, this same people

---

[27] It seems that there are, in *Caliban parle* and in the entirety of Guéhenno's work, two readings of the marginality of the people, whose compatibility is not at all

finally says no and gives free expression to a legitimate desire for happiness and material well-being. And in a climax of bourgeois arrogance, the owners of property then read this very demand as proof of the non-existence of Caliban and those like him. Since the whole world turns bourgeois, the real people, the poor and the workers, disappear. Vain denial, Caliban assures us: "When they say I no longer exist, they hope, I suppose, to muster courage: they deny me so as not to fear me" (Guéhenno 1962b: 6). What is more, he now has higher ambitions than ever before; the bourgeois will find peace nowhere: "My destiny is [...] European. Being Prince of Milan is no longer enough; I want to be master of the world. Beaten here, I get on my feet again somewhere else" (Guéhenno 1962b: 18).

The brutality, the self-assured and derisive tone, the contempt, all is intent on waking the upper classes from their sweet ideological dreams: the world is running straight into a conflict which will lock money and labour in an inexorable battle. Caliban seems to be less inspired by 1789 than by 1917. This is not to say that socio-economic inequality and all it entails is central to Caliban's real preoccupations. On the contrary, his critique of

---

clear. The first reading focusses on the fundamental difference of popular culture from high culture and the human sciences (history and sociology), a difference that is constantly under threat – for instance from the intellectual who thematises it – but that must be preserved at all cost (see a.o. Guéhenno 1939: 61ff; 1961; 1962b: 44ff). In this connection, Guéhenno's reflections are rather of a sociological and anthropological nature, and they anticipate by a few decades the contemporary interest in every-day culture, micro-history, etc. (Certeau, Maffesoli, Farge, Ginzburg). Yet this first dimension is clearly overdetermined – though never quite eclipsed – by a political reading of marginality: the meaning of the popular referent is here reduced to a question of social exclusion (Guéhenno 1962b: 91-92) that needs to be remedied in the name of a universalist humanism. The distinction between these two readings will be clear: in the first case, the intellectual universalism constitutes a threat that risks destroying the heterogeneity of the popular form of life – it is systematically accompanied by a self-criticism on the part of Guéhenno; while in the second case, this same humanism is the medium through which the redemption of the excluded is announced. It should be added here that in the course of Guéhenno's career the first reading clearly wins out, even though the tension never quite disappears.

money is only an appetiser followed by the main course of resistance to the intellectuals of the time. What precisely does he hold against them? A question rendered more difficult by the fact that Caliban's rage is elicited by diverse intellectual misdemeanours. First and foremost, the intellectuals, men of letters or *savants*, are largely responsible for the carnage of 1914. Renan's profound aspiration, the reign of knowledge, has been realised but the dream immediately degenerated into a veritable nightmare for those who had to suffer its consequences. That is the real treason of the intellectuals that should have been denounced: "The *savants* have recently tried out their monarchy. They have exerted an "unlimited terror," but it was less beautiful than Mr Renan had envisaged. Their "truth" was the driving force all right; their calculations, when put to the test, proved to be exact, and none of us would dream of doubting the unimpeachable nature of the 75 or of the 405 [shells]" (Guéhenno 1962b: 57-58). Or again: "between the mandarins that ignore us and the technicians that see us only as utilities, what do they want us to become?" (Guéhenno 1962b: 57). Indeed, what good is reason if it only serves the purpose of propaganda or of human murder: "One thing is certain: the spirit, in continuing its treason, will justify our violence" (Guéhenno 1962b: 59). Second, next to the ideologues and the narrow-minded engineers, [28] there are the beautiful souls, those who turn away from the sublunary to take delight in their own psychological and moral refinement, those who take turns in playing devil or angel even as they try to delude the others into believing that they suffer real torments. Farcical impostures. Caliban makes fun of this falsely fragile self-indulgence which has turned "the Spirit" into "a bloated king [*roi fainéant*]" (Guéhenno 1962b: 52). Nothing more execrable than these "Fools of the Spirit" (Guéhenno 1962b: 54): "They try out ideas like they try out women, they give in to anything and give themselves to nothing" (Guéhenno 1962b: 53).[29] The last category of intellectuals targetted by Caliban is that of the

---

[28] Elsewehere, Guéhenno does not hesitate to name those he attacks and will continue to attack, to wit Barrès (Guéhenno 1962c: 131-56; 179: 22-28; 1987: 119, 172) and especially Maurras (Guéhenno 1957: 50-1)

[29] The one intellectual whose subtle quietism and narcissistic egoism Guéhenno will never tire of denouncing is Gide: see Guéhenno 1939: 43ff; 1973: 126-27, 132-33, 301 and *passim*; 1977: 172ff and *passim*; 1979: 192-201. For Gide's reaction, see

intellectuals who seek to resuscitate Catholicism: "The old God whom we have so long kept alive in our prayers does not resign himself to dying. It's always like that with gods" (Guéhenno 1962b: 66). This movement of restoration must be denounced, the real nature of this dead deity disguised as a living God must be revealed. The rejection of the present is announced for the sake of the future: "If I hate today, it is in the name of tomorrow, not because I regret yesterday" (Guéhenno 1962b: 73). The future shall not be Christian but humanist (Guéhenno 1962b: 72).[30]

Notwithstanding his many reservations about the intellectuals, Caliban is an educated man himself. His acerbic invective at times makes us almost forget that, from the outset of his discourse, this devourer of intellectuals inscribes himself directly in Renan's lineage. He is one of those he condemns. Which in its turn destabilises the speaker's enunciative position. Are we dealing with a man of the people or with a schizophrenic intellectual whose education comes to disturb his populist vocation? A question that is difficult to answer, since both alternatives are equally true. Caliban is of very humble, popular origin but, at the same time, he has a

---

Gide 1992: 1231-32. In many respects, Guéhenno's critique astonishingly resembles that formulated by Sartre at the end of the 30s: see Sartre 1995: 262ff, 282ff, 292ff. At any rate, this severe judgement of those who anxiously abstain from all political commitment makes *Caliban parle* a frontal attack on the theses defended by Benda in his *Trahison des clercs* (1927). On this score, see also Guéhenno 1973: 36 and 1977: 30-33.

[30] Caliban takes pains to clearly distinguish the so-called "humanism" of the bourgeoisie from the authentic humanism that is social, universal and egalitarian: Guéhenno 1962b: 36-67. This distinction must have escaped Sartre. In *La Nausée*, the "Self-Taught Man" is presented to us as the very caricature of socialist humanism. Roquentin makes fun of him and compares the Self-Taught Man to Guéhenno: "by a curious phenomenon of mimeticism, [the Self-Taught Man] resembles that poor Guéhenno" (Sartre 1981: 143). The editors comment: "Sartre did not harbour any particular animosity against Guéhenno [...]. Guéhenno himself said he could not understand why he had been attacked by Sartre in this fashion" (Sartre 1981: 1782). See also Guéhenno 1957: 228; 1973: 410 and 1969: 16, where the author, speaking of the events of May 1968, alludes to a "false Prospero" who "put himself at the head of all those rebelling false Calibans" and who, no doubt, is Sartre, considering the context of the passage.

formative intellectual past. He is a man of the in-between, caught between an originary past forever faded – or so it seems – and the high culture that simultaneously seduces and disgusts him. "I was almost a traitor" (Guéhenno 1962b: 28), he confesses.[31] The temptation may be almost irresistible, but Caliban does not give in. The Great War brings him closer to his own again (Guéhenno 1962b: 41ff),[32] and, at any rate, he is a crafty one, a tactician: "Who cares for being a master and a turncoat! Success is essentially bourgeois. Succeeding is not what matters" (Guéhenno 1962b: 39).

Unfortunately, wanting to be a tactician does not make you one. It is impossible, in fact, to taste the apple of Culture without being poisoned by it. All too anxious to present proof of his genuine origin in the people, Caliban tends to suppress what fatally separates him from this same people. A man of culture, he is intent on inventing a form of revolt that would be in conformity with his culture. Caliban speaks of the people, for the people, in the name of the people, yet he no longer belongs to it. Coming from a man destined to remain an intellectual, profoundly marked by intellectual values such as an ascetic moral rigour, the defence of the people's right to material well-being can only ring false. It cannot be the last word. The true intent of the revolution must be the advent of a superior civilisation rather than the pursuit of happiness, that is to say: the revolutionary intent must be in accordance with the universally human and elevated contents of Culture. Morality is all, politics or economics are nothing. All this transpires clearly the moment the October Revolution comes under discussion. Caliban hesitates: he affirms his full support of the event, and then, in one and the same gesture, makes an about-face: "We have been participating in a strange adventure these last few years. I

---

[31] The chapter entitled "Difficult faithfulness" (Guéhenno 1962b: 27-47) is by far the most autobiographical in *Caliban parle*. It recounts certain cultural experiences of Caliban which were soon to reappear, perhaps even literally (e.g. the resemblance between Sycorax and Guéhenno's mother), in the later autobiographical writings: see esp. Guéhenno 1961, 1987 and 1957 – an autobiographical sequence of sorts.

[32] See also Guéhenno 1987, which deals with the years of the war. This account comprises some of the most sombre and most acerbic pages of Guéhenno's oeuvre.

do not yet know what to think of it, I tell myself different stories"
(Guéhenno 1962b: 59). Why should the revolution frighten this self-
confessed revolutionary? Let us return to the text to see what is at stake.
On the one hand, as was said, Caliban does not hide his enthusiasm for
this "strange adventure" that is 1917: "The formulas of liberation,
intellectual and abstract, that we invented in the West of Europe have
taken on real life and spirit in such a place, they have been charged with
soul" (Guéhenno 1962b: 60). Attempts had been made to break the
resistance to the Tsar's regime by prison sentences and exile, but to no
avail: "The war [...] arrived, and the prince of the country was foolish
enough not to win it; then all could clearly see what the Calibans had been
saying all along: that he was in reality cruel and stupid. They had hardly
returned to Russia and already they were leaders of the people"
(Guéhenno 1962b: 60-61). "Never," Caliban concludes, "has there been a
more positive, more practical, and more realist attempt at happiness"
(Guéhenno 1962b: 61). On the other hand, what worries Caliban is the
hard political pragmatism of the Bolsheviks, the violence of the new
regime, in short, the "realist methods" (Guéhenno 1962b: 62) with which
the Bolsheviks show themselves excellent students of the political order
they have just overthrown: "Nothing more bourgeois than a Bolshevik, in
a way. The most wily, most hypocritical, most pharisaical bourgeoisie is
his model and the origin of his methods. He matches trickery with
trickery, compromise with compromise, ranting with ranting, violence
with violence. Cunning with craftier cunning" (Guéhenno 1962b: 61-62).
The second threat is that of a rampant materialism that could degrade the
revolutionary ideal into a banal pursuit of 'happiness.' Petty instant
material gratification risks suffocating the revolutionary body, the
revolution might just die of lack of spirit: "Ah! Prospero, why have you
abandoned us? [...] At this moment when I invoke your help, am I so
certain that my fellows will still accept your assistance? Perhaps it is
already too late. Already they have become accustomed to relying on
themselves only. They are certain of victory, and I can already glimpse the
order they will institute on their own: a Middle Age. They could establish
a new Church, an order of the heart; perhaps they will be happy. But is
that all it is about? If you had been with us, Prospero, I know our victory
would be more beautiful: a Renaissance; and we would perhaps be less
happy, but more noble" (Guéhenno 1962b: 63).

The situation does not bode well. Was Renan right after all, when he proclaimed in his *Caliban* that the revolution and the people are realist and empiricist? At the very beginning of his discourse, Caliban still asks himself: "But could he not say with equal justice: 'The revolution is idealism'?" (Guéhenno 1962b: 2). But that revolution, the revolution operated by and for the Spirit, is not (yet) of this world. What is, on the contrary, beyond doubt is that Caliban's remarks bear witness to a state of mind that is, to say the least, hybrid,[33] strangely similar, by the way, to that of many contributors to *Europe* who also welcomed the events of 1917 and their fallout but who at the same time pleaded in favour of a revolution that would be spiritual and moral rather than material and political. The people may well effect a revolution, they ignore its true

---

[33] Incidentally, the reader will find even more striking instances of this ambiguity in Guéhenno's texts and articles from the 30s, which either clearly mark their distance from communist ideas (see esp. Guéhenno 1962c: 201-26), or embark on a defence of the international communist movement and the USSR, for reasons that are often more strategical than ideological (but can we tell the difference?). Thus Guéhenno is extremely severe in his judgement of Gide's 1937 *Retour de l'URSS* (Guéhenno 1939: 43ff, 85ff, 213-40; Gide 1950) while around the same time he minimises the significance of the Moscow Trials (Guéhenno 1939: 241-53). This ideological hesitation was not favourably received by more radical communists who, from the publication of *Caliban parle* onwards, denounced Guéhenno's indecisive attitude: see e.g. Poulaille 1930: 178-82. Here, for instance, is what Poulaille, the indefatigable propagandist of proletarian art, has to say about *Caliban parle*: "*Caliban parle* is a very beautiful book, its spirit is clear and straightforward. Yet what the author does not realise is that this book that should touch the working public, can only reach them in snatches. Here is the chink in the armour, Guéhenno. You speak of life through the approximation of life, you speak of it through the life of books. The people for whom the book is intended have not read Renan and only a very little Shakespeare. And Prospero, Ariel, Caliban, are allegories, as if you would have talked to them about Demos, they have trouble following you. And this obliges you to Renanise at times. You are closer to Renan than to Michelet in this book with this language that is not, cannot be, and has no need to become the language of Caliban, the actual Caliban. You have not betrayed him, no, but you have betrayed yourself. The culture that is to be given to the people will be ineffectual if it is boring. The task is to bring the people to fiction, to the symbol through life, that life that is closest to their own" (Poulaille 1930: 180)

sense. That is why the intervention of the Spirit and the intellectuals – two terms that are easily interchangeable – is required.[34] Is Guéhenno's Caliban a man of the people? Nothing is less certain. At the end of his book, the author himself drops his enunciative mask: "Caliban speaks! Some pretence! I find it hard not to fall out of character. How can the grain of your voice be heard in these pages? [...] It is too true that Prospero and his magic have perverted me" (Guéhenno 1962b: 109). And Guéhenno goes on to denounce his own discursive imposture: "The real Caliban does not know he is Caliban" (Guéhenno 1962b: 110). All *mise en discours* inevitably falsifies the reality in whose name it is designed.[35] Still, this lucidity in no way leads to resignation. Guéhenno does not abandon his faith in the possibility of the arrival of an authentic voice: "These pages in which you will not want to recognise yourself and which may appear to betray you, will be censured [by our masters] for having been exclusively inspired by your interest. Unfaithful though I may be, they will only censure my fidelity" (Guéhenno 1962b: 112).

Enunciative ambiguity, ideological ambivalence, these are doubtless the most salient traits of a species of intellectual that tried, in the course of the twenties and thirties, to defend a fully European humanitarian ideal while steering clear of the simultaneously seductive and murderous excesses of Stalinism and fascism. The majority of them ended up being crushed by the weight of extreme ideological pressure, others simply were unable to resist the ideological Sirens' song and abandoned this third route. Guéhenno, for one, did not cop out. He continued to devote himself to

---

[34] In the eyes of these intellectuals, and contrary to what the communists hold, the revolution by no means signifies a break with the existing cultural tradition. The idea of the revolution pertains to the intellectual heritage of humanity, which, in its turn, gives rise to discourses that pass without difficulty from Descartes and Pascal over Voltaire to Lenin and Marx: see a.o. Guéhenno 1962c: 201-26; 1979: 230-34. This further explains the hostility of these same intellectuals towards all proletarian sectarianism.

[35] Guéhenno returns to this question of enunciation in his autobiographical writings where he is almost forced to say I without ever feeling wholly at ease, seeing that the line between an I-witness and an I-Narcissus is so thin: see e.g. Guéhenno 1961: 17ff; 1977: 10ff.

the fate of the Calibans, he never ceased to register his doubts and hesitations over his gesture of speech, and, more painfully, he was not spared disappointment. After an effort of seven years, Guéhenno leaves *Europe* in 1935: he can no longer tolerate the interference of the publishing house – of money – and he is tired of communist attempts to take over the journal. But Caliban does not remain silent: he pursues his struggle against the forces of darkness of the time in *Vendredi*, a popular weekly with a considerable circulation founded by Guéhenno, Chamson and Viollis in 1935, which, however, after its initial success, ended in failure.[36] At the end of the thirties, everything is ready for a new drama. Munich, the phoney war, the war, Nuremberg, such is the infernal cycle humanity passed through between 1938 and 1945. Guéhenno remains silent, submissive, and suffers from the servitude and the war. He also begins to mistrust a little that being that has played such a dirty trick on the world, Caliban. Hitler, Stalin, and Mussolini were men who had come from the people and who were staunchly supported by the people (Guéhenno 1962b: xii-xviii, 249-60; 1969: 45ff; 1973). True, his faith in humanity remains substantial, but his intellectual and moral reservations will never disappear. In the post-war period, Guéhenno regularly returns to Caliban and to Prospero in his struggle against new threats: consumer society, television, fashion, Americanism, technology, etc. (Guéhenno 1969: 25-68). Given the semi-culture that seems to reign everywhere, one imperative question demands to be considered: how to reconcile Prospero and Caliban? The very possibility of Guéhenno's humanist creed depends on the answer to this question, and what his post-war work shows is that the answer is never quite unequivocal: at times Guéhenno believes in and

---

[36] See Prochasson 1993: 224-29. Concerning Vendredi, Guéhenno later wrote: "This time, Caliban was really going to speak" (Guéhenno 1957: 203). Yet the way in which Guéhenno explains the title of the journal shows that the enunciative ambiguity of *Caliban parle* has by no means disappeared: "Friday [Vendredi] was an old childhood friend. When, at fifteen, I started to learn English, I found no better method than to embark on a translation of Robinson Crusoe. Friday made me think of that saviour and master, Robinson, that hero who, in the shipwreck of all he loved, had had to recreate the world entirely by himself, which seemed to us, in our exalted mood, a fairly accurate image of what we ourselves had to do" (Guéhenno 1957: 199-200)

defends the complementarity of Prospero and Caliban, at times he returns to the theme of the culture of the masters, which brutally denies the beauty and wealth of popular, ordinary culture. All in all, he remains, throughout his life, a prisoner of the undecidable ambiguity that already riddled *Caliban parle*: "I cannot make up my mind to choose between these two characters in the human comedy and to decide which is the more important. The one and the other have been my life-long preoccupation" (Guéhenno 1969: 27). The fact that in a constellation where others never ceased being seduced by one dream of purity or another, Guéhenno deliberately wanted to run the risk of this ambiguity, makes his intellectual enterprise fragile, programmatically hesitating, but all the more unique.[37] Through him, an age voices its agony, its tragic and irrevocable ambiguity.

Conclusion

"I am the craftsman of the revolutions, fooled by the revolutions. [...] It's always the same farce." In a first reading, these utterances from the beginning of *Caliban parle* would simultaneously express both Caliban's lucidity and his revolt in the face of the past. They thus signify exactly the opposite of what they say. This, in fact, amounts to a fundamentally

---

[37] From the end of the thirties onwards, Guéhenno grows more and more critical towards the issue of political commitment. Henceforward, his reflections are less intent on adjudicating between different ideologico-political position than on the fundamentally hybrid nature of the modern human condition which seems to exclude any truly clear-cut choice. Yesterday's ideologue is superseded by today's moralist, who thematises the innumerable ways in which saying is distanced from doing and the other way about. Ambiguity is thus transformed into a fully-fledged existential category. The most visible fallout of this turn can be registered in the autobiographical writings and in the impressive trilogy on Rousseau (Guéhenno 1948, 1950, 1952), which reads like a simultaneously historical, social and psychological phenomenology of the modern intellectual and his or her desire for purity. Once again, the parallel with Sartre – who had also, in his *Carnets de la drôle de guerre*, brilliantly called into question the very possibility of a fully authentic existence – is striking. Except that Sartre seems to have followed the opposite trajectory, leading from the moralist to the ideologue.

optimistic reading that firmly believes in the possibility of leaving behind the farce once and for all, a reading that betrays Guéhenno's Caliban's most profound, most vital desire: the desire to reside in the true. Nonetheless, and despite the declared intention that underlies Guéhenno's discourse, we can equally affirm that the farce will never end. Indeed, Guéhenno himself admits as much in the epilogue: it is not Caliban who speaks, it is I, Guéhenno, who have styled myself as the mouthpiece of those who never speak. Still, Guéhenno never fully thinks through the *political* implications of his discursive *mise-en-scène*, he remains convinced of the legitimate, *re*-presentative nature of his tale. Avowal and denial go hand in hand and must go hand in hand lest the discursive and ideological edifice crumble completely. Guéhenno vaguely senses what he will never be able to admit: just like Renan-Prospero, he enlists the *Other* – the one who is situated well below discourse, culture and politics – in an intellectual project for intellectuals: he *inscribes* the Other. This schizophrenia that dares not or cannot declare itself fully is called Caliban. It characterises, as we saw, the singularity of Guéhenno's discourse, but it also turns out to be symptomatic of a constellation of problems that haunts European modernity at least since the eighteenth century and that profoundly links together the various modern ideological formations (whether they be of the left or of the right) as so many responses to one single fundamental question: what is *legitimate* power, how can the State or power in general adequately and acceptably represent the *Voice* of the people? An urgent question, but also perhaps one that is unanswerable: can those who do not speak be made to speak? What do politicians and intellectuals do when they put themselves *in the place of?* Fundamental questions, to be sure, which, in the analysis, all bespeak the necessity of a critical sociology of those who receive a mandate or believe themselves to be in possession of one, a sociology which, it would seem, risks upsetting the legitimacy of innumerable discourses *on* the social and political legitimacy of discursive practice. From this perspective, Guéhenno's utterances can also be read as an involuntary avowal: it's always the same farce, and the present tale, Guéheno's tale, is yet again and always a farce. Someone is missing here, despite his *nominal* presence: Caliban. This missing Other *makes* (the others) speak, Michel de Certeau would say.

Translated by Ortwin de Graef

References

Angenot, Marc. 1989. *1889. Un Etat du discours social.* Québec: Le Préambule.

Arendt, Hannah. 1985. *Essai sur la révolution* [1964]. Paris: Gallimard.

Barbusse, Henri. 1921. *Le Couteau entre les dents. Aux intellectuels.* Paris: Eds Clarté.

Beaumarchais, Marie-Alice de. 1984. "Renan Ernest." in Jean-Pierre de Beaumarchais. Daniel Couty. Alain Rey. *Dictionnaire des littératures de langue française, vol. III (P-Z).* Paris: Bordas, 1890-94.

Benda, Julien. 1927. *La Trahison des clercs.* Paris: Grasset.

Bernard, Jean-Pierre. 1972. *Le Parti communiste français et la question littéraire. 1921-1939.* Grenoble: Presses Universitaires de Grenoble.

Certeau, Michel de. 1988. *L'Ecriture de l'histoire* [1985]. Paris: Gallimard.

—. 1990a. *La Possession de Loudun* [1970]. Paris: Gallimard.

—. 1990b. *L'Invention du quotidien 1. Arts de faire* [1980]. Paris: Gallimard.

Foucault, Michel. 1988. *Les Mots et les choses. Une archéologie des sciences humaines* [1966]. Paris: Gallimard/NRF.

Furet, François. 1995. *Le Passé d'une illusion. Essai sur l'idée communiste au XXe siècle.* Paris: Laffont-Calmann-Lévy.

Gaulmier, Jean. 1985. "Renan (Ernest)." In *Encyclopaedia Universalis.* Corpus 15 (Pozzo-Rococo), 888-89.

Gide, André. 1950. *Littérature engagée.* Paris: Gallimard.

—. 1992. *Journal. 1889-1939* [1951, 1939]. Paris: Gallimard/NRF.

Guéhenno, Jean. 1939. *Journal d'une révolution. 1937-1938.* Paris: Grasset.

—. 1948. *Jean-Jacques I. En marge des «Confessions».* Paris: Grasset.

—. 1950. *Jean-Jacques II. Roman et vérité.* Paris: Grasset.

—. 1952. *Jean-Jacques III. Grandeur et misère d'un esprit.* Paris: Gallimard/NRF.

—. 1957. *La Foi difficile.* Paris: Grasset.

—. 1961. *Changer la vie. Mon enfance et ma jeunesse.* Paris: Grasset.

—. 1962a. *L'Evangile éternel. Etude de Michelet* [1927]. Paris: Grasset.

—. 1962b&c. *Caliban parle, suivi de Conversion à l'humain* [1928, 1930]. Paris: Grasset.

—. 1969. *Caliban et Prospero, suivi d'autres essais.* Paris: Gallimard/NRF.

—. 1973. *Journal des années noires* [1947]. Paris: Gallimard.

—. 1977. *Dernières lumières, derniers plaisirs.* Paris: Grasset.

—. 1979. *Entre le passé et l'avenir (Articles d' «Europe»).* Paris: Grasset.

—. 1987. *Journal d'un homme de quarante ans* [1934]. Paris: Grasset.

Kermode, Frank, ed. 1994. *The Arden Edition of the Works of William Shakespeare. The Tempest* [1954]. London/New York: Routledge.

Kriegel, Annie. 1974. *Communismes au miroir français. Temps, cultures et sociétés en France devant le communisme.* Paris: Gallimard/NRF.

Librowski, S.J. 1985. *Guéhenno. An Inter-war Intellectual.* PhD. Thesis. University of Warwick.

Lottman, Herbert R.. 1981. *La Rive gauche. Du Front populaire à la guerre froide.* Paris: Eds du Seuil.

Luhmann, Niklas. 1989. *Gesellschaftsstruktur und Semantik. Studien zur Wissensoziologie der modernen Gesellschaft. Bd. III.* Frankfurt am Main: Suhrkamp Verlag.

Maricourt, Thierry. 1994. *Dictionnaire des auteurs prolétaires de langue française. De la Révolution à nos jours.* Amiens: Encrage Editions.

Morel, Jean-Pierre. 1985. *Le Roman insupportable. L'Internationale littéraire et la France (1920-1932).* Paris: Gallimard/NRF.

Ory, Pascal. 1979. "Introduction." In Guéhenno 1979: 7-11.

Poulaille, Henry. 1930. *Le Nouvel âge littéraire.* Paris: Valois.

Prochasson, Christophe. 1993. *Les Intellectuels, le socialisme et la guerre. 1900-1938.* Paris: Eds du Seuil.

Psichari, Henri. 1977. "La pensée et l'influence d'Ernest Renan." In Pierre Abraham and Roland Desne, eds. *Manuel d'histoire littéraire de la France. vol. 5 (De 1848 à 1913).* Paris: Editions Sociales, 131-37.

Renan, Ernest. 1878. *Caliban (Suite de La Tempête).* Paris: Calmann-Lévy.

—. 1888. *Drames philosophiques.* Paris: Calmann-Lévy.

—. 1890. *L'Avenir de la science. Pensées de 1848.* Paris: Calmann-Lévy.

Rioux, Jean-Paul. 1978. "Caliban ne parlera plus." *Esprit*. 23 (4): 283-4.

Rolland, Romain. 1916. *Au-dessus de la mêlée* [1915]. Paris: Librairie Olendorff..

—. 1935. *Quinze ans de combat, 1919-1934*. Paris: Rieder.

—. 1975. *L'Indépendance de l'esprit. Correspondance entre Jean Guéhenno et Romain Rolland. 1919-1944*. Paris: Albin Michel.

Sartre, Jean-Paul. 1981. *Oeuvres romanesques*. Paris: Gallimard/NRF.

—. 1995. *Carnets de la drôle de guerre. Septembre 1939 – mars 1940*. Paris: Gallimard/NRF.

Sirinelli, Jean-François, ed. 1993. *L'Histoire des droites en France*. 3 vols. Paris: Gallimard.

Sternhell, Zeev. 1985. *Maurice Barrès et le nationalisme français*. Bruxelles: Eds Complexe.

Vaughan, Alden T. and Virginia Mason Vaughan. 1991. *Shakespeare's Caliban: A Cultural History*. Cambridge: Cambridge UP.

Browning Born to Wordsworth

Intimations of Relatability from Recollections of Early Monstrosity

Ortwin de Graef

If you could see the you that I see when I see you see me you'd
see yourself so different believe me.

(Rollins, "Low Self-Opinion")

– But why would you even want to move the earth?
– How can I not want it, when my entire chain of reasoning
has made it hypothetically possible?
– So? Non sequitur, surely?
– But that is just the point: not only is the chain always
stronger than its weakest link, it even binds when links are
missing – especially when links are missing.

One mark of strong writing, perhaps, is the critical relation it entertains
with the readings it receives, allows for, or suffers. Wordsworth famously

stated that poems "cannot read themselves,"[1] but then Wordsworth
famously stated many things that cannot just be taken as read. As a
principled objection to the monumentalisation of the poem as a
transcendental significator engaged in authoritative self-interpretation, the
verdict may stand. Yet such an interpretative practice, intent on the auto-
consolidation of the poem's self as only ever the same, is precisely not a
reading: texts (provided they are strong texts) cannot interpret themselves,
which is why they must read the readings they receive, allow for, or
suffer.

Wordsworth's own Immortality Ode is a case in point. It is not my
primary concern here, but a few remarks on its reading can plot a
circuitous yet enabling passage towards the core of this essay, Robert
Browning's reading of another *monstre sacré* of English Letters in his
dramatic monologue "Caliban Upon Setebos; or, Natural Theology in the
Island." My principal interest throughout will be the relationary rhetoric
that informs both poems and their interpretations as critical documents in
our rage for the relatable.

* * *

As is the case with many of Wordsworth's more ambitious writings, the
anthology-piece we now know (though perhaps no longer by heart) as
"Ode: Intimations of Immortality from Recollections of Early Childhood"
has a complex history of composition. The poem's canonical 11-stanza
version, carrying the directive title just quoted and with an epigraph from
"My Heart Leaps Up," was published in 1815, some eight years after its
first publication under the starker title "Ode," and with an epigraph from
Vergil's *Eclogues* ("Paulo maiora canamus"). It had been completed in
substantially this form by March 1804, but the first four stanzas, ending
on the ringing questions "Whither is fled the visionary gleam?/ Where is it
now, the glory and the dream?" (ll.56-57), were already written in March
1802. Wordsworth recited these stanzas to Coleridge in early April of that
year and Coleridge promptly responded in his verse epistle "A Letter

---

[1] "Preface to Poems (1815)" (Wordsworth 1989: 629). The fact that Wordsworth's
"read" should be read as "recite" is appropriate in ways I shall not further explore
here.

to . . .," which was published, after considerable revision and condensation, as "Dejection: An Ode" exactly half a year later, on Wordsworth's wedding-day, October 4th. Wordsworth's later extension of his poem, then, can in its turn be read as a response to Coleridge's reading – which is to say that Coleridge's Ode effectively transformed Wordsworth's culminating questions of 1802 into the opening movements of a fully-fledged alternative ode rehearsing and, after a fashion, answering these questions. In 1843, Wordsworth told Isabella Fenwick that "[t]o the attentive and competent reader the whole [of the definitive Ode] sufficiently explains itself" (1985: 428), but bearing in mind this whole's compositional history, it would be more accurate to say that it tries to explain the whole of the four 1802 stanza's by turning them into a part of the 1804 whole.

As we cannot go into the detail of this intricate exchange here,[2] I only want to insist for a moment on the decisive modulation of the initial stanzas' questioning finish into the definitive Ode's apparently confident genealogical answer. The 1802 stanzas start out by remembering "a time when meadow, grove, and stream/ The earth, and every common sight,/ To me did seem/ Apparelled in celestial light" (ll.1-4).[3] In the "now," even as the speaker still registers the beauty of things, this splendour is a thing of the past: "Turn wheresoe'er I may,/ By night or day,/ The things which I have seen, I now can see no more." (ll.7-9) The melancholy attending this loss, however, is apparently lifted in a "timely utterance" (l.23), further unspecified, granting the speaker the strength to ward off grief on "[t]his sweet May-morning" (l.44) and to enjoy the abundant vitality surrounding him – "I feel – I feel it all" (l.41) – "I hear, I hear, with joy I hear!" (l.50)

Fifty lines is a good, round number, and in the absence of any obvious formal requirements to further extend the poem, this final exclamation,

---

[2] For some instructive comments in this connection, see Gill 1990: 200-6, 228 and Servotte 1992: 45-7.

[3] Unless indicated otherwise, all Wordsworth quotations in this essay are from Stephen Gill's Oxford Authors edition. Line numbers for the Ode consequently refer to the first published version of 1807.

carrying as it emphatically does the sense of an ending proper to moments of spiritual recovery, could have been a perfect (though hardly critically satisfactory) finish. Yet already in the first version, Wordsworth adds a singular retraction returning the poem to the mild despondency registered in its first half:

> I hear, I hear, with joy I hear!
> – But there's a Tree, of many one,
> A single Field which I have looked upon,
> Both of them speak of something that is gone:
> The Pansy at my feet
> Doth the same tale repeat:
> Whither is fled the visonary gleam?
> Where is it now, the glory and the dream? (ll.50-57)

As indicated above, it was only after Coleridge's response (which, to put it all too crudely, can be read as something like: the gleam has not exactly fled, for it was never even there in the first place, not before you put it there: "we receive but what we give,/ And in our life alone does Nature live" ["Dejection: An Ode," ll.47-48]) that Wordsworth began to rehearse these questions. The seven stanzas that "completed" the poem in 1804 indeed hold up something of an answer, albeit an answer that adjusts the perspective of the initial question: it is not the visionary gleam that has fled somewhere; it is we who have progressively (or regressively) fallen away from its glory from the moment of our birth:

> Our birth is but a sleep and a forgetting:
> The Soul that rises with us, our life's Star,
> Hath had elsewhere its setting,
> And cometh from afar:
> Not in entire forgetfulness,
> And not in utter nakedness,
> But trailing clouds of glory do we come
> From God, who is our home:
> Heaven lies about us in our infancy! (ll.58-66)

Upon which the poem piously abandons itself to a passionate development of this variation on a neo-Platonic theme. The specific – and by no means straightforward – nature of this further development need not concern us here. Instead, what I wish to retain is Wordsworth's strategic translation of the "time" in the opening lines of the poem – a "time" specified only as preceding the "now" when he "knows" that "there hath past away a glory from the earth" (l.18) – into, specifically, the time of "infancy." The obvious attractiveness of this specification is that it triggers a reassuringly intelligible narrative of growth, whereby the "fading" of the "vision splendid" (l.73) is understood as a corollary of a process of *Bildung* culminating in the "sober" (l.197) lucidity of "the philosophic mind" (l.185). The further advantage of this ontogenetic pattern is that it posits a solid ground on which the fading of the gleam can be recorded: the identity of the Man's body with that of the blessed Babe trailing clouds of glory ensures the lasting inscription of this glory and renders it accessible to, as the final title states, recollection. "Whither is fled the visionary gleam?": We left it behind – that is: *we* left it behind, *I* left it behind, and to the extent that I can recollect who I was in an identity encompassing my history, I can commemorate and preserve it for the day when I return to my source. We recollect but what we have received:

> What though the radiance which was once so bright
> Be now for ever taken from my sight,
>> Though nothing can bring back the hour
> Of splendour in the grass, of glory in the flower;
>> We will grieve not, rather find
>> Strength in what remains behind,
>> In the primal sympathy
>> Which having been must ever be
>>> (ll.178-85)

Hence: Intimations of Immortality from Recollections of Early Childhood. *Q.E.D.*

And yet. In the notes compiled by Isabella Fenwick in 1843, Wordsworth tries to answer some reservations readers of the Ode had registered:

> To that dream-like vividness and splendour which invests
> objects of sight in childhood every one, I believe, if he

would look back, could bear testimony, and I need not
dwell upon it here – but having in the Poem regarded it
as presumptive evidence of a prior state of existence, I
think it right to protest against a conclusion, which has
given pain to some good and pious persons that I meant
to inculcate such a belief. It is far too shadowy a notion
to be recommended to faith as more than an element in
our instincts of immortality. But let us bear in mind
that, tho' the idea is not advanced in revelation, there is
nothing there to contradict it, and the fall of Man
presents an analogy in its favor. Accordingly, a
preexistent state has entered into the popular creeds of
many nations, and among all persons acquainted with
classic literature is known as an ingredient in Platonic
philosophy. Archimedes said that he could move the
world if he had a point whereon to rest his machine.
Who has not felt the same aspirations as regards the
world of his own mind? Having to wield some of its
elements when I was impelled to write this Poem on the
'Immortality of the soul' I took hold of the notion of
preexistence as having sufficient foundation in humanity
for authorizing me to make for my purpose the best use
of it I could as a Poet. (Wordsworth 1985: 428)

This authoritative comment is often cited as evidence of Wordsworth's
questionable deference to orthodoxy in his old age – an attempt to make
amends for the Ode's deviant Platonic inversion of the Pauline line in 1
Corinthians 14:11, but this is to overlook the passage's opening appeal to
the self-evidence of the presumptive evidence itself: the self-evidence of our
pre-existence not as Immortal Soul but, precisely, as a child whose primal
sympathy with all that is we can recollect. In this imperious appeal to the
allegedly obvious, Wordsworth effectively erases the tracks of his
translation of the 1802 stanzas into the ontogenetic narrative of the 1804
sequence. Put more simply: perhaps the true fulcrum here is not any
Platonic notion stored in our collective memory but the specific
imposition of our childhood as a source of meaning – a source of which
we are the river underway to the "immortal sea" (l.163).

The pattern involved here – epitomised in the bull "I was a fine child, but they changed me" – is that of a saving sense of identity achieved through the postulate of a genetic continuity between, in Coleridge's terms, present "personal identity – *Ego contemplans*" on the one hand, and, on the other, "the visual image or object by which the mind represents to itself its past condition, or rather, its personal identity under the form in which it imagined itself previously to have existed. – Ego contemplatus" (72-73).[4] That Wordsworth was sensitive to the slightly perverse critical defamiliarisation of this "natural" pattern of personal identity persistent through time is subtly suggested in the epigraph from his own "My Heart Leaps Up" which he placed over the 1815 version of the Ode:

> The Child is Father of the Man;
> And I could wish my days to be
> Bound each to each by natural piety.

You wish. The desire for a participation in this legitimating bond is indeed recognised *as* desire, as a wish rather than as the apparent truism of identity through time. The Child is *Father* of the Man: as Joyce might have said of such male bonding, "Paternity is a legal fiction" – an imposition of logic and coherence on the basis of an absurd assumption that is as fictional as is the neo-Platonic doctrine of gradual amnesia. Through the patently counterfactual *hysteron proteron* of his epigraph, Wordsworth foregrounds the anxious appropriation of fact into meaningful sequence that interests us here: the genealogical invention of an entity as the explanatory origin of a present condition, an entity whose fictional nature as explanatory origin is masked by an *implicit* appeal to material evidence – in this case, flesh and bones and sensory organs that persist through time and are figured, on the basis of this very persistence, as undeniable evidence of what is precisely *not* evident.

The further pertinence of the childhood-fulcrum to our argument here is its explicit function as a social cement. As a space of splendid vision to

---

[4] For an excellent reflection on the purport of this pattern for the Ode, Wordsworth and Romantic thought, see Christensen 1994: 460ff. On the intimately related issue of Wordsworth's characteristic attempts to prefigure his own death, see de Man 1993: 81ff.

which "everyone, [...] if he would look back, could bear testimony," it serves as a foundational topos for human (or at least male) society – making the Ode into a veritable *Discourse on the Origin of Similarity*.[5] Things are speeding up. The social extension of the argument to the postulate of a shared ontogenetic narrative of nativity can hardly avoid triggering a further massive expansion of the genetic imperative, allowing us to raise the stakes by moving backwards towards the birth of the species. The question whether we must or indeed even can bind ourselves with this chain of reasoning is what this essay is about.

***

In the Romantic period, natural science could still be fun.

(David Knight, "Romanticism and the Sciences")

In his *Discours sur l'origine et les fondemens de l'inégalité parmi les hommes* Rousseau justifies his notorious dismissal of factual evidence by taking recourse to an instructive analogy:

> Il ne faut pas prendre les Recherches, dans lesquelles on peut entrer sur ce Sujet, pour des vérités historiques, mais seulement pour des raisonnemens hypothétiques et conditionnels; plus propres à éclaircir la Nature des choses qu'à montrer la véritable origine, et semblables à ceux que font tous les jours nos Physiciens sur la formation du Monde. (132-33)

As Jean Starobinski points out in his editorial notes, for Rousseau's 1755 French reader the reference here is to works such as Buffon's *Théorie de la Terre* and Maupertuis' *Essai de Cosmologie*. But some hundred years later, in the wake of geological science's principled (though not therefore always

---

[5] In this connection, it is fitting that Wordsworth should have explicitly characterised the gradual socialisation of the growing child, the "little Actor" (l.102), as a mimetic imperative: "As if his whole vocation/ Were endless imitation." (ll.106-07)

substantiated) insistence on the truth of its historical evidence, the analogy backfires and a very real monster slouches towards the hypothetical State of Nature. Enter Caliban – or perhaps not quite.

It is the hottest time of the day on the island. Prospero and Miranda are asleep and Caliban, who should be "drudg[ing] at their task" (1.21)[6] is "cheat[ing] the pair" (1.22), sprawling "flat on his belly" (1.2) in the "cool slush" (1.4) of his cave, looking out over the sea and "talk[ing] to his own self" (1.15), "Letting the rank tongue blossom into speech." (1.23) The theme of his soliloquy is "that other, whom his dam [Sycorax] called God" (1.16): Setebos. Caliban knows that talking about Setebos is forbidden, yet he feels safe to "speak [...] his mind" (1.268) under the triple protection of his cave, the heat (Setebos dwells in the cold) and the third person which, like Caesar, he applies to himself throughout his monologue (give or take a few significant exceptions). From this presumptive point of safety, Caliban speculates on Setebos's motives in creating the world and its creatures. The organising principle that powerfully punctuates this exercise is analogy: throughout, the logic of Caliban's catechism is "So He." Setebos has created the world and its creatures in a spirit of resentment: living in eternal cold like a fish in an icy stream, He longs for, and in this longing creates, a warmth He cannot live in; unable to be what He is not, like a Caliban wishing he was a bird, He creates "what Himself would fain, in a manner, be" (1.62); Himself subordinate to a higher "something" (1.129) which Caliban calls the "Quiet" (1.137), He makes a "bauble-world" (1.147) of which He is lord and master, just like Caliban imitates Prospero, etc. On the basis of this understanding of the dynamics of creation, Caliban then sketches a rule to live by: if Setebos created the world in a spirit of vicarious pleasure, endowing what He is not with what He Himself lacks, "the best way to escape His ire/ Is, not to seem too happy" (1.257), giving Him the impression that life is hard and that His creature Caliban envies Him more than He envies him. Perhaps, Caliban continues, such a charade may even lull Setebos to terminal sleep, but as he murmurs this blasphemous conclusion, clouds slide across the sun and Caliban sees a raven whom he suspects is Setebos's spy. Fearing divine punishment, he prostrates himself and promises penitence:

---

[6] Quotations from Browning are taken from Kenyon's Centenary edition.

His thunder follows! Fool to gibe at Him!
Lo! 'Lieth flat and loveth Setebos!
'Maketh his teeth meet through his upper lip;
Will let those quails fly, will not eat this month
One little mess of whelks, so he may 'scape! (ll.291-95)

"so He" (l.43), "So He" (l.97), "so He" (l.108), "So He" (l.126), "so He"
(l.169), "so He" (l.199), "So He" (l.240) – "so he may 'scape!" (l.295) So?

Ever since its first publication in *Dramatis Personae* in 1864, this question
has occupied Browning's readers. Whether or not Caliban has succeeded in
escaping Setebos's wrath, he certainly seems to have escaped decisive
critical classification. If in Wordsworth's Ode the child in its primal
sympathy with divine splendour is a pre-eminently enabling mediating
figure precisely by virtue of its obvious (though highly problematic)
appeal to a shared sense of saving incorporation, Browning's monster
seems to incarnate no such immediate pertinence. Wordsworth's blessed
babe figures the material fact of our birth into a fictional fulcrum on
which we may hope to lean as we try to move our mind towards some
kind of resolution; Browning's Caliban just seems to figure as a fiction,
intent only on letting its rank tongue blossom into impertinent speech.

As if there could ever be a pure as if: clearly, "Caliban Upon Setebos" also
calls out for pertinence, and such pertinence has been abundantly granted
– which is not to say that the call did not fall on deaf ears. Very broadly
speaking, all the interpretations of the poem I have come across have
sought to solve the riddle of Caliban by identifying him as some type of
transitional creature, an incarnation of the missing link, or as a parodic
figure conceived as a vehicle for "a profound criticism of
anthropomorphically believing humanity as Browning and as we have
known it" (Maclean 1987: 9). My argument here will not be that of these
Caliban is both at once – that is in fact the understanding most of these
interpretations arrive at (see e.g. Gridley 1972: 114-17 and Jack 1973: 263-
68) – but rather that he is indeed at once both yet also, and crucially,
neither. This I take to be the poem's resistance to its hermeneutic
recuperation and my intention in the following pages is to recognise this
resistance by considering more closely some representative responses to
Browning's text.

Erasmus joked that Plato thought 'our "necessary ideas [of good and evil]" arise from the pre-existence of the soul' – and that they 'are not derivable from experience' – which Darwin capped by adding 'read monkeys for preexistence [of the soul].'

(Adrian Desmond and James Moore, *Darwin*)

It has been an inept conception of ancient and also recent Philosophy of Nature to regard the progression and transition of one natural form and sphere into a higher as an outwardly-actual production which, however, to be made clearer, is relegated to the obscurity of the past. [...] A thinking consideration must reject such nebulous, at bottom, sensuous ideas, as in particular the so-called origination, for example, of plants and animals from water, and the origination of the more highly developed animal organisms from the lower, and so on. [...] It is a completely empty thought to represent species as developing successively, one after the other, in time. Chronological difference has no interest whatever for thought.

(Hegel, *Philosophy of Nature*, § 249)

Browning probably began composing Caliban's monologue in 1859 and his readers have been quick to envelop the poem in the mythical aura of that date. 1859 is, after all, the year in which Darwin finally published *The Origin of Species*, and while the divisive question of the descent of Man did not quite make it in these pages yet, the figure of the ancestral monkey and its monstrous progeny already loomed large. What must more specifically interest us here is the curious preferential pattern in which this issue was repeatedly cast, most famously perhaps in the titanic clash between Bishop Wilberforce and Thomas Henry Huxley at Oxford in 1860. In the course of this notorious polemic, the anti-Darwinian Bishop

asked Huxley whether it was through his grandfather or his grandmother
that he claimed descent from an ape, to which Huxley is claimed to have
offered the devastating answer that he would rather have a miserable ape
for a grandfather than a man who abuses his talent and authority by
"introducing ridicule into a grave scientific discussion."[7] Some ten years
later, in the famous closing paragraphs of *The Descent of Man*, Darwin
presented his own variation on this comparative theme by stating that he
would as soon be descended from monkeys and baboons – creatures he
credited with acts of heroism and compassion – as from savages such as
those inhabitants of Tierra del Fuego whose delight in torture, bloody
sacrifices, infanticide, wife-enslavement, indecency and "grossest
superstitions" he had observed with horror during his voyage on the
Beagle (1899: 634).

The semi-conscious irony in these two venerable chestnuts of Darwinian
lore is, of course, that evolutionary processes are superbly indifferent to
whatever Messrs. Huxley and Darwin may or may not prefer and that, at
the end of the day (i.e. now), we are all related to monkeys, savages and –
horresco referens – Bishop Wilberforces. What this irony masks is the
deeply distressing implication of maximised relatedness – the sense that, as
the final sentence of the *Descent* has it, "Man still bears in his bodily frame
the indelible stamp of his lowly origin" (634), that every human being is
riddled with material connections that stubbornly resist the kind of
reassuring narrative that Wordsworth's Ode read into our bodies. Not in
utter nakedness indeed: what hair we have left links us to the beast we
descend from (cf. Darwin 1899: 57). Something of this distress indeed
shines through in the phrasing of Darwin's observation that "[h]e who has
seen a savage in his native land will not feel much shame, if forced to
acknowledge that the blood of some more humble creature flows in his
veins" (Darwin 1899: 634) – the point being the telling elision of the
logically inevitable "also" between the subject and the verb of the closing
clause: *that* is the implication we are indeed *forced* to acknowledge – we are
all family: baboon, Bishop, barbarian.

---

[7] For an entertaining reconstruction of this famous exchange between Soapy Sam
and Darwin's Bulldog and of the mythopoeic modulations it has received, see
Gould 1992: 385-401. Further context can be found in Desmond 1994: 276ff.

Or are we? And if we are, what does this mean? How do we come to terms with this anxiety of connection, this disturbing sense of material participation, this pathos fed by savage blood in our veins? Most classically: How do we determine where the animal turns barbarian and the barbarian man (of God), given that God Himself, who used to be in charge of these comforting demarcations, has been ruled out of court? Hegel decreed that such questions of chronological difference have "no interest whatever for thought" (20), but they certainly had a profound interest for the fevered imagination of Darwin's contemporaries. Darwin himself regally ruled that the impossibility to fix any "definite point" as the transition between the pre-human and the human was "a matter of very little importance" (Darwin 1899: 184),[8] yet what is scientifically – or indeed dialectically – of very little importance is often precisely what will not go away,[9] and to many readers of "Caliban Upon Setebos" Browning brings a measure of relief for this anxiety. As a direct recourse to the Creator has become problematic, the interest of Browning's response, as understood by these readers, is that it addresses the problem of relatedness precisely by explaining the emergence of the very notion of God as an explanatory force – by readmitting God into court as evidence rather than as judge, "using the poem to bring Darwin's theory of evolution to the test" (Melchiori 1992: 96), the test of relatability.

Darwin's marked outrage at the savage Fuegians' "grossest superstitions" bespeaks the implicit assumption that a rudimentary sense of religion

---

[8] A verdict echoed by one of his most prominent spokesmen in our time, Richard Dawkins, who suggests that "there is a good case for not even trying to pin down the precise identity of ancestors" (284).

[9] One of the clearest contemporary expressions of science's impotence to adequately address the questions generated by its own findings remains Matthew Arnold's 1882 "Literature and Science" – as in the following passage: "for the generality of men [...], when they have duly taken in [Mr. Darwin's famous proposition] that their ancestor was 'a hairy quadruped furnished with a tail and pointed ears, probably arboreal in its habits,' there will be found to arise an invincible desire to relate this proposition to the sense in us for conduct, and the sense in us for beauty. But this the men of science will not do for us, and will hardly even profess to do." (1958: 495)

(retrospectively recognised as superstition) is a crucial feature in the transition from the animal to the human. From an evolutionary perspective, this means that what has to be accounted for is the development of this religious sentiment, and Huxley, for one, seems to have thought that this is exactly what Browning had achieved: "a scientific representation of the development of such [religious] ideas in primitive man" (quoted in Mermin 1992: 203). Huxley's interpretation has been implicitly or explicitly echoed ever since in the many commentaries on Caliban that seek to place him as an imaginative incarnation of the missing link. A relatively recent representative instance of this tradition is John Howard's "Caliban's Mind," and in the following pages I shall consider Howard's argument in some detail – not because his is a particularly good or bad account of the poem, but because his interpretive strategy allows us to understand more clearly the governing assumptions of any interpretation that proposes to name Caliban as the missing link.

Howard understands the poem as "a clear picture of [...] a primitive subhuman who contemplates God in the only way he can" (225), yet after some minimal critical development, this picture turns out to be badly focussed. Browning, so the argument goes, "created a character who represents something early and undeveloped, something which is far back in the evolutionary scale" (227), in an endeavour "to capture the limitations of the subhuman mind when confronted with religious speculation" (224) – in other words, the missing link caught in the proto-religious act of linking, explaining himself to himself by imposing a rudimentary coherence on his situated existence. The binding principles in this worldview are "spite, envy, vexing and propitiation" (233), a powerplay of bleak cruelty Caliban has "derived from the rude forces of the nature that he inhabits" (229). It is this simple-minded logic of direct derivation that allegedly captures "the limitations of the subhuman mind" in its inability to attain the "abstract knowledge" proper to "the fully developed human" (230). Browning's enactment of the absence of such knowledge in his transitional monster would thus implicitly credit us, "fully developed humans," with the power of abstraction that can then figure as our saving distinction from our savage ancestry and all is well with the world.

But what exactly is this "abstract knowledge"? Caliban's "point of view," Howard argues, is that of "a perceptive but unscientific mind" (227), the mind of a subhuman who understands all that is in a spirit of resentment and cruelty derived from the "rude forces" of his "fierce world" (229). The implication might be that a higher scientific awareness would somehow yield an abstract knowledge articulating a coherent vision that would be more comforting. If our access to abstraction already offers us a reassuring formal distinction from the subhuman, this narrative still requires some more substantial development – yet faced with such substantial vision as has been forthcoming from evolutionary science, the picture turns from injury to insult. If Caliban's world is resentful and cruel, the logic read into life by Darwinian science is one of blind indifference, an affront not just to our desire for a salvational dynamic but, more painfully, to our narcissistic yearning for any kind of motivated development in which we can recognise ourselves as meaningfully special.[10] Being possessed by this knowledge is not likely to assuage the anxiety of material connection Browning's "scientific" representation of subhuman thought is supposed to have addressed.

It is no accident, then, that Howard – whose reading of Caliban as a subhuman missing link is, as suggested, fairly representative – should shy away from this bleak conclusion in a momentous shift of perspective. In a first highly significant preparatory move, Caliban's subhuman mind is reread as the mind of a child: "Like the child, he reads direct causes into the effects, thus inferring the nature of the Creator in the only way he can understand him. Like the child, he sees simple, direct relationships, not scientific distinctions," and, like the child, he only "understands by simple analogy" (232). Thus Caliban's cruel reasoning, the scientific representation of which could hardly be said to generate a comforting phylogenetic narrative, is partly redeemed on the basis of its putative analogy with a child's analogical thought, and lest this return to a less disturbing ontogenetic *Bildungsgeschichte* be judged insufficient, Howard adds one more predictable and definitive turn:

---

[10] On Freud's famous characterisation of Darwinian science as a second blow to humanity's self-image, see Beer 1985: 12. Further seminal thoughts on the scientific self-erasure attendant on this blow can be found in Levine 1993.

> The one essential element which Caliban cannot deduce
> about God is his loving nature. [...] Caliban has clearly
> found the power and intelligence of crafty Setebos, by
> looking at the 'work i'the world,' but he cannot find the
> good. Revelation is necessary for that, and Caliban, being
> something primitive and below humanity, cannot receive
> it. (232)

With one imperious stroke, the question raised by evolutionary science is
spirited away: the "abstract knowledge" Caliban cannot attain turns out to
be not the coherent pattern of scientific distinction but the assurance of
divine love that can be "deduced" by humanity which has "received" it
from God in the visionary gleam of Revelation. We deduce but what we
have received. The missing-link-reading starts out by casting Browning's
Caliban as a scientific representation of subhuman thought intent on an
enabling identification of the savage blood linking us to our history and
thus on a consolidation of our distinction as fully developed humans; to
put it more defensively, the poem is understood as a diagnostic enterprise
committed to a responsible representation that can ward off the threat of a
creeping migration of primitive matter even as it recognises the scientific
fact of our participation in that matter. Suddenly, however, this "clear
picture" is miraculously developed into a fundamentally non-scientific,
indeed *radically* abstract and overexposed snapshot of salvational history.
The material implication of man in his monstrous origin is cunningly
transsubstantiated through divine intercession and all is well with the
world. The indelible stamp has been overwritten, the missing link is lost
again.[11]

Yet was Browning's Caliban ever a missing link in the first place? Who
put him in that place? Not Browning's poem: all we are given is Caliban's

---

[11] This is as good a place as any to underscore that such a miraculous transmutation
need not as blatantly abandon the scientific frame as is the case here. Indeed,
secular versions of the same salvational relation were prominent in the Darwinian
camp as well, most notably for our purposes in Huxley's modulation of evolution
into an emancipatory dynamic (cf. Desmond and Moore 1992: 508). Here, too,
man's descent from a "bestial savage" (508) is no sooner admitted than it is erased
in an edifying narrative of inexorable progress..

analogical catechism fuelled by his acute observation of the world around him and framed by two square-bracketed passages, also spoken by Caliban, the first of which sets the stage while the second ends Caliban's disquisition with his attempts to escape the divine wrath he fears he has incurred. John Woolford has suggested that these square-bracketed passages indicate an "editorial intervention fragment[ing] the internally unbroken utterance of [the] speaker into ranked 'levels'" (161), but what is most striking is that this 'ranking' in no way establishes an authorial connection between Caliban's "rank tongue" and the human eyes that read him. According to Howard, "Browning takes pains to fix [Caliban] somewhere below man in [the] great hierarchy" (231), but even in these editorial framing passages, where such fixing would be eminently possible, that is precisely what does not happen: Browning does *not* say "not in utter hairlessness but trailing clouds of monstrosity do we come." Neither does he deny it.

"Caliban Upon Setebos" is certainly not the strongest of poems, but it does display considerable critical power in its emphatic foregrounding of the linkthink it has suffered from its readers. Not only is the poem's speaker obsessively engaged in an attempt to link all that he so acutely senses in a Great – if Dispiriting – Chain of Being; not only does the author emphatically abstain from explicitly inserting his speaker in such a chain; the poem also conspicuously stages the very enterprise of linking in such a way that it prefigures the fallacies of linkthink it could hardly hope to escape. One recent blatant misreading of the poem may help to briefly illustrate the excessive and significant obviousness of this prefigurating strategy.

***

Analogy would lead me one step farther, namely, to the belief that all animals and plants are descended from some one prototype. But analogy may be a deceitful guide

(Darwin, *The Origin of Species*)

> *... and to him that ordereth his conversation aright will I*
> *shew the salvation of God.*

(Psalms 50:23)

In their impressively researched "cultural history" of Shakespeare's Caliban, Alden T. Vaughan and Virginia Mason Vaughan also devote a page to Browning's Caliban, whom they characterise as "an amphibian – half man, half fish – who lives on the margins of humanity but reveals essential human traits such as selfishness and self-deception." (109) For this description of Caliban as an amphibian missing link, they rely on a passage that "summarizes Browning's conception of Shakespeare's fishlike monster" (110)

> a sea-beast, lumpish, which he snared,
> Blinded the eyes of, and brought somewhat tame,
> And split its toe-webs, and now pens the drudge
> In a hole o' the rock and calls him Caliban. (ll.163-66)

What is wrong with this conception of Caliban is that it is no such thing. Nowhere in the poem is Caliban credited with fishy features: true, he sprawls in the cool slush of his cave, but he does so "With elbows wide, fists clenched to prop his chin" (l.3) and kicking "both feet" (l.4); he has two arms (l.6), a "round mouth" (l.125), a "scalp" (l.175), thumbs (l.227), fingers (l.271), teeth and lips (l.293). That is all we know of Caliban's physique. The passage quoted by Vaughan and Vaughan in fact figures as part of Caliban's account of Setebos's creating the world and its creatures by way of compensation for His own subordination to "the Quiet" – a practice Caliban characteristically understands by analogy with his own imitations of Prospero: Caliban has made himself a grimoir, a magic wand and an enchanter's robe; he keeps a "four-legged serpent" (l.158) and "saith she is Miranda and my wife" (l.160); "for his Ariel" he keeps "a tall pouch-bill crane" (l.161); and the web-footed creature Vaughan and Vaughan call Caliban in fact is Caliban's Caliban, a poor sea-beast he has enslaved just as Prospero enslaved him: "'Plays thus at being Prosper in a way,/ Taketh his mirth with make-believes: so He." (ll.168-69)

Vaughan and Vaughan's mistake may be marginal but it is instructive in
that it foregrounds the poem's peculiar pronominal patterns, its constant
permutation of shifters in hierarchical sequences punctuated by Caliban's
Caesarean self-reference: the "he" (l.163) they take to be Prospero is
Caliban, the "him" (l.165) they take to be Caliban is the sea-beast. It is
important to stress that this pattern is peculiar but by no means
undecidable: indeed, on any attentive reading the poem's shifters cannot
fail to fall into place. Yet they only do so when the reading observes the
mechanical regularity that obtains within the text's frame, and the
significance of Vaughan and Vaughan's mistake is that they disturb this
regularity precisely by trying to link up Caliban in a chain that exceeds
the frame of the fiction. Or, more accurately, in a double chain: a
narrative of cultural history – "Caliban's odyssey," as their final chapter
has it – and a narrative of natural history embedded within this cultural
lineage – the narrative also imposed on the poem by Huxley and Howard
featuring Caliban as the missing link (more specifically, as Darwin's
hypothetical aquatic ancestor of man[12] – hence the erroneous insistence on
Caliban's "amphibian" features).

It would appear, then, that Caliban's conspicuous pronominal-analogical
antics indeed ironically prefigure and pre-empt the numerous
interpretations that have sought to place him as the missing link. Vaughan
and Vaughan somewhat carelessly stumble into the textual trap,[13] but
Howard's far more sophisticated interpretation ultimately makes the same
mistake by inserting Caliban into a chain of its own making. Clearly,
Howard can tell his "he"'s from his "he"'s – yet his persistent attempts to
render the poem's meaning in terms of our "we" are governed by the same

---

[12] A reading "made more explicit," as Vaughan and Vaughan note (1991: 110), in
Daniel Wilson's 1873 *Caliban: The Missing Link*.

[13] That Vaughan and Vaughan are not primarily intent on an attentive reading of
Browning partly excuses them. The same cannot be said for Joseph Bristow, whose
reconstruction of Browning's models of understanding is marred by his misreading
Caliban's fanciful impersonation of his flute's disrespectul reference to "his great
round mouth" (l.125) as Caliban's "imagining Setebos with his 'great round
mouth'" (123). The fact that even Browning scholars are confused by Caliban's
shifters further justifies our insistence on the importance of this level of the letter.

pronominal licence that powers Vaughan and Vaughan's, and indeed
Caliban's, clasificatory enterprise. Next to these missing-link-
interpretations, however, there is an alternative standard interpretation of
Browning's poem that focusses explicitly on Caliban's pronominal
analogisms and thus might seem to avoid these pitfalls. (It doesn't.)

According to this second canonical interpretation, the key to the poem
has nothing to do with Caliban's place in the evolutionary scale but must
instead be sought in its subtitle, "Natural Theology in the Island," and in
its epigraph, taken from Psalm 50, "Thou thoughtest that I was altogether
such a one as thyself." Michael Timko, a representative exponent of this
interpretation, rightly points out, in explicit opposition to Howard, that
"there is nothing to show that the poem is necessarily directly connected
with Darwinism" (142), and, taking his cue from the subtitle, proposes
instead to read the monologue as a topical satire on the kind of "scientific"
religious speculation inspired by works like Joseph Butler's 1736 *The
Analogy of Religion, Natural and Revealed* and William Paley's 1802
Natural Theology – speculations in which theological truth is made
"dependen[t] on analogy" consolidated by "constant references to
empirical proof" (145) rather than to divine Revelation.[14] For Timko,
Caliban is a "rationalist" (142) "presenting a highly conventional,
orthodox view of theology, one supplied and advocated by such staunch
churchmen as Butler and Paley" (143), and Browning invented him as a
caricaturesque vehicle for his "ideas on the dangers of too much
dependence on intellect and reason in matters of faith" (142), thereby
fashioning his dramatic monologue as "poetic proof of his strong faith"
(150).

Now, it seems quite possible that Browning indeed had something like
this in mind – the directive subtitle suggests as much and, as Timko
convincingly points out, such an interpretation could be comfortably
confirmed with reference to various other works in "the canon of
Browning's 'religious' poetry" (143). The only problem is that the poem's

---

[14] Like the missing-link-interpretation, this interpretation too had already been
duly registered by Browning's contemporaries. See e.g. Litzinger and Smalley 1970:
220.

speaker is patently *not* a "staunch churchman" advocating orthodox natural theology, as Timko indeed almost recognises (half-contradicting his previous rejection of references to Caliban's "place in the evolutionary scale" [142]) when he states that "[t]o see Caliban only as a primitive subhuman is to take the poem much too literally" (143) – implying that, read literally, Caliban is at least also something other than an orthodox defender of natural theology, something of a missing link. The predictable point we must make here is that to interpret Caliban as a satirical version or monstrous antetype of Butler or Paley requires taking massive recourse to yet another variation on Caliban's pronominal-analogical permutations – even while Timko's intent is precisely to demonstrate that Browning's poem is a satire on analogical reason itself. Let me try to illustrate this by considering in some more detail Timko's central claim that "[t]he basic questions in the poem are those concerning the nature of God, His relationship to human beings, and His method of revealing Himself to these human beings." (146)

The only suggestions "in" the poem that these are indeed its "basic questions" occur in the subtitle and the epigraph, yet these can hardly be called straightforward clues to Caliban's soliloquy. Earlier on in his essay, Timko briefly sketches the continuing importance of natural theology in Browning's time, characterising its mid-Victorian version in the *Bridgewater Treatises*, with Elie Halévy, as an attempt "to reconcile Christian doctrine with the conclusions of modern physiology" and concluding that "[a]s the epigraph to the poem (*Psalms*, 50:21, "Thou thoughtest that I was altogether such a one as thyself") indicates, Browning knew exactly where the real danger to his emotional gnosticism lay." (145) Timko does not deem it necessary to specify exactly what this means, but given that Browning's "emotional gnosticism" involves a "skeptical view of human knowledge" (143), the implication must be that natural theology is to be dismissed because it fashions God in the image of (hu)man (knowledge). This, however, raises some considerable problems. First, if Timko wants us to understand that Caliban, as a natural theologian, is guilty by implication of thinking that (his) God is altogether such a one as himself, the difficulty is that that is exactly what Caliban does not think. To Caliban's mind, his very existence is dependent on his not being altogether like Setebos, who made him, precisely, as "what Himself would fain, in a manner, be" (l.62). True, this desire itself is

projected by Caliban onto Setebos by analogy with Caliban's own desire
to be what he is not, but this imposition of identity on the basis of a
shared desire for difference already indicates that matters are rather more
complex than Timko's blanket judgement allows for. Yet the pattern
becomes more interestingly complex when we recover the context of the
epigraph: for the "thou" God addresses in verse 21 from Psalm 50 is not
any general pronominal stand-in for "man" but quite specifically names
"the wicked" (50: 16), guilty of all kinds of evil: "These things hast thou
done, and I kept silence; thou thoughtest that I was altogether such an one
as thyself: but I will reprove thee, and set them in order before thine
eyes." (50: 21) God's wrath, then, descends not so much on "man" for
having thought of God as similar to himself but, with important precision,
on the wicked who think God, too, walks their wicked ways. God's
"saints," "those that have made a covenant with me by sacrifice" (50: 5),
are pointedly not included in the "thou" denounced in verse 21 – their
erring is altogether of a different kind.

It appears, then, that Timko's confident understanding of the epigraph as a
clear denunciation of natural theology's attempt to understand God in
analogy with man is predicated on a misread pronoun. Whatever else the
epigraph may mean, as a Bible-thumper's key to the poem it picks more
locks than Timko's hermeneutic desire bargained for.[15] For even if we
accept, for the sake of argument, that the epigraph was intended by
Browning as a forceful (though unfelicitously chosen) Biblical curse on the
heads of all natural theologians, it still is not clear how this can be
unambiguously fed into the poem. For (I must return to my wearying
rhetorical question) was Caliban ever a natural theologian, let alone a
human being, in the first place? Who put him in that place? Timko argues
that the poem's basic questions concern the nature and relation of God
and man and that

---

[15] Just to give one further instance: both F.G. Kenyon (in his edition of the *Works*,
xxxii) and Barbara Melchiori argue that the reference to Psalm 50 in fact supports
the missing-link-interpretation of the poem Timko seeks to invalidate with this
same reference. The fact that Melchiori's suggestion also makes Caliban "a
counterpart of [...] the Jews at a certain part of their development as a race" (98) is
perhaps unintended but significantly there.

Caliban, who is pondering these questions, reasons, like Butler and Paley, inductively. He is the complete Baconian. Limited to his senses (unlike man, Browning would stress), he depends on them, just as Butler and Paley, while admitting that man is not limited to his senses, do. (146)

In the space of three sentences, we are treated to a display of substitutive fireworks that might even put Caliban himself to shame: Caliban ponders the relation of man (which he is not) and God and he does this like the men of God Butler and Paley even while, unlike man, as Browning would say (but does not), he is limited to his senses and depends on them just like the men of God Butler and Paley who admit nonetheless that they are not limited to them. Just who is guilty of unlawful analogical reasoning here? As if in response to this question, Timko immediately continues by saying that "Caliban is always consistent, always resorting to analogies; 'so He' is his favourite expression. He also, like Butler and Paley, is aware of..." – never mind what he of the "so He" is also aware of just like those who are like him: Timko is always consistent, always resorting to analogies; "like Butler and Paley" – or even "so they, Butler and Paley" (148) – is his favourite expression. The title of his essay, "Browning upon Butler," is either a masterful stroke of self-irony or conclusive evidence of his damaging blindness to the analogical nature of his reduction of the poem to a rejection of natural analogy.

None of this is to say, however, that we should not mind what Timko has to say, as I have just brutally suggested. Timko's interpretation is not simply wrong. On the contrary, like Howard's and, to a lesser extent, Vaughan and Vaughan's, it is simply correct, precisely in the sense that it mimetically responds to the poem's obsessive foregrounding of analogical-pronominal permutation. To interpret Caliban as a "perceptive but unscientific" creature (Howard 1966: 227) incarnating "the limitations of the subhuman mind" (224), or, on the contrary, as a "spokesman, and a very shrewd one, for what many would consider a highly developed intellectual point of view" (Timko 1965: 143) ultimately incarnating the "reduction to absurdity" (147) of "the rational, scientific approach to problems" (143) proposed in this "natural reasoning" (147), is in both cases to inscribe him in just the kind of "geneanological" narrative whose condition of possibility is critically challenged in the text of Browning's poem. As said, this challenge takes shape in the poem's excessive performance of analogical and pronominal permutations that eminently make sense in the frame of its fiction but never allow for a transfer to the "real" narrrative its readers require. Indeed, the frustration any reading of "Caliban Upon Setebos" is bound to encounter not only resides in the fact that it is by no means clear what the poem *is* "really" about, it ultimately derives from the understanding that this lack of recognisable, relatable pertinence is itself the poem's impertinent point. Such rank impertinence is hard to swallow: in fact, it can only be rejected, but there are different ways to get caught up in this apotropaic gesture.

***

> *A soul shall draw from out the vast*
> *And strike his being into bounds,*
>
> *And moved through life of lower phase,*
> *Result in man, be born and think*
> *And act and love, a closer link*
> *Betwixt us and the crowning race*
> *[...]*
> *Whereof the man that with me trod*
> *This planet, was a noble type*
> *Appearing ere the times were ripe*
>
> (Tennyson, *In Memoriam A.H.H.*)

> *Needless to say, this fly with segmented appendages instead of wings, and a pair of legs assuming the structure of a mouth part, is only a monstrous Drosophila. But it is clearly what I have called a "hopeful monster." If such a monster were formed in nature and found a proper niche to which it were preadapted, the major step toward formation of a new class would have been accomplished.*
>
> (Richard B. Goldschmidt, "Ecotype, Ecospecies, and Macroevolution")

The most obvious way to recuperate Caliban's impertinence generates interpretations that are simply correct in that they register the poem's geneanological structure by mechanically imitating it in a frame of higher relevance. As E. Warwick Slinn has argued, "in Caliban's world [...] objects and events are misread signs, signs that gain meaning through being absorbed into his own version of a hermeneutic circle" (62) – to which we must add that it is just such an absorption Caliban himself suffers at the hands of the many hermeneutic monster-tamers who seek to classify him as a telling figure enabling a narrative of definitive meaning. In fact, the reason why Browning's Caliban has proven to be such a particularly irrestible challenge is arguably his seductive (but fallacious) availability for insertion into the hyperhermeneutic circle whose centre is everywhere and whose circumference is nowhere. It is indeed not surprising that both Howard and Timko should ultimately locate the truth of the poem in the presence-by-absence of divine Revelation, the supreme narrative of evidence for what is not evident. Both recognise the poem's concern with materiality, both see it as a response to the demands of scientific evidence, both criticise Caliban's geneanological processing of material evidence – both end up with the Word made flesh, a position they can only attain after a hermeneutic leap of divination that leaves behind the stubborn evidence (or lack of it) of the text.[16] Both move the poem towards resolution on the basis of a fulcrum that is just not there: the very idea, carried only by unwarranted analogy, that Caliban is a figure in our human narrative at all, a hopeless monstrosity prefiguring the hopeful monster that is the true Christian anticipating the Second Coming. The force of this hermeneutic interpretation is that, like Wordsworth's hermeneutic self-recollection in the Ode, it allows us to make sense of ourselves by geneanologically figuring forth a human homecoming as the true conclusion to Caliban's Odyssee: as Freud memorably said, "analogies, it is true, decide nothing, but they can make one feel more at home." (72)

Yet in its marked refusal to connect Caliban's isle to what we think of as our human continent, Browning's text stubbornly persists as a

---

[16] For some further thoughts on hermeneutic divination and related matters, see my "Dead Herrings" (1994) and *Titanic Light* (1995: 70).

prefigurative critique of geneanological reason itself – a critique precisely
of these reassuring, analogical, simply correct interpretations. To realise
this resistance is itself a first step towards another way of coming to terms
with it – rejecting it nonetheless, but this time in what hopes to
approximate a critically true reading, not a simply correct interpretation.
The point is not to simply reject hermeneutic interpretations like those I
have been savaging here: they are important precisely in their enactment
of the seriousness of the predicament "Caliban Upon Setebos" addresses,
the "lack of a transcending principle" (Maclean 1987: 15). Yet these
hermeneutic interpretations fail themselves to genuinely address this
"profoundly tragic issue" (15) by assuming, in a decisive divination, that it
has already been resolved into a chain of transcendental meaning. What a
true reading of the poem proposes instead is a displacement of this
resolution that recognises its origin in, indeed, a serious predicament
intimately conditioned by its *literary* existence as a genuine question. To
this genuine question of literature, hermeneutic interpretation is the
inevitable but constitutionally premature answer, and the best we can
hope to do is to insist that the link between literature and its meaning is
still missing.

That this is not an easy task should be evident by now – even if only
because what I have sketched in this essay so blatantly fails to be the true
reading I celebrate here. A failure further compounded in this very
celebration: for is not the assumption that "Caliban Upon Setebos" *is* a
genuine literary question itself a thoroughly hermeneutic imposition?
Who made it a poem in the first place? Browning did, by inscribing his
words in the work of Shakespeare; I did, compensating for my decision
not to insert the text in the hermeneutic body of Browning's corpus (as
can and has been excellently done) by binding it instead to Wordsworth's
Immortality Ode on the basis of a tenuous conceptual analogy. It is not
enough to know this. Perhaps it doesn't even help.

I have expressed it all insufficiently, and will break the chain
up, one day, and leave so many separate little round rings to
roll each its way, if it can.

(Robert Browning, *Letter to Julia Wedgwood*,
31 Dec. 1864)

For is Browning even a poet? An unsigned review of *Dramatis Personae* in
The Athenaeum for June 4th 1864 points up the relevance of this perversely
trivial question:

> 'Thou thoughtest that I was altogether such an one as
> thyself,' says the quotation attached to Mr. Browning's
> 'Caliban,' but most assuredly no one ever thought Mr.
> Browning like unto any other poet! He could not if he
> would, and he would not if he could. He pioneers his
> own way, and follows no one's track for the sake of ease
> and smoothness. (Litzinger and Smalley 1970: 219)

How then can we recognise him as a poet – as, indeed, "one of our very
few living poets [whose] book is a richer gift than we shall often receive at
the hands of poetry in our time" (221)? All we have are traces. Yet the
track takes care of itself.

Browning died in 1889 and was buried in Westminster Abbey's Poets'
Corner. On this occasion, Henry James wrote a brilliant commemoration,
speculating how Browning "would have enjoyed prefiguring and playing
with the mystifications, the reservations, even perhaps the slight buzz of
scandal, in the Poets' Corner, to which his own obsequies might give rise"
among the "corporate company" of those already buried there (1966: 12-
13):

> A good many oddities and a good many great writers
> have been entombed in the Abbey; but none of the odd
> ones have been so great and none of the great ones so
> odd. There are plenty of poets whose right to the title
> may be contested, but there is no poetic head of equal
> power – crowned and recrowned by almost importunate

hands – from which so many people would withhold the distinctive wreath. All this will give the marble phantoms at the base of the great pillars and the definite personalities of the honorary slabs something to puzzle out until, by the quick operation of time, the mere fact of his lying there among the classified and protected, makes even Robert Browning lose a portion of the bristling surface of his actuality. (13)

Give me a firm tombstone on which to stand, and I will tell you what you were and were to be. So Shakespeare, so Wordsworth, so Browning. But the other portion will remain. So Hölderlin, perhaps.

References

Arnold, Matthew. 1958. "Literature and Science." In Buckler 1958: 486-501.

Beer, Gillian. 1985. *Darwin's Plots. Evolutionary Narrative in Darwin, George Eliot and Nineteenth Century Fiction.* London: Ark.

Bloom, Harold, ed. 1992. *Caliban (Major Literary Characters).* New York: Chelsea House.

Browning, Robert. 1912. *The Works of Robert Browning (Centenary Edition), 10 vols.* Ed. F.G. Kenyon. London: Smith Elder & Company.

Buckler, William E., ed. 1958. *Prose of the Victorian Period.* Cambridge, Mass.: The Riverside Press.

Christensen, Jerome. 1994. "The Romantic Movement at the End of History." *Critical Inquiry* 20: 452-76.

Coleridge, Samuel Taylor. 1983. *The Collected Works of Samuel Taylor Coleridge, Vol. VII: Biographia Literaria, or Biographical Sketches of My Literary Life and Opinions, I.* Ed. James Engell and W. Jackson Bate. Princeton: Princeton UP.

Cunningham, Andrew and Nicholas Jardine, eds. 1990. *Romanticism and the Sciences.* Cambridge: Cambridge UP.

Darwin, Charles. 1878. *The Origin of Species by Means of Natural Selection, or the Preservation of Favoured Races in the Struggle for Life*. Sixth Edition. London: John Murray.

—. 1899. *The Descent of Man and Selection in Relation to Sex*. Second Edition. New York: D. Appleton & Co.

Dawkins, Richard. 1988. *The Blind Watchmaker*. Harmondsworth: Penguin.

De Graef, Ortwin. 1994. "Dead Herrings. 'You must have mistaken the author.'" *Textual Practice* 8: 239-54.

—. 1995. *Titanic Light. Paul de Man's Post-Romanticism, 1960-1969*. Lincoln: U of Nebraska P.

De Man, Paul. 1993. *Romanticism and Contemporary Criticism. The Gauss Seminar and Other Papers*. Ed. E.S. Burt, Kevin Newmark and Andrzej Warminski. Baltimore: Johns Hopkins UP.

Desmond, Adrian. 1994. *Huxley. The Devil's Disciple*. London: Michael Joseph.

Desmond, Adrian and James Moore. 1992. *Darwin*. Harmondsworth: Penguin.

Drew, Philip, ed. 1966. *Robert Browning. A Collection of Critical Essays*. London: Methuen.

Freud, Sigmund. 1964. "The Dissection of the Psychical Personality." *The Standard Edition of the Complete Psychological Works of Sigmund Freud, Vol.XXII (1932-36): New Introductory Lectures on Psycho-Analysis and Other Works*. Trans. and ed. James Strachey *et al*. London: Hogarth Press.

Gibson, Mary Ellis, ed. 1992. *Critical Essays on Robert Browning*. New York: G.K. Hall.

Gill, Stephen. 1990. *William Wordsworth. A Life*. Oxford: Oxford UP.

Goldschmidt, Richard B. 1980. "Ecotype, Ecospecies, and Macroevolution" [1948]. In *Richard Goldschmidt: Controversial Geneticist and Creative Biologist*. Ed. Leonie K. Piternick. Basel: Birkhäuser, 140-53.

Gould, Stephen Jay. 1992. *Bully for Brontosaurus. Further Reflections in Natural History*. Harmondsworth: Penguin.

Gridley, Roy E. 1972. *Browning (Routledge Author Guides)*. London: Routledge & Kegan Paul.

Hegel, G.W.F. 1970. *Philosophy of Nature, Being Part Two of the "Encyclopedia of the Philosophical Sciences."* Trans. A.V. Miller, with foreword by J.N. Findlay. Oxford: Clarendon Press.

Howard, John. 1966. "Caliban's Mind" [1963]. In Drew 1966: 223-33.

Jack, Ian. 1973. *Browning's Major Poetry*. Oxford: Clarendon Press.

James, Henry. 1966. "Browning in Westminster Abbey" [1890]. In Drew 1966: 11-6.

Knight, David. 1990. "Romanticism and the Sciences." In Cunningham and Jardine 13-24.

Levine, George. 1993. "By Knowledge Possessed: Darwin, Nature, and Victorian Narrative." *New Literary History* 24 : 363-91.

Litzinger, Boyd and Donald Smalley, eds. 1970. *Browning. The Critical Heritage*. London: Routledge & Kegan Paul.

Maclean, Kenneth. 1987. "Wild Man and Savage Believer. Caliban in Shakespeare and Browning." *Victorian Poetry* 25: 1-16.

Melchiori, Barbara. 1992. "Upon 'Caliban Upon Setebos'" [1968]. In Bloom 1992: 195-108.

Mermin, Dorothy. 1992. "Browning and the Primitive" [1982]. In Gibson 1992: 202-25.

Rousseau, Jean-Jacques. 1964. *Oeuvres complètes, III: Du contrat social/Ecrits politiques*. Gen ed. Bernard Gagnebin and Marcel Raymond. Paris: Gallimard.

Servotte, Herman. 1992. *Stem en visioen. Engelse dichters en het verdwijnen van God*. Kapellen: DNB/Uitgeverij Pelckmans.

Slinn, E. Warwick. 1991. *The Discourse of Self in Victorian Poetry*. Houndmills: Macmillan.

Timko, Michael. 1965. "Browning upon Butler; or, Natural Theology in the English Isle." *Criticism* 7: 141-50.

Vaughan, Alden T. and Virginia Mason Vaughan. 1991. *Shakespeare's Caliban. A Cultural History*. Cambridge: Cambridge UP.

Woolford, John. 1988. *Browning the Revisionary*. Houndmills: Macmillan.

Wordsworth, William. 1985. *Poems in Two Volumes, and Other Poems, 1800-1807 (The Cornell Edition of the Complete Poetical Works)*. Ed. Jared Curtis. Ithaca: Cornell UP.

—. 1989. *William Wordsworth (The Oxford Authors)*. Ed. Stephen Gill. Oxford: Oxford UP.

The Survival of the Prettiest

Transmutations of Darwin in José Enrique Rodó's *Ariel*

Maarten van Delden

Two Versions of Darwinism

Darwin's theory of the origin of species opens up two very different perspectives on the relationship between human beings and the other creatures of the natural world. The idea that the differences among the species are the result of the continuous struggle for life in which all organic beings must engage, a struggle in which only the fittest survive, may justify a sharply hierarchical view of existence, with a clear ranking of the various forms of life, and a firm sense of humanity's more advanced position in comparison with other species. This is reflected in the constant use in Darwin's work of binaries such as "weak" and "strong," or "higher" and "lower." Yet Darwin's claim that all beings are ultimately descended from "one primordial form" (1985: 455) can also lead to a vision of all the earth's species as bound together by the most intimate ties of resemblance. Darwin spends many pages in *The Descent of Man* attacking the idea that there exists "an impassable barrier" separating humanity from "all the

lower animals" (I, 49).[1] In demonstrating in painstaking detail how in
matters ranging from bodily structure to mental faculties humanity shares
most of its characteristics with other organic beings, Darwin deals a severe
blow to what he describes as "that arrogance which made our forefathers
declare that they were descended from demi-gods" (I, 32), and restores a
sense of humanity's embeddedness in the natural world. Darwin makes it
clear, moreover, that there is no need to feel shame at humanity's lack of a
distinguished pedigree, for, he writes, "no one with an unbiassed mind can
study any living creature, however humble, without being struck with
enthusiasm at its marvellous structure and properties" (I, 213).

Alden T. Vaughan and Virginia Mason Vaughan's account of Darwinian
interpretations of Shakespeare's Caliban suggests that these interpretations
tended to follow the latter pattern. The Darwinian view of Caliban as
missing link, "somewhere between brute animal and human being," as an
"educable" creature with "an evolving sensibility," and therefore as a figure
for "the nineteenth-century belief in humanity's continuing progress and
ability to improve itself" (Vaughan and Vaughan 1991: 110-13), contrasts
with the seventeenth- and eighteenth-century view of Caliban as a symbol
of human depravity, as well as with the twentieth-century view of him as
an emblem of "the inexorable, ineradicable evil within the human psyche"
(Vaughan and Vaughan 1991: 114). In the Darwinian scenario described by
the Vaughans, Caliban represented an earlier stage in the ascent of
humanity. It was a stage, however, that he, too, could rise above. Given
the existence of these associations in the late nineteenth and early
twentieth centuries, it is interesting that the Uruguayan essayist José
Enrique Rodó should have used the figure of Caliban in his *Ariel* (1900) to
represent not the past of humanity, but its potential future. Rodó's
immensely influential essay, cast in the form of a lecture by a teacher
known as Prospero, treats a variety of subjects, including the value of
being young, the importance of a well-rounded personality, the
relationship between the good and the beautiful, and the strengths and

---

[1] *The Descent of Man* was first published in two volumes in 1871. The Princeton
UP edition I have used for this article is a facsimile reprint which includes in one
volume the two volumes of the original edition. References in parentheses in the
text are to volume and page number.

limitations of democracy. But the essay's most notorious section is the one in which Rodó links the United States of America, the very embodiment of the nineteenth-century ideology of progress, with the base and backward Caliban. When Rodó observes in *Ariel* how the North Americans give "the greatest prominence to the bold and astute struggle-for-lifer" (1988: 240; 85),[2] he is implying that the United States offers the clearest exemplification in the social realm of the laws which according to Darwin governed the natural world. For Rodó this was something to be lamented rather than celebrated, as the Social Darwinists of the era did.[3] This is why Caliban was for Rodó not so much what Latin America had left behind, but rather what he feared the continent might become if it followed in the footsteps of the nation which after its victory in the Spanish-American War of 1898 was already beginning to look like the most powerful on earth. Yet even while Rodó's depiction of Caliban as the United States marks a clear turning away from an influential Darwinian paradigm, it is remarkable how heavily Darwinian is Rodó's language in *Ariel*. While he may disapprove of the naked struggle for life he sees in the United States, Rodó speaks again and again in *Ariel* of "evolution" and "selection" as inevitable and even desirable processes. What, then, is Rodó's exact relationship to Darwinism? Does he use a Darwinian terminology only to swerve away from Darwinian principles, or does he in fact remain within a Darwinian framework? And what can an answer to these questions tell us about Rodó's use of symbols from Shakespeare's *The Tempest*?

---

[2] While quotations from *Ariel* are provided in English, page references are to both the Spanish original and the English translation, in that order. I have made some changes in Margaret Sayers Peden's translation. All other translations from Spanish texts cited in this article are mine.

[3] Jonathan Howard writes that "In late Victorian society in England and more especially in America a peculiarly beastly form of social climbing, 'Social Darwinism,' was established under Herbert Spencer's slogan 'The survival of the fittest.' The evolutionary law was interpreted to mean victory to the strongest as the necessary condition of progress" (89). Howard insists that such ideas had very little to do with Darwin, who "was unable to see how evolution in biology could have any but the feeblest analogical resemblance to the evolution of society" (v).

Darwin in Uruguay

The introduction of Darwin's theories into Latin American intellectual discourse was part of the broader phenomenon of the last quarter of the nineteenth century labelled "the ascendancy of positivism" by Charles Hale. While conceding that there is "no accepted definition" of the term, Hale argues that central to positivism was the belief in "the scientific method" as "man's only means of knowing" (383). There is no question that in these years Darwin was among the most influential practitioners of this method. When Rodó speaks, as he repeatedly does in *Ariel*, of the lessons of science, it is important to recall that some of the most important of these lessons were first propagated by Darwin. Arturo Ardao points out that in the specific case of Uruguay positivism was absorbed primarily in its English rather than its French guise, which means that Uruguayan intellectuals gravitated towards Darwin and Spencer rather than Comte (Ardao 1950: 15). Thomas Glick suggests that in 1860 eighteen year old William Henry Hudson, the future writer and naturalist, and the son of an Anglo-Argentine rancher, became the first person in the River Plate region to read *The Origin of Species* after his brother brought him a copy from England. It is likely that Darwin's work first reached Uruguay via a similar route, since there were many English ranchers in Uruguay, too (Glick 1989: 101). In fact, the first extended debate in Uruguay on Darwinism took place within the *Asociación Rural* (Rural Association), an organization founded in 1871 with the aim of promoting the modernization of the nation's agrarian sector (Glick 1989: 85). The *Asociación Rural* published a journal that became for a while the principal forum for the presentation of Darwin's ideas in Uruguay (Glick 1989: 95). It wasn't until a few years later that Darwin's thought became a subject of debate in academic and other intellectual circles as well. Arturo Ardao, overlooking the role played by the *Asociación Rural*, describes the polemic that unfolded in 1876 between José Pedro Varela and Carlos María Ramírez in the Montevidean newspaper *El Siglo* as the first occasion on which Darwinism was explained in Uruguay (Ardao 1950: 84-5). It is clear, though, that whatever the precise starting-date may have been for the assimilation of Darwin's work into Uruguayan intellectual debate, for a significant period of time in the late nineteenth century, Darwinism played an important role in Uruguayan cultural life. It is not surprising, then, that the work of José Enrique Rodó should bear Darwin's imprint.

This is not to say that there is any explicit discussion of Darwin in Rodó. There is no mention of Darwin in Clemente Pereda's *Rodó's Main Sources*, and the index of Emir Rodríguez Monegal's edition of Rodó's *Obras Completas* (Complete Works) lists only two references to Darwin. One reference appears in *Motivos de Proteo* where Darwin is mentioned along with Humboldt and Haeckel as somebody whose career illustrates the usefulness of travel to the development of the natural sciences (423). The other reference is to the passage in *Ariel*, which I discuss in more detail below, where Rodó supports his argument for the importance of beauty in the process of evolution by referring to Darwin's theory of sexual selection, though without mentioning Darwin by name. But Darwin was clearly important to Rodó even if he rarely referred to him. Darwin's theories shaped the intellectual climate of the era, and Rodó did not escape their impact. Nancy Leys Stepan perhaps best captures Darwin's role in Latin American intellectual life when she writes that "the social Darwinisms taken up by intellectuals and scientists served as 'meta-languages' providing rich, multivalent frameworks for the analysis of the history of the Latin American peoples and their destinies" (1991: 41). The workings of this Darwinian framework in *Ariel*, and in particular its bearing on Rodó's reading of the Shakespearean figures who anchor his meditation on Latin American identity, are the subject of this essay.

From Natural to Aesthetic Selection

Although Darwin did not use it in the first edition of *The Origin of Species*, the word "evolution" eventually became firmly linked to his name. Rodó makes frequent use of the term in *Ariel*. Even more remarkable is the number of times Rodó uses the word "selection," another concept with strong Darwinian connotations. "Selection" and its cognates appear around twenty times in an essay of just over seventy pages in the English translation. Like Darwin, Rodó uses the word "selection" to express a conception of life as a process that produces higher and higher forms. But whereas Darwin offered a very precise description of the mechanism that fuels the process of selection, Rodó uses the term in a much looser fashion.

And where Rodó hints in the direction of an answer to the question of how the process of selection operates, his ideas constitute an almost direct inversion of Darwin's position. This is clear from the fact that for Darwin selection is always "natural," whereas for Rodó it is normally "spiritual" or "intellectual."

Darwin's theory of natural selection is remarkable for its elegance and economy.[4] The central idea in his theory is that the world exists in a state of flux. The concept of natural selection identifies the basic rule that governs the changes constantly taking place in the natural world. In developing his theory, Darwin began by uncovering the materials with which natural selection works. He drew attention in the first place to the fact that individual members of a species always differ at least slightly from each other, and in the second place to the fact that variation of this kind is to some degree hereditary. He then suggested that the gradual accumulation from one generation to the next of individual differences in a certain direction could result – given enough time – in the transformation of one species into another. But in order to make his theory work, Darwin needed to identify the precise mechanism of evolutionary change, that is, he needed to explain why change was in one direction rather than another. He found his answer in Thomas Malthus's *Essay on Population* (1798). Malthus had noted that all living creatures have a tendency to multiply beyond the capacity of the environment to sustain them. All creatures were consequently condemned to struggle with each other to obtain what they needed in order to survive. Borrowing Malthus's key insight, Darwin gave the name "natural selection" to the check imposed on the free multiplication of the species by the fact of the earth's limited resources. Variations that proved useful in the struggle for life were likely to be preserved, while unprofitable variations were eliminated. By projecting such a process onto a vast time-scale, one could see how evolution might result in the extinction of some species, as well as in the emergence of new, better adapted ones.

---

[4] My summary of Darwin owes a great deal to Jonathan Howard's very useful book.

It is clear from this account that for Darwin evolution is guided entirely by material factors, and, moreover, that it is an ongoing and unpredictable process that is contingent in the case of any given species on the circumstances in which it happens to find itself in a particular place and time. Darwin states very clearly that he believes in "no law of necessary development" (1985: 348). Yet Darwin's work promoted a genealogical perspective on the natural world. He believed that "community of descent" offered the main criterion according to which species ought to be classified (1985: 404). A similarly genealogical way of looking at culture and society was extremely common in the late nineteenth century. Rodó, for example, relies heavily in *Ariel* on the notion of descent in order to define Latin American culture, since he believes that this culture is what it is in the first place because of its specifically Latin heritage.[5] At the same time, Rodó fails to heed Darwin's cautionary note concerning the contingent element in the process of evolution. For Rodó clearly believes that the preservation, refinement and handing down of this Latin heritage to future generations is part of a transcendent historical pattern. It is to this process that he applies the term "selection." But what exactly is the mechanism that makes this process advance?

We have seen that in Darwin natural selection consists of the efforts which all organisms must undertake to adapt to their material conditions. Towards the end of *Ariel* there is a passage in which Rodó speaks in a Darwinian manner of "conditions" and "adaptation," but veers sharply

---

[5] Lily Litvak suggests that the emergence in the last decades of the nineteenth century of the idea of a Latin identity was related not only to political and economic developments of the period, but also to the fact that the "Darwinist and evolutionist propaganda which acquired such prominence in Europe after about 1860 emphasized the idea of the biological existence of different human races, some of which, thanks to their energy, vigor or intelligence, were more succesful in the struggle for life than others, and were therefore superior" (Litvak 1980: 12-13). While such views were most often used to explain and legitimate the rise of the Northern European nations and the United States (the Saxons), they also led to the elaboration of a discourse on Latin identity, which at times sought to explain the relative decline of the Latin nations, and at times exalted these nations as a source of alternative values in a world increasingly dominated by the Saxons.

away from Darwin's actual position when he suggests that in the case of human beings the key conditions to which they must adapt are not the material ones that affect them in the present, but rather a set of imaginary conditions linked above all to the idea of the future. "We are capable of progress," Rodó claims, "only to the extent that we know how to adapt our acts to conditions that are increasingly distant from us in space and time" (247; 96). Since adaptation and selection are two sides of the same coin, we can conclude that for Rodó the agent of selection is not a material force but an ideal. As a projection of the future, the ideal frees us from the material conditions of life. In fact, so powerful is the mind's potential for projecting itself beyond its present circumstances that it can achieve body-altering effects. In Rodó's eyes, "Thinking races reveal in the increasing capacity of their crania the thrust of [...] internal activity" (245; 94).

Selection is driven from within the individual mind. At the same time, it engages a culture as a whole. The notion of selection is linked to certain exceptional individuals (the well-rounded self discussed in the second section of *Ariel*), as well as to entire cultures and ethnic groups (the Ancient Greeks, and in modern times, Latins rather than Saxons). Thus we see the curious mixture of individualism and culturalism that characterizes Rodó's thought. But what type of culture does Rodó associate with the notion of selection? It is, as we have just seen, the culture of specific ethnic groups, but more important is the fact that it is a spiritual and, above all, aesthetic culture (for which certain ethnic groups are assumed to possess a greater affinity than others). So Rodó can speak in one breath of "the interests of aesthetic culture and spiritual selection" (224; 58), and can state elsewhere in *Ariel* that "the sense of the select has its most natural adaptation" in the realm of art (227; 64).

But to get a clear picture of the role of aesthetics in the process of selection, we need only turn to the first page of *Ariel*. Rodó describes there the bronze statue of Ariel that presides over Prospero's classroom. It was, in fact, because of his custom of sitting beside the statue of Ariel that the "venerable old teacher" (1988: 206; 31) had come to be known as Prospero. According to Rodó, "Shakespeare's ethereal Ariel symbolizes the noble, soaring aspect of the human spirit." He is "the ideal towards which human selection ascends, rectifying in the superior man the tenacious vestiges of Caliban, symbol of brutal sensuality, with the this sentence the subject of "rectifying," that is, the agent wielding the chisel of life, can be either Ariel himself or human selection. My own preference is for the latter reading, since there is something slightly awkward about the picture of Ariel wielding the chisel with which he sculpts himself. It makes more sense to think of Ariel as the product of the workings of human selection, while Caliban remains behind as unselected, unsculpted humanity. But whichever reading we prefer, it is clear from this passage that art is the force that drives the process of selection, for it is art that grants "sculptural solidity" (1988: 207; 32) to Ariel's image. In *Ariel* human evolution operates through aesthetic rather than natural selection.

The importance to society of an aesthetic culture is asserted throughout *Ariel*, but it is treated most directly in the essay's third section, where Rodó argues that ethics and aesthetics, the good and the beautiful, are indissolubly linked to each other. Near the end of this section appears the passage in which Rodó draws on Darwin's work on sexual selection. Having asserted that ideas are more effective when they are granted aesthetic form, Rodó proceeds to draw an analogy from the natural world:

> Thus it is that in the evolution of life, some of the enchanting ornamentations of nature that may seem to result from a superfluous capriciousness – the song and bright plumage of the birds, and, to attract the pollinating insect, the color and perfume of the flowers – have actually played, among the elements in the struggle for life, a very practical role; offering higher motives for the attractions of love, they have ensured that the most beautiful within a species survive over those less fortunately endowed. (1988: 221; 55)

The idea of sexual selection is for Darwin supplementary to that of natural selection. He introduces the topic briefly in *The Origin of Species*, and treats it at greater length in *The Descent of Man*. In the earlier work, he writes that sexual selection "depends, not on a struggle for existence, but on a struggle between the males for possession of the females; the result is not death to the unsuccessful competitor, but few or no offspring" (1985: 136). Another way of putting it would be to say that in the case of natural selection the prevailing environmental conditions select, whereas in the case of sexual selection the females of each species select. The question then is by what means the males try to obtain advantage over each other. Darwin is led at this point to introduce a somewhat extraneous element into his theory. While noting that males in some cases engage in outright combat with each other, Darwin also draws attention to the more peaceful methods of contest in use in the natural world. Many males, especially among birds, attempt to seduce and conquer the females by the beauty of their song or appearance, rather than by their superior strength: "The rock-thrush of Guiana, birds of Paradise and some others, congregate; and successive males display their gorgeous plumage and perform strange antics before the females, which standing by as spectators, at last choose the most attractive partner" (137). Such habits explain why the males and females of the same species sometimes differ so sharply, for it is clear, according to Darwin, "that female birds, by selecting during thousands of generations, the most melodious or beautiful males, according to their standard of beauty, might produce a marked effect" (137). What is difficult to explain, however, is from where the females derive their standard of beauty.

In *The Descent of Man* Darwin concedes that his account implies "powers of discrimination and taste on the part of the female which will at first appear extremely improbable" (1981: I, 259). He admits that it is an "astonishing fact" (II, 400) that the females of many animal species should possess an "aesthetic capacity" (II, 401). But he insists that only the assumption that females do indeed possess such a capacity can explain certain traits of male behavior. For Darwin "the extraordinary attitudes assumed by the male during the act of courtship, by which the wonderful beauty of his plumage is fully displayed" (II, 93) must serve some purpose. He notes that beauty is sometimes "a source of danger" (II, 97) for its possessor, a fact that makes sense only if we acknowledge that "the power to charm the female has been in some instances more important than the power to conquer other males in battle" (I, 279). The advantages provided by physical beauty within the arena of sexual selection sometimes outweigh the disadvantages the same trait may entail within the general struggle for life. But to identify the functional element that explains male aesthetic display does not mean that one has also explained the female taste for the beautiful. Darwin can only remove the aura of purposelessness that attaches to certain aspects of male behavior by transferring it to the female. For what fuels the female aesthetic capacity remains a mystery in Darwin's system.

The traces of this gendered reading of the relationship between beauty and utility can also be found in Rodó. In the paragraph following the passage in which he speaks of the role of beauty in the process of evolution, Rodó concedes that his account may produce some mortification in "A person gifted with an instinctive love of beauty," since he has proceeded "through a series of arguments grounded in a principle other than the independent and selfless love for beauty" (1988: 221; 55). Rodó justifies his approach by pointing out that "higher principles do not always triumph in the case of large numbers of individuals" (222; 55). As a propagandist of beauty, Rodó feels that he must construct an argument that will not just persuade a few refined souls (who, in any case, do not need to be persuaded), but will in fact capture the imagination of the masses. Since the masses do not naturally experience a love of beauty, it is necessary to lure them into aesthetic appreciation by revealing how what is beautiful is also often useful: "If you propose to popularize respect for the beautiful, begin by illustrating the possibility of harmonious accord among all legitimate human activities, for you will find that an easier task than to convert the multitude directly to a love of beauty for beauty's sake" (222; 56). The brief passage about sexual selection becomes in Rodó's own reading the illustration of a rhetorical and pedagogical technique, as well as an allegory of the usefulness of beauty. But the theory of sexual selection can only be read as allegorical in this sense if we focus on the behavior of the male. What drives the female, that is, what practical advantage she gains when she selects a male for his beauty rather than his vigor, remains an enigma.

Rodó: Positivist or Idealist?

There are two different readings of Rodó's relationship to positivism. One group of critics believes that Rodó breaks with the positivist hegemony of the late nineteenth century, while another group argues that Rodó remains within the positivist paradigm. My reading of the Darwinian element in *Ariel* provides some measure of support to each position. Given the way Rodó transforms Darwin's materialist reading of evolution into an aestheticist one – Rodó's aspiration towards beauty replacing Darwin's struggle for life – it is understandable that José Miguel Oviedo should claim that "The idealism of *Ariel* [...] was a symptom of the failure of nineteenth-century positivism and its blind adherence to science and pragmatism" (1990: 50). At the same time, my reading of Rodó's use of Darwin's ideas on sexual selection serves to indicate that Rodó also remains in places solidly within Darwin's pragmatic, utilitarian framework. Rodó emphasizes the goal-directed nature of male aesthetic display in the animal world rather than the more perplexing, mysterious nature of the female taste for the beautiful not only because he is automatically drawn to the male perspective, but also because pragmatic explanations have in the end a much stronger appeal for him than some of his idealistic, aestheticist statements might lead us to believe. This aspect of *Ariel* helps account for the claim made a long time ago by Alberto Zum Felde that "Rodó's idealism was simply positivism dressed up as humanist literature" (100), or for Charles Hale's more recent insistence that "Though Rodó was heralded as the prophet of a new idealism, much of *Ariel* was cast in a positivist mould" (415).

There is, of course, also Rodó's own view of his relationship to positivism to be considered. In "Rumbos Nuevos" (New Directions), an essay on the Colombian writer Carlos Arturo Torres, first published in 1910, Rodó discusses the recent move away from positivism. He uses the term "neo-idealism" to describe the new orientation he sees in intellectual life, both in Europe and Latin America. But Rodó neither observes nor advocates a wholesale rejection of positivism. While he believes that ideals rather than considerations of utility should guide human behavior, he continues to regard positivism as the "corner-stone of our intellectual formation" (521). But the lessons of positivism need to be absorbed into a new synthesis that transcends the limitations of positivism. In Arturo Ardao's words, Rodó was part of "the *fin-de-siècle* movement which wanted to go beyond positivism, without essentially negating it" (1971: 242).

I do not believe that my reading of *Ariel* lends support to this view of Rodó as the creator of a synthesis between positivism and what he calls idealism. There are indeed elements of both orientations present in *Ariel*, but rather than coherently combined into a new synthesis, they are superimposed on each other in an arbitrary, unsystematic manner. Rodó's use of terms such as "species," "adaptation," "evolution," and "selection" carries the clear suggestion that he is working within a Darwinian framework, but in substituting an aesthetic for a biological mechanism at the heart of the evolutionary process, Rodó turns Darwin's theory upside down. Rodó's biologizing vocabulary becomes merely a way of drawing on the authority of the natural science of the day so as to buttress a position that in fact bears very little relationship to that science. Rodó declares that it is unnecessary for him to comment on the criticisms levelled at "the revelations of natural science" (223; 57), since he takes it for granted that his readers understand the value and importance of these revelations. He also asserts that science is, along with democracy, one of "the two essential pillars upon which our civilization rests" (228; 65). Yet in practice he uses a scientific terminology in order to give weight to a piece of work which, by the standards of the authority Rodó himself invokes, has no scientific value whatsoever.

Roberto González Echevarría has drawn attention to the element of "ideological imposition" in *Ariel* (1985: 26). He points to Rodó's deployment of images related to acts of inscription, of cutting, and of chiselling, and argues that these images betray an understanding of communication as "doing violence to an implied other" (27). I would suggest that these images should not be read as commenting exclusively on the problem of comunication; they must be placed, also, in the context of the period's broader concern with the issue of evolution, and in particular in relation to the Darwinian view of selection as an unremittingly harsh, violent process. Some of this violence is absorbed into Rodó's description of selection as the sculpting of humanity, that is, as the gradual chiselling away, or elimination, of lower forms. The element of ideological imposition of which González Echeverría speaks is reflected much more obviously in the way Rodó uses a vocabulary derived from natural science while ignoring the assumptions embedded in this vocabulary. But what about the passage in *Ariel* about beauty and sexual selection? Doesn't Rodó hew very closely to Darwin's position here? Isn't this evidence of the seriousness with which Rodó uses scientific arguments? To prove that it isn't one need only recall Rodó's almost embarrassingly frank acknowledgment of the reasons for his interest in the theory of sexual selection. It is not so much that this theory allows him to make a point about the importance of beauty in the natural world, as that the theory is assumed to possess a special power over the minds of the masses. Rodó introduces an anecdote drawn from the researches of natural scientists not because it is true, but because it promises to be effective in the pursuit of a specific socio-political goal.

Up from Caliban

The question that remains is what light this reading of the Darwinian element in *Ariel* can cast on Rodó's relationship to the history of interpretations of Shakespeare's Caliban. There are, in fact, only three references to Caliban in *Ariel*. The first is the description of Caliban as a symbol of "brutal sensuality" at the start of the essay. The second reference is to Ernest Renan's view of democracy as the "enthronement of Caliban" (223; 58). The third and last reference occurs just before the end of the essay where Rodó speaks of Ariel's perseverance despite being "conquered a thousand times over by the indomitable rebellion of Caliban" (248; 98). Caliban's role within the essay's overall argument must, then, largely be inferred. José Miguel Oviedo has complained that the principal inference made about Rodó's Caliban – that if Ariel is Latin America, then Caliban must be the United States – has no basis in the text (1990: 49). But if the dichotomy between Ariel and Caliban is to make any sense, it must be related to the other dichotomies – spirit vs. matter, aesthetics vs. utility, the United States vs. Latin America – around which Rodó structures his argument. If Ariel represents the spiritual, aesthetic culture of Latin America, then coherence requires that Caliban should embody the materialist, utilitarian culture of the United States.[6] But Ariel and Caliban are not simply opposites. They also have much in common. Each represents a form of progress. Caliban symbolizes the progress driven by the naked struggle for life that rules in the United States, while Ariel stands for the progress of the spirit, a progress that is at the same

---

[6] Emir Rodríguez Monegal (1977: 80) shows how the study of Rodó's sources lends additional credibility to the notion that Caliban represents the United States. He argues that Rodó took the idea from Paul Groussac, who in a speech he gave in Buenos Aires in May 1898 described the United States as possessing an "unformed and calibanesque body."

time a return to the sources of Western civilization.[7] Moreover, in Rodó's
view, Ariel's type of progress cannot take place without Caliban's help.
This is clear not only from explicit statements such as "the work of North
American Positivism will serve the cause of Ariel," or "History clearly
demonstrates a reciprocal relationship between the progress of
utilitarianism and idealism" (242; 88), but also from the way Rodó on the
first page of his essay describes how the chisel of human selection sculpts
the ideal form of Ariel out of the shapeless mass of Caliban. This vision of
the interconnectedness of the two figures emerges in yet another passage
where Rodó exploits an analogy with natural science. Near the end of
Ariel, Rodó speaks of how "the laws of science tend to sanction and
strengthen the spirit of democracy," since these laws have demonstrated
"the enormity of the role reserved for the anonymous and obscure in any
stage of universal evolution" (230; 68-69). As an example of how science
"enhances the dignity of the humble," Rodó mentions how it has taught
us to see "in the oscillations of the formless, primitive cell all the impulses
of ascendant organic life" (230; 69). In this tiny, shapeless cell we recognize
one more of Rodó's images of Caliban. And in calling on his readers to
acknowledge the dignity and importance of the "anonymous" and
"obscure" in the scheme of life, Rodó may even be seen as anticipating the
Third-Worldist interpretation of Caliban offered by critics such as
Roberto Fernández Retamar. However, having extracted from the natural
science of his time this lesson in egalitarianism, Rodó quickly proceeds to
remind us that science also "proves that hierarchical order is a necessary
condition for all progress," and that "Relationships of dependence and
subordination among individual components of society, and within the
individual himself, are a principle of life" (230; 69). Thus Caliban is put
back into place, and the version of Darwinism that sanctions a sense of
distinction and hierarchy finally triumphs.[8]

---

[7] See my essay "The Banquets of Civilization" for a discussion of the role of
Ancient Greece in *Ariel*.

[8] Gordon Brotherston, in his excellent introduction to the Cambridge UP edition
of *Ariel*, argues that Rodó follows the French essayist Alfred Fouillée in staking
out a position in between the extremes of "hierarchy and equality" represented by
"the aristocratic and democratic schools of thought" (5). My analysis of Rodó's

160 *Maarten van Delden*

References

Ardao, Arturo. 1950. *Espiritualismo y positivismo en el Uruguay.* México: Fondo de Cultura Económica.

—. 1971. *Etapas de la inteligencia uruguaya.* Montevideo: Universidad de la República.

Brotherston, Gordon. 1967. "Introdúction." *Ariel* by José Enrique Rodó. Cambridge: Cambridge UP, 1-19.

Darwin, Charles. 1981. *The Descent of Man, and Selection in Relation to Sex.* Princeton: Princeton UP.

—. 1985. *The Origin of Species by Means of Natural Selection or the Preservation of Favoured Races in the Struggle for Life.* London: Penguin Classics.

Glick, Thomas F. 1989. *Darwin y el Darwinismo en el Uruguay y en América Latina.* Montevideo: Universidad de la República.

González Echevarría, Roberto. 1985. "The Case of the Speaking Statue. *Ariel* and the Magisterial Rhetoric of the Latin American Essay." *The Voice of the Masters. Writing and Authority in Modern Latin American Literature.* Austin: U of Texas P, 8-32.

Hale, Charles A. 1986. "Political and Social Ideas in Latin America, 1870-1930." *The Cambridge History of Latin America.* Vol.IV. Ed. Leslie Bethell. Cambridge: Cambridge UP, 367-441.

Howard, Jonathan. 1982. *Darwin.* New York: Hill and Wang.

Litvak, Lily. 1980. *Latinos y anglosajones. Orígenes de una polémica.* Barcelona: Puvill.

Oviedo, José Miguel. 1990. *Breve Historia del Ensayo Hispanoamericano.* Madrid: Alianza.

---

aestheticization of the Darwinian discourse on natural selection indicates in the first place that Rodó's aestheticism is not, as Brotherston maintains, "incidental" and "uncharacteristic" (9), but rather an integral element in his outlook, and in the second place that Rodó finally inclines much more towards the hierarchical and aristocratic pole rather than the egalitarian and democratic one.

Pereda, Clemente. s.d. *Rodó's Main Sources*. San Juan, P.R.: Imprenta Venezuela.

Rodó, José Enrique. 1988. *Ariel. Obras Completas*. English translation by Margaret Sayers Peden. Austin: U of Texas P, 206-49.

—. *Motivos de Proteo. Obras Completas*, 308-495.

—. 1967. *Obras Completas*. Ed. Emir Rodríguez Monegal. Second edition. Madrid: Aguilar.

—. "Rumbos Nuevos." *El Mirador de Próspero. Obras Completas*, 514-24.

Rodríguez Monegal, Emir. 1977. "The Metamorphoses of Caliban." *Diacritics* 7 (3): 78-83.

Stepan, Nancy Leys. 1991. *"The Hour of Eugenics". Race, Gender, and Nation in Latin America*. Ithaca: Cornell UP.

Van Delden, Maarten. 1990. "The Banquets of Civilization. The Idea of Ancient Greece in Rodó, Reyes and Fuentes." *Annals of Scholarship* 7 (3): 303-21.

Vaughan, Alden T. and Virginia Mason Vaughan. 1991. *Shakespeare's Caliban. A Cultural History*. Cambridge: Cambridge UP.

Zum Felde, Alberto. 1930. *Proceso Intelectual del Uruguay*. Vol. II. Montevideo: Imprenta Nacional Colorada.

Caliban in the Weimar Republic

Arnold Zweig on Antisemitism

Barf Philipsen & Georgi Verbeeck

Caliban, Trinculo and Ariel

In the tumultuous years after the First World War Caliban returned on the cultural stage, appearing this time in the Jewish world of Central Europe. In 1927, during the Weimar Republic, the German writer Arnold Zweig (1887-1968) published a voluminous essay called *Caliban or Politics and Passions*.[1] Still, it was not *Caliban* that made the year 1927 into a turning point in Zweig's biography.[2] Born in the Silesian town Glogau as the son of a Jewish shopkeeper, the young Zweig became aware of his

---

[1] First published as A. Schweig [sic] *Caliban oder Politik und Leidenschaft. Versuch über die menschlichen Gruppenleidenschaften dargetan am Antisemitismus* (Potsdam: Gustav Kiepenheuer Verlag, 1927). A recent extended edition (Weimar: Aufbau Taschenbuch Verlag, 1993) also includes an essay on "The Function of Antisemitism," an "Introduction" (1929), and a "Necessary Preface" to the second edition, written in 1960, and a comment by Detlev Claussen (*Vor dem Sturm. Zu Arnold Zweigs Essay über den Antisemitismus aus dem Jahre 1927*).

[2] On Zweig's biography, see Wenzel 1978, Midgley 1980, Hermand 1990 and 1992.

literary vocation during his studies at different German universities, where he attended lectures in modern languages and literature, history, philosophy and psychology. By 1927 he had already produced an impressive number of novels, short-stories, drama's, literary and cultural-political essays and other writings, including editions of the complete works of Büchner, Lessing and Kleist. Although the respectable *Kleist-Preis* was awarded to his second drama *Ritualmord in Ungarn. Jüdische Tragödien in fünf Akten* (Ritual Murder in Hungary. Jewish Tragedies in Five Acts) (1914), it was not until his anti-militarist novel *Der Streit um den Sergeanten Grischa* (The Battle for Sergeant Grischa) had appeared in the autumn of 1927, that Zweig turned almost overnight into a writer of world-wide fame. Encouraged by this unexpected success, Zweig seized the opportunity to edit or re-edit some material on which he had been working in the past – especially his extensive research on antisemitism and its relation to nationalism – in order to present it to a larger public.

Caliban was certainly the most ambitious and large-scale product of this research. Its subtitle, *Essay on Human Group Affects Demonstrated by the Phenomenon of Antisemitism*, emphasizes both subject and methodology: Zweig's study is indeed an extensive description and analysis of the phenomenon of antisemitism, allegorically represented by Shakespeare's Caliban as the embodiment of what Zweig defined as the *Differenzaffekt* (discriminating affect):

> Yes, his [Shakespeare's] Caliban was the personification of instinct, particularly of my 'discriminating affect' itself. Caliban lives beneath Good and Evil – a guy to be pitied, despite his hurling fury. Lust, anger, hatred, revenge, fear, superstitious worshipping of the fetish and a mass of undifferentiated power control him. No doubt, he was the discriminating affect, confirming what I had discerned in the soul of the group [...]. (Zweig 1993: 11)[3]

This archaic, instinctive aversion and rejection of cultural otherness, rooted (as Zweig argued) in the collective psyche of an ethnic group, finds

---

[3] All translations by the authors. As far as we know, there is no English translation of Zweig's *Caliban* available.

its polar counterpart in a correlative *Zentralitätsaffekt* (centralizing affect) that articulates the hyperbolic self-esteem of that same collectivity, allegorized by the figure of Shakespeare's Trinculo:

> As the discriminating affect is inextricably bound to its opposite, the centralizing affect, being the drive that wants every group of people to believe that the world is turning around them, one wonders where its partner is – where was this intoxicating seductive instinct, without which no fight, no war, no collective effort nor achievement would come about? I found it, I found Trinculo, under Caliban's cloak. (Zweig 1993: 11)

Finally, Shakespeare's airy Spirit Ariel is invoked as the symbol of man's ability to transcend this entanglement in dark passions, representing the enlightened, creative alternative to the destructive forces:

> What William Shakespeare, the greatest of all poets, observed as Caliban during his life, he could also have perceived from a higher level as a puppet, from which at due time would rise an Ariel: the winged Eros of Phantasy freeing itself from the driving instinct, the creative Eros, escaping from the bubbling chaos of fear, anxiety, hatred, contempt, egocentrism and lust between the people or groups and heading unanimously for the great divine tasks and aims of which Man has shown himself again and again, at least mentally, capable; and capable he really is, when he succeeds in transcending the limits, the circle in which the instinct is trying to lock him. (Zweig 1993: 296)

According to its author, *Caliban* should be read as a *Sach- und Kampfbuch*, both a scholarly study and polemic essay (Zweig 1993: 13). It is almost impossible to summarize the contents of this book, which is moreover based on a collection of separately published essays written over a period of several years. One cannot but be struck by the minute phenomenological description and analysis of a caleidoscopic cultural and political reality, seen through the eyes of a learned and passionate writer who likes to show his poetical skill by mixing all kinds of literary and non-literary registers and genres and creating a rather hybrid and unfortunately also rather inconsistent text. The extensive encyclopedic material is forced into an allegedly 'scientific,' 'methodic' systematic frame, illustrating Zweigs rather naive enthusiasm about the great scientific discoveries of his time (psycho-analysis, phenomenology, sociology and biology) as well as his confidence in a, at that time, new and promising ideology (Zweig 1993: 12). The overtly respectful, though not completely justified dedication to *Vater* Sigmund Freud and the gradually increasing eschatological pathos of a 'supranational organisation' to which mankind may finally ascend, after having freed itself from the chains of earthly passions and unjust social conditions, stress the romantic Freudo-Marxist perspective of Zweig's *Caliban*. But before going into that matter, some light must be shed on the intellectual and historical background of this work.

Arnold Zweig: Looking back at a Jewish Experience in Germany

Undoubtedly, the allegorical reference to Caliban implies indirectly a second reference to the Great War as the historical *Tempest* that brought the 'discriminating affect' to the surface. The mechanical mass destruction (*Materialschlachten*) of the First World War had been a major traumatic event for Zweig as for most men of his generation, who saw their ideals and beliefs shattered (Gay 1968, Laqueur 1974). Untill then Zweig, who had got his share of antisemitism in his youth, had fled more or less in a world of refined intellectual and esthetic pleasures, convinced of the romantic maxim that art and philosophy would 'educate' mankind and overcome empirical differences and tensions. Though the student's former enthousiasm for an idealist philosophical canon including Plato, Spinoza, Kant, Husserl, and Scheler never really faded, the experience of the Great War opened his eyes to the ideological mechanisms behind the façade of the cultural superstructure as wel as to the entanglement of politics and passions. His very early admiration for Sigmund Freud's work and – more important than that – his therapy, which had actually helped him to deal with his own emotional problems (Zweig was treated for the first time in 1924), had grown stronger after his reading of Freud's essay *Modern*

Thoughts on War and Death (1915), in which Freud analyzed the suspension of the taboo on killing during the massacres of the First World War. The founder of psycho-analysis, "our new Odysseus," became one of the most powerful influences in Zweig's intellectual career. It was this complex of ideas, experiences and perspectives that built the ideological substrate of the literary case-study of Sergeant Grischa's unjustified execution. Zweig used it to criticize authoritarian rule in Wilhelminian Germany, taking nevertheless a highly moralist and enlightened stance that confirmed his humanistic belief in the actual educability of mankind. As an attempt to 'work through' the apocalyptic experience of the war, *Grischa* became almost exemplary and trendsetting.

Zweig's admiration for the German cultural tradition (especially the literary and philosophical canon) was not only a way to repress the antisemitic experiences of his childhood. It was also the expression of a deep identity crisis, typical of a generation of Jewish intellectuals, torn between the historical heritage of Judaism and the West European, in this case German culture to which they owed their education and their artistic and intellectual career (Gay 1979). His gradually growing insight into the inextricable entanglement of German nationalism and antisemitism developed into a painful dilemma for the admirer of the German *Kulturnation* (cultural nation). But this growing dilemma of being a German Jew[4] mirrored still another tension at the heart of Jewish culture itself, internally divided by the geographical and social distance between Eastern and Western Jewry. Zweig started writing for Jewish periodicals like *Der Jude, Die jüdische Rundschau, Freie zionistische Blätter* and ultimately *Der neue Orient.*

Zweig's essays on East European Jewry, the Palestinian question and – his favorite subject – antisemitism reveal his strong humanistic view on mankind. But the estheticizing and generalizing tenor of the young author's works was now forced into the background by a more historical and sociological interest, not in the least in the fate of the chassidic Jewish culture in Eastern Europe with which he had had intensive contact during

---

[4] See A. Silbermann, "Deutsche Juden oder jüdische Deutsche? Zur Identität der Juden in der Weimarer Republik." In Grab and Schoeps 1986: 347-55.

his stay in Kowno (Kaunas) at wartime. He dedicated a larger work to East European Jewry called *Das ostjüdische Antlitz* (The Eastern Jewish face) (1920), an extensive typological and anthropological essay illustrated with 50 lithographies by his friend Hermann Struck. Nevertheless, his rather Rousseauistic concept of the East European Jewish community still revealed his inclination towards an idealistic and romantic perspective, criticizing as he did modern liberal West European civilization (including the Western Jews) as the result of what might be called a *Verfallsgeschichte*. Zweig's defence of East European Jewry despite (or because of) their cultural and social deprivation brought him into conflict with those Western Jews who advocated a process of assimilation.

In view of the often sharp social and cultural contrasts within European Jewry, *Caliban* gains a new but fundamental dimension. Zweig's basic concept of the 'discriminating affect' could be seen as a theoretical tool in the analysis of both antisemitism and the tensions *within* the Jewish community. *Caliban* therefore crystallizes, as one critic argues, Zweig's own position as a German Jew between East and West (Claussen in Zweig 1993: 331-33). Differences in political, social and cultural living conditions had given rise to the geographical division of European Jewry. The image of the impoverished masses in the East and growing migration to Western Europe and North America since the last decades of the nineteenth century (with a second wave after the Russian revolution) had encouraged xenophobic reactions even within the Jewish community. To Western Jews the confrontation with the newcomers recalled their own painful experience of emancipation. East European Jews who had largely remained attached to religious orthodoxy and traditional ways of living generally challenged the notions of integration and assimilation current in Western bourgeois society. Among, the legacy of oppression and deprivation endorsed at the same time the hope for an own Jewish homeland. The tensions between *Ostjudentum*, German-Jewish assimilation and Zionism encouraged Zweig's belief in Socialism as the natural political and ideological vehicle of what he envisaged, in the tradition of Martin Buber's anti-nationalist Zionism, as the messianic destiny of Jewish culture.[5]

---

[5] See also Mosse 1985.

Antisemitism in the Weimar Republic

In a period of relative stability, in which the devastating effects of the Great Depression were still lying ahead, antisemitism played only a marginal political role in the Weimar Republic, which was slowly recovering from the defeat as well as from its revolutionary aftermath.[6] That explains the perhaps astonishing opening lines of Zweig's *Caliban*, in which the author calls antisemitism "a third-rate problem" (Zweig 1993: 9). The rather stable republican coalition prevented extremist parties from coming up. Though antisemitic undertones prevailed in most of the right-wing parties – e.g. the *Deutschnationale Volkspartei* (DNVP) (German National People's Party) – the latter never gained substantial political power and were moreover closely watched by Jewish organisations like the *Central-Verein deutscher Staatsbürger jüdischen Glaubens* (Central Association of German Citizens of Jewish Faith). The liberal centre did not assume a clear position, though many members of the two liberal parties were actually the target of antisemitic assaults. Political Catholicism (especially *Zentrum* [Centre]) oscillated between the remnants of traditional anti-judaism and the rejection of antisemitic excesses, whereas Socialists and Communists fought antisemitism as an ideology that kept the masses from its actual struggle for Socialism.

Not as a political factor but more as a 'cultural code' antisemitism became widespread in the twenties.[7] Opinions on modern Jewry as the embodiment of a 'subversive' intelligentsia or of a 'decadent' metropolitan society became very popular. Antisemitism was actually a postponed reaction to the Jewish emancipation of the previous century.[8] Their prominent presence in public life and their oft-emphasized progressive role therein turned the Jews into favourite targets of conservative cultural

---

[6] A brief introduction to the role of antisemitism in the Weimar Republic is provided by H.-A. Winkler, "Anti-Semitism in Weimar Society." In Strauss 1993: 196-205.

[7] On antisemitism as a 'cultural code' in modern German history, see in particular Volkov 1990.

[8] See various contributions in Rürup 1987.

policies. In the Weimar Republic, as had equally been the case in the Wilhelminian age, the social vanguard of antisemitism consisted of the educated middle classes and the academic corps, the so-called *Bildungsbürgertum*. The success of antisemitism reflected the social promotion of many Jews. In the mutual interaction between emancipation and antisemitism social competition and aversion played a decisive role.

Only in the final stage of the Weimar Republic the gradually growing NSDAP turned antisemitism into a functional instrument of ideological cohesion. With more success than his right-wing predecessors Hitler used the abstract *Feindbild* (enemy image) of the 'Eternal Jew' as the vehicle of a new mass movement, welding together all the different parts of his program: anti-Bolshevism, anti-liberalism and a radical 'ethnic' nationalism. Yet it was not antisemitism but the social and economic program that made the National Socialist movement attractive for large groups of voters. From the perspective of the social, economic and political crisis of the Weimar Republic antisemitism was not the breeding ground but the product of National Socialism.

One cannot but acknowledge the merits of Zweig's detailed and subtle observations of the phenomenon of antisemitism pervading all cultural and social levels of the early Weimar Republic, as well as his general interpretation of antisemitism as the cornerstone of the German *Feindbild* and therefore a signal of a frustrated national identity.[9] Zweig considered it as a painful, yet necessary moment in the growth of modern nationalism. At the same time his analysis articulated a reflection on the so-called German *Sonderweg* (special path), referring to a critical theory in German historiography that already existed before the Second World War. According to this theory, Germany's own, specific historical evolution is radically different from the development of other Western nations, because the liberal bourgeois revolution that had started off the process of gradual democratization in those countries, had never taken place in

---

[9] On *Feindbilder* (images of the enemy) in nineteenth- and twentieth-century German history, see also H.-M. Bernhardt, "Voraussetzungen, Struktur und Funktionen von Feindbildern." In Jahr & Mai & Roller 1995: 9-24.

Germany.[10] The virulent power of antisemitism is thus linked by Zweig to the specific social conditions caused by the ambivalent modernization of Germany in the nineteenth century.[11]

Measured by the results of recent historical and social research, Zweig's analysis shows many flaws. The influence of modern sciences on 'biologist' race theories remains – very significantly for that matter – unmentioned. Moreover, insufficient light is shed on the differentiation of the historical evolution from a broad but vague anti-Jewish attitude to anti-Judaism and eventually modern antisemitism. For Zweig as for most of the leftist and liberal intelligentsia of the Weimar Republic antisemitism was an outmoded problem, as it allegedly still is in the present day.[12] As a 'cultural code' it had certainly left its mark on the political and intellectual climate during the interbellum, but it had not provided a blueprint for persecution and genocide. Considering the developments after 1933, Kurt Tucholsky's letter to Zweig in December 1935, shortly after the passage of the Nuremberg Racial Laws, might nevertheless apply to the years before Hitler's take-over as well: "a country is not only that what it does – it is also that which it stands, which it tolerates" (Tucholsky 1935: 336).

Marxism, Psycho-Analysis and the Historiography of Antisemitism

Zweig's life-long admiration of Sigmund Freud is well-known and the influence of the latter's ideas on Zweig's work has long been acknowledged.[13] Zweig's contribution to the reception and popularization of psycho-analytical terminology may be called considerable. He was one of the first writers to make explicit use of Freud's discoveries and long before the idea of *Verdrängung* (repression) became a key concept in the

---

[10] For a detailed discussion of the German *Sonderweg*, see Grebing 1985: 11-22.

[11] See also Peukert 1987: 13-31.

[12] For a comment on antisemitism in present-day Germany, see Benz 1995.

[13] See e.g. A. Tilo Alt, "Zur Psychologie der Beziehungen zwischen Arnold Zweig und Sigmund Freud." In Midgley & Müller & Lambrechts 1993: 124

post-war remembrance of the Nazi-experience, it was introduced by Zweig to describe his generation's pathological relation with the first *Kriegserlebnis*, the experience of the First World War (Zweig 1993: 21-22).

Yet, Zweig's popular reading and adaptation of Freud has always remained very controversial and a target of firm critique, not in the least by the adored predecessor himself. Though Freud never launched his critique directly at Zweig, with whom he had a a good relation and whose works he read with great interest, his letters to Zweig show nevertheless his tacit but strong reservations about the latter's transposition of his theory to the political and cultural level.[14] Especially Zweig's concept of *Gruppenleidenschaften* (group affects) rooted in a collective psychic zone radically diverges from Freud's mass psychology, in which the point of reference remains the individual 'I' – the cornerstone of Freud's enterprise, which may be "a member of a herd of people, organizing itself at a particular moment for a particular purpose" (Freud 1974: 115). Freud's study *Massenpsychology und Ich-Analyse* (Mass Psychology and Ego-Analysis) from 1921 had been very clear on this, yet Zweig's own theoretical account gives the impression that he had either not read or just not understood this crucial text. Zweig generally tended to confuse Freud's theory of 'mass psychology' with his own conception of 'social psychology,' hence advocating a popular variation of traditional 'anthropological' psychology. The fact that Zweig's analysis of a collective psyche and its overt social-psychological dimension ignored the difference between Freud and his dissident 'students' Jung and Adler, must have been unbearable for the founding father of psycho-analysis.

But then, one should not forget that Zweig's respect for Freud actually originates in his own positive experiences with the curing power of psycho-analysis, and it is exactly this therapeutic dimension that attracted him most as a possible political instrument. "The Freudian therapy is even considered as a way of self-curing for the Jewish 'group-Ego,' suffering from an inferiority complex" (Midgley 1989: 17). According to Zweig:

---

[14] Claussen 1993: 329-33 and Midgley 1989: 16-18.

That's why, from the perspective of the group-Ego 'Jewish people' Freud's theory of neurosis, rooted in his and Breuer's research on hysteria, has the effect of a regeneration of a recovering organ in an affected body, that is still capable of curing itself. [...] In the great group-Ego lives the desire to recover from this dissociation that dares to affect the substance of life itself. Freud's ingenious insight [into the mechanism of neurosis] appears like an intuition into an entelechy, inherent in every organism. (Zweig 1993: 178-79)

From Zweig's popular cultural and political Freudianism it was just a small move to Marxist analysis:

The atheistic and materialistic Socialism of the Marxist thrust [...] is today a church and a religion like any other on earth. It denies the spiritual freedom and divine origin of man in a 'scientific' determinism, dedicated to the dogma of a coercive development of social situations according to materialistic, political-economic laws. It strives for the abolition of classes and of class-ruling, going beyond all national frontiers towards the international, supranational society of productive people. And all this through a change of situations, through practical, political measures, through outside activity. Because man is considered as a product of Nature and Society and appears moreover to be alienated through social circumstances from his nature, being the object of changing influences, Marxism aims at the improvement of the social conditions and is convinced that, once those depraving conditions are abolished, the originally pure nature of Man will come to the surface, allowing for a purification and amelioration of the human kind with fewer and less exacting didactic means. This belief is complementary to ours, which does not need to be exposed here. (Zweig 1993: 308)

The last sentence of this long quotation, taken from the last chapter ('Antisemitism and German Youth'), is an indirect reference to Zweig's psycho-analytical approach which indeed doesn't need to be made more explicit, as it was clear from the very beginning. But Zweig now links it explicitly to a Marxist stance, which he considers as complementary to his 'Freudian' method, or vica versa, since Zweig was particularly interested in reintroducing spiritual categories in the cultural and political discourse-categories that he seemed to miss in the Marxist approach. The question remains, whether Freud's rather technical analysis of the psychic apparatus allows for an identification with idealist concepts like 'soul,' 'spirit' etc. This shows once more how Zweig's rather amateurish application of psycho-analytical terminology equals a comparably reductionistic reception of Marxism, merging together into a very early example of 'vulgar' but basically romantic Freudo-Marxism.

One of the characteristics of Freudo-Marxism that is undoubtedly at stake in *Caliban* is the 'functionalist' approach of antisemitism, reducing the anti-Jewish ideology to an epiphenomenon that is caused by an underlying social field of influence (Verbeeck 1990: 385-96). "As long as we know about the existence of the antisemitic affect, it has been used as a means to something else. Needless to say that the forces that have made use of it, did not create it; but without them antisemitism would never have become such a functional attitude..." (Zweig 1993: 317). Since the fall of the Second German Empire antisemitic feelings and agitation had functioned as an outlet for the tensions caused by the post-war revolutionary crisis:

> German post-war antisemitism is an instrument
> deliberately used to unburden the German group soul, as
> it turned out to be a very appropriate way to soothe
> momentarily the high tension on the political scene in
> the years between 1919 and 1923 and later. The more
> these emotional tensions within the German community
> diminish, the less they need antisemitism for an outlet.
> For that reason the stabilization of the Mark caused the
> rudest forms of antisemitism – and only those forms are
> efficient enough to be used as a vehicle for something else
> – to lose year by year their publicity and power. (Zweig
> 1993: 318)

Nevertheless even Zweig seemed to understand that a one-sided approach of antisemitism as a 'national affect' would leave out the broader social-historical process (Zweig 1993: 318-321). This was the point of departure for his critique of capitalism. Together with the psycho-analytical approach, it cleared the path for the methodological dialogue between Freudianism and Marxism. Antisemitism was linked by Zweig to the different stages in the historical development of capitalism: a basically archaic, agrarian type; industrial capitalism with its financial and commercial backbones, and finally its conflict with the working classes. The discriminating affects, latent during the period of agrarian capitalism, were activated by the shift in the means of production during the industrial revolution. It is no coincidence that anti-Jewish stereotypes turned up at the end of the nineteenth century, when agrarian-based capitalism was confronted with the 'Jew' as tradesman, as huckster and finally as Socialist agitator.

Zweig had good reasons to regard the First World War as a decisive turning point. Up till then the old balance of power in the East Elbian territories had remained unchanged. The Prussian nobility had managed to maintain its grip on the political, administrative and military institutions, whereas the new classes had not yet succeeded in breaking the vitality of this power complex. It was not until the elite in Eastern and Central Europe – not just in Germany, but also in Russia, the Habsburg empire and Turkey – threatened to collapse under the blows of the conquering enemies, that they lost their former social status and glory in the eyes of their own people. Practically everywhere the new capitalist class inherited the grandeur and the way of life of the old aristocracy. The real anger for the lost glory had to be focused now on the danger coming 'from below,' the masses: their blind obedience had turned to revolt against the old rulers whom the war had shown up as lousy leaders. Frustrated *Differenzaffekte* burst out in the revolution of 1918/19, originating though in the process of transformation in the nineteenth century. *Caliban* reveals the social fractions within society: the growing revolt of the masses and the acts of revenge by the upper classes. Very significant in this respect is a quotation from Oscar Wilde that Zweig adapted and used as a motto for

Caliban: "The rage of the nineteenth century is the rage of Caliban, seeing his own face in a glass."[15]

Both Marx and Freud had a strong influence on the conventional perception of antisemitism. Yet, in their reductionist form both Marxism and psycho-analysis tend to underestimate the ideological nature of antisemitism, reducing it to a phantasm that supposedly veils the 'real' conflicts on the level of social and economic relations or in the psychosomatic domain. Because of its ideological character antisemitism is considered then as an epiphenomenon without compelling effects on the real historical and social process, an incident affecting an orginally healthy social and psychological substance that can be restored by curing the symptoms. This kind of rationalism – an inheritance of the Enlightenment – may be a heavy burden on the study of the history of ideas. A wholly different and more conventional tradition in historiography defines ideology after Hannah Arendt as 'the logic of an idea,' forcing us to examine ideologies as 'points of departure for action.' National Socialist Ideology in general and antisemitism in particular lend themselves very well for this approach.[16]

Katharsis ton Pathematon: Curing the Differences

Zweig's rather popular Freudo-Marxist reduction of antisemitism to an epiphenomenon – a symptom that will disappear when the socio-psychological conditions and circumstances have changed – has a rather paradoxical outcome, considering the fact that in Zweig's view the finality

---

[15] "Die Wut des neunzehnten Jahrhunderts ist die Wut Calibans, der sein Antlitz im Spiegel erblickt" (Zweig 1993: 8). The original version of Oscar Wilde's *Preface* to *The Picture of Dorian Gray* is slightly different: "The nineteenth century dislike of Realism is the rage of Caliban seeing his own face in a glass. The nineteenth century dislike of Romanticism is the rage of Caliban not seeing his own face in a glass" (see Vaughan and Vaughan 1993: 112-13).

[16] "Never has the Enlightenment grounding of Marxist and Freudian social criticisms been so clearly revealed as in their approaches to National Socialism" (Pois 1986: 23).

of the Marxist revolution is supposed to be the restoration of an almost mystical, supranational organization of peoples, loving and respecting each other. As in his earlier works Zweig still remains attached to a romantic form of Socialism.[17] He does not hesitate to recall the 'metaphysical' substance of people, freeing themselves from their fallen 'empirical' state through 'repentance' (Zweig 1993: 29-30). The religious overtones of this word, containing the idea of confession and purification, are made explicit in Zweig's invocation of Caliban in the introductory pages:

> Poor fellow, forever condemned to rage on an island, since the blindness of your fury concealed from your sight the bridges between you and another person, another group, the great community of men, you hothead and driven instigator: you too shall serve for something good! Whether you want it or not – you must after all bring about your own salvation! For the evil that is in you is no original evil but the expression of your raging against the chains of your own defigured, unarticulated spellbound being. We invoke you: and perhaps, perhaps, this will free you from your malicious skin? (Zweig 1993: 16)

It soon becomes clear that the 'methodological' thrust of Zweig's work is actually the result of an obsessive, almost invocatory repetitiveness of themes and arguments, a quasi-poetical 'working-through' of traumatic and neurotic experiences. They articulate the central didactic core of the author's enterprise and underscore his optimistic belief in the therapeutic, actually sublimating, 'cathartic' effects of knowledge and language. Exorcising Caliban by the power of the Word is Zweig's programmatic intention :

---

[17] The discourse of romantic or 'utopian' Socialism often remained largely interwoven with religious metaphors. This refers to a basic problem in the classical interpretation of Marxism, according to which Marxist ideology could be seen as 'secular eschatology.' As in Zweig's case, however, idealist goals and ambitions are hardly compatible with the materialist presumptions in Marxist theory of history and society.

> Yes, affects can be controlled, their fixation can be dissolved, they can be purified: by means that are both amazingly simple and amazingly hard to realize, like for instance: confession of the affects, articulating the repressed meanings. The fear of spirits in singular persons as well as groups can be exorcised or abreacted by making them conscious of what they fear: actually the forces of nature around them and within them. In the same manner the destructive and poisening force of the discriminating and centralizing affect can be exposed by the acknowledgement that their cause is the fear and the desire for each other. (Zweig 1993: 266-67)

Concepts like 'abreaction' and 'purification' occur so often that they become the *Leitmotive*, the guiding principles of a literary rather than 'scientific' discourse (Midgley 1989: 17). Zweig cannot hide his real vocation, nor his deepest conviction: art as the principle of sublimation (Ariel) is the only real remedy for all the negative affects that tear apart the people of the earth. And one is hardly surprised, when Zweig recalls the effects of Greek Tragedy on Greek culture and on the birth of democracy. He refers more than once to one of the classics of his youth: Nietzsche's *Birth of Tragedy* which, according to Zweig, "deals (unconsciously) with the function of art as abreaction of group affects, art that is to say: literature, more specifically drama" (Zweig 1993: 226). But it is definitely Aristotle, "the great phenomenologist of the Classics" who designated the function of drama as "the purification of instincts" (Zweig 1993: 218). Zweig is torn between the observation that our times have lost the sense of tragedy, that we have replaced the tragic scene by sporting events, and the hope of restoring this sense, "the sociological function of drama and the actually political significance of reading [novels]":

> Drama, it seems to me, has the function to represent and make tolerable the tensions within a community, to disarm the threatening passions within a group or between groups, to spiritualize them and sublimate them in symbolic catastrophes instead of letting them really occur. This, it seems to me, was the vision of the great sociologist Aristotle, as he put the *katharsis ton*

pathematon, the purification of passions, at the centre of his reflections on drama. (Zweig 1993: 226-27)[18]

Zweig does not hesitate to consider his work as a 'service' to mankind and this didactic and prophetic attitude seems to culminate in the dramatic and programmatic appeal to the young generation to adopt the democratic and socialist ideology and 'to beware of the Right.' This apostrophic finale seems to be conceived as a refutation of the appalling introductory statements about the actual addressees: the "representatives of a lost generation, who are no longer among the living" and whose bones "have since long been rotting under the earth" (Zweig 1993: 14). The reference to the traumatic experience of the Great War reveals the deeper motivation of *Caliban*, which is to write a memorial for the dead as well as for the world they belonged to, a world of illusions which Zweig nevertheless tries to resuscitate by sublimating the apocalyptic experience and rewriting it into a instructive tragedy: "Think of those [who are dead] because they are the ones that are missing today, and not ignoble was the material of their soul, as they rushed to perdition" (ibid.).

Though this may still be a brave and admirable attitude in the twenties, the same idealistic and optimistic rhetoric in the 'necessary preface to the second edition,' written in 1960, becomes painfully outdated. After his return from exile in Palestine in 1948, Zweig had become a highly esteemed author and citizen of the German Democratic Republic, ultimately completing a transformation from 'utopian' to 'scientific Socialism,' or orthodox Marxism. Zweig looked back upon Caliban's moderate success and minor influence, mainly due to both the Cold War and the failure of Freudo-Marxist theory.[19] He readily acknowledged the failures and shortcomings in his work (Zweig 1993: 324). Of necessity, Zweig distanced himself from his previous theme of interest and was forced to reject Zionism. The 'Jewish question' as well as the legacy of

---

[18] "των τοιουτων παθηματων καθαρσιν" ("Tragedy is a representation [...] accomplishing by means of pity and terror the catharsis of such emotions") (Aristotle 1989: 49 b28). See also: Politics VIII, 5: 1339 b42 - 1340 a27 and 1341 b32 - 1342 a 18.

[19] For a critical evaluation of the Freudo-Marxist theory of antisemitism, see also Cramer 1979.

Freud were drastically erased from the collective memory of the 'other Germany' (Verbeeck 1990). The problem of antisemitism would finally have lost its relevance since the abolition of capitalism and the establishment of 'real existing Socialism.'[20]

Zweig however remained firmly attached to his moralizing credo. It exposes, according to a post-war observer, Zweig's blatant blindness for the epochal difference between the time before and after 'the fact Auschwitz' – a 'fact' that has thoroughly disrupted the tradition to which Zweig seemed unconditionally dedicated at first sight, the tradition of European Enlightenment, that since Francis Bacon has believed in the possibility to control both outer and inner nature by the acquisition and application of knowledge.[21] But even this belief in Rationalism remains ambivalent, since Zweig feels urged to appeal to the irrational, pedagogical effects of the tragic:

> That the transformation of our society in a Socialist world will also contribute to the purification of all group affects, is not something we just dare to hope – we are working on it. The tragedy, hidden behind antisemitism and the lust for war of our bourgeois society, will lead in this way to Aristotle's Katharsis hepatematon [sic],[22] still in this century. The floods of blood and tears will then not have flown in vain into the river of the past, and our children and grandchildren will look upon us, survivors, as upon the rider on the Bodensee, who didn't know that between him and the abyss there was only the frozen water of a severe winter. (Zweig 1993: 328)

It may be symptomatic for Zweig's lifelong optimistic attitude that he doesn't refer to the unexpected catastrophic end of Schwab's famous

---

[20] On the theoretical foundations of the Marxist attitude towards the 'Jewish question,' see Silberner 1983.

[21] Claussen in Zweig 1993: 338, and Claussen 1994.

[22] See note 18.

ballad: after his ride on the frozen sea that cracks when he is already in safety at the other shore, the rider dies of postponed fear and – perhaps – shame at his own naivety.

References

Aristotle. 1987. *Poetics*. Translated by R. Janko. Indianapolis/Cambridge: Hachett Publishing Company.

Benz, W., ed. 1995. *Antisemitismus in Deutschland. Zur Aktualität eines Vorurteils*. München: Deutscher Taschenbuch Verlag.

Claussen, D. 1994. *Grenzen der Aufklärung. Die gesellschaftlichen Genese des modernen Antisemitismus*. Frankfurt a.M.: Fischer Taschenbuch Verlag.

Cramer, E. 1979. *Hitlers Antisemitismus und die 'Frankfurter Schule.' Kritische Faschismus-Theorie und geschichtliche Realität*. Düsseldorf: Droste.

Freud, S. 1974. "Massenpsychologie und Ich-Analyse [1921]." *Studienausgabe (1972-1976)*. Frankfurt a.M.: Fischer.

Gay, P. 1968. *Weimar Culture. The Outsiders as Insiders*. New York: Harper & Row.

—. 1979. *Freud, Jews, and the other Germans*. New York: Harper & Row.

Grab, W. and J.H. Schoeps, eds. 1986. *Juden in der Weimarer Republik*. Stuttgart/Bonn: Burg Verlag.

Grebing, H. 1985. *Der 'deutsche Sonderweg' in Europa 1806-1945. Eine Kritik*. Stuttgart/Berlin/Köln/Mainz: Kohlhammer.

Hermand, J. 1990. *Arnold Zweig*. Reinbek: Rowohlt.

—. 1992. *Engagement als Lebensform. Über Arnold Zweig*. Berlin: Sigma.

Jahr, C. and U. Mai and K. Roller, eds. 1995. *Feindbilder in der deutschen Geschichte*. Berlin: Metropol Verlag.

Laqueur, W. Z. 1974. *Weimar. A Cultural History 1918-1933*. London: Weidenfeld.

Midgley, D. 1980. *Arnold Zweig. Zu Werk und Wandlung 1927-1948*. Königstein/Ts.: Athenäum.

—, ed. 1989. *Arnold Zweig. Poetik, Judentum und Politik. Akten des Internationalen Arnold-Zweig-Symposiums aus Anlaß des 100. Geburtstags, Cambridge 1987.* Bern/Berlin/Frankfurt a.M./New York/Paris/Wien: Peter Lang.

—, H.H. Müller and L. Lamberechts eds. 1993. *Arnold Zweig. Psyche, Politik und Literatur. Akten des II. Internationalen Arnold-Zweig-Symposiums, Gent 1991.* Bern/Berlin/Frankfurt a.M./New York/Paris/Wien: Peter Lang.

Mosse, G. L. 1985. *German Jews beyond Judaism.* Bloomington: U of Indiana P.

Peukert, D. J. K. 1987. *Die Weimarer Republik. Krisenjahre der Klassischen Moderne.* Frankfurt a.M.: Suhrkamp.

Pois, R. A. 1986. *National Socialism and the Religion of Nature.* London/Sydney: Croom Helm.

Rürup, R. 1987. *Emanzipation und Antisemitismus. Studien zur 'Judenfrage' der bürgerlichen Gesellschaft.* Frankfurt a.M.: Fischer Taschenbuch Verlag.

Silberner, E. 1983. *Kommunisten zur Judenfrage. Zur Geschichte von Theorie und Praxis des Kommunismus.* Opladen: Westdeutscher Verlag.

Strauss, H. A., ed. 1993. *Hostages of Modernization. Studies on Modern Antisemitism 1870-1933/39. Germany, Great Britain, France.* Current Research on Antisemitism, 3/1. Berlin: de Gruyter.

Tilo Alt, A., ed. 1995. *Arnold Zweig. Berlin, Haifa, Berlin. Perspektive des Gesamtwerkes. Akten des III. Internationalen Arnold-Zweig-Symposiums, Berlin 1993.* Bern/Berlin/Frankfurt a.M./New York/Paris/Wien: Peter Lang.

Tucholsky, K. 1962. *Ausgewählte Briefe 1913-1935.* Reinbek: Rowohlt.

Vaughan, A.T. and V. Mason Vaughan, 1993. *Shakespeare's Caliban. A Cultural History.* Cambridge: Cambridge UP.

Verbeeck, G. 1990. "Marxism, Antisemitism and the Holocaust." In *Leo Baeck Institute. Yearbook,* Vol. XXV, 385-396.

Volkov, S. 1990. *Jüdisches Leben und Antisemitismus im 19. und 20. Jahrhundert.* München: C.H.Beck.

Wenzel, G., ed. 1978. *Arnold Zweig 1887-1968. Werk und Leben in Dokumenten und Bildern*. Berlin: Aufbau-Verlag.

Zweig, A. 1927. *Caliban oder Politik und Leidenschaft. Versuch über die menschlichen Gruppenleidenschaften dargetan am Antisemitismus*. Potsdam: Gustav Kiepenheuer Verlag.

The Forgotten Caliban of Aníbal Ponce

Kristine Vanden Berghe

In 1935, the Argentinian Marxist Aníbal Norberto Ponce (1898-1938) writes the essay "Ariel or the agony of a stubborn illusion."[1] Its publication places the author amongst a series of Latin American intellectuals who use Shakespeare's *Tempest* to illustrate and enforce their ideological beliefs. Ponce, however, is not referred to in the *Tempest*-bibliography. This neglect makes it necessary to start this paper with an elaborate presentation and explanation of Ponce's text. In a second part, we will discuss the reception and influence of Ponce in Latin America and show that his approach bears a remarkable resemblance to some later Latin American interpretations of the relation between Caliban and Ariel, a resemblance which obviously sheds doubt on Vaughan and Mason Vaughan's assertation that Ponce "had little overt influence on the Caliban-metaphor" (1991: 155).[2]

---

[1] The text – with the Spanish title "Ariel o la agonía de una obstinada ilusión" – was published in 1938 in Mexico, where the author had gone into voluntary exile. The work was later republished in Cuba in the volume 'Humanismo Burgués y humanismo proletario' (Imprenta Nacional de Cuba, 1962). Only the latter edition will be referred to in what follows.

[2] The authors only devote the following sentence to Ponce's essay: "Similarly [to Guéhenno], Argentinian Aníbal Ponce's *Humanismo burgués y humanismo proletario* (1938) favorably identified Caliban with the exploited masses in partial refutation of Renan" (1991: 155).

Ariel as a petty bourgeois

The text "Ariel or the agony of a stubborn illusion" is part of a series of lectures, Humanismo burgués y humanismo proletario,[3] which Ponce gave as a professor in Argentina.[4] The series consists of two parts. The first part, a study about the development of bourgeois liberalism, ends with the lecture "Ariel or the agony of a stubborn illusion." This text at the same time functions as a transition to the second part, about proletarian humanism. Ponce distinguishes four different stages in the evolution of bourgeois liberalism, which he illustrates on the basis of four case studies, devoted successively to Erasmus, Shakespeare, Renan and Romain Rolland.[5]

Ponce discusses Erasmus as the first exponent of bourgeois liberalism. Erasmus is the typical intellectual of old: he is 'virtue' itself, but at the same time petty and narrow-minded: "This extraordinary man, who represented like no one else bourgeois humanism, possessed all the virtues which assured him of an intellectual kingdom, all the narrow-mindedness of a man of letters, which thrived in his cold soul and his secluded room" (52).[6] Two more characteristics are high-lighted in the author's portrayal of Erasmus: the dependence of the intellectual with regard to the upper

---

[3] Ponce defines the two kinds of humanism as follows: "On the one hand, a handful of rich people to whom culture should be a gift of a happy few; on the other hand, millions of free people who, after having renewed their souls by abolishing private property, have opened the hitherto unaccessible doors to the platonic banquet" (34-35).

[4] More in particular, those lectures were given at the Colegio Libre de Estudios Superiores de Buenos Aires.

[5] Chronological references abound in Ponce's text. The author reminds the reader that "Shakespeare composed the prodigious symphony of *The Tempest* one century after Erasmus's *Praise of Folie* [sic]" (81-82), and that "two and a half centuries after *The Tempest* [...] an illustrious spokesman of the bourgeoisie [Renan] resumed the legend of Ariel and Caliban" (90). Moreover, Ponce seems to consider himself as part of this historical development. In an "Advertencia" at the beginning of the volume, he notices: "The pages of this volume were written on the occasion of the four-hundredth birthday of Erasmus, and the jubilee of Romain Rolland" (32). The author seems to make use of references like these to highlight both the continuity and the progress of bourgeois humanism.

[6] All translations by Bart Maddens.

class and his elitist way of thinking. On the one hand, Ponce clearly pities the bourgeois intellectual: "Life for the humanists was hard. On the payroll of the powerful, they occupied a position at the bottom" (58). But at the same time, he emphasizes the advantages which the position of intellectual entails: "Thus, according to Erasmus, only the elite had a right to discuss the questions that were important for the world. The elite! Erasmus was perhaps the first one to foster this belief, which was the key-stone of bourgeois humanism, and which has reappeared ever since under various guises amongst 'intellectuals' and 'men of letters'" (76).

According to Ponce, the bourgeois humanist holds a permanent position in the societal game. Within the economical and political field, he is entirely dependent on the secular authorities. But he is master of the game on his own ground: within the field of intellectual production, he fiercely defends the borders of the "champ de la production restreinte." And that renders him, in Ponce's eyes, an unworldly and elitist intellectual. In this regard, the author repeatedly stresses the function of the Latin language as a boundary-mark, which safeguards the elitist nature of the cultural field. In spite of the lack of explicit references to Shakespeare, the link is undeniably there: Ponce's portrayal of Erasmus as a (relatively) subservient and unworldly intellectual is perfectly in line with more recent interpretations of the Ariel-character.

Ponce's lecture about Erasmus is followed by another about *The Tempest*. It is beyond doubt, Ponce alleges, that this play is a metaphor of the humanist's fate: "On the unknown island where Shakespeare takes us, we will see how *all the dreams of humanism and all the ideas already apparent in the works of Bruno and Erasmus* unfold, hidden behind masks and symbols" (82, Ponce's emphasis).[7] Shakespeare manages to represent an entire society and *Zeitgeist* through four characters: "Prospero is the enlightened tyrant, esteemed in the age of the Renaissance, Miranda stands for his descendants, Caliban for the suffering masses, and Ariel for the aerial genie, unrelated to real life" (83). Miranda, one of these four, is immediately discarded by Ponce: "Prospero, Ariel and Caliban: humanism

---

[7] Earlier in the text, Ponce had briefly dealt with Giordano Bruno, whose expression "crédula locura" (59) he had mentioned, i.e. that which the bourgeois humanists thought proper for the common people.

would not have needed anything else" (83). The Prospero-character is the next one to fade away. Ponce obviously does not need him to make his case. The twin characters of Ariel and Caliban remain and form the subject of the next lectures.

Ponce identifies Caliban with the oppressed masses all over the world. He is usually depicted as an ugly "red monster," but this can be explained as a projection on behalf of an unfair master: "an enormous injustice inflicted by a master" (84). Ponce thus unquestionably stands out as the first Latin-American who straightforwardly proposes a marxist interpretation of the Caliban-figure. While Rodó considered Caliban as the foreign oppressor, *in casu* the United States, Ponce is now transforming him into a symbol of the oppressed class, *in casu* the "red" proletariat.

Still, as indicated by the title of his text, Ponce pays more attention to the figure of Ariel, or the pole of 'passive' thought. Consequently, as far as the structure of the text is concerned, the picture that is drawn of Caliban is only of marginal importance and is largely a derivative of the picture of Ariel. A few explicit strokes suffice to finish the portrait of Caliban. He is the 'actor,' represented as the 'human being' or the 'complete human being' (86). The figure of Caliban, though of minor structural importance in Ponce's text, is essential to its meaning, because it is the necessary condition for Ariel's existence: "Ariel would not enjoy his spiritual freedom in the air, if Caliban did not carry the wood to the stove next to which Prospero re-reads his old books" (87).

In spite of this relationship of mutual dependence, Caliban and Ariel are contrasted by the author. Both pursue mutually exclusive goals, which is made clear by the fact that both are connected with opposite paradigms. Ariel is the 'spectator' who is nothing but 'mind' and 'intelligence.' He stands for 'freedom,' 'the belief in rational values,' 'the disapprovement of action' and 'the pernicious voluptuousness of intelligence' (87), as a result of which any interest in wordly affairs on behalf of the intellectual is considered as treason (86). In other words, Ponce's analysis is based on an opposition between living and thinking. This representation of the intellectual field implies a radical distinction between the intellectual community and 'real life': "On the one hand, then, those who live, and on the other those who think" (87).

Ponce's assessment of the views of Renan – the third bourgeois humanist on his list – is predictable: Renan acknowledges the rise of the proletariat, but underestimates its possibilities. However, when the Argentinian tries to counter Renan's opinion on this matter, his argument takes a strange turn. Up to this point, he had extolled Caliban as a symbol of the proletariat, which, in its turn, was identified with 'life' and the 'complete human being.' It now becomes evident that this human being was not so complete after all. For Ponce reproaches the bourgeoisie with not letting the proletariat share in its scientific and philosophical endeavours. In other words, the 'complete human being,' embodied by Caliban, now appears ignorant: "From Erasmus to Shakespeare, from Shakespeare to Renan, the bourgeoisie has, in the course of its development, never bridged the gap between the cultures of the different classes" (93).

The opposition between thinking and living is thus translated into an opposition between the educated and the ignorant human being. This translation explains why Ariel takes center stage in the text. Though a 'proletarian humanist' and communist, Ponce obviously also attaches a lot of importance to the functions of knowledge and thinking, which he disparagingly denounces as 'passive.'

Romain Rolland: from Petty Bourgeois to Proletarian Humanist

At the end of Ponce's essay, it is made clear that the rise of the proletarian era does not render the functions of knowledge and thinking irrelevant. Romain Rolland is the fourth bourgeois humanist discussed by Ponce. According to the author, this French intellectual embodies the transition to the proletarian era.[8] Actually, Ponce's essay and more in particular its title unmistakably refer to Rolland. In *Quinze ans de combat*, Rolland

---

[8] The choice of Rolland appears to be related to the fact that he functioned as an example for leftist intellectuals in Argentina. Rolland, Barbusse, and Anatole France, together with the French group *Clarté*, had a special influence on those intellectuals, according to Graciela Montaldo (1989: 382).

describes the intellectual process which he had gone through as the agony
of a 'stubborn illusion' (1935: VII).[9]

In his analysis of Roland's development, Ponce keeps focussing on the
characteristics of a bourgeois intellectual, always associating him with the
same familiar elements: he is still the 'mind,' the 'intelligence' and the
'gauzy tunic' ('túnica de gasas'). Moreover, Ponce now alleges that the
modern, humanist intellectual lives in a dream world. When reflecting, he
is enclosed by 'blindness' ('ceguera'), inspired by the belief in a 'pretended
independence' ('pretendida independencia,' 98). 'Infatuation' and 'false
assumptions' resemble the expressions Rolland uses in *Quinze ans de
combat*, as do 'the deceit of this ideology' ('engaño de esa ideología'),
'delusion' ('fantasma') and 'imaginary treasures' ('tesoros imaginarios')
(quoted by Ponce, 100). The modern humanist intellectual, Ponce
contends, has always been a victim, as the case of Rolland shows. He is an
Ariel, who has the illusion of being independent, but he is actually playing
the game of the established bourgeoisie. The ideal of independence is
nothing but an illusion, which a lot of intellectuals keep clinging to.

If the bourgeois Ariel lives in a dream world, this implies that the
proletarian one enjoys a 'complete life.' One has the impression, though,
that Ponce finds it difficult to properly conceive the figure of the
proletarian humanist. This figure is indeed described in very abstract and
romantic terms as, for instance, 'splendour' ('resplandor') (98), 'ardour of
life' ('hervor de la vida') (98) or 'dawning world' ('mundo naciente') (99).
Hence, the answer to the key question of the entire volume – what does it
take to become a proletarian humanist? – is too vague and general to serve
as practical guide-line. The "good" intellectual "marches proudly in the
ranks of the proletarian revolution" and "has recreated the only
environment in which Intelligence and Mind can prosper" (99). Those
reflections can hardly be considered practical guide-lines with regard to the

---

[9] Terán's comment in 'Aníbal Ponce o el marxismo sin nación' suggests that Ponce
could just as well have written about himself. He too evolves from a thorough
scepsis about the capacities of the people toward avowed Marxism: "he made an
ideological U-turn, rejecting socialism in his youth and later on adhering to it in a
progressive and general manner" (1986: 144). Although this cannot be concluded
from the essay under discussion, it is possible that Rolland and Ponce have met:
both made a voyage to the Soviet-Union in 1935 (cf. Rolland's *Voyage à Moscou*).

question that time and again has dogged the Latin-American intellectual community: does the intellectual have to join the masses in carrying out manual work, in order to serve them? Or does his task rather consist in developing his intellectual and artistic talents in the service of the people? Ponce obviously is unable to give an unequivocal answer to this question. What is more, he does not even pose the question. Still, the first part of the volume ends with the following sentence: "Our noble Ariel starts to fly above the vast earth on the wings of revolutionary fire" (101). In this final image of Ariel, the earthliness of Caliban and the spirituality of Ariel go hand in hand: Earth, fire and revolution soar high on the wings of the mind. The blending of both paradigms refers to the intellectual who combines intellectual work with preparing the revolution.

Ariel and Caliban in the Era of Proletarian Humanism

The character of Ariel disappears entirely in the second part of the volume, which deals with proletarian humanism. The opposition between mind and manual labor, connected with Ariel in the first part, is now applied to the proletariat itself. "Without the rise of the proletariat, Ponce asserts, it would never have been possible to blend theory and praxis, intelligence and desire" (101).

Ponce's belief in the possibilities of the proletariat is to a large extent the direct result of a study tour in the USSR. His admiration for the Soviet Union's growing power and impressive economic successes in the thirties is actually an important key to understanding the text. When Ponce attends a performance of *Richard III* by Shakespeare in Leningrad, the audience consists of enthusiastic labourers, who gave evidence of a keen interest in culture. Ponce is delighted about what he calls a new kind of Caliban: "the wretched red monster which Shakespeare had so much calumniated in Caliban, might he not be present, with a new soul, in that immense hall in which the hammer and the sickle have replaced the crown and the eagle? Facing the reddish curtain on which three glorious dates are endlessly repeated – 1871, 1905, 1917 – a world which was new, but which Shakespeare could not image, tells us how little we already know about man, and how man can start realizing what we had not thought possible, as soon as he is put in control of himself, rich with technical powers and with the culture of centuries" (141).

It seems, at first sight, that the opposition between Caliban and Ariel is now lifted, the proletariat equally fulfilling the two functions embodied by both figures. And yet, the opposition is subtly restored by the author's above cited mention of Caliban, in which he implicitly opposes 'el hombre' to 'we': in the past, we did not grasp the possibilities of mankind. In other words, the intellectual (Ariel) had no idea of what the proletariat (Caliban) was capable of. In the same sense Shakespeare, the intellectual, is contrasted with the new world of the proletariat. Ponce cannot dissolve this opposition, much as he would like to do so. In addition, he himself does not live up to the ideal of the new intellectual either. Not only did he never do any manual labour, he also does not address the proletariat in what could have been a form of educational prose. He continues to write about the proletariat, but he does so as an intellectual before a public of peers. In doing so, the author himself works to maintain the subject-object relationship between the intellectual and the proletariat. As far as Ponce is concerned, the proletariat is only marginally involved in the praxis of writing. Ponce writes as an intellectual, for an intellectual audience, about the task of an intellectual and about the enemy, who is an intellectual as well. Our analysis thus corroborates Terán's thesis that Ponce, contrary to many other filocommunist intellectuals, continued to attach a lot of importance to the role of the word.[10] On the other hand, our study contradicts Vaughan and Mason Vaughan's assertion that Ariel silently disappeared during the twenties and thirties. Although Ponce does indeed explicitly talk about an agony, his text in many ways indicates that the interest in the bourgeois intellectual was still very much alive in the thirties.

---

[10] Terán associates Ponce with an "Intellectualism which, even in 1933, made him hail 'the supremacy of the intellectuals in the moment of rebellion and urgent action'" (1986: 160). The similarity between Ponce and Rodó is striking, in this sense that they both address the academic community by means of a didactic discourse.

A Forgotten Author

In spite of its innovative approach to the Caliban-Ariel relationship, certainly in comparison with other Latin-American interpretations, Ponce's text has only sporadically been referred to. The reception of the text by two eminent Caliban scholars, Emir Rodríguez Monegal and Roberto Fernández Retamar is characteristic of this misjudgment.

Rodríguez Monegal, famous literary critic and Uruguayan 'neighbour' of Ponce, does not ever mention Ponce's essay. This omission is understandable as far as Rodríguez Monegal's introduction to the collected works of Rodó is concerned.[11] Rodó's *Ariel* is thirty-five years older than Ponce's. Hence, Rodríguez Monegal could at best have dealt with the possible influences of the former on the latter.[12] More puzzling is the silence about Ponce in "The metamorphoses of Caliban," a later essay by Rodríguez Monegal. In this text, the author, at that time professor at Yale University, lists the various characteristics that have been ascribed to Caliban in the course of history. Amongst other things, he alleges that the monstrous traits ascribed to Caliban in *The Tempest* and in the works of later authors disappeared for the first time in the interpretation of Mannoni.[13] Yet Ponce, an author belonging to the same culture area as Monegal and writing in Spanish about a decade before Mannoni, had made

---

[11] Rodríguez Monegal edited two editions of the complete works of Rodó. The first edition dates from 1954. In the edition of 1967, the introduction and the other comments remain the same, and some unpublished texts of Rodó are added.

[12] Or he could have discussed the differences between them. This is what Mabel Moraña does when he states that Rodó's work is a clear example of what Ponce would describe as 'humanismo burgués.' In the work of Rodó can be found "The parameters of a voluntaristic and stabilizing humanism, of a 'bourgeois humanism,' as Aníbal Ponce would define it afterwards" (1987: 662).

[13] More in particular, Rodríguez Monegal writes: "It was the task of a French psychoanalyst, O. Mannoni, to save Caliban from his detractors and present him not as an object of scorn but as a pitiful victim of colonization" (1977: 78). He also mentions the contribution of Fanon and Césaire: "Caliban is a revolutionary while Ariel is the intellectual who sells his rights for some crumbs from his master's table. Mannoni, Fanon and Césaire practised a political reading of *The Tempest*: a reading which inverts the functions of the roles the major characters play and uses Shakespeare's prototypes to serve the needs of twentieth-century ideologies" (1977: 79).

a revolutionary and undeniably sympathetic portrait of Caliban and had written critically about Ariel.[14] Rodríguez Monegal's negligence clearly shows that Ponce, unlike Rodó, is not an obligatory reference amongst Latin-Americans. This may be partly due to Ponce's uncritical defence of the Soviet system, although it is also possible that Ponce's book simply did not get a good distribution outside of Argentina.[15]

Although Aníbal Ponce's work continues to be relatively little known, the cultural entrepreneurs of the Cuban revolution have to a certain extent saved it from oblivion. In 1962 *Humanismo burgués y humanismo proletario* was republished in Havana. In his preface, "Vida, Obra y Muerte de Aníbal Ponce," the Cuban cultural ideologist Juan Marinello carefully tries to incorporate Ponce in the anti-imperialistic ideology of the Cuban revolution: "This combative author, who was the president of the organising commission of the Latin American Congress against imperialist war, in Montevideo in March 33, and who left us highly valuable texts which denounce the voracity of the yankees, would have been the first to publish vigorous reflections in the defence of our case" (1962: 27).[16]

One of the most famous Cubans to have written about Caliban is the literary critic Fernández Retamar. As he is an ideologue of the Castro-regime, and the opposite and rival of Rodríguez Monegal, we can expect him to pay attention to Ponce's contribution.[17] Contrary to Rodríguez

---

[14] Moreover, Rodríguez Monegal does not once mention the earlier, largely similar interpretation of Guéhenno. As concerns Ponce, it is not clear whether he was familiar with the French author. In any case, Guéhenno is not mentioned in *Humanismo burgués y humanismo proletario.*

[15] Rodó, on the other hand, is said to have contributed a lot to the distribution of his own essay *Ariel* (cf. for example Real de Azúa 1976: XX).

[16] Marinello also puts a lot of emphasis on Ponce's americanism, an americanism, however, that certainly cannot be traced back to the text itself. The Cuban contends, for instance, that Ponce's ideas were particularly beneficial to Argentina and Latin-America (1962: 13), and attaches a lot of importance to the fact that he wrote in Spanish: "His language is the Spanish of America, which he wanted all the authors on this side of the ocean to use" (1962: 21).

[17] In *Calibán. Apuntes sobre la cultura en nuestra América* (México: Diógenes, 1972), Fernández Retamar writes condescendingly about Rodríguez Monegal in his capacity as director of the review *Mundo Nuevo* (1972: 75). In his turn, Rodríguez Monegal accuses the Cuban, in 'The Metamorphoses of Caliban,' of not entirely

Monegal, he does indeed mention the text of Aníbal Ponce. According to the author, "the observations of the Argentinian Aníbal Ponce are much more shrewd than the Caliban-interpretations of Guéhenno" (1972: 25).[18] The Cuban praises Ponce for freeing Caliban of his bestial traits and associating the figure with the oppressed masses. He also thinks highly of Ponce's remarks about Ariel as a humanist intellectual. Fernández Retamar concludes as follows: "We are dealing here with one of the most intelligent essays that have ever been written about this topic in our America [read: Latin America]" (1972: 25).

Still, even Fernández Retamar, though a fellow Marxist-Leninist, is not unequivocally positive in his comments on Ponce. This is apparent, to begin with, from his relative lack of attention to Ponce after all. How come Retamar merely devotes one single paragraph to an author to whom he is ideologically very much akin? The 'but' that follows the above cited praise explains the reserve. Ponce has made an 'error' by isolating the issue from the Latin-American context: "But this analysis, though performed by a Latin-American, is still exclusively focused on the European world" (1972: 25-6).[19] Taking into account the political context at the time

---

knowing what he is talking about: "All these aspects of Rodó's work seem to have escaped Fernández Retamar's attention" (1977: 82). We are dealing here with one of the many polemics between the two figure-heads of Latin-American literary criticism. Nevertheless, both authors mainly refer to the same 'Caliban-authors,' and both try to fit the essay *Ariel* by Rodó in their own pattern of thinking, in spite of their fundamental objections against some of his ideas. Fernández Retamar, for instance, praises Rodó's anti-imperialism: "As concerns Rodó, while it is certain that he was mistaken about the symbols, as already explained, it is no less certain that he managed to make clear who was the principal enemy of our culture in his time, as in ours. And this is much more important" (1972: 31). One may therefore wonder what grounds Juan Marichal has to claim that Fernández Retamar's *Calibán* is directed against Rodó as the author of Ariel: "Since 1925, there existed a marked hostility towards Rodó, that culminated, so to speak, in the essay of the Cuban poet Roberto Fernández Retamar, *Calibán*, written in 1972. In the essay, the author of *Ariel* is decribed as the prototype of the so-called 'colonial' writer" (1978: 79).

[18] The criticism of Fernández Retamar on Guéhenno is extremely vague. In note 21, he writes about "the incapacity of Guéhenno to deal with this topic in depth."

[19] It is true that Ponce has little eye for the specific situation of the subcontinent. The Argentinian historian Oscar Terán considers this absence of any form of Latin-American awareness as one of the most important aspects of Ponce's

Retamar wrote, it is possible that the 'Latin-Americanisation' of the debate was ideologically correct because of the growing criticism that Cuba was imitating the Soviet Union. The ideologues of the Castro-regime did indeed try to defend themselves by emphasizing the so-called Latin-American nature of the revolution. It is thus probable that Ponce was condemned to oblivion in Cuba because he failed to interpret the Caliban-figure from a specifically Latin-American perspective.

This leads to the conclusion that the two mayor Latin-American critics mentioned are only interested in the subject of *The Tempest* and Caliban to the extent that it can be 'Latin-Americanised' and 'indianised.' Linking the Caliban-figure to issues of Latin-American identity is deemed more valuable or ideologically more useful than the universal approach advocated by Ponce himself. The Caliban-character has to be interpreted as a metaphor for the neo-colonial yoke under which the average Latin-American labours. From this perspective, the association of Caliban with the international labour class is obviously considered inadequate, even to a Marxist like Fernández Retamar, whom we should expect to honour the ideals of international class solidarity.

Nevertheless, in spite of the fact that Fernández Retamar clearly takes his distance from Ponce, there are some striking similarities between the two

---

discourse. Ponce's Eurocentrism is not that surprising, however, in view of the fact that Europe has traditionally been a more important point of reference to Argentina than Latin-America. But the absence is not evident either, since the period in which Ponce's ideas came to maturity coincided with a crisis in Argentina, involving a succession of political incidents and continual social unrest. This crisis inspired a lot of other Argentinian intellectuals to become more concerned with their country. Roberto Arlt's novel *Los siete locos* dates from 1929. Martínez Estrada publishes his *Radiografía de la pampa*, followed by *La cabeza de Goliat* in 1940, two books containing bitter reflections about Argentina and its culture. Juan Marichal, on the other hand, pays a lot of attention to the introspective attitude of the generation of the thirties: "The generation of 1930 consists of a group of introspective intellectuals. I almost dare say that they are the most alienated intellectuals of the entire Latin American history. They are intellectuals who consider solitude as an inevitable quality of their professional state" (1978: 95). If this is a correct assessment, Ponce's essay can also be read as an implicit answer to that attitude, although the essay contains no explicit indications that would justify such an interpretation.

authors.[20] To start with, Fernández Retamar describes the 'old intellectual' in exactly the same terms as Ponce. He who should possess knowledge is portrayed as miserably ignorant. Ponce reproaches the bourgeois intellectual with "The profound *ignorance* of social problems, brought about by living in the clouds for centuries on end" (emphasis added). Fernández Retamar, in his turn, complains about the intellectual's "*lack of knowledge*, if not depreciation, of our concrete social reality, both in the past and the present" (1972: 84, emphasis added). Moreover, both critics associate the ignorant intellectual with the dying class by which he is nurtured. Ponce is sorry for the intellectual who is dependent on the goodwill of the bourgeoisie: "The bourgeoisie spoils and decorates them as many times as suits them" (98). In the same way, Fernández Retamar highlights the ambiguity of the relationship: Ariel has to choose between Caliban and Prospero "with whom he appears to be on the best of terms, but whose timid servant he remains" (1972: 82).

The most striking similarity, though, involves the ambiguity of the task of an intellectual. Ponce's image of Ariel as a hybrid creature of both earth and air, wings and revolution appears in almost exactly the same form in Fernández Retamar's text. The Cuban uses the image with regard to the exemplary role of Che Guevara: "[Guevara], himself a radiant and aerial example, such as has never existed before, proposes that Ariel ask Caliban the privilege of a place in his glorious and energetic ranks" (1972: 95).

The debate about the task of the intellectual, which is so crucial in Latin-America, seems to be trapped in a repetitive spiral, oscillating between the idealistic and the materialistic point of view. However much the dilemma of the intellectual is formulated, it is unlikely that we will ever get a clear

---

[20] It would be incorrect not to mention some considerable differences between the authors. For one thing, as already said, Fernández Retamar places the problem in a specific Latin-American framework. A second important difference concerns the tone of their texts. Ponce denounces the 'corruption' of the bourgeois liberal in a non-agressive way. According to him, the bourgeois does not realise that he is wrong, and becoming aware of his mistake involves a lot of 'agony.' Fernández Retamar's discussion of the bourgeois Ariel is much sharper and much more polemic. He points an accusing finger at Ariel, whom he identifies with Borges, Fuentes and Rodríguez Monegal (1972: 61-72).

and unequivocal answer, not even from those authors who pretend to have found it.

Translated by Bart Maddens

References

Fernández Retamar, Roberto. 1972. *Calibán. Apuntes sobre la cultura en nuestra América* [1971]. México: Diógenes.

Marichal, Juan. 1978. *Cuatro fases de la historia intelectual latinoamericana 1810-1970*. Madrid: Fundación Juan March y Ed.Cátedra.

Montaldo, Graciela. 1989. *Yrigoyen, entre Borges y Arlt (1916-1930)*. Buenos Aires: Contrapunto.

Moraña, Mabel. 1987. "José Enrique Rodó." In L. Iñigo Madrigal (coord.), *Historia de la literatura hispanoamericana, Tomo II. Del neoclasicismo al modernismo*. Madrid: Cátedra.

Ponce, Aníbal. 1962. *Humanismo burgués y humanismo proletario*. La Habana: Imprenta Nacional de Cuba.

Rodó, José Enrique. 1954. *Obras completas. (Editadas, con introducción, prólogo y notas por Emir Rodríguez Monegal)*. Madrid: Aguilar.

—. 1976. *Ariel, Motivos de Proteo. (Prólogos de Carlos Real de Azúa, notas y cronología: Angel Rama)*. Caracas: Biblioteca Ayacucho.

Rodríguez Monegal, Emir. 1977. "The Metamorphoses of Caliban." *Diacritics* 3: 78-83.

Rolland, Romain. 1992. *Voyage à Moscou (juin-juillet 1935)*. Paris: Albin Michel.

—. 1935. *Quinze ans de combat, 1919-1934*. Paris: Rieder.

Terán, Oscar. 1986. *En busca de la ideología argentina*. Buenos Aires: Catálogos Editores.

Vaughan, Alden T. and Virginia Mason Vaughan. 1993. *Caliban. A Cultural History* [1991]. Cambridge: Cambridge UP.

Auden's Caliban. Man's "Drab Mortality"

Herman Servotte

Auden's *The Sea and the Mirror* (1944) is, so the subtitle tells us, *A Commentary on Shakespeare's "The Tempest."* It is a commentary of a very special kind. The term "commentary" usually indicates a discussion by an outsider on such subjects as the structure, the meaning, the themes and the relevance of the play. But that is not what Auden is interested in. At the moment when *The Tempest* reaches its end, Auden summons the Shakespearean characters back onto the stage, and has them voice their opinion about what happened to them on the island. In succession one hears Prospero taking leave of Ariel (I), the supporting cast which includes all the other characters each of whom formulates his deepened awareness of self (II), and, in a third section, Caliban addressing the audience (III). The characteristics of Shakespeare's dramatis personae are sometimes changed to suit Auden's particular ends. What he aims at is the exploration and the analysis of the different stages man has to go through in his search for selfhood. As for Ariel and Caliban, they are still what they were in *The Tempest*. Ariel is imagination, art; Caliban is the disgusting monster, malevolent but powerless enemy of whatever is noble and pure.

Inspired by Kierkegaard, especially by *The Sickness unto Death* (1849), Auden makes a distinction between people who are aware of the human predicament and those who are not. A second distinction concerns the degree of success with which people have been able to combine opposite poles in their being. For Auden, man is a divided creature appropriately called "the double man." That term was the original title of the American edition of *A New Year Letter*, which was written a few years before *The Sea and the Mirror*. The dualism hinted at has nothing in common with the Platonic dualism between soul and body or with a metaphysical dualism between time and eternity. It is anthropological, i.e. proper to man in all human experiences, manifesting itself in tensions between contrary values and truths. In most, if not all, human situations Auden detects such polar oppositions. They have to be acknowledged, accepted and transcended into a higher unity. One may think here of the Hegelian dialectic which moves from thesis to the contrary antithesis and reconciles them in the superior synthesis.

Some examples may help to clarify this statement. Auden believed that man, although determined by a number of factors, was also a free being. Both in judging the other person and in living one's own life, one had, according to Auden, to find the way between the Charibdis of absolute freedom and the Scylla of absolute necessity. Or, to take another example, it was possible to live as if man were merely finite and to neglect the infinite pole of his existence. To ignore or, worse, to try and destroy one pole, was to mutilate the human being. Man's desire and his task is to create his self in history. In the play Prospero and Alonso can be considered as the most advanced in mental and moral integrity; not only are they conscious of the human predicament, they have achieved the required synthesis in life, and they are now ready to die. All the other characters have also made some progress but they still have a long way to go. In this essay on Caliban I need not further belabour this point. It was, however, necessary to recall it to mind in order to understand who is Caliban, and how he functions in Auden's poem. He is the subject of our interpretation.

In the first part of *The Sea and the Mirror*, Prospero's farewell to Ariel, brief mention is made of Caliban:

> But Caliban remains my impervious disgrace.
> We did it, Ariel, between us; you found on me a wish
> For absolute devotion; result – his wreck
> That sprawls in the weeds and will not be repaired:

My dignity discouraged by a pupil's curse,
I shall go knowing and incompetent into my grave.

Two remarks are in order here: first, contrary to Shakespeare's Prospero, Auden's Prospero feels responsible for Caliban whom he considers as evidence of his failure to achieve perfection. Caliban is not merely an obstacle Prospero might avoid or ignore. His existence manifests a flaw in Prospero's being. Initially he was indeed Prospero's pupil, and then something went wrong.

This brings me to my second remark. The respective part of each party in the harm done to Caliban is not clear. But obviously Ariel has spotted and exploited Prospero's weakness: "you found on me a wish for absolute devotion." Ariel's role in damaging Caliban is underlined, even though the exact nature of his guilt in corrupting Caliban is far from clear. But if he is also responsible for Caliban's depravity he can hardly be considered as the "good" antagonist of the "bad" Caliban. As for Prospero's role, that is indicated by the enigmatic "wish for absolute devotion." Is that a desire to be served with an absolute devotion or, on the contrary, a desire to serve others with absolute devotion? In both cases what went wrong was Prospero's sense of the relativity of things and humans. In giving, or demanding, "absolute" devotion Prospero forgets that he is, and remains, a finite creature. No man can act out of absolute devotion, and no man must demand absolute devotion. His failure to reconcile his desire for perfection with the lucid awareness of the human being's weaknesses, is Prospero's "original sin"; but, as will be shown later, that is a "felix culpa."

Prospero, Ariel and Caliban cannot simply be contrasted as the good and the bad, or as victim and criminal. And there is another turn of the screw. A few lines later, Prospero, who is watching the band of the shipwrecked, states that they "have been soundly hunted by their own devils into their human selves." They have, in other words, reached a certain degree of selfhood. They owe this progress in humanity, not to a good spirit, but to their own devils. Can we not, putting two and two together, assume that Prospero has undergone a similar evolution? In that case, Ariel's guile and whatever Caliban represents have been beneficial to Prospero's growth as a human being; he owes his success to his failures.

In his *New Year Letter* Auden had already written about the devil in a similar vein:

> For how could we get on without you
> Who give the *savoir-faire* to doubt you
> And keep you in your proper place,
> Which is, to push us into grace.

This is precisely the service which Ariel and Caliban have rendered to Prospero; they have pushed him into grace, the former by tempting him with the lure of absolute devotion, the latter by refusing the absolute devotion which he craved.

Kierkegaard, who – in the forties – is never a long way away, believed that in his search for selfhood man could go through three stages, each of which was marred by failure. In the first stage, the aesthetic one, man lives in the moment, motivated by the pleasure principle; he has no sense of direction, as he allows the stimuli from outside to dominate his life. He may stay in that stage, but when sickness and death come nearer he will inevitably be disappointed and look out for a better way of life. He can then enter the ethical stage: deciding to become a real self, beyond time, he sets up an ideal and tries to realize it. But that will prove too demanding a task for the human being who is no absolute master of his self and its destiny. As soon as man despairs of ever becoming ethically good, the way lies open for the religious stage in which he abandons the self, expecting from God what he cannot achieve himself, and, paradoxically, receives his self from God. Kierkegaard's example here is Abraham who was ready to sacrifice his son to God and in the same instant received him back from God. Thus Prospero is led from failure to failure, from despair to despair until he reaches the stage where he can leave the world behind and abandon himself to the divine mercy. The psychic powers, which bring about this awareness of one's despair, are, in *The Tempest*, replaced by the hypostazes Ariel and Caliban. Whatever they represent, they goad him into becoming himself, without realizing that their temptations actually lead him to the very spot they wanted him to miss. They are good and bad at the same time; man must at the same time obey and disobey them, a paradoxical task which cannot be effectively fulfilled.

So far we have seen Caliban through the eyes of Prospero and against the background of Auden's concept of man. In the second section Caliban is notably absent, but in the third part of *The Sea and the Mirror*, Caliban himself unexpectedly takes the floor and delivers a long speech in highly elaborate, almost Jamesian, prose. That speech is difficult to connect with the character Prospero calls "a wreck" or with Shakespeare's monster. With its carefully tortuous syntax, its studied imagery, and the devious subtlety of its thought it is a far cry from the gibberish Shakespeare attributes to Caliban and from the speechlessness Prospero's references to him imply. There is, then, more to him than Shakespeare or Prospero had led us to believe.

He does not, however, speak in his own name. Presumably sent by the absent author to answer the audience's outraged questions, Caliban "speaks their echo." He acts as if he were the audience's spokesman, which is tantamount to saying that he considers himself – or pretends to be – their representative. Although they are reared in the British dramatic tradition which can combine elements that would be mutually exclusive on the classical stage, the audience cannot accept Caliban's presence – or so Caliban says. In a superbly ambiguous indictment he accuses the author of so "introducing Him to them among whom He doesn't belong" with the result that "He couldn't appear as anything but His distorted parody." The ambiguity of the third person pronoun used here matches the bewilderment of the audience; they no longer know Ariel from Caliban and, in consequence, where they themselves belong. Are they Caliban's or Ariel's? Whether the Sakespearean play idealises or represents life, Caliban – or Auden? – always assumes that the audience are of Caliban's party as much as they are of Ariel's party. The ambiguity of the two creatures, which was discovered at the end of the first part, is again made manifest.

Not surprisingly, the audience feel insulted. But they are even more apprehensive of what this theatrical trick might entail for their daily lives. "Is it possible that, not content with inveigling Caliban into Ariel's kingdom, you have also set loose Ariel in Caliban's?" What they fear is the uncontrolled crossing of the borderline separating real life from its poetic representation. In their view the poetic, which is the realm of Ariel, should be immune from the contamination of the real; and the real, which is where Caliban belongs, ought to be shielded from the intrusion of art and imagination that are Ariel's. Hence their cry, as relayed by Caliban:

> We want no Ariel here, breaking down our picket fences
> in the name of fraternity, seducing our wives in the name
> of romance, and robbing us of our sacred pecuniary
> deposits in the name of justice.

The serious problem referred to in these comic lines, is that of the relation between art and life, mirror and sea. Elsewhere Auden had written that "poetry makes nothing happen" ("In Memory of W.B. Yeats") and that "poetry could be no midwife to society," thus allocating to art and life their proper sphere. Nevertheless he strongly opposed Yeats's contention that one had to choose either the perfection of life or the perfection of the work. Both, he maintained, were to be cultivated. The origin of art was to be located in man's "desire for both beauty and truth" (*The Dyer's Hand*, 337-338); and that poem would be satisfactory which led the reader into "a verbal earthly paradise [...] because of its contrast to our historical existence" and which, at the same time, provided us "with some kind of revelation about our life" and helped to "free us from self-enchantment and deception"(ibid.). Clearly, what the audience think about the relation art and life, is not acceptable to Auden; and Caliban, whose sayings are supposed to originate in the audience, expresses Auden's misgivings about the audience's views. For Auden, art is not, as it is for the audience, an escape from the real world, but the creation of a world in which the mimetic desire for truth and the poetic longing for beauty have contributed.

In order to approach the problem from a different angle, Caliban returns to what he calls "my officially natural role," which is to express the ideas of his creator on the subject. In order to do that he describes an artist's growth under the positive influence of inspiration. In this passage Ariel is what in another language game would be called "the muse." Working in perfect synergy with him the artist believes himself to be the creator of the work of art. But things change; the collaboration between artist and muse turns into sullen opposition; worst of all, the helper who one thought Ariel was, has suddenly been transformed into a gibbering fist-clenched creature with which you are all too unfamiliar, for this is the first time indeed that you have met the only subject that you have, who is not a dream amenable to magic but the all too solid flesh you must acknowledge as your own; at last you have come face to face with me.

Ariel's place has been taken by Caliban; or, more accurately, Ariel has turned into Caliban. Are they, perhaps, but the two sides of one coin? And if they are, is their relationship then similar to the famous dichotomy of Dr Jekyll and Mr Hyde? Is one beautiful, good-natured and creative, whereas the other is, symmetrically, ugly, base and destructive? Or is the relationship a much closer one?

To answer that question one should look at the relation between the artist and the two antagonists. The text shows clearly that Caliban is but an aspect of the artist's personality. The artist discovers himself when he looks into Ariel's unblinking eyes and sees himself reflected there in the guise of Caliban. It is Caliban whom he sees in the mirror. Should we not draw the logical conclusion, and also equate the author and Ariel? In other words, both Ariel and Caliban are but projections of the artist's soul, admirable when Ariel is in command, disgusting when it is Caliban-like.

We have come a long way from Shakespeare's creatures. His basic opposition between the ugly and the beautiful can be interpreted as the opposition of nature versus culture, or nature versus grace, or the ignorance of the savage versus the knowledge of the white man, but it always keeps the two poles apart. In Shakespeare these poles are to be found in different individuals; it is a social difference, opposing man to man, and sex to sex, and culture to culture. Here however, the opposition is internal to the individual and it is to be found within every man. Once again, the motive of the double man manifests itself. The enemy is not lurking outside, waiting for the propitious moment to strike, he is inside man. Man is a divided subject, inhabited by the Other.

It is not surprising that the last part of Caliban's long speech, in which he again addresses the audience about their questions, should be uttered by Caliban "on behalf of Ariel" and himself. There may have been enmity between them, or they may have ignored each other so far, but now they turn out to see eye to eye. They must answer the petitions and prayers of the humans who solicit their guidance for the last leg of their life's journey. Ariel and Caliban will scrupulously realize their deepest wish, that is, they will give them their desire for all eternity. "Tel qu'en lui-même enfin l'éternite le change," to use Mallarmé's comment on Poe's death.

Those who choose Caliban have, so Caliban tells them (us?), heard his "reiterated affirmation of what [their] furnished circumstances categorically are"; those who opt for Ariel are more attracted "by his successive propositions as to everything else they conditionally might be." Translated into Kierkegaardian terms the choice between the two antagonists can be seen as the choice between necessity and possibility. Caliban's followers have become so painfully aware of the determinisms governing their lives that they despair, and hope for a deliverance which Caliban cannot give; he can only bring them to the world of pure necessity, thus confirming their existential choice for all eternity. In Caliban's words:

> when you so cry for deliverance from every and any anxious possibility, I shall have no option but to be faithful to my oath of service and instantly transport you [...] to that downright state itself.

Ariel's followers, on the contrary, have believed in possibility, and ignoring all determinisms, tried hard to change the world. Their demand for a world without conditions will result in Ariel's leading them into a world of pure possibility. To quote Caliban again:

> Obliged by the terms of His contract to gratify this other request of yours, the wish for freedom to transcend *any* condition, for direct unentailed power without *any*, however secretly immanent, obligation to inherit or transmit, what can poor shoulder shrugging Ariel do but lead you forthwith into a nightmare [...], a state of perpetual emergency and everlasting improvisation where all is need and change.

Caliban and Ariel are obviously allegorical representatives of the psychological powers at work in man. Here they are shown in their impact on man's eternal fate. But their influence is not limited to that aspect of life; it manifests itself on more than one level of human experience. To give but a few examples: as far as their temperament is concerned, Ariel seems to represent utopian hope and Caliban nostalgic memory. On the political level the basic opposition manifests itself as the conflict in man between progressiveness versus conservatism; psychologically as his hesitation between reason versus emotion, existentially as the ethical attitude versus the aesthetic one. These polarities are not isomorph. Conservatism and emotion may have in common the backward look, but they also have many points that are not common. Similarly, the ethical attitude may share some points with reason, and the esthetical attitude may play on emotions, but though they have points in common they are not identical; they do not cover the same ground. So Caliban and Ariel can, depending on the context, represent distinct but related poles: or, to formulate this differently, each pole is situated in different non-concentric circles, which overlap only partly. That makes for the richness of Caliban's picture in Auden, but also for the difficulty to pin him down. He is much richer than the usual interpretations given of him.

Obviously, a unilateral reliance on either Caliban or Ariel, leads to despair, i.e. to the failure to become oneself. It follows that Caliban and Ariel are equally important in man's life. It is, then, no longer possible to reject or to neglect Caliban and his like on the pretext that they differ from us. When one has become aware of Caliban as of the other in us, one also realizes that to reject that other would be to diminish the self. It is, of course, a good thing to get rid of one's weakness, but as the present essay has shown, Auden would undoubtedly counter with the idea that we need our devils to become ourselves. Our mistakes can be considered as a "felix culpa."

One might object that the dualism between us and Caliban may indeed have been overcome, but that the solution makes for a rebirth of the dualism between, this time, Caliban and Ariel, or between the temperaments that choose for them; the conflict between them has become an internal one in each of us. Precisely, but the relation which was conflictual has now become dialectic, or, to use an image, it is of the seesaw type. The higher Caliban rises, the lower Ariel descends, and vice versa. In the words of Caliban about the drama:

> the dramatist, who, in representing to you your condition of estrangement from the truth, is doomed to fail the more he succeeds, for the more truthfully he paints the condition, the less clearly he can indicate the truth from which it is estranged, the brighter his revelation of the truth in its order, its justice, its joy, the fainter shows his picture of your actual condition in all its drabness...

Up goes the one, down the other. One cannot achieve the perfect balance between both, unless both fail to get the upper hand and the seesaw is at rest in a precarious untenable equilibrium.

That is the moment of awareness of failure, when you do no longer know what to do and yet know that you have got to move forward to become what you are, when you no longer know whether to choose Ariel or Caliban and always forget the difference between them. At that moment the Other manifests itself, not *in propria persona* but as the condition of possibility for you to become yourself. For it is only when there is an open space that you can move forward into the unknown; it is only when the other is already present in you as a mere potentiality that you can change and become that other. You discover the truth of what a French schoolboy of sixteen wrote to a friend: "Je est un autre" (Rimbaud). That enigmatic statement can mean many things. It refers to, among other things, the distance separating one's present from one's future, one's own image of self from that which others have of it; it also refers to the driving power behind one's desire and which is not to be fathomed by consciousness. Prospero's "I am that I am" is but one side of the coin. Its reverse side shows Rimbaud's maxim: "Je est un autre." They have to balance each other.

The impossibility of such a synthesis manifests itself in the evident lack of success of the play our lives are involved in. Yet, at the very moment when this failure becomes painfully obvious, we do at last "see ourselves as we are." The end of Caliban's speech turns back to the beginning of the play when Prospero made the discovery "I am that I am." That authentic self-awareness is the necessary condition for the entry into what Auden calls that "Wholly Other Life." But now it no longer means what it meant in Prospero's mouth. He recognized his guilt, and in so doing escaped from the lures of the imagination in a wilderness of mirrors. Here, the selfknowledge accepts the rift in one's being and trusts the Other to lead one on the road to selfhood.

As if to illustrate that truth, Ariel is given the last word. In the postscript he speaks for the first time in *The Sea and the Mirror*, and refers to Caliban as "drab mortality." We can see now why Caliban had to speak in the name of the audience. He is indeed their representative. Far from being a debased creature, differing from other more fortunate ones, he is, in his ugliness, in his brutishness, in his lies and lust, "one of us." No outsider he, but yet another "poor bare forked animal." Even Ariel, the idealistic dreamer, owes his existence to Caliban: he is the "fleet persistent shadow cast by [Caliban's] lameness [...] helplessly in love with you." And it is to Caliban's unfulfilled desire, to his lack of truth and authenticity, that Ariel owes his existence and the human being his salvation. "Hunted by his devils" i.e. by Caliban, "into his human self," man is finally brought to the moment of decision where he can accept mortality and failure, and in deep trust start "sailing alone, out over seventy thousand fathoms." That is the – Kierkegaardian – metaphor Auden adopts to describe the act of faith.

As long as Caliban is there, Ariel will also be there. Neither can exist without the other; and the end of their partnership, "when our (i.e. Caliban's and Ariel's) falsehoods are divided," is unavoidably death, "one evaporating sigh." But the prompter, who keeps the play going, echoes "I." This is deeply significant. For in this passage, the subject "I" owes his existence to the song of Ariel which, in turn, owes his being to Caliban, "drab mortality."

The play is over, and we are now in a better position to situate Caliban. He cannot be what we thought he was and what he certainly was in Shakespeare's play. There the repulsive, uneducated creature so utterly different from what we think we are can be seen by us as the obvious representative of the other(s) whether they be physically deficient, socially inferior, ethnically different, or culturally alien. Shakespeare's Caliban is the stranger, the other; and as such he can be left behind to rust in the weeds, or be ignored as he is in the second part, or be turned into a figure of derision or hatred. What such a creature cannot do is what he actually does in the third part, i.e. to speak in the name of Shakespeare, to voice the opinions of the crowd and in this way to reveal himself as one of us.

In *The Sea and the Mirror* that is done on several levels. In the play the characters must leave their former selves and adopt new ways of life; and the author himself must find an equilibrium between his mimetic desire and his will to transform reality. In life the choice of one pole, be it Caliban or Ariel, leads to an eternity of sameness; one can escape that determinism only if one corrects this unilateral choice by the option for the Other. As this is the main movement of the text, one needn't be surprised when the awareness of the play's awfulness calls up what Auden calls "that Always Opposite which is the whole subject of our not knowing." Neither the sea of life nor the mirrors of art in isolation, but the sea and the mirror – or Caliban and Ariel – together can achieve a marred perfection. *The Sea and the Mirror* announced itself as a commentary on *The Tempest*. That is what it is, indeed. But the discussion on the relation between art (the mirror) and life (the sea) in the play, becomes a discussion about the relation between what we actually are and what we hope to become; and the Shakespearean play reveals itself as an allegory of Kierkegaardian philosohy. At the same time it expresses Auden's acceptance of "drab mortality." The poet, who had written in 1939 about man as

> the living creature [...]
> Mortal, guilty but to me
> The entirely beautiful ("Lullaby")

reiterates here that he finds "the mortal world enough," by declaring himself in love "with drab mortality." What there is, beyond mortality, is, as he announces in the *Preface*,

> silence
> On the other side of the wall;
> And the silence ripeness,
> And the ripeness all.

It needed a Caliban to make that discovery.

Cruising against the Id

The Transformation of Caliban in *Forbidden Planet*

Tim Youngs

The question of why the director of *Lassie Come Home* should have turned to a science-fiction version of the "puppy-headed monster," as Caliban is called by Trinculo (II.ii.154-55),[1] is not one I shall doggedly pursue. However, if we take seriously Leo Marx's claims that the "topography of *The Tempest* anticipates the moral geography of the American imagination" (Marx 1964: 72), then Fred McLeod Wilcox's 1956 film *Forbidden Planet* may offer us a glimpse of what had become of that imagination in the decade after the Second World War.

Leo Marx sees the prophetic quality of *The Tempest* as lying in its plausible presentation of a pastoral retreat which it then denies (1964: 71-72). As with his statement that "Prospero's situation is in many ways the typical situation of voyagers in newly discovered lands" (1964: 35), Marx concedes that this is neither a new nor a uniquely American theme, but he insists that both ideas possess a special significance in the American context since the American experience illustrates them so vividly:

---

[1] Wilcox directed *Lassie Come Home* in 1943. This information may be found in, among other places, Brosnan 1991: 55.

> I am thinking of the remote setting, the strong sense of
> place and its hold on the mind, the hero's struggle with
> raw nature on the one hand and the corruption within
> his own civilization on the other, and, finally, his
> impulse to effect a general reconciliation between the
> forces of civilization and nature. [...] an unspoiled
> landscape suddenly invaded by advance parties of a
> dynamic, literate, and purposeful civilization. It would
> be difficult to imagine a more dramatic coming together
> of civilization and nature. (Marx 1964: 35-36)

Marx's terms are revealing of a certain tradition in a way that perhaps he did not intend: the setting can hardly be "remote" or "newly discovered" to its indigenous population. The identification of raw nature is not an uncomplicated perception but an ideological construction dependent upon civilization's idea of itself. Nonetheless, the kinds of setting, struggle and attempted reconciliation he outlines are exhibited in *Forbidden Planet*, which, set in 2257 A.D., is a reworking and updating of *The Tempest*.[2] Even where the film appears to depart from Marx's terms, the result is a more complicated reinforcement of them. The planet on which the action occurs is not, we learn, unspoiled, but it seems so on the surface since: "There are no cities, ports, roads, bridges, dams. There's just no sign of civilization at all."[3] What we learn of the civilization that did exist certainly denies this as a pastoral retreat. Some of the parallels with Shakespeare's play will be apparent from the following summary of the film, which will also highlight some of the themes I wish to look at.

---

[2] John Brosnan reports that *The Tempest* "happened to be special effects man Irving Block's favourite play, and it was Block, along with writing collaborator Allen Adler, who wrote the story for the movie (the screenplay was written by Cyril Hume). Block also had a strong interest in mythology and incorporated several basic mythological themes into the story (for example, when Altaira loses her virginity she also loses her power over her wild animals)" (1991: 55).

[3] These words are spoken by Gerry, a crew member on the United Planets spaceship as it surveys Altair IV prior to landing. In fact, the native inhabitants, the extinct Krel, built underground, a reflection of the film's psychological theme and of contemporary fears of nuclear war, as will become clear.

Commander Adams and his all-male (and, it seems, all-white) crew land on the planet Altair IV in their spaceship United Planets Cruiser C57D, hoping to discover the fate of a previous mission. The aims of the United Planets vessels are the conquest and colonisation of space. Adams and his men encounter philologist Dr. Morbius (the Prospero figure), who tells them that only he and his wife, Julia Morrison (who is now dead), survived beyond the first year on the planet. The rest of the crew were killed by dark forces, torn limb from limb by something devilish which never showed itself. "Always," says Morbius, "in my own mind, I seem to feel the creature is lurking somewhere close at hand, sly and irresistible, and only waiting to be reinvoked for murder." Now Morbius's only companions are his innocent daughter Altaira (the Miranda figure) and Robby the robot, who (like Ariel) has incredible powers at his master's disposal. Morbius reveals that he and his wife differed from their late companions only in their "special love for this new world and our boundless longing to make a home here far from the scurry and strife of humankind," and so were "utterly heartbroken when [a] vote was taken to return to Earth."

Morbius asks that allowances be made for his daughter, who has "never known any human being except her father."[4] Altaira's innocence is displayed in her lack of self-consciousness ("I so terribly wanted to meet a young man and now three of them at once") and her imperviousness to innuendo. She is accused by Adams of having no feelings and nothing human in her mind, and is told that she should dress less provocatively. She has already been having lessons from Lieutenant Farman on how to kiss, but when she instructs Adams to kiss her, a tiger, which she has always previously been able to tame, springs to attack her. Adams kills it with his laser-like gun.

---

[4] This is one of a number of hints of an incestuous relationship. However, it would be wrong to say, as Margaret Tarratt has done, that Morbius's "suppressed incestuous desires are clearly implied to be at the root of *all* the trouble" (1970: 39; emphasis added). Morbius's possessiveness (which, of course, echoes Prospero's) should rather be seen as evidence of his more general will to power.

Morbius tells Adams about the Krel,[5] the former inhabitants of the planet, who had been ethically and technologically a million years ahead of humanity and had reached outwards to Earth before humanity's existence. However, they had experienced a catastrophe two thousand centuries ago. Adams argues that humans need the Krel's knowledge but Morbius, who declares "Perhaps I do not choose to be dictated to in my own world," insists that humans are not ready for the Krel's knowledge and he alone will decide what of their knowledge to impart and when to do so. He will answer exclusively to his own conscience and judgement.

Adams's spaceship is attacked and one of his crew killed by an invisible monster. The form of this monster is only revealed when it passes through the electrical currents of a protective fence erected by the crew. A cast is made from its tracks, showing a claw measuring thirty-seven inches by nineteen, belonging to a four-footed type of creature although the tracks are those of a biped. This, we are told, goes against every known law of evolution.

Adams, with the help of Altaira, who has soon grown to love him, gets into Morbius's laboratory and discovers the Krel's technology, including a brain-scanning machine, which Adams's companion, Doc, tries with fatal results. However, before dying, Doc is able to tell his commander that the Krel forgot that their machine, which projects thought as matter, would also register their subconscious selves, the monsters from the id. The physical manifestation of their lust for revenge and destruction had catastrophic results. Morbius shows no sympathy when Doc dies, saying simply that he should be buried with the other victims of human greed and folly. This callousness stirs Altaira to announce that she will desert her father and leave with Adams.

When Adams points out that the Krel forgot their own subconscious hate and their lust for revenge and destruction, Morbius's utopian view of them is destroyed. Adams realises that the monster must be Morbius's own id

---

[5] Spellings of the Krel vary, with some critics writing "Krell." For consistency I shall use Krel throughout, except where quoting from critics who use the alternative spelling. Spellings of Robby and Altaira also vary but I follow the orthography of the film's credits.

and that it is this that was responsible for killing his fellow crew members because of his urge to rule. "We're all part monsters in our subconscious, so we have laws and religion," Adams proclaims. He tells Morbius that Altaira has bound herself to him (Adams) body and soul, and accuses Morbius of displaying a primitive rage at Altaira's disobedience and of wanting no one to challenge his egomaniac empire.

Morbius asks to be killed to save himself and the others from his id, which is outside trying to break in. He has Adams, whom he now calls "son," push the Krel's self-destruct button which will destroy the planet. He remains on Altair IV, while Altaira flees to safety with Adams and the others. On the Cruiser, which is navigated by Robby, the crew and Altaira watch on the monitor as the planet explodes.

My focus in this essay will be on the implications of the symbolic transformation of Caliban to id. This is not to say that Shakespeare anticipated Freud or that they were describing the same creature. Rather, it is to say that the beast against which humanity identifies itself is protean. (The various identities ascribed to Caliban by other characters in the play also suggest this.) The shape of the beast will shift as its environment changes. Alterations in the intellectual and social context, combined with the generic influences of representation, will affect its appearance. Whether or not there is an essential essence that remains unchanged beneath the altered features, it may be impossible to judge.

Mark Rose has written of Caliban that he

> represents, among other things, the unregenerate, earthy
> side of man – original sin, we should say if we were to
> read the play as a Christian allegory – that must be
> restrained in order to found a civil society. Drawing
> upon the popular mythology of Freudian psychology,
> the id-monster of *Forbidden Planet* represents something
> analogous, and the possibility of translating Caliban into
> such a figure indicates the continuity between certain
> older forms of self-alienation and our own. (1981: 177-78)

This idea of continuity between older and modern forms of self-alienation risks flattening out important differences of historical context which must be considered alongside any generic or thematic affinities. Representations of monstrosity may serve to objectify beastliness and distract from the local conditions that decide what is monstrous. An examination of *Forbidden Planet* will show that the concerns it reflects have as much to do with discontinuities as with continuities. Since this film has been accurately labelled a "Freudianized sci-fi version of *The Tempest*" (Biskind 1984: 108), the effects of both of these intellectual and generic descriptors need to be considered.

In "Civilization and Its Discontents," Freud wrote that

> it is impossible to overlook the extent to which civilization is built upon a renunciation of instinct, how much it presupposes precisely the non-satisfaction (by suppression, repression or some other means?) of powerful instincts. This 'cultural frustration' dominates the large field of social relationships between human beings. [...] it is the cause of the hostility against which all civilizations have to struggle. (1991a: 286-87)

In both *The Tempest* and *Forbidden Planet*, as in many other works, the motifs of travel and bestiality are employed in the expression of the repressed. These motifs seem, if not transcendent, then at least enduring, while the emergence of new cultural forms, fostered in part by new technologies and in part by intellectual developments, may modify the particular representation of the repressed figure. Here I am thinking specifically of the impact of the theories of Darwin and Freud, which gave simian and subterranean imagery new significance, and of the film technology that was not available (obviously) to Shakespeare. In the nineteenth and twentieth centuries, Darwinism and Freudianism have given Western observers of "savagery" and the "primitive" a discomfiting shudder of kinship that Shakespeare's contemporaries might either not have felt or could have shrugged off. One can no longer examine social repression without inspecting oneself. As Rosemary Jackson has said, "it is in the unconscious that social structures and 'norms' are reproduced and sustained within us, and only by redirecting attention to this area can we begin to perceive the ways in which the relations between society and the individual are fixed" (1981: 6).

Freud's statements that the ego is "that part of the id which has been modified by the direct influence of the external world"; that the id has its pleasure principle denied by the reality principle of the ego, with the ego seeking to "bring the influence of the external world to bear upon the id and its tendencies"; and that the "ego represents what may be called reason and common sense, in contrast to the id, which contains all the passions" (1991b: 363-64), all suggest the connectedness of what we might otherwise try to separate as culture and nature. More succinctly, "For the ego, perception plays the part which in the id falls to instinct" (364). This is not an ahistorical conception. It suggests quite clearly that perceptions and representations of the id will shift and be influenced by the historical situation and by the prevailing ideological constructions of nature. After Darwin, for example, it is more likely that we should see Prospero and Caliban as conflicting tendencies within a single entity, and after Freud it is almost inevitable that we should do so. If we forget, then we may end up sharing the fate of Morbius and the Krel, fatally neglectful of our own destructive instincts. We must therefore try to establish both the specific nature of the id in *Forbidden Planet* and its temporal disguise, especially as the genre of the fantastic has been said to perform its "most transgressive function" when it engages in the "subversion of unities of self" (Jackson 1981: 83).

The authors of a book on transformations of Caliban have claimed that after the two world wars and the holocaust of the Second, writers "Influenced by Freudian analysis of the darker side of human nature – the sexual and violent impulses lurking beneath the surface – [...] saw Caliban as a symbol of the inexorable, ineradicable evil within the human psyche" (Vaughan and Vaughan 1991: 114). This view of the id and of Caliban as a symbol of evil manages with startling brevity to diminish Shakespeare, Freud and later writers. However, the Vaughans seem to be on stronger ground when they go on to remark that

> The creators of *Forbidden Planet* seem to have projected
> post-World War II terrors onto Shakespeare's original
> savage. Their interpretation of Caliban as the id, the
> thing of darkness within us that we must acknowledge as
> ours, is patently Freudian in an era groping to
> understand the senseless cruelties of the 1930s and

1940s./ However educated or civilized humans think
they are, *Forbidden Planet* suggests, this beast lurks
within, ready to pounce and destroy. Morbius endures
Prospero's timeless problem of maintaining order and
decency without himself being transformed into an evil ◄
monster who abuses power and authority. The film is
also postwar in its emphasis on nuclear power as a
potential source of destruction – of civilization and of
the planet itself. [...] *Forbidden Planet*'s concerns,
particularly in its portrayal of Caliban [...] were
especially appropriate for the 1950s. (Vaughan and
Vaughan 1991: 206)

It might appear odd that having emphasised the importance of the
historical context, the Vaughans should then undermine it by dismissing
the cruelties of the 1930s and 1940s as "senseless" (when in fact they were
often predicated on a frightening appeal to a perverted sense of reason),
but there is evidently something about the nature of beastliness that
encourages a shrugging acceptance of its eternal presence.

On the question of the postwar context, the 1940s and 1950s have been
seen by many as:

a period during which the United States went through
some of the most profound and disturbing changes of its
modern history – changes that altered national direction,
shifted the ideological mood, shifted and enlarged the
nation's world role, and re-directed American
consciousness. (Temperley and Bradbury 1981: 243)

And in a study of *Forbidden Planet*'s "double vision of its futuristic
world," J. P. Telotte points to the contrast in the 1950s between the
"economic prosperity and the great consumer access to technology it
facilitated," on the one hand, and the "cold war fears, especially the
looming potential for a technological self-destruction, a nuclear holocaust"
(1989: 26-27), on the other.

Telotte is certainly right to remark that the power the United States
enjoyed on the world stage, together with its growing domestic

prosperity, provided a sense of equilibrium that was in tension with the atomic threat that underlay it. In 1950 Joseph McCarthy had begun his witch-hunt of suspected communists and their sympathisers (though McCarthy was censured by the Senate in 1954). The Korean War ended in 1953, the same year as the execution of the Rosenbergs for atomic espionage and just three years before the release of *Forbidden Planet*. The political introspection caused by McCarthyism and the sociological inspections inspired by this perception of material well-being and conformity might well give an impression of an externally confident but inwardly uncertain people. Surveying some of the contemporary critiques of that society, Temperley and Bradbury have written that "never had a people possessed so much in worldly goods, or, apparently, been so troubled in spirit on that account" (1981: 259).[6] What seems to have been so troubling to the "spirit" was the growing feeling that in the domestic sphere physical comfort and technological convenience left an essential side of human nature unfulfilled, while in its global and military context technology was perceived increasingly as a threat to human existence itself. Many people felt too that the introduction of "technological rationality [...] into every sphere of life was crushing individuality and driving out spirituality," while a "significant sign of the renewed perception of the technological threat" was its contribution to the "sombre mood [that] had descended on science fiction ever since the bombing of Hiroshima" (Kumar 1987: 403).

The dichotomy that emerges here parallels the basic Freudian structure of the civilised and pre- or uncivilised identities, with the reality principle of

---

[6] This idea is given perhaps its most famous expression in Arthur Miller's *Death of a Salesman*, first published in 1949. Miller's opening stage directions indicate very clearly both of these opposing strains and their manifestation in the physical world and in fantasy: "An air of the dream clings to the place, a dream rising out of reality. The kitchen at centre seems actual enough, for there is a kitchen table with three chairs, and a refrigerator. But no other fixtures are seen. [...] The entire setting is wholly or, in some places, partially transparent [...] Whenever the action is in the present the actors observe the imaginary wall-lines, entering the house only through its door at the left. But in the scenes of the past these boundaries are broken, and characters enter or leave a room by stepping through a wall on to the forestage" (Miller 1961: 7).

the former being accepted as necessary and inevitable while the loss or submergence of the latter's pleasure principle is nevertheless lamented. It is not surprising, then, that commentaries on that society should inherit this model, with non-conformity identified with – and by some celebrated as – unreason. As one assessment has it:

> Despite the Eisenhower equilibrium, the romanticization of anarchic unreason, and the insistence that a conflict rather than a consensus model of society was necessary, were central themes of the Fifties. Hence, among certain intellectuals and writers, as well as among many of the affluent young, the issues of the Sixties – social and sexual repression, minorities, race, poverty, the military-industrial complex, and the politics of global interference – were already alive. (Temperley and Bradbury 1981: 261)

The language used here by Temperley and Bradbury – a romanticised anarchic unreason and the insistence upon conflict threatening to undermine an equilibrium – appears far from neutral, but I am less interested in what their own views might be than in how these terms, which were widely used at the time, are taken as symptomatic of the era. After all, whether or not we detect a sniff of disapproval from these two critics, we can easily find celebrants of the non-rational in contemporary literature, such as Ken Kesey's *One Flew over the Cuckoo's Nest* (1962) and Herbert Marcuse's *Eros and Civilization* (1956) and *One-Dimensional Man* (1964). Almost as a kind of inverted and internalised primitivism, there is an attraction to the pre- or non-technological aspect of humanity as it struggles to free itself from the stifling grip of the military-industrial-bureaucratic complex. So it is that critics have been able to write that the "Fifties was a time in which the whole structure of radicalism and conservatism, romanticism and stoicism, *the id and the ego*, seemed to be realigned" (Temperley and Bradbury 1981: 265; emphasis added). Thus the id comes to represent that which has been repressed but not eradicated by technological civilisation, while the need for its repression now becomes a matter for vigorous debate. Fittingly, science fiction of this period "moved from outer space to 'inner space.' It concerned itself not with journeys to outer planets but with journeys to the interior" (Kumar 1987: 404).

Science fiction and other forms of the fantastic are well suited to the revelation of the interior or the visualisation of the repressed, as Rosemary Jackson has noted:

> fantasy characteristically attempts to compensate for a lack resulting from cultural constraints: it is a literature of desire, which seeks that which is experienced as desire and loss./ In expressing desire, fantasy can operate in two ways (according to the different meanings of 'express'): it can *tell of*, manifest or show desire [...] or it can *expel* desire, when this desire is a disturbing element which threatens cultural order and continuity [...] In many cases fantastic literature fulfils both functions at once, for desire can be 'expelled' through having been 'told of' and thus vicariously experienced by author and reader. (Jackson 1981: 3-4)

Telotte rightly points to the troubled ambivalence on which the crisis of *Forbidden Planet* largely depends, though it is worth noting at once that Telotte's assumptions exclude (as do conventional views of the economy in the 1950s) the socially repressed: those for whom the supposed national prosperity and the claimed domestic access to technological products meant very little. It is important, also, to note that the projection of an external enemy provided a distraction from those internal elements which did not conform to the desired national image. These two processes – the identification and sustenance of an outward foe and the management of those within who did not fall into line – were exemplified by McCarthyism in particular and by the cold war in general. It is between these poles of exclusion and incorporation that the film operates in its navigation of attraction and repulsion. In this it echoes *The Tempest*, for there the portrayal of Caliban's plight shows the unattractive side of colonialism – "I lov'd thee And show'd thee all the qualities o' th' isle [...] and here you sty me/ In this hard rock, whiles you do keep from me The rest o' the island," Caliban complains to Prospero (I.iii.338-46) – even as colonial activity in fact proceeded. In both *The Tempest* and *Forbidden Planet* final liberation works ultimately in the ideology of the texts to justify the practice of repression which has subliminally been questioned.

Many critics have shown that an ambivalence towards technology is characteristic of science fiction. The genre allows both for an exploration of the positive potential of science and for a warning against possible consequences of its use or misuse. This dual perspective may be detected even in those examples of science fiction that do not foreground the issue. In an intelligent discussion of the genre, Mark Rose has sensibly argued against recomposing an early text like *Frankenstein* under the influence of a generic idea that did not come into being until well after it was written (1981: 5). He observes that "In any case, as the original name 'scientific romance' suggests, science fiction is perhaps most fruitfully regarded as a transformation of earlier forms of romance," and notes that "Wizards and magicians – Spenser's Archimago or Shakespeare's Prospero – are common in early forms of romance." Rose continues thus:

> Indeed, at the core of all romance forms appears to be a Manichean vision of the universe as a struggle between good and bad magic. [...] Time machines, rocket ships, and other technological wonders – all signs of the power of science – generally, but not always, function in science fiction as equivalents to white magic. Science is usually opposed by nature, and the narrative of science-fiction stories typically involves a struggle between mystified versions of science and nature conceived as ultimate antagonists. (Rose 1981: 7-9)

And so "Science [...] is often both humanity's magic and its magical opponent" (Rose 1981: 39). To this extent, further comparisons can be made between *The Tempest* and *Forbidden Planet*. Alden and Virginia Vaughan have noted that although the film "abandons Shakespeare's language entirely, its central conflict between the conveniences of technology and the terror of science's destructive power captures the serious elements of Prospero's magic" (1991: 200). Morbius's command to Adams to push the button that destroys Altair IV spectacularly removes the Krel's scientific achievements and their harmful projection of Morbius's inner self, while freeing Adams, his crew, and Altaira from further threat. We may be reminded here of Prospero's announcement that "this rough magic I here abjure" (V.i.50-51), a renunciation which liberates both Ariel and Caliban, and which is uttered when Prospero will be removing himself from the island and from any further plotting by Caliban. We have already heard of the strength of Prospero's magic in the service of colonialism when Caliban says in an aside: "I must obey: his Art is of such pow'r, It would control my dam's god, Setebos, And make a vassal of him" (I.ii.374-75).

Seeing science fiction as displacing religion and as representing a "secular transformation of religious concerns" (1981: 50), Rose points to what he discerns as a fundamental contradiction "between science fiction's materialistic ideology and its status as a romance form concerned with essentially religious material and committed to a vision of the world as a conflict between good and bad magic" (44). For the genre, he asserts, this is an empowering contradiction. Of the tension between spiritualistic and materialistic world views which he believes to be central to modern culture, he writes that it is "likely to become particularly evident" at times of "social stress such as the 1960s in the United States [...] as dissenters from the predominantly pragmatic and materialistic culture express their position by aligning themselves with various spiritualistic movements" (45). The stresses of the 1960s were already in evidence in the 1950s, the decade that saw the production of *Forbidden Planet*, a film which belongs to a genre whose main cultural function is to mediate between the spiritual and the material, the human and the non-human (45-49).

In the view of many critics, including Rose, science fiction provides a forum for the exploration of concerns about industrialism and technology. The ambivalence resulting from a widespread feeling that material benefits have been obtained at the cost of a connectedness with nature is reflected in the way that the genre treats the relationship of its human characters with its mechanical figures. Rose is only one critic to have traced this preoccupation back to the industrial revolution since

> As a genre science fiction comes into being not only as a medium for expression of the feeling of separation from physical nature, the alienated senses both of space and time, but also for the expression of the feeling of social disconnection that accompanied urbanization and industrialization. (141)

If the genre mediates in this way, then perhaps the most obvious image of how it does so is to be found in the element which frequently identifies it: the machine. Rose has written of this:

> The role of machines in science fiction is double. Machines typically mediate between the human and the nonhuman, serving as the agency through which man explores and protects himself from the cosmos. But at the same time, as versions of the nonhuman, machines may represent a threat to humane values. (139)

In *Forbidden Planet* ambivalence towards machines is central to the plot. Robby the robot, the Ariel-like figure, is man's servant. I use the gendered noun deliberately since, as some critics have observed, Robby performs those domestic tasks which – especially in 1950s America – had been identified as women's duties. Pete Boss argues that in occupying this role Robby usurps women's station and is thus a "threat to established notions of the sexual economy of the home" (1990: 60). According to Boss, this threat is further felt because Morbius's wife is dead (Boss thinks we are tempted to "speculate that Mrs Morbius has disappeared, not from natural causes but natural wastage") (60), and because the liberation of Altaira from the domestic activities now performed by Robby has freed her to gain a degree of knowledge and independence that embarrasses Adams and his companions. This, in my opinion, overestimates the extent to which Altaira is "presented to Adams as a problem of order" (61). It is true that Adams rescues Altaira from what seems to be the "'incorrect' incestuous affections of her father and the casual, extramarital involvements offered by the 'space-wolf' Lt Farman" (61), but Altaira's naïveté undermines the seriousness of any threat she may otherwise pose. The mocking of Altaira's social innocence is also a conservative kick against social declarations of female equality. In any case, the film makes it quite clear that the problem lies not with Robby's performance of Altaira's tasks but with Morbius's chilling insistence on her intellectual education at the expense of her emotional roundedness. Indeed, soon after Adams's acquaintance with Altaira, Morbius tries to reassure the Commander that Altaira will become fully human by saying that he supposes she will have to visit Earth one day for her "natural development." Altaira is not the grave threat Boss suggests she is, and the relative ease with which Adams,

Ferdinand-like, places himself as "the proper object of her affections" (62), demonstrates the smooth restoration of the hierarchies of gender and rank: he is, after all, the Commander.

The equivalence between women's and Robby's roles reinforces ideas of female servitude and therefore of man's mastery over machines and women. Peter Biskind has written that Robby "was the latest thing in labor-saving devices, a Waring Blender, Mixmaster, and Electrolux vacuum cleaner all rolled up into one" (1984: 106). The robot performs household tasks directly, allowing the woman to concentrate on other designated female tasks, including the instruction of this mechanical servant. When the spaceship's (male) cook wondered if the robot was male or female, he was told by Robby, who had been monitored to answer to this name for their convenience, "In my case, Sir, the question is totally without meaning." Robby's male voice seems to have led some critics to overlook this declaration, but it is important because in its desexing of technology it provides reassurance that greater technology need not overturn familiar gender roles.

On the other hand, the fact that it is technology in the form of the Krel's brain scanner that releases the Krel's and Morbius's id shows the inability of humanity to control machinery absolutely. The projection of the return of the repressed signals our failure to have machinery denature us completely. The resolution is a complex one. The natural, in the shape of the id, is monstrous and ought to be repressed. That it has not been kept subdued is a result of Morbius's ambition, which appears more selfish than Promethean. His obsessive and individualistic quest for knowledge is therefore seen as unnatural, emphasising the need for someone of humanity, like Adams (whose name suggests a new beginning), to exercise sane judgement over the machinery and its uses. This safe harnessing is witnessed in the escape of Adams and his crew from the planet. Inside their spaceship they watch the destruction of the planet on a television monitor.[7] Furthermore, the spaceship, as Boss notes (1990: 64), is itself navigated by Robby. This final accommodation with science, with technology "back in the driver's seat" (Biskind 1984: 111), seems to be

---

[7] I owe this last point to Mark Jancovich.

overlooked by Telotte (1989: 26-27), who reads the ending as one in which the characters and the narrative turn away from the alluring technology the film has earlier presented.

Morbius mediates between the human and the technological because he embodies them in extremis; as Rose has observed (1981: 177), "Apparently the epitome of cold intellect, the scientific reason embodied, Dr. Morbius is in fact a man of intense passions that he has never acknowledged." This is suggested not just by the film's narrative but by its visual arrangement: "a secret passage in [Morbius's] study opens to the underworld of the Krel machines, a vast subterranean realm of enormous power that suggests the hidden power of Morbius's mind" (177).[8] The implication is not that Morbius should indulge his passions but that he should acknowledge and therefore better control them, just as we have heard Prospero say of Caliban that "this thing of darkness I Acknowledge mine" (V.i.275-76). The better balanced Adams is able to accommodate both aspects of humanity, resulting in a convenient settlement of the questions raised in the film. It is hard not to conclude that in so doing the film is also reaching a reconciliation with contemporary fears that nuclear technology will obliterate the human species. The film's closure reassures us that, whatever the threats posed by mavericks, sensible and trustworthy leaders will reassert their authority to the benefit of all. At the same time, Altaira's education into female experience and her union with Adams comforts us that the machine age need not entail a denial of natural feeling though of course what we see here is a naturalization of an ideological view of how women should behave, with Altaira yielding herself physically and spiritually, body and soul. In these respects, the film both reflects and contains the two main anxieties about technological society in the 1950s.

There is another sense too in which *Forbidden Planet* works toward an accommodation with technology, and this becomes apparent when we consider it as a film, for film is itself a technological medium. The narrative is transmitted through applied technology:

---

[8] On images of the underground in relation to technology, see Williams 1990.

> in its foregrounded use and representation of technological hardware, the film is a showcase for the wonders of applied science, both through its futuristic speculation on the development of utility science – robots, space-ships, free and unlimited power-supplies – and in the advanced special effects commissioned by MGM to herald its typically prestigious entry into the field. This operates as part of a mutually reinforcing process, whereby barely plausible pseudo-scientific ideas draw an implicit authority from the state-of-the-art technology by which they are realised on film. This, in turn, allows judgements on the merits of the technology offered by the text to feed back into our perceptions of present-day developments. (Boss 1990: 59)

Viewers of the film are, simply by watching it, accepting the benefits of technology. As Pete Boss has observed, the visual representation of Morbius's monstrous id "offers a paradoxically triumphant aspect of technological endeavour" (1990: 64). If the repressed returns, it does so to be contained in the mode of telling. Anti-technological films, if not an oxymoron, are self-deluding. Biskind is undoubtedly right to say that the "emphasis on the monster from the id lets technology off the hook" (1984: 110), though to put it like this, as if technology could otherwise be blamed independently seems puzzling. He is less convincing when he writes that

> In *Forbidden Planet*, people betray technology, nature betrays culture. Trouble comes from 'human error.' [...] people are still imperfect, insufficiently machinelike. They harbor dark, irrational forces, primitive throwbacks to their natural origins. Neither Morbius nor the Krel, the race that knew too much, were up to their own technology. (Biskind 1984: 110)

In fact, the Krel are not human and neither, in his misanthropic aloofness, is Morbius. It is an anti-social, overly ambitious individual who has betrayed technology, and it is an alien race that has built that technology. There is no sign of a dangerously unstable id in any of Adams's crew. Indeed, their mild flirting with Altaira always leaves her in control, and when Adams orders her to dress and behave in a more becoming way her potential as a disruptive force vanishes. She is incorporated as her father enacts his own expulsion and expiration.

Adams's spaceship is a *United Planets* Cruiser. It is united by its crew's colour and gender. It roots out the non-conformist, forces him to recant and witnesses his death along with the fall of his empire.[9] It leaves with his daughter as a trophy whose willingness to depart is supposed to objectify its values, and it utilizes his science. Adams's men confront not only Morbius's id but Morbius *as* id. The id has been repressed. This Caliban has no language in which to curse or state his case. In this film, "force not therapy is the solution to the problems of the self" (Biskind 1984: 135). The forces of civilisation are free to continue their conquest and colonisation of space.

References

Biskind, Peter. 1984. *Seeing is Believing. How Hollywood Taught Us to Stop Worrying and Love the Fifties*. London: Pluto Press.

Boss, Pete. 1990. "Altair IV Revisited. *Forbidden Planet* (1956)." *Movie* (Winter 1990).

Brosnan, John. 1991. *The Primal Screen. A History of Science Fiction Film*. London: Orbit.

Freud, Sigmund. 1991a. "Civilization and Its Discontents." In A. Dickson, ed. *Civilization, Society and Religion*. Harmondsworth: Penguin Books.

—. 1991b. "The Ego and the Id." In A. Richards, ed. *On Metapsychology. The Theory of Psychoanalysis*. Harmondsworth: Penguin Books.

Hulme, Peter. 1992. *Colonial Encounters. Europe and the Native Caribbean 1492-1797*. London: Routledge.

---

[9] There is an echo here of Prospero's final recognition by Caliban (V.i.294-97), who "repudiates his claims *of his own volition*. [...] This is the wish-fulfilment of the European colonist: his natural superiority voluntarily recognized" (Hulme 1992: 132).

Jackson, Rosemary. 1981. *Fantasy. The Literature of Subversion.* London: Routledge.

Kermode, Frank, ed. 1964. *The Arden Edition of the Works of William Shakespeare. The Tempest* [1954]. London/New York: Routledge.

Kumar, Krishan. 1987. *Utopia and Anti-Utopia in Modern Times.* Oxford: Basil Blackwell

Marx, Leo. 1964. *The Machine in the Garden. Technology and the Pastoral Ideal in America.* Oxford: Oxford UP.

Miller, Arthur. 1961. *Death of a Salesman. Certain Private Conversations in Two Acts and a Requiem.* Harmondsworth: Penguin Books.

Rose, Mark. 1981. *Alien Encounters. Anatomy of Science Fiction.* Cambridge, MA.: Harvard UP.

Tarratt, Margaret. 1970. "Monsters from the id." *Films and Filming* (December 1970).

Telotte, J.P. 1989. "Science Fiction in Double Focus. *Forbidden Planet.*" *Film Criticism* 13: 3.

Temperley, Howard and Malcolm Bradbury. 1981. "War and Cold War." In M. Bradbury and H. Temperley, eds. *Introduction to American Studies.* London and New York: Longman.

Vaughan, Alden T. and Virginia Mason Vaughan. 1991. *Shakespeare's Caliban. A Cultural History.* Cambridge: Cambridge UP.

Williams, Rosalind. 1990. *Notes on the Underground. An Essay on Technology, Society and the Imagination.* Cambridge, MA: The MIT Press.

Caliban, Culture, and Nation-Building in the Caribbean

A. James Arnold

Postcolonial and neocolonial rewritings of Shakespeare's *Tempest* in the Caribbean region since the decade of decolonization in the 1960s will frame the present discussion. I shall leave out of consideration both George Lamming's *Pleasures of Exile* (1960), which was doubtless the first effort to appropriate *The Tempest* as a paradigm for understanding new relations of race, class, and nationhood in the Caribbean, and Roberto Fernández Retamar's "Calibán" (1971), which is treated elsewhere in this volume. The Martinican co-founder of the negritude movement, Aimé Césaire, gave a full-fledged treatment of the subject in 1969 in his *Une tempête, d'après "La tempête" de Shakespeare: Adaptation pour un théâtre nègre*, which has been translated as *"A Tempest" Based on Shakespeare's "The Tempest": Adaptation for a Black Theatre* (1986). The Barbadian poet-historian Edward – soon to be Kamau – Brathwaite included a poem entitled "Caliban" in his collection *Islands*, also published in 1969. Although Brathwaite did not yet know Césaire's play, his interpretation of Caliban as representative of the vast majority of the population of the Caribbean islands aligned itself neatly with the negritude vision he had found in Césaire's early poetry, notably in his *Cahier d'un retour au pays natal (Notebook of a Return to the Native Land)*, which functions as intertext in Brathwaite's "Caliban."

Black Cultural Nationalism and the Ideology of Roots

My real subject is the ideological investment that motivates Caribbean treatments of *The Tempest* in such a way as to present the dramatis personae as representative of the Caribbean nation, either in its immediate post-independence or post-revolution phase (Brathwaite) or in its prolonged neocolonial phase (Césaire). Both writers identify in one way or another with Caliban as the postcolonial subject of History. Prospero risks becoming a bit of a bore. For our authors Prospero is no longer the wizard who commands storms, unless these are cyclones of inappropriate technology and development or tourism schemes imported by the imperial powers. Indeed, Prospero in these Caribbean Tempests becomes allegorically reduced to one or another version of American imperialism, although Brathwaite maintains a British imperial presence by placing a purring Jupiter automobile next to a Chrysler in the second stanza of his poem "Caliban."

The first canto of Brathwaite's "Caliban" is largely devoted to an evocation of prerevolutionary Havana, with its officially sanctioned vice industry that catered to wealthy tourists from puritanical North America. The canto concludes with a superposition of three dates, the thrust of which is to tie the current plight of Caliban, as a symbol of the nation, to the history of the region since Columbus's first voyage. Here are the concluding lines of the first canto of "Caliban":

> It was December second, nineteen fifty-six.
> It was the first of August eighteen thirty-eight.
> It was the twelfth October fourteen ninety-two.
>
> How many bangs how many revolutions?[1]

---

[1] The glossary that accompanied the original edition of *Islands* in 1969 was reprinted as back matter in *The Arrivants: A New World Trilogy* (London: Oxford UP, 1973). In the new edition the glossary was meant to accompany *Rights of Passage* and *Masks* as well, which may explain the shift from "this poem," in 1969, to "these poems," in 1973 (p. 271).

The last date is universally recognized; the second – Emancipation Day in the ex-British West Indies – only slightly less so; the first in order is the date from which revolutionary Cuba dates its own history.

Césaire provided the historical frame for his play outside the text itself, in an interview that has been cited less than it deserves.[2] He related that in rewriting the roles of Caliban and Ariel for his *Tempest* [...] *for a Black Theatre* he thought about the Black Power movement and Martin Luther King, Jr. Thus, the allegorizing thrust of the play pulls it in the direction of the struggle for racial equality and civil rights in the U.S. Given the fact that the Black Power movement was making serious inroads in the English-speaking Caribbean at the precise moment when Césaire wrote his *Tempest,* and given that Edward Brathwaite's name change to Kamau is part and parcel of that same movement, we find a quite remarkable ideological alignment of Brathwaite and Césaire with respect to the cultural remapping of Caribbean societies, implicitly or explicitly, in the work of both writers at this date.

It is in rewriting the role of Ariel that our authors reveal the orientation of their cultural project most clearly. Quite curiously, from the U.S. perspective Césaire claimed to have in mind, he labelled his Caliban "A black slave," which is fair enough, but his Ariel is called "A mulatto slave." It is important for our purposes here to recognize that, although a mulatto middle class has long existed in the U.S., even and perhaps especially during the long period of *de jure* racial segregation, in recent history mulatto has not been an operative term in U.S. discourse on ethnicity, which has broken down into a rigorous manichaean opposition of white and black (whatever the preferred term signifying *black* may have been at a given moment). In other words, even if we credit Césaire's claim that his Caliban is in some sense a "Malcolm X" figure and his Ariel a "Martin Luther King, Jr." figure, they are made to play these roles out according to

[2] Césaire discussed at length his conception of Ariel and Caliban in his interview with Lucien Attoun, published in *Le théâtre 1970-'71* (1971: 99-116). René Richard developed this material in "Césaire et Shakespeare: *Une tempête* de Césaire et *La tempête* de Shakespeare," published in *Actes du colloque sur le théâtre négro-africain* (1971: 126-27).

the Caribbean script that assigns more or less specific values to the race *and* class designations of blacks and mulattos respectively. I shall use the term *ethnoclass* to describe this phenomenon.

Césaire had, however, correctly understood that the Black Power movement, even in the Nation of Islam version that Malcolm X embraced for a time, was the historical heir to his own negritude project of the 1940s (Arnold 1986). At the end of the 1960s and the beginning of the 1970s the Black Power term *bourgies* (for bourgeois) was levelled at the established Negro middle class, as it was then designated in the U.S. Insofar as Dr. Martin Luther King, Jr. had emerged as a prominent member of that class and as the foremost proponent of non-violent integration into the capitalist system in the United States, he effectively resembled for Césaire, and for many other like-minded Caribbean intellectuals, members of the mulatto ethnoclass whose interests were best served by influencing the direction taken by the existing socioeconomic system. This Marxian analysis, as I have already suggested, has several points in common with Brathwaite's cultural nationalist project.

Whereas Césaire marginalizes the mulatto figure in his *Tempest*, making Ariel little more than a flunkey, the agent of Prospero's trickery with no part to play in an eventual liberation of the island, Brathwaite elides this figure altogether in the opening lines of his poem "Caliban":

> Ninety-five per cent of my people poor
> ninety-five per cent of my people black
> ninety-five per cent of my people dead
> you have heard it all before, O Leviticus O Jeremiah O
> Jean-Paul Sartre. (191)

From his *Development of Creole Society in Jamaica* (1971) to *Contradictory Omens* (1974) and on to the poems of *X/Self* (1987) Brathwaite has made clear what he means by his unlikely "Ninety-five per cent" figure, which bears no relation to the demographics of, say, Trinidad or Guyana. For Brathwaite as for Césaire, the *essential* or core element in Creole society is the black element, which should be considered normative in all aspects of national culture. As he put it in *Contradictory Omens*, "the acceptance of the culture of this black ex-African majority as the paradigm and norm for the entire society" (1977: 30) is necessary for cultural wholeness in Jamaican society.

Black cultural nationalism, formulated either as Martinican negritude or as the Nation-language project propounded by Brathwaite, is exemplary of Roots thinking. The paradigmatic situation for Roots thinking about nation and culture is the type of tree whose great taproot plunges deep into the soil from which it draws its sustenance. The taproot rhetorically figures ethnicity conceived as a unique origin or stock from which all positive value is supposed to derive. Once we describe the paradigm in terms of its indispensable elements, we can better see how it functions as a response to the Eurocentric paradigm to which the old imperial powers, and the neocolonial powers of today, habitually refer. The other feature of the taproot paradigm of nation and culture that requires mention here is its totalitarian logic, by which I mean its tendency to exclude all sources of positive value other than those presumed to belong to one's own ethnic stock. This feature underlies Brathwaite's discourse on creole society and culture, as it underlay the negritude ethos Césaire had worked out on the eve of World War II. It leads to such "logical" conclusions as Brathwaite's referring to East Indian West Indians in *Contradictory Omens*, a witty form of exclusion from the true nation. (In *Contradictory Omens* Brathwaite in fact considers the Indo- and Sino-Caribbean populations under "Post-Emancipation Problems," thus signifying that they cannot be true Creoles.) The same features of exclusion were present in a paper tabled at the inaugural meeting of the Australian Association for Caribbean Studies, where an early version of this article was read. Steve Spencer, in a paper on "The Arena of Test Cricket: The Struggle for Ethnic Domination in Guyana," followed the lead of the Guyanese social scientist Ralph Premdas in referring to Afro-Guyanese as Africans ([forthcoming]: 2). The totalitarian logic I have just described represents an extreme form of the binarism familiar to specialists of postcolonial cultures. It is, I believe, a historically conditioned response to the logic of the colonizer.

Césaire and Brathwaite: Intertexts

Brathwaite's poem "Caliban" exhibits in its structure – and in its place within the poetic economy of *Islands* – other features that tie it to Césaire's negritude vision. "Caliban" has three numbered sections. The passages cited earlier all occur in the first section, which is more descriptive than the other two. Section one represents the colonial period up to 1956 and ends on the question: "How many bangs how many revolutions?" (35). Section two is choppy and rhythmically insistent, by contrast, as it develops the persona of the contemporary Caliban as a Carnival reveller who "like to play/ pan/ at the Car-/ nival" (35). This section is punctuated by images of the ship, the "[...] ship/ where his free-/ dom drown" (36), which the reader takes to be a reenactment of the crossing of the Middle Passage. From the evocation of the (slave) ship in the historical past, the poem's second section moves to a paroxystic image that unites Carnival with spiritually significant physical movement: "dip-/ ping down/ and the black/ gods call-/ ing back/ he falls/ through the water's/ cries/ down/ down/ down/ where the music hides/ him/ down/ down/ down/ where the si-/ lence lies" (36).

At this point the second section ends. The third and final section dramatizes the limbo dance that section two had rhythmically and metaphorically evoked. The author made a recording of *Islands* for Argo Records in 1973. On that recording Brathwaite sings in a thin, high voice the passages of section three that are printed in italic in the published text (37-38). Section three, then, renders explicit and actualizes as performance the metaphoric and rhythmic strength that had built up in the central part of the poem: "And limbo stick is the silence in front of me/ [...] / *limbo/ limbo like me/* long dark deck and the silence is over me/ [...] / stick is the whip and the dark deck is slavery [...]" (37). The limbo dance, as enacted poetically by the voice, thus becomes the agency of spiritual transformation. Caliban's going down to the beat of the Carnival pan in part two is finally linked to the gods of Africa, who are the agents of transformation of the new Creole self even before arrival in the New World: "down/ down/ down// and the drummer is calling me// *limbo/ limbo like me//* sun coming up/ and the drummers are praising me// out of the dark/ and the dumb gods are raising me" (38).

The short, final movement of section three opposes an abrupt, affirmative elevation of the new self to the old. Immediately after "and the dumb gods are raising me," we read: "up/ up/ up// and the music is saving me// hot/ slow/ step// on the burning ground" (38). The now upright speaker steps onto the burning ground of the new land, having received his spiritual renewal from the gods of Africa. On this note the poem ends.

Césaire's long poem *Cahier d'un retour au pays natal* (*Notebook of a Return to the Native Land*) has an identical structure. In *Modernism and Negritude: The Poetry and Poetics of Aimé Césaire* I demonstrated that this foundational text of the negritude movement has a tripartite structure that presents the agonistic transformation of the speaker and his society from a physical, metaphysical, and historical position of horizontality (flat, passive, immanent) through a central transformation of the speaker that is metaphorically figured by a going down (just as in Brathwaite's "Caliban"), and a spiritual crisis preparatory to an abrupt rising up on the deck and in the very rigging of the slave ship. The final section, marked by exclusive images of verticality, transcendence, and potency, prefigures Brathwaite's "Caliban" quite clearly (Arnold 1981: 165). An intertextual reading suggests a further, formal intention with respect to "Caliban"'s placement within *Islands*. In the original edition of 1969 the author signalled his formal intention that *Islands* be read as one long poem in five cantos, as follows: I. New World; II. Limbo; III. Rebellion; IV. Possession; V. Beginning. "Caliban" is the third of six texts in the Limbo canto, which is itself concerned with the transformative experience of the limbo dance. "Caliban" is also a *mise en abyme* of the structure of both the Limbo canto and the entire long poem. The transformation of the Afro-Caribbean Caliban's consciousness through his contact with the old gods of Africa has prepared him to tread the "burning ground" of the New World. "Caliban" radiates out in all directions from its crucial position within the long poem, providing a concentrated source of dramatized history and a locus of value for the culture hero of the black Creole struggle to come.

Brathwaite's "Caliban" and the long poem *Islands* of which it is such a crucial part are heroic in the same sense that Césaire's negritude poetry of the 1940s had been heroic. The enemy is readily identifiable. Only the spiritually transformed Afro-Caribbean hero, black and male, can

effectively challenge him. As we have already seen, all the black male
Other's others are written out of the historical struggle.

Caliban, Miranda, and Sycorax in Brathwaite's Essays

Shakespeare's Caliban was to become an archetypal figure for Brathwaite
between the publication of *Islands* in the late 1960s and the early 1980s. A
series of lectures he gave at the Centre for Commonwealth Literature and
Research of the University of Mysore, India, in 1982 repeatedly returned
to the dramatis personae of Shakespeare's *Tempest* as an interpretive grid
through which to read Caribbean history and the history of its literature.
Thus, in "An Alternative View of Caribbean History" (1984) Brathwaite
reads the entire history of the colonization, the people, and the resultant
culture of the Caribbean allegorically with reference to *The Tempest*.
Concerning Caliban's failure to make the revolution on Prospero's island,
we learn that it is, in the first instance, Miranda's fault:

> And the person who is given the responsibility for
> teaching Caliban the language is Prospero's daughter,
> Miranda, which introduces another factor into the
> equation: Here is a young woman who is used as a kind
> of broker to encourage Caliban to move away from his
> mother culture, his mother language, and toward the
> language and culture of Prospero. And as a result, when
> Caliban attempts a revolt against Prospero, Prospero is
> able to anticipate the nature of that revolt [...]. (45)

Miranda is not the only female agent in Caliban's dilemma. Brathwaite
posits a choice not made, and a crucial error committed, by Caliban:

> Of course Caliban can also remember his own mother's
> language. And that's where the debate about the use of
> dialect, whatever worth is given to it, becomes crucial.
> Because, we in the Third World have English as an
> official language, English as a language of education,
> English as a language of interpretation. But all of us still
> retain, to a greater or lesser degree, the language of the

mother; and as artists we do have the responsibility of choice. We do not have to use only Prospero's language in our efforts to understand ourselves, and to express ourselves; we still have the mother's milk of language to fall back on. (45)

At this point in Brathwaite's argument, the focus shifts to Sycorax, Caliban's mother, who is identified as the potential transmitter of an alternative culture. She is "an archetype for our protest [...] [and] [...] the kind of woman, that is very common [...] to all parts of the Third World" (44):

> Here is this woman who is the carrier, the keeper, the protector of the native culture. She possessed this island and she gave birth to her son Caliban, who was then impris[o]ned and indentured to Prospero. The woman herself, Sycorax, was banished, she was imprisoned, but the point about her is that she became submerged... Now applied to culture, this woman Sycorax has not been able to contribute to Caribbean culture, but she still carries within herself, she still carries in a submerged manner, the very essence of the native culture. Sycorax, in other words, carries the secrets of a possible alternative culture for the Caribbean. (44)

This very stimulating evocation of Sycorax as the potential matrix or womb of cultural renewal in the Caribbean might have opened onto a longer development of the role of women in the Caribbean and the Third World. It did not; rather, Brathwaite's Indian audience in Mysore heard, and later read, that "[Sycorax] becomes a paradigm for all women of the Third World, who have not yet, despite all the effort, reached that trigger of visibility which is necessary for a whole society. Most of our women are not given the same kind of natural privileges that men have, and most of our women are not given opportunities to express themselves fully outside of the domestic framework. We know this in your country and we know this in ours in different ways" (44).

In short, the paradigmatic Sycorax must still, throughout the Third World at the beginning of the 1980s, tend the home fires and communicate nation language to all her little Calibans through her mother's milk. To the extent that the paradigmatic Sycorax, fundamental and even primary with respect to Caliban, communicates only through her mother's milk, then her role as an agent of cultural change in fact collapses into a purely natural function. Even Sycorax, although she is the mother of Caliban, can only communicate *naturally* to her son the elements he will need to become the sole, gendered agent of change in postcolonial society. The tendency to push Sycorax back into her natural function as mother suggests that, within Brathwaite's discourse, the day when she will realize her own *cultural* potential in the Third World may never come. Thus, in the debate over the respective roles of nature and culture, Caliban is on the side of culture once again, whereas Sycorax finds herself relegated to the familiar role of nature. If we read the destiny of Sycorax side by side with Brathwaite's condemnation of Miranda as an agent of imperialism, it becomes apparent that the women in the play are, in one way or another, pushed into the background despite Brathwaite's best avowed intentions.

From Roots to Rhizomes

The Roots paradigm, although literary in the first instance, makes claims for the nation-building process in the contemporary Caribbean. It describes what Benedict Anderson (1983) has called "imagined communities." The Roots paradigm as it is manifested in Césaire's and Brathwaite's treatment of Caliban represents a clear failure to imagine the nation (in Anderson's sense) as something more inclusive than one's own ethnoclass. The basic problem with Fernández Retamar's vision (1989) is that everything depends upon the success of the revolution, which is supposed to sweep away all class distinctions. Apart from the grave doubts that have arisen in the wake of actual socialist revolutions in this century, peoples of color have had legitimate concerns over the absolute subordination of race or ethnicity to social class. Indeed, Aimé Césaire resigned from the Communist Party of France in 1956 over this very issue.

In the decade of the 1980s a new paradigm for imagining the Caribbean nation with a more inclusive sense of *communitas* emerged. The Cuban novelist and essayist Antonio Benítez-Rojo and the Martinican poet, novelist, and essayist Edouard Glissant wrote important essays that propounded a rhizomous theory of cultural identity. Both writers explicitly envisaged their conception of the nation in opposition to the binarism we found in Césaire and Brathwaite's readings of *The Tempest*. Here is the rather highly imaged and literary description of the rhizome state offered by Benítez-Rojo in *La isla que se repite* (1989), translated as *The Repeating Island* (1992):

> The rhizome state can be understood starting from the rhizome of the vegetable world. It is a botanical anomaly if compared to a tree. It is subterranean, but it is not a root. It sends out multiplications in all directions. It is a labyrinth in process. It can be understood also as a burrow, or as the system of tunnels in an anthill. It is a world of connections and of trips without limits or propositions. In a rhizome one is always in the middle, between the Self and the Other. But, above all, it should be seen as a nonsystematic system of lines of flight and alliance that propagate themselves ad infinitum (Benítez Rojo 1992: 291, n.24).

Elsewhere in the same book Benítez-Rojo acknowledges his debt to the French philosophers Gilles Deleuze and Félix Guattari, from whom he borrowed the notion of the rhizome. In *Poétique de la relation* (A Poetics of Relating, 1990), Glissant makes the same point in slightly less highly imaged language, as follows:

> Gilles Deleuze and Félix Guattari have criticized the notion of *root* and [...] of *rootedness*. The root is unique; it is the stock that takes everything to itself and kills all around it. Over against this notion they set the rhizome, which is a multiple root, spreading in fibrous systems through the earth or the air, without any stock developing into an inevitable predator. Thus the notion of *rhizome* would maintain the fact of being rooted but would challenge the idea of a totalitarian root. Rhizomous thought would refer to what I call a poetics of Relating, according to which all identity extends itself in relation to an Other. (Glissant 1990: 23)

I cannot develop these notions here in the detail they deserve. They have been fully worked out by Keith A. Sprouse and Román de la Campa in a literary history of the Caribbean that is currently in press. The rhizome theory of identity, as put forward by Glissant and Benítez-Rojo, is not a utopian vision. There is no incompatibility between the conceptualization of Caribbean identity as a rhizomous state and the manifestly conflictual relations that pertain between ethnic groups and social classes throughout the region. The most important point to be made is that the rhizome paradigm offers a way out of the deadly oppositions that binary logic traps us in, whether the specific model be Eurocentric, Afrocentric, or Indocentric.

In the recently completed introduction to *Monsters, Tricksters, and Sacred Cows* (a volume I edited with the help of a dozen cultural anthropologists, historians, and literary comparatists) I argued this same point at greater length, citing a literary example of this process from the Eastern Caribbean. In the sub-plot of Earl Lovelace's novel *The Dragon Can't Dance* (1979), one finds just the sort of conflictual representation of nationhood centering on ethnicity that has, to my mind, real critical value in the postcolonial world. Lovelace's representation of the fortunes of the "Indian" couple, Boya and Dolly Pariag, in counterpoint to the evolution of the black Creole residents of Calvary Hill goes through stages of extreme suspicion, violent rejection, and eventual grudging acceptance. *The Dragon Can't Dance* also contains a fictionalized critique of the Roots paradigm of nationhood in the farcical representation of the bad johns on the corner taking over a police jeep and issuing confused Black Power slogans as they cruise around Port-of-Spain until they literally run out of gas. We may take this to be a reply to Brathwaite's reading of *The Tempest* as well as a reply to Césaire.[3]

---

[3] In two of Earl Lovelace's plays one finds echoes of Césaire's *Cahier/Notebook* that, taken together, testify to an ongoing engagement with his work. In *Jestina's Calypso* the phrase "You have come home to your native land," spoken by one character to another, suggested the title of the poem. However, in *The New Hardware Store* the reference to "Amazons [...] Dahomey, prince of Ghana, doctor of Timbuktu" replicates intertextually this passage in the *Cahier/Notebook*: "No, we have never been *amazons* of the king of *Dahomey*, nor *princes of Ghana* [...] nor

Finally, a shift of critical vision away from the old ethnoclass paradigm of culture and the nation toward a rhizomous one will certainly involve a reordering of the value judgments we have placed on many Caribbean literary works of the recent past. In order to present a convincing example of literature that corresponds to the rhizomous paradigm I was obliged to abandon Caribbean rewritings of *The Tempest*. My best judgment on this point is that rewritings of *The Tempest*, which were most fruitful in holding up a mirror to the Eurocentric and imperial discourse of the colonial past, have now largely run their course.[4] I expect that in future Caribbean artists and writers who appeal to a more inclusive sense of *communitas* will do so on the basis of popular culture models such as Carnival, as Lovelace did in *The Dragon Can't Dance*.

References

Anderson, Benedict. 1983. *Imagined Communities. Reflections on the Origin and Spread of Nationalism*. London: Verso.

Arnold, A. James. 1981. *Modernism and Negritude. The Poetry and Poetics of Aimé Césaire*. Cambridge/Massachusetts/London: Harvard UP.

—. 1986. "Les Afro-Américains et Césaire. Un exemple de transculturation double." *L'Amérique et l'Europe: Réalités et représentations* 2: 63-74.

—. "Monsters, Tricksters, and Sacred Cows." Forthcoming in *Monsters, Tricksters, and Sacred Cows*. New World Studies. Charlottesville/London: UP of Virginia.

[doctors] in *Timbuctoo*." The Césaire quotation is taken from the Emile Snyder translation of the *Notebook* (Paris: Présence Africaine, 1971: 96; emphasis added). Compare the Lovelace quotations in *Jestina's Calypso & Other Plays* (1984: 36, 72).

[4] A world of explanation is in order here. The appropriations of *The Tempest* I have discussed in this article are exemplary of Counter-Modernism, to use Theo D'haen's term (in "(Post)Modernity and Caribbean Discourse," forthcoming). I plan to develop elsewhere the notion that D'haen's Counter-Modernism correlates to Roots responses to *The Tempest*, whereas D'haen's notion of Counter-Postmodernism would gain by being correlated to rhizomous visions of culture in the Caribbean and in the Caribbean diaspora.

Benítez-Rojo, Antonio. 1992. *The Repeating Island. The Caribbean and the Postmodern Perspective*. Durham/New York: Duke UP.

Brathwaite, Edward. 1969. *Islands*. London: Oxford UP.

—. 1977. *Contradictory Omens* [1974]. Savacou Monograph N.°1. Mona: Savacou Publications.

—. 1984. "An Alternative View of Caribbean History." In *The Colonial Encounter. Language*. Powre Above Powres 7. University of Mysore: Center for Commonwealth Literature and Research, 43-65.

Campa, Román de la. "The Discourse on Theory in the Caribbean. Benítez-Rojo and Glissant." Forthcoming in A. James Arnold, ed. *A History of Literature in the Caribbean*, Vol. III. Amsterdam/Philadelphia: John Benjamins.

Césaire, Aimé. 1969. *Une tempête d'après "La tempête" de Shakespeare. Adaptation pour un théâtre nègre*. Paris: Seuil. Translated into English by Richard Miller as *A Tempest Based on Shakespeare's "The Tempest". Adaptation for a Black Theatre* [1986]. New York: Ubu Repertory Theater Productions.

—. 1971. *Le théâtre 1970-'71*. Paris: Bourgois.

D'haen, Theo. "(Post)Modernity and Caribbean Discourse." Forthcoming in A. James Arnold, ed. *A History of Literature in the Caribbean*, Vol. III. Amsterdam/Philadelphia: John Benjamins.

Fernández Retamar, Roberto. 1989. *Caliban and Other Essays* [1971]. Translated by Edward Baker. Minneapolis: U. of Minnesota P.

Glissant, Edouard. 1990. *Poétique de la relation*. Paris: Gallimard.

Lovelace, Earl. 1984. *Jestina's Calypso & Other Plays*. Caribbean Writers Series 32. London: Heinemann.

Richard, René. 1971. "Césaire et Shakespeare: *Une tempête* de Césaire et *La tempête* de Shakespeare." In *Actes du colloque sur le théâtre négro-africain*. Paris: Présence Africaine.

Spencer, Steve. [1995]. *The Arena of Test Cricket. The Struggle for Ethnic Dominance in Guyana*. Unpublished paper tabled at the inaugural conference of the Australian Association for Caribbean Studies, held at Queensland University, 12-15 July 1995.

Countering Caliban

Fernández Retamar and the Postcolonial Debate

Nadia Lie

> *What a sobering and inspiring thing it is therefore not just to read one's own side [...].*

> (Edward Said, *Culture and Imperialism*)

In 1971 an essay entitled "Calibán" appeared in the Cuban journal *Casa de las Américas.*[1] It had been written by the journal's editor-in-chief Roberto Fernández Retamar (Havana, °1930) and soon gained a very wide circulation in Latin America and beyond. The article's success can be attributed to its polemic character, and to its programmatic promise of a form of literary criticism which would take into account Latin America's specific cultural identity. It is largely due to this programmatic aspect that the article has managed to withstand the ravages of time. Stronger, "Calibán" has turned into the figure-head of "la nueva crítica

[1] I would like to thank Jürgen Pieters, Kristine Vanden Berghe and Peter Venmans for their critical comments on this essay. An earlier version was read carefully by Bruno Bosteels.

latinoamericana," an influential movement which explicitly prefers a more
contextual approach to text-immanent interpretation.

In recent years, however, the essay has acquired yet a new dimension:
Retamar[2] has increasingly become associated with "postcolonial" thinkers
such as Edward Said and Gayatri C. Spivak. On the back of the 1989
English book translation of "Calibán," Retamar is praised for his
"meticulous efforts to dismantle Eurocentric colonial and neocolonial
thought," and in his foreword Fredric Jameson considers "Calibán" to be
"the Latin American equivalent of Said's *Orientalism*" (viii). Six years later,
in an interview published in *Critical Inquiry*, Retamar is placed alongside
Fanon as "one of the precursors of what has come to be known as
postcolonial discourse" (Diana and Beverley 1995: 421).[3]

In a recent reader, postcolonial studies are presented as "based in the
'historical fact' of European colonialism, and the diverse material effects to
which this phenomenon gave rise" (Ashcroft e.a. 1995: 2). There is much
diversity of opinion as to the precise chronological and geographical
significance of "postcolonialism," but thematically speaking, especially
"the confrontation between colonized and colonizing culture" or
"between margin and centre" is highlighted (D'haen 1993: 12). Next to a
specific research domain, postcolonialism attempts to offer a series of
"alternative reading practices" (Ashcroft e.a. 1989: 45) through a critical
and "oppositional" way of reading texts (Slemon 1995a: 45). Two concepts
are central to this reading: the contextual-social embeddedness of texts and
the status of the Other. Both concepts are fundamentally connected: the
alternative reading approach views the contextual dimension as essentially
having to do with power (Skura 1991: 222), and power involves processes
of image (de-)formation with regard to races and cultures (Bhabha 1992:
437). The task of a postcolonial critic then is to check how literary,
scientific and other texts in their "worldliness" (Said 1984) form part of

---

[2] A condensed form of his family name, which is *Fernández* Retamar, will be used
in this essay.

[3] Even though he does not explicitly object to this association, Retamar remarks:
"The world as we know it is not so much postcolonial as neocolonial" (Diana and
Beverley 1995: 421).

"the mechanics of the constitution of the Other" (Spivak 1993: 90), and to allow the suppressed voices to speak again (Said 1984: 53).

To illustrate what an oppositional reading practice can yield, the example of *The Tempest* is often cited. To Ashcroft e.a. (1989: 190), *The Tempest* is "perhaps the most important text used to establish a paradigm for post-colonial readings of canonical works." The alternative reading strategies that were applied to it by people like Brown (1985), Hulme (1985, 1986) and Greenblatt (1988, 1990a, 1990b) re-site this "timeless" work as part of a broader "colonial" discourse, and Prospero and Caliban are turned into a kind of archetypal colonizer and colonized.[4] Yet, such re-siting has always been with us, if not in the critical centre, then in the creative periphery, viz. in the form of critical, "counter-canonical" (Tiffin 1992) rewritings of *The Tempest*: African and Caribbean writers have long reconsidered Shakespeare's masterpiece through the eyes of the oppressed Caliban. The fact that the periphery has thus preceded the centre has given rise to a conviction referred to implicitly or explicitly in many postcolonial books: people from the margin are better, more attentive readers, because, being direct victims of oppression, they are more sensitive to "refractory places" in literary works (Barker and Hulme 1985: 204) or to "false universality claims" in literary theories (Ashcroft e.a. 1989: 12). Thus, little by little a kind of reversal of terms has developed. After having stood in the shade of the centre for many decades, the margin now suddenly appears as the outstanding place for reflection on literature and literary criticism. It therefore comes as no surprise that postcolonialism has lately made a thorough search for forerunners of its ideas in what used to be called "the Third World" (Williams and Chrisman 1994: 15). And that is how post-colonialism came across someone like Retamar.

Being a critical rethinking of *The Tempest* and at the same time a representative voice from the margin, Retamar's "Calibán" assumes a

---

[4] These alternative readings are sometimes also associated with "new historicism." According to Meredith Anne Skura, the link between *The Tempest* and the New World was already established at the beginning of the nineteenth century, but the new historicists go further than that and "claim that the New World material is not just present but is right at the centre of the play" (1992: 222).

privileged position in the debate. Even Edward Said, generally considered to be the founding father of postcolonialism, acknowledges the essay, and treats it as an example of what he calls "the culture of resistance" that originated in the (ex-)colonies as a reaction against "imperialism" (Said 1994: 275-78). Said's own oppositional reading practice, which he himself prefers to call "contrapuntal," however, is mainly reserved for the (many) Western masterpieces which he discusses. This in itself legitimate corpus demarcation might inadvertently convey the impression that voices from the "margin" dispose of a kind of ideological virginity, that they are less "worldly" than Western texts. In the following analysis, I will therefore approach Retamar's "Calibán" not so much as a "postcolonial text," but rather as a document that can be analyzed by means of "postcolonial reading strategies." My attitude towards postcolonialism as a literary-theoretical movement will thus resemble the attitude of postcolonial critics towards Western theory: I will not repudiate it, but recycle it for new use (Ashcroft e.a. 1989: 168).

Latin America as a Cultural Community

"Calibán" presents itself as an essay on cultural identity. Starting from a question put by a European journalist, "Does a Latin American culture exist?" (3), Retamar advances two propositions. The first proposition claims that Latin America does indeed have a specific cultural identity which distinguishes it from all other continents. The second proposition has it that, as a culture area, Latin America shows two diametrically opposed traditions: one of denying its cultural identity, and one of affirming it.

Retamar's first proposition constitutes a reaction to the repeatedly surfacing belief that Latin America is a mere reflection of Western European culture because its inhabitants speak Spanish and Portuguese. Retamar endorses the claim that Latin America suffered intense linguistic colonization, but also argues that these Western languages, together with the conceptual apparatus that is linked to it, are being used in Latin America's very own way. In this respect, Caliban forms the most adequate symbol of Latin-American culture: Caliban learns to speak thanks to Prospero, but at the same time he uses this knowledge to curse Prospero.

Or, to put it in Caliban's own words as cited by Retamar (6): "You taught me language, and my profit on't/ Is, I know how to curse. The red plague rid you/ For learning me your language!" (I.ii.362-64).

The second proposition amounts to a critique of those who present Latin-American culture as a homogeneous or at least harmonious whole. Once again using *The Tempest* as an analogy, Retamar considers Latin America to be the setting of the conflict between Prospero and Caliban over the rightful ownership of the island. This time Prospero symbolizes the imperialist invader and Caliban represents the wrongfully oppressed people. Retamar wants Latin-American writers and intellectuals to take the side of the suffering people of the continent, or, in other words, to take Caliban's side. Caliban thus becomes a two-fold symbol: he refers to a certain social class (group) – the "people" opposed to the "exploiters" – but at the same time also to a cultural community – "Latin America." Latin-American writers and intellectuals in turn are associated with yet another character from *The Tempest*: Ariel.[5] He is the one that has to choose between Prospero and Caliban, in favour of or against the invader, in favour of or opposed to Latin America.[6] If he chooses for Latin America and rejects the invader, he belongs to the real culture of the continent, if not, to the "anti-America" of the westernized, colonial writers. Both traditions are to be found on Latin-American territory, but, says Retamar, they are radically irreconcilable.

Similar to what is done in some postcolonial readings of *The Tempest*, then, Retamar relocates a character that was traditionally seen as rather marginal in the plot, i.e. Caliban, as central to the story. He considers

---

[5] Retamar explicitly borrows this interpretation from Aníbal Ponce and Aimé Césaire.

[6] According to Retamar, "There is no real Ariel-Caliban polarity" (1989: 28). Basing herself on this passage, Spivak claims that "Retamar locates both Caliban and Ariel in the postcolonial intellectual" (1985: 245). The exclusive symbol of the intellectual, however, is Ariel, and if anything is "located" in Ariel, it is the *conflict* between Caliban and Prospero. There are other points of Spivak's reading of Retamar's essay that are rather problematic, as has been indicated by Retamar himself (1993: 240).

Caliban not as the disobedient slave, but rather as the oppressed native. He sees him not as "the wrong side" of the piece, but rather as "the other side" (Nixon 1987: 575). Retamar, however, goes even further than that and, via a gesture which he terms the "dialectics of Caliban," he attempts to identify with the distorted picture given by Caliban's Other, i.e. Prospero, to turn it into a "mark of glory" (16). His identification is primarily based on the verbal behaviour of Caliban, "the curse," but also on the name "Caliban," which via the anagram "cannibal" would directly refer to the Caribbean.[7] What's more, Retamar pays attention to the role of Ariel in *The Tempest*: the story could have turned out differently if Ariel had chosen Caliban's side, instead of Prospero's. If one looks at it from that angle, Retamar's essay constitutes a "counter-canonical strategy" towards Shakespeare's play in two ways. First, he claims the negative symbol of otherness as the symbol of identity. Second, he presents *The Tempest* as a "possible" story, the end of which is connected with Ariel's position. In this way, *The Tempest* becomes a play dealing with intellectual responsibility, with choices.

However, Retamar's "Calibán," next to a reaction to *The* Tempest, is just as much a reaction to another text, viz. to *Ariel* (1900) by the Uruguayan writer José Enrique Rodó. Rodó sees in Ariel the true symbol of Latin America; Caliban, on the other hand, only represents the imperialistic Northern part of the continent. The background to this comparison is that Ariel is equated with art and spirituality, while Caliban is considered a materialistically inclined Philistine. With his essay, Retamar wants to pay homage to his Uruguayan predecessor, the centenary of whose birth was being commemorated in 1971, the year of publication of "Calibán." Nevertheless, Retamar also states quite plainly that Rodó is mistaken as to the symbols used, even though Rodó's essay is equally anti-imperialistic. "Our symbol then is not Ariel, as Rodó thought, but rather Caliban. This

---

[7] "More important than this is the knowledge that Caliban *is* our Carib" (Retamar 1989: 9). According to Vaughan and Vaughan (1991: 146), this directly referential interpretation gives Retamar's essay a unique position within the "Third World interpretation" which is "symbolic, not historic"; "it adopts Caliban for what he represents to the observer, not for what Shakespeare may have had in mind".

is something that we, the *mestizo* inhabitants of these same isles where Caliban lived, see with particular clarity" (14).[8]

As a "counter-canonical" essay, then, "Calibán" has to be analyzed in a dual perspective: not only as "countering" a Western masterpiece – the usual approach in postcolonial studies, but likewise "countering" a non-Western essay. This immediately makes clear that, at least as far as Retamar's "Calibán" is concerned, a concept like "master-piece" does not only apply to the literature of the old colonial power, but likewise to Latin America's own literature. The double intertextuality invoked moreover has immediate repercussions on the interpretation of "Calibán": as a rethinking of *The Tempest*, Caliban is opposed to Prospero, that is, if one follows the colonizing reading of Retamar's time. In the Latin-American tradition, however, the name "Caliban" immediately evokes that of "Ariel." Such being the case, it should not come as a surprise to find the final section of the essay entitled "And Ariel now?"

The Padilla-Affair

The question about Ariel should be linked to the specific circumstances in which Retamar's essay was written, or, to put it differently, it should be related to its own immediate "context." As was said before, the interaction between text and context forms an important topic in all readings which can be termed postcolonial. The idea that there exists something like a "dominant" context can especially be found in Barker and Hulme (1985). The label "dominant" arouses questions as to "the assumption about what

---

[8] The word "mestizo" in this context functions to mark the opposition with the Uruguayan Rodó, who comes from a part of Latin America where racial blending is minimal. It represents an attempt by Retamar to explain the other perception of Caliban within Latin America itself. Said presumably bases himself on this excerpt when he claims that Retamar prefers Caliban to Ariel, because the former would better match "the Creole or *mestizo* composite of the new America" on the basis of its "strange and unpredictable mixture of attributes" (Said 1994: 257). Said thus, however, fails to take into account the most essential motivation for the symbolic value of Caliban in Retamar's essay: the linguistic, oppositional relation with his ruler.

we mean by the 'relevant discursive context', about how we agree to determine it, and about how we decide to limit it" (Skura 1992: 230). Fifteen years after publishing "Calibán," Retamar himself launched an appeal for his essay to be read against the background of certain events. It goes without saying that such an appeal for contextualization again derives from a certain context and that it is not because the author himself points at the relevance of the contextual factors that he is necessarily "right." However, the essay providing our working hypothesis concerning the "dominant context" – "Calibán revisitado" (1986) – was included as a kind of epilogue in the English translation of "Calibán" and thus acquires a privileged status as compared to other statements on "Calibán's" context.

As a concrete example of contextual influences that played a role in the genesis of his essay, Retamar refers to "the affair Padilla": "If it [the essay] is now disengaged from that polemic, or if that polemic is not taken into account, it is evident that the meaning of 'Caliban' is betrayed" (53). Of course several different versions of the polemic exist, but a summary of what happened could go like this. Padilla stands for Heberto Padilla, a Cuban poet who, after having been jailed for one month in 1971, pleaded guilty to contra-revolutionary activities. As he himself openly declared to the Cuban Writers' League, his principal fault was that he had reviled a novel by a Cuban writer, and had sung the literary praises of a "traitor of the Revolution": Guillermo Cabrera Infante. Padilla's imprisonment and his public declaration produced a general outcry among a large group of leftist intellectuals who up till then had been supporting the Cuban Revolution. As a result of these events, two open letters to Fidel Castro were published in *Le Monde*, signed by prominent intellectuals such as Jean-Paul Sartre and Mario Vargas Llosa. The first letter asks for additional information about the sudden arrest of Padilla, and expresses the concern that "sectarian" tendencies might resurge in the Cuban Revolution.[9] In the second letter, Padilla's public statement is directly linked up with the practice of self-criticism under Stalin, and it is strongly condemned. In between the publication of the two letters, a speech by Fidel Castro,

---

[9] The term "sectarianism" was used in Cuba in the sixties to refer to the dogmatic joining of the communist model of the Soviet Union. Most documents dealing with the affair-Padilla are to be found in Libre 1971 and Casal 1971.

delivered at the *First National Congress on Education and Culture*, has to be situated. In that speech, Castro severely criticizes the signatories for their interference in Cuba's internal affairs, and he denies them further access to the island. Together with the second letter, the speech put an end to the good relations obtaining between the Castro-regime and many intellectuals within Latin America and beyond.

Even though Retamar emphasizes the significance of the polemic for the genesis of his essay, he especially highlights one aspect of it: the at first sight unnecessarily sharp tone in which the controversy was carried on. Significant in this respect is the following passage: "I do not demand that readers familiarize themselves with all the material that surfaced in the heat of the polemic, but rather that they recall its bitterness" (53). Nonetheless, a "postcolonial reading strategy" will precisely attempt to uncover the ways in which the context is present in "Caliban," how this affair "exists at the same level of surface particularity as the textual object itself" (Said 1983: 39) and how the contextual background, as an instance of intertextual background, can increase the understanding of the essay (Barker and Hulme 1985: 192).

From Context to Text

What immediately strikes us is that the context, as it is described by Retamar in 1986, is only marginally present in "Calibán." References to the events concerning Padilla are casual and indirect. The author, for instance, does briefly refer to "a Cuban writer's one month in jail" (30) and to the accusation of "deformations in our revolution" (40), but the term "stalinism" is never dropped and the name Padilla is left unmentioned.

In fact, the term "marginal," as I used it in my previous paragraph, should also be interpreted in a literal sense: the two most important references to the events of 1971 are to be found at the beginning and end of the essay. The opening question by the European journalist, "Does a Latin American culture exist?", is presented as "one of the roots [of] the recent polemic regarding Cuba" (3). The commotion about Padilla, interpreted abroad as a political issue, thus appears as a problem with essentially cultural reasons. This legitimizes the essay's further treatment of the affair in the form of a meditation on cultural identity. The second explicit link with the Padilla-case is given in the final passage on Ariel.

> More recently we have not been lacking either in individuals who attribute the volcanic violence in some of Fidel's recent speeches to deformations – Caliban, let us not forget, is always seen as deformed by the hostile eye – in our revolution. (40)

With an air of naturalness, the parenthetic clause switches from the symbol of Caliban to the Cuban Revolution, that is to say to Fidel Castro. The linking of both concepts is supported by the emphasis which is laid on the aspect of "voice": the "volcanic violence" of Castro's speeches fits in with Caliban's cursing. At the same time, Retamar uses another, new aspect of Caliban in the context of the polemic: his looks. By presenting the reproach of ideological "deformation" via the character of Caliban and calling it a deliberate deformation by "the hostile eye," it becomes neutralized. These two aspects – appearance and verbal behaviour – thus indirectly legitimize the analogy between the symbol Caliban and the man Fidel Castro, who in that way also becomes associated with Latin America and "the people." In other words, what looks like a repressive act in the eyes of the enemy turns out to be a measure taken to serve "the people," and what the signers of the letters attribute to "deformation or to foreign influence " (i.e. stalinism), according to Retamar goes back to "an attitude that is at the very root of our historical being" (40).[10]

My analysis hitherto implies that Ariel's choice between Caliban and Prospero amounts to a choice for or against the Cuban Revolution, that is, for or against Fidel Castro. To put it differently, the Padilla-case forms a

---

[10] The link Castro-Caliban also surfaces in a self-reflexive passage of the essay. Retamar defends the choice of a Western symbol for a Latin-American concept of identity by citing Fidel Castro, who states that marginal peoples don't necessarily have an own name apart from the one that was given to them by their oppressors (16). If you look at it from that angle, the choice for the symbol of Caliban is not so much "ironic" (Vaughan and Vaughan 1991: 162), but historically and culturally determined.

touchstone for the two opposed cultural traditions of the continent. The specific interpretation of Caliban and Prospero as oppressed/oppressor, and the association of Caliban with Latin America as a cultural community then gives an indication as to what is the *right* choice to make. Siding with Castro equals remaining loyal to one's origins as a Latin-American intellectual. Those that turn against Castro, on the other hand, betray their identity. It follows that the geographical concept "Latin-American" is rewritten into a discursive-cultural notion and becomes part of a logic of gain and loss, or rather, of reward and punishment. The fact that this happened in an essay that is written by the editor-in-chief of *Casa de las Américas* ("House of the Americas") and published in the journal of that same name, is significant. In the years after, the journal would set itself up as defender of "authentic" Latin-American culture and would thus function as a site of in- and exclusion (Lie 1996: 237-75).

Marginal as they are, the casual references in "Calibán" to the "external" context therefore activate, through the Shakespeare-characters, a network of positive and negative associations which are advantageous to Castro. This brings us to the *performative* character of the essay "Calibán": put back in its contemporary context, the text turns out to support the official Cuban viewpoint in the affair Padilla. But there is still another way to show the text's performative character. Following Barker and Hulme's analysis of *The Tempest* (1985), we can interpret the notion of "context" also as a collection of texts with which "Calibán" has intertextual relations. Rather than with explicit references, we are then dealing with lexical and narrative connections.

From this angle, Retamar's essay clearly echoes Castro's speech at the *First National Congress on Education and Culture*. Especially Retamar's description of "the recent polemic regarding Cuba" at the beginning of his essay is revealing in this respect.

> We were discussing, naturally enough, the recent polemic regarding Cuba that ended by confronting, on the one hand, certain bourgeois European intellectuals (or aspirants to that state) with a visible colonialist nostalgia; and on the other, that body of Latin-American

writers and artists who reject open or veiled forms of
cultural and political colonialism. (3)

The affair Padilla is treated here as a confrontation between supporters and
opponents of colonialism, and an identical depiction of the facts figures in
Fidel Castro's speech. Castro calls Padilla's friends "accomplices of mental
colonialism" and he considers the struggle against "cultural colonialism" to
be the main task of the Cuban officials of culture.

> We have revealed that other, subtle form of colonization,
> a form that might even be harder to eradicate than
> economic imperialism or colonialism. We are alluding to
> cultural imperialism, to political colonialism, an evil
> which we have discovered to exist on a large scale.
> (Castro 1971: 26; translated by L.H.)

Castro's speech could also explain why direct references to the affair
Padilla are so rare in "Calibán": that the "Westernized" intellectuals make
such a big fuss over the case to Castro proves their petty bourgeois
mentality. "Let them publish their stories and snags in one or the other
literary journal. That should suffice. Our problems are of a totally
different nature: they have to do with the underdevelopment you left us in
and have to overcome it" (Castro 1971: 26-27; translated by L.H.). As a
result, the theme of cultural identity becomes the only opportunity to
make the affair Padilla a subject of discussion without calling the suspicion
of being petit bourgeois on oneself.

Making it into a subject of discussion however does not mean that the
topic becomes "discussable," it only implies that it is "acceptable,"
"legitimate" to talk about it. In his speech, Castro depicts the letter-signers
as "intellectual rats," "poisoners" and "intriguers," and the affair Padilla is
compared to intellectual "rubbish" and "backbiting" (Castro 1971: 26-28).
By changing this kind of "volcanic violence" into an essay on Shakespeare
and cultural identity, Retamar manages to tailor a political speech to a
cultural field, or to translate it in literary terms.

One important difference between Retamar's essay and Castro's speech
remains: via Ariel Retamar introduces the idea of a conscious *choice*. As
was said before, Castro's speech formed the closing of a major event: the

First National Congress on Education and Culture. Here we meet with the
institutional context in which Retamar's essay was published in Cuba, a
context that is missing with "Caliban revisited," but that, following for
instance Greenblatts analysis of *The Tempest* (1988), certainly deserves
particular attention.[11] Both in Cuba and outside, the congress is nowadays
considered the starting point of "The Grey Quinquennium," a period in
which strictly ideological criteria were expected to create a new kind of
"popular culture." The message underlying Padilla's "self-criticism" and
other such events that took place in subsequent days, seems to have been
precisely that Castro's politics were *not* to be debated in principle. The
Congress marks the definite end of the relative autonomy which the
cultural field had enjoyed throughout the sixties. Now, by emphasizing
the aspect of "choice," Retamar manages to transform a politics of culture
which at that very moment is being imposed rather heavy-handedly by the
political authorities on the intellectual field into a matter of individual
choice. The implied message is that the Cuban Ariels have *chosen* this
cultural policy *out of their own free will*[12] and that they now invite their
Latin-American brothers to do the same. The final section, "And Ariel

---

[11] If we take into account Greenblatt's analysis, we can moreover state that the
position of Retamar's "Calibán" towards Castro's speech shows remarkable
parallels with the position of Shakespeare's *Tempest* towards the so-called Bermuda
pamphlets, in particular William Strachey's letter. In both cases there are clear
institutional influences at work: Retamar is editor of *Casa de las Américas*, a journal
which is subsidized by the Cuban government, and through his membership of the
King's men, Shakespeare is shareholder of the Bermuda-company, of which the fleet
runs ashore in Bermuda. In both cases one could speak of an authority-crisis,
situated in a rather idyllic setting (Virginia, Cuba), which leads to a series of
draconic, social measures. Both in Retamar and Shakespeare, this context is
rendered "negotiable" by including it into the text in a creative way.

[12] It is therefore highly problematic to say, as is done by Peter Hulme, that "his
[Retamar's] role as editor of *Casa de las Américas* seemed to offer some guarantee
that Castro's famous phrase 'within the revolution, everything' might still have
some recognizable meaning (after the Padilla-case)" (1992: 78). It is precisely what
follows in Castro's speech of 1961, namely "against the revolution, nothing," that
is the central theme of Retamar's essay (1989: 43-45, my translation; Baker wrongly
translates "contra" as "outside").

Now?", ends with the image of Caliban inviting Ariel to take up his position in the "rebellious and glorious ranks" (45).

The Voice of the Other

Even though in the final section of his essay Retamar calls on Ariel to side with Caliban, almost all of the preceding pages are devoted to the Ariel that has taken Prospero's side, at least in Retamar's opinion. We thus arrive at the second postcolonial point of interest: "How can we know and respect the Other?" (Said as quoted in Williams and Chrisman 1993: 8).

We mentioned earlier that Retamar associates the letter-signers with the Ariel that sides with Prospero. It is, however, not so much this Ariel which is criticised, but rather the "members of his family" in the Latin-American tradition. Retamar is critical of writers-intellectuals like Jorge Luis Borges and Carlos Fuentes for being slavishly attached to Western culture, and he consequently brands them as essentially "colonial" writers. In the case of Borges, especially his exaggerated intertextuality with Western sources is rejected. As far as Fuentes is concerned, his literary-critical work *La nueva novela hispanoamericana* (1969) is zoomed in on. Retamar claims that the structuralist reading method which Fuentes in this work applies to Latin-American writings leads to a radical negation of the latter's historical and cultural specificity.[13] He moreover states that the "cultural colonialism" which Borges and Fuentes are deemed guilty of places them alongside right-wing political thinkers and implies a repudiation of the Cuban Revolution.[14]

---

[13] This critical comment on structuralism brings Retamar's essay again very close to post-colonialism as a theoretical movement which aims at bursting false universality claims as put forward by for instance some forms of structuralism (Ashcroft e.a. 1989: 12).

[14] Borges condemned the Cuban Revolution already in 1961 at the time of the invasion of the Bay of Pigs, while Fuentes only openly came to criticize Castro as a direct result of the Padilla-affaire. This time difference, however, according to Retamar does not alter the fact of their essentially identical viewpoint.

One Latin-American author deserves special mention in the present context: Domingo Faustino Sarmiento. This Argentinian writer, who eventually became president of his country, is believed to be the forefather of the Latin-American intellectuals that took Prospero's side. To be precise, Sarmiento's most important work *Civilización y Barbarie* (1845) is seen as the material embodiment of Prospero's voice in Latin America. As it happens, the two concepts in the title express the essence of the *discourse* with which Prospero wins the Latin-American intellectuals over for his cause: he plays the role of bringer of "civilization" and he depicts the native Calibans as "barbarians." The natural habitat of culture (even political culture) is Europe or West, his message goes. By means of this ideology, Prospero manages to take possession of the continent, to deprive the real Calibans of their country, and even to extirpate them outright.[15]

Still, a "postcolonial" reading of a text does not only involve an attempt to identify the voice of the Other. It also implies that we approach the issue as seen through the Other's eyes, that we take in a "contrapuntal" viewpoint (Said 1994).[16] This mental exercise has been undertaken by Spivak (1985) and especially by Chanady (1990), who both query the relationship of self-identification with the indigenous population of his country, which Retamar as an intellectual has entered into. Both authors define "the Other" as a text-external concept: "the Maya, the Aztecs, the Incas, or the smaller nations of Latin America" in Spivak's analysis (1985: 245), "the Amerindian" in Chanady's (1990: 42). Retamar's "dialectic of Caliban," however, implies that this self-identification itself produces a

---

[15] It would take many more years before the Cuban José Martí would burst this discourse. In *Nuestra América* ("Our America", 1895) he claims that "civilización" is actually tantamount to "falsa erudición." Because of this interpretation, Retamar places Martí at the basis of that other family of Latin-American intellectuals: those that take Caliban's side.

[16] Cf. "Post-colonial counter-discursive strategies involve a mapping of the dominant discourse, a reading and exposing of its underlying assumptions, *and the dismantling of these assumptions from the cross-cultural standpoint of the imperially subjectified "local"* (Tiffin 1995: 98, emphasis added); "More explicitly, the critic is responsible to a degree for articulating those voices dominated, displaced or silenced by the textuality of texts" (Said 1984: 53).

new Other: Prospero in Shakespeare's play, Sarmiento within the Latin-American tradition.[17] Taking in a contrapuntal position thus comes down to viewing the issues raised in Retamar's essay from the perspective of *Civilización y Barbarie* or of *The Tempest*. But how can one do that? How does one take the viewpoint of a dead writer or of a fictitious character?

One possible answer to this question is obvious: one can let Sarmiento or Shakespeare speak, namely by going back to their original texts. Reversal of perspective then entails the reversal of the relation between the text which is commented upon and the text that is doing the commenting, for also this relation is essentially one of power: the commentator decides which passages will or will not be discussed and thus creates an *image* of the text that is being commented on. By rereading Sarmiento and Shakespeare integrally, with Retamar's arguments at the back of our mind, new passages come into relief which, without being directly related to the Cuban situation in 1971, can nevertheless broaden our view on it in a contrapuntal way.

Two Contrapuntal Readings: Sarmiento and Shakespeare

What attracts attention while reading Sarmiento in the light of Retamar's essay 150 years after date, are the many points of agreement between both texts on a purely discursive level. Sarmiento and Retamar, even though they appear in "Calibán" as polar opposites within Latin-American culture, turn out to make use of essentially the same rhetorical strategies to build their arguments. In both works a Latin-American concept is being symbolized by a proper name: "Calibán" in Retamar's essay, and "Facundo" in Sarmiento's work. That Caliban is a literary character, while Facundo Quiroga stands for a historical – be it only legendary – person is of marginal importance in this context, for Facundo loses his directly referential function as Sarmiento's argument unfolds. He becomes the symbol of a typically Latin-American way of ruling a country, as it was at the time of the publication of *Civilization and Barbarism* embodied by the

---

[17] Retamar clearly posits: "The *other* protagonist of *The Tempest* [...] is not of course Ariel, but rather Prospero. There is no real Ariel-Caliban polarity" (1989: 16).

dictator Juan Manuel de Rosas. Besides, the main title of Sarmiento's book is precisely "Facundo," after Facundo Quiroga, and not, as Retamar writes, "Civilization and Barbarism."

A second resemblance is that both Sarmiento and Retamar construe their argument on the basis of strong contrasts: Prospero versus Caliban, Civilization versus Barbarism, Sarmiento versus Martí, for or against dictator Rosas, for or against Castro. Most striking, however, is that Sarmiento pays as much attention as Retamar does to the relation between language and power. Sarmiento does not only condemn Rosas' regime, he also analyses it. He states explicitly that this regime owes its power not only to a repressive police force, but that it does so just as much to its use of a rhetoric which conceals the oppression going on. In this rhetoric, the concept of "America" plays a crucial role. To many Latin-American countries, the Argentinian dictator Rosas appeared as the defender of "(Latin) America," and with his crass remarks directed against the European powers, which condemned and boycotted his regime, he won the respect of many on his own continent. But, as Sarmiento sneers, Rosas was only able to formulate his torrents of abuse in the language of the Western powers which he detested: "and you speak evil in the language of these foreigners!" (220). Nowhere could the analogy between Caliban and Rosas/Facundo be shown more clearly than in this passage, except maybe in the explicit depiction of Rosas as the "cannibal of Buenos Aires" (140), which immediately brings to mind Retamar's etymologic reflections on the name "Caliban."

There is also an important difference between the two symbols, a difference which in a way runs parallel to the reversal in the quote from Sarmiento, where the emphasis is on the shared language, and not on the cursing. If Facundo can be compared to Caliban, then Sarmiento's personage certainly is a power-ful Caliban. Facundo was a "caudillo," who ruled over other local potentates, and Rosas was a "dictator" ruling over the whole of Argentina. In Sarmiento, the hybrid symbol which Retamar sets up around Caliban again breaks up into two parts: Latin America and the oppressed people. Facundo and Rosas do indeed symbolize Latin-American barbarism, but at the same time they represent "rulers" who oppress their own people via a certain rhetoric. If we are aware of the fact that Sarmiento condemns the dictator for oppressing intellectuals and artists like himself, for doing this in the name of a certain notion of "America," and finally, for hurling reproaches at those foreign powers that put pressure on him by means of a blockade, his book *Civilización y Barbarie* becomes an act of criticism *avant-la-lettre* of the Castro-regime, comparable to the criticism that was ventilated by Padilla's supporters in 1971.

In short, the same book in which Retamar recognizes the so-called "language of Prospero," with its dichotomy between "civilization" and "barbarism," contains an analysis of "the language of Caliban" as soon as the latter accedes to power. While Retamar presents Caliban merely as a cursing creature and therefore as a negation of all that Prospero stands for, Sarmiento engages in filling in the words Caliban would use if given the floor. What does he say and do when he becomes the more powerful? Does he really differ that much from that other ruler, Prospero? And particularly, how does a concept like "cultural identity" function in a concrete situation of power? Retamar thinks Sarmiento's book furnishes evidence that an ideal picture of Western culture can be used to oppress the Latin-American people, but Sarmiento demonstrates that the same holds true for exaggerated pictures of any native "(Latin-)American" identity. Sarmiento's book thus raises questions as to Caliban's *rhetoric* in Retamar's essay itself. Why this emphasis on the notion of "our America"? Whose interests are being served with it?

The issue of Caliban's rhetoric could also be investigated in *The Tempest* itself. In Shakespeare's play too, Caliban makes use of rhetorical figures, but notably these are not related to the notion of "cultural identity," but to another concept central to Retamar's essay: "oppression." The concept concretely emerges in the first act, in which Prospero and Caliban provide us with two versions of the history predating the action of the play. According to Caliban, he himself was king of the island until Prospero's arrival there. At first, Prospero behaved civilly towards Caliban, and therefore Caliban gladly showed him around on the island. Suddenly however, Prospero's attitude towards his generous host changed, and Caliban was confined to a cave and treated as if he were a slave. Especially this version of the facts has been drawn attention to in postcolonial readings of *The Tempest* (Hulme 1986). It also plays a crucial role in Retamar's essay, legitimizing the identification of Caliban with the Carribean (Retamar 1989: 14).

A contrapuntal reading, however, prompts us to also listen without prejudice to Prospero's version. Even though he starts by calling Caliban a "most lying slave" (I.ii.347), he does not contradict Caliban's account of what happened. Instead, he completes it by revealing that Caliban's present situation results from his attempt to rape Prospero's daughter, Miranda. If it is true that "Caliban's account of the beginning of the relationship is allowed to stand unchallenged" (Hulme 1986: 125), then it is equally right to claim that Caliban at this point does not contradict Prospero's version, but rather confirms it: "O ho, O ho! would't had been done!/ Thou didst - prevent me; I had peopled else/ This isle with Calibans" (I.ii.350-52).

The so-called untruthfulness of Caliban in this respect has got nothing to do with what Caliban says, but rather with what he does *not* say. By keeping silent about his own contribution to his oppression, Caliban insinuates that Prospero was after the island from the start and that he managed to trick Caliban out of it by cunning and feigned friendliness. The rhetorical figure of *ellipsis* is thus doubly distorted: it embellishes the picture we get of Caliban, and it deforms Prospero's image. Caliban turns into the erroneously oppressed slave, whereas Prospero becomes the oppressor eager for power. Prospero's intervention corrects this picture by replacing the terms "oppressor/oppressed" by something like "father/punished person." This also introduces a third character on the scene: Miranda. On Miranda, the one who in fact had bothered most to teach Caliban to speak, Caliban also perpetrated an act of "usurpation" by trying to rape her. If it is true that colonial discourse often represents women as symbolizing the colony (Spurr 1994: 170), it follows that Caliban himself can be called a kind of colonizer. As in the Sarmiento-reading, the two oppositional characters thus come closer to one another; the concept of "effacement" or "euphemization," which "new historicists" have brought to bear on Prospero's usurpation of Caliban's island (Brown 1985: 64) could perhaps also bear on Caliban himself.

The rhetorical dimension of Caliban's oppression, which of course has its roots in reality, reappears when Caliban hatches a plot against Prospero. In slightly different words he uses the image of Prospero as the cunning oppressor once again: "[...] I am subject to a tyrant, a sorcerer, that by his cunning hath cheated me of the island" (III.ii.40). This time, however, Caliban not only witholds that he has tried to rape Miranda, he also keeps silent about the fact that he considers himself to be the first king of the island. One of the ways to urge Stephano (and Trinculo) to oust Prospero is by promising them that Stephano will become the new king of the island, with Caliban serving as "true subject." Rather than absolute freedom, Caliban looks for "a new master," and on several occasions he volunteers to kiss Stephano's foot as a token of his complete subordination. In his new contacts, Caliban thus uses his negative self-image of "oppressed person" in a positive way: as "subject."[18] It not only demonstrates that images of "oppression" can be used out of self-interest, but it also makes clear that a discourse of "resistance" can be directed against one specific master, and not against another one. In *The Tempest*, Caliban uses language not only to curse his former master, but also to serve and flatter his prospective master. It is telling that, while performing his dance of joy, Caliban has no trouble combining the notions of "freedom" and "new master" (II.ii.185-86). It is precisely in this regard that a major difference with Ariel can be observed. Even though Retamar does not see any fundamental polarity between Ariel and Caliban (1989: 16), their attitude towards the notion of "freedom" in *The Tempest* differs greatly: Ariel's rendering of services has got everything to do with Prospero's promise to release him by the end of the play. One could therefore say that Ariel does *not* take Prospero's part: Ariel merely sides with himself.

---

[18] Prospero also uses the imagery of power and oppression supplied in the first act in his self-designed plot. To be more precise, Prospero introduces Ferdinand to Miranda as someone who came to the island as a spy in order to take it from him, thus in fact consciously reproducing Caliban's discourse. He especially makes use of the image of Miranda as "sex object," offered to him by Caliban, and translated in terms of the possibility of marrying her off.

We thus once again arrive at a point where we have to consider the "affair" which was the topic of the moment in 1971. The questions raised by Shakespeare in Retamar's essay run as follows: To what extent does the discourse on oppression serve the interests of a new master: Castro? What is the exact significance of the Cuban Ariel elaborating this discourse? In this context we should mention that the Padilla-affair witnessed the dissolution of the editiorial board of *Casa de las Américas*, which from 1965 onwards had been led by Retamar. The non-Cuban members of the old editorial staff, especially Julio Cortázar and Mario Vargas Llosa, had been directly involved in the polemic: both signed the first letter, and the second letter even turned out to have been written by Vargas Llosa. What's more, several of the signatories had previously published in the journal *Casa de las Américas*. Retamar's severity towards this group is therefore probably also influenced by his desire to openly distance himself from his ex-colleagues and to protect concrete institutional interests, among which his own...

Conclusions and Previews

A contrapuntal reading of "Calibán" calls attention to the possible abuse of exactly those concepts which Retamar, by means of the dual symbol Caliban, emphasizes: "Latin America" and "oppressed people." In view of the great importance of this kind of notions in postcolonial discourse itself (be it in the more general form of "cultural identity" and "margin"), it follows that the much advocated attention to "the rhetoric of empire" (Spurr 1995) might have to be complemented by what could be termed "the rhetoric of the colony." It goes without saying that this does not imply that colonialism has not existed, nor does it deny that the pernicious effects of colonialism continue to be visible. What it does, however, hint at is that those people that live in the "margins," are not "better readers" – if they are at all – simply on the basis of their oppression by the West, but also because of concrete, local interests. At a moment when postcolonialism has according to some become the scene of "newfound power" (Dirlik 1994), the task of a culture critic has grown beyond trying "to hear the accents of Caliban" (Greenblatt 1990b: 232) and now also has to include attempts "to decipher his power."

"The power of Caliban," however, is also located in the symbol of Caliban itself as he appears in *The Tempest*. According to Vaughan and Vaughan (1991: 289), the Caliban-metaphor has, due to Shakespeare's play's lacking of a "sixth act," built-in limitations which render it less applicable to newly liberated nations: "what he [Caliban] does with his new freedom, is beyond the metaphor." In the Cuban essay, however, it is precisely this lacking of a sixth act which prevents that questions are asked about how authority is exercised by a regime that claims to have liberated itself from (neo-)colonial powers. That this question was open to discussion shows from a contextual approach of Retamar's essay. Similar to the ellipsis in Caliban's story, then, this "non-dit" within the Caliban-symbolism allows for a productive dimension.

All in all, it seems highly problematical to classify Retamar's "Calibán" in categories like "counter-canonical" or – in Said's case – "culture of resistance." Such labels at least presuppose that one is specific about what one is offering resistance to, and that one allows for the possibility that the answer is multiple, or ambivalent. If we place Caliban back into the context of the Padilla-polemic, the essay rather seems to become part of "the culture of acceptance" or "legitimation."

It is likely that here we have also come across Retamar's main motive to finally bid farewell to his personage in 1993 (ironically, he did so in the epilogue to a Cuban republication of his essay). Rather than the disappearance of world-scale decolonization-movements, which according to Nixon (1987: 576) and Vaughan and Vaughan (1991: 282) reduced the force of attraction of the Caliban-icon, the specific background of the crisis in the Castro-regime seems to have made a further association with this personage problematic to Retamar. The epilogue nevertheless contains a passage which might prove to be very interesting for the future "postcolonial" reception of "Calibán." In "Adiós a Calibán," Retamar no longer presents his essay as a polemic with others, but rather calls it an internal dialogue. To prove his point, he refers to his continuing admiration for Borges. It follows from this statement that Retamar no longer applies the "dialectics of Caliban" only to Western culture, but also to that other Latin-American tradition, which he used to call inauthentic. One could say that he again translates "the wrong side" into "the other side," but this time within his own essay.

Thus he comes close to that other recycling of Caliban in recent Latin-American cultural criticism. Some years after the publication of "Calibán," Emir Rodríguez Monegal, Retamar's arch-enemy on issues literary, claimed Caliban to be the most adequate emblem for those writers that Retamar treats as non-authentic. It is precisely the use of intertextuality by someone like Borges, whom Retamar accuses of mimicry and of cultural colonialism, that perfectly fits the metaphor of "cannibalism" associated with Caliban. Intertextuality then stands for creative linguistic activity, for cultural cannibalism. This in turn leads us to that other voice of postcolonialism which we have heard so little in this essay: Homi K. Bhabha (1994). His alternative approach to phenomena like "mimicry," and his critical questioning of binary ways of thinking get us to understand that also a contrapuntal viewpoint still rests on the distinction between two terms: Caliban and Prospero, centre and margin. It is possible that this postcolonial movement in the years to come will allow us not only to "canonize" or to "counter" Retamar's text, but also to rewrite it as the point where the two Calibans meet.[19]

Translated by Liesbeth Heyvaert

References

Ashcroft, Bill, Gareth Griffiths and Helen Tiffin. 1989. *The Empire writes back. Theory and Practice in Post-Colonial Literatures*. London/New York: Routledge.

—, eds. 1995. *The Post-Colonial Studies Reader*. London/New York: Routledge.

Barfoot, C.C. and Theo D'haen. 1993. *Shades of Empire in Colonial and Post-Colonial Literatures*. Amsterdam/Atlanta: Rodopi.

---

[19] Maarten van Delden ([1994]) recently suggested that there might be a connection between the concept of "curse" which is so central to Retamar's "Calibán," and the notion of "parody," which critics like Emir Rodríguez Monegal have drawn attention to in their "cannibalist" interpretation.

Barker, Francis and Peter Hulme. 1985. "Nymphs and Reapers Heavily Vanish. The Discursive Con-texts of *The Tempest*." In Drakakis 1985: 191-205.

Bhabha, Homi K. 1992. "Postcolonial criticism." In Greenblatt and Gunn 1992: 437-465.

—. 1994. "Of Mimicry and Man. The Ambivalence of Colonial Discourse." In *The Location of Culture*. London/New York: Routledge, 85-92.

Bloom, Harold, ed. 1992. *Caliban (Major Literary Characters)*. New York/Philadelphia: Chelsea House Publishers.

Brown, Paul. 1985. "'This Thing of Darkness I Acknowledge Mine.' *The Tempest* and the Discourse of Colonialism." In Dollimore and Sinfield 1985: 48-71.

Casal, Lourdes. 1971. *El caso Padilla. Literatura y Revolución en Cuba. Documentos*. New York: Nueva Atlantida.

Castro, Fidel. 1971. "Discurso de clausura del Primer Congreso Nacional de Educación y Cultura." *Casa de las Américas* 65-66: 21-33.

Chanady, Amaryll. 1990. "Latin American Discourses of Identity and the Appropriation of the Amerindian Other." *Sociocriticism* 6 (1-2): 33-48.

D'haen, Theo. 1993. "Shades of Empire in Colonial and Post-Colonial Literatures." In Barfoot and D'haen 1993: 9-16.

Delden, Maarten van. [1994]. *Two Views of Latin American Cosmopolitanism*. Paper delivered at the XIVth Congress of ICLA. Edmonton/Alberta (in press).

Diana, Goffredo and John Beverley. 1995. "These Are the Times We Have to Live In. An Interview with Roberto Fernández Retamar." *Critical Inquiry* 21 (2): 411-33.

Dirlik, Arlif. 1994. "The Postcolonial Aura. Third World Criticism in the Age of Global Capitalism." *Critical Inquiry* 20 (2): 328-56.

"Documentos [relacionados con el caso Padilla]." *Libre*. 1971. N.° 1.

Dollimore, Jonathan and Alan Sinfield, eds. 1985. *Political Shakespeare. New Essays In Cultural Materialism*. Ithaca and London: Cornell UP.

Drakakis, John, ed. *Alternative Shakespeares*. London/New York: Routledge.

Fernández Retamar, Roberto. 1989a. "Caliban. Notes Towards a Discussion of Culture in Our America" [1971]. In Fernández Retamar 1989c: 3-45.

—. 1989b. "Caliban Revisited" [1986]. Fernández Retamar 1989c: 46-55.

—. 1989c. *Caliban and Other Essays*. Translated by Edward Baker. Foreword by Fredric Jameson. Minneapolis: University of Minnesota Press.

—. 1993a. "Calibán, quinientos años más tarde." *Nuevo Texto Crítico* 11: 223-44.

—. 1993b. "Adiós a Calibán." *Casa de las Américas* 191: 116-22.

Greenblatt, Stephen J., 1988. "Martial Law in the Land of Cockaigne." In *Shakespearean Negotiations*. Berkeley: University of California Press, 129-98.

—. 1990a. "Culture." In Frank Lentricchia and Thomas McLaughlin, eds. *Critical Terms for Literary Study*. Chicago and London: University of Chicago Press, 225-32.

—. 1990b. "Learning to Curse. Aspects of Linguistic Colonialism in the Sixteenth Century" [1976]. In *Learning to Curse. Essays in Early Modern Culture*. New York/London: Routledge, 16-39.

— and Giles Gunn, eds. 1992. *Redrawing the Boundaries. The Transformation of English and American Literary Studies*. New York: The Modern Language Association of America.

Griffiths, Trevor. 1983. "This Island's Mine. Caliban and Colonialism." In *Yearbook of English Studies* 13: 159-80.

Hulme, Peter. 1986. *Colonial Encounters. Europe and the Native Caribbean 1492-1797*. London: Methuen.

—. 1992. "Towards a Cultural History of America." *New West Indian Guide* 66 (1-2): 77-81.

Lie, Nadia. 1996. *Transición y transacción. La revista cubana "Casa de las Américas" (1960-1976)*. Gaithersburg, Md./Leuven: Ed. Hispamérica/Leuven UP.

Nixon, Rob. 1987. "Caribbean and African Appropriations of *The Tempest.*" *Critical Inquiry* 13: 557-78.

Padilla, Heberto. 1971. "Intervención en la Unión de Escritores y Artistas de Cuba." *Casa de las Américas* 65-66: 191-203.

Rodríguez Monegal, Emir. 1977. "The Metamorphoses of Caliban." *Diacritics* 3: 78-83.

Said, Edward. 1984. *The World, the Text and the Critic* [1983]. London: Faber and Faber.

—. 1994. *Culture and Imperialism* [1993]. London: Vintage.

Sarmiento, Domingo Faustino. 1970. *Facundo. Civilización y barbarie* [1845]. Buenos Aires: Espasa-Calpe.

Skura, Meredith Anne. 1992 (1989). "The Case of Colonialism in *The Tempest*" [1989]. In Bloom 1992: 221-48.

Slemon, Stephen. 1995a. "The Scramble for Post-Colonialism" [1994]. In *The Post-Colonial Studies Reader* 1995: 6-45.

—. 1995b. "Unsettling the Empire. Resistance Theory for the Second World" [1990]. In *The Post-Colonial Studies Reader* 1995: 104-113.

Spivak, Gayatri Chakravorty. 1985. "Three Women's Texts and a Critique of Imperialism." *Critical Inquiry* 12: 243-61.

—. 1994. "*Can the Subaltern Speak?*" [1988]. In Williams and Chrisman 1994: 66-111.

—. 1987. *The Post-Colonial Critic. Interviews, Strategies, Dialogues.* Ed. by Sarah Harasym. London: Routledge.

Spurr, David. 1994. *The Rhetoric of Empire. Colonial Discourse in Journalism, Travel Writing and Imperial Administration* [1993]. Durham and London: Duke UP.

Tiffin, Helen. 1995. "Post-Colonial Literatures and Counter-Discourse" [1987]. In *The Post-Colonial Studies Reader* 1995: 95-98.

Vaughan, Alden T. and Virginia Mason Vaughan. 1991. *Shakespeare's Caliban. A Cultural History.* Cambridge: Cambridge UP.

Williams, Patrick and Laura Chrisman, eds. 1994. *Colonial Discourse and Post-Colonial Theory. A Reader* [1993]. New York/London: Harvester/Wheatsheaf.

"I'll be wise hereafter"

Caliban in Postmodern British Cinema

Chantal Zabus & Kevin A. Dwyer

As far as one looks in the "dark backward and abysm of time," the iconic Caliban that prevails is the *sui generis* colonized subject, be he Indian American, Latin American or African. It has of late been fashionable to favour or look for a post-colonial reading of Caliban and to see *The Tempest* entirely in relation with "the salvage and deformed slave."[1] This *fin-de-siècle* (and end of millennium) has therefore supposedly restored the colonized's script and his/her apocryphal version of colonial history.

In light of such blatantly political readings privileging the race and ethnicity of the Caliban-figure, two British postmodern filmic adaptations of Shakespeare's play, Derek Jarman's *The Tempest* (1979) and Peter Greenaway's *Prospero's Books* (1991), appear somewhat out of place. By foregrounding the Europeanness of the story (which in the original play is restricted to Milan while the main setting is a Caribbean island) and ignoring the New World setting and the Caribbean source (Gates's shipwreck off Bermuda in 1609), both Jarman and Greenaway have retrieved and investigated the controlling myths of the English

---

[1] See Zabus 1994.

Renaissance and of "European culture" which is, despite its contemporary multi-ethnic aspect, still perceived as a self-defining and mutually definable notion. The words of MacCabe about Jarman – that the latter is "trying to rescue, from underneath the monument of the nation, the last ethnic minority – the English" (1992: 9) – are equally applicable to Greenaway. Jarman's and Greenaway's adaptations are therefore a regeneration of Europe into *The Tempest* story. Their cultural conservatism inevitably goes hand in hand with a professed lack of concern for the post-colonial potentialities of the play.[2]

Written in a time of colonial expansion (1611), *The Tempest* has logically been reread and rewritten as a manifesto of decolonization and a myth of transatlantic imperialism, rooted in the central metaphor provided by the colonial encounter between Prospero and Caliban.[3] Most postcolonial writers and critics have therefore identified not with the Moor Othello (with the possible exception of Eldred Jones's 1965 critical study of the African in English Renaissance drama in *Othello's Countrymen*) or their Carib ancestor Man Friday but with Caliban, who best conveys the leprosy of colour and its concomitant cultural mulattism.

It is on Caribbean soil that Caliban has had the most durable career, firstly because West Indian writers have readily identified with the very site of Caliban's island not far from "the still vexed Bermoothes"(I.ii.229) in the Caribbean basin; and second, because Caliban originally comes from Africa ("Argier"; I.ii.261) and, through the painful experience of the Middle Passage, emigrated to the island and has thus a common ancestry with West Indians. Caribbean writers have thus recognized the

---

[2] See Ciment 1991, passim; and Sutton 1980. Further referred to as Ciment and Sutton, respectively.

[3] See a.o. D.O. Mannoni's *Prospero and Caliban: the Psychology of Colonization* (1950); Philip Mason's *Prospero's Magic* (1962); D.G. James's *The Dream of Prospero* (1967); Aimé Césaire's vehement attack against Mannoni in his "Discourse on Colonialism" (1950); Frantz Fanon's *Black Skin, White Masks* (1952); J.P. Clark's "The Legacy of Caliban" in *The Example of Shakespeare* (1970); and Janheinz Jahn's chapter on "Caliban and Prospero" in his *History of Neo-African Literature* (1968).

contemporary relevance of the Prospero/Caliban relationship to the postcolonial discourse.[4]

Outside of the Caribbean, and the corpus of Shakespeare studies where he is often an Amerindian,[5] Caliban has been variously recuperated by African writers and ideologists (e.g. Sithole, Chinweizu, wa Thiong'o, Nwankwo) as well as by American and Latin-American critics (e.g. Baker, Sánchez, Retamar).[6] The claim that Caliban is a Latin-American "mestizo" probably comes closest to the original text for, as Skura reminds us, "Sycorax, Caliban's mother, through whom he claims possession of the island [...] came from the Old World herself or at least from eastern-

---

[4] Caribbean writers and critics have touched on such issues as rape and language-as-curse or, as Derek Walcott put it, "language-as-enslavement" (in "The Muse of History." In J. Hearne, ed. *Carifesta Forum 76: An Anthology of 20 Caribbean Voices*, 111-28). It is also useful to discuss Caliban's curse in terms of "the new englishes" and the inscription of language variance in postcolonial texts. If we except Frantz Fanon, the earliest use of Caliban as colonized subject in the Caribbean can be traced to the Barbadian George Lamming, who has explored the inconclusiveness of the play: f.i. Miranda is actually raped in *Water with Berries* (1971), Caliban journeys to Milan/London in *Pleasures of Exile* (1960). Also, Caliban resumes his former status as king of the island in Césaire's play *Une tempête* (1969), so far the only full-scale rewriting, to the point of inversion, of the play outside Britain. Both Lamming and C.L.R. James have identified Caliban with Toussaint l'Ouverture, the Negro leader of the slave revolt in Haiti. See also Stoll 1984.

[5] See Hantman 1992, A.T. Vaughan 1988. This point will be again driven home in Vaughan and Vaughan 1991.

[6] The notion of Caliban as a Negro rather than a "freckled whelp" was anticipated by Zimbabwean writer Ndabaninai Sithole in his *African Nationalism* (1959); it was taken up by the Nigerian Nkem Nwankwo in his poem "Caliban to Miranda" (1969), by Chinweizu (1987) as well as by the Kenyan Ngugi wa Thiong'o in *Homecoming* (1972). Houston Baker (1986) sees Caliban as "the Afro-American spokesperson" whereas Retamar (1971, 1989) and Sánchez (1976) have proposed Caliban as the symbol of the Latin-American "mestizos." See Roberto Fernández Retamar 1989. Caliban has indeed been recuperated as an icon of "modern utilitarian barbarism" by Hispanic American poets such as the Uruguayan José Enrique Rodó and Nicaraguan poet Rubén Darío.

hemisphere Argier (Algiers). She is a reminder that Caliban is only half-native, that his claim to the island is less like the claim of the Native Indian than the claim of the second generation Spaniard in the New World" (Skura 1989: 50). What transpires in these various appropriations is that Caliban is Black or a man of colour, except in e.g. Québec where he is redefined as the "nègre blanc d'Amérique," after Vallières' phrase. Seguin's Caliban in the novel of that name (1977) shares with the Black post-colonial writer a preoccupation with Caliban as a cultural mulatto or "hybrid," who needs to sever his symbiotic ties with Prospero, a need palpable in Québec's separatist policies.[7]

What all of these rewritings of The Tempest bring out is Caliban's ability or predisposition, already inherent in the ambivalent nature of Shakespeare's text (a monster speaking the most poetic lines of the play), to be appropriated within minority discourse. This has been further pursued by Western rewritings which do not turn to Caliban as a colonized subject but to a fashionable, "politically correct" array of the wretched of Europe: women, the underclass, the homosexual, the "blind" (in that respect, it is significant that Jack Birkett, who plays the role of Caliban in Jarman's film, is a blind actor).

In British postmodern literature, Caliban is often the underdog whereas Prospero is a master-minder and an islanded magus, as in John Fowles's The Magus (1977) or in Iris Murdoch's The Sea, the Sea (1978). Prospero is the typical, orphaned, childless, old professional "artist" or enchanter paired off, as is usual with Murdoch, with a benevolent "saint." Although one might perceive in him a creeping insanity, he remains throughout the owner of white or black magic, a control-freak and manipulator of others and events. The ubiquity of Prospero on the British postmodern scene may point to the fact that the Old World is reflecting on the abjuration of its "rough" magic.

In so far as postmodernism questions the dominant ideology by signaling a "crisis of cultural authority" and enacts "a critique of liberal humanist

---

[7] The explanation for the germination of such a novel in the soil of Québec lies in Max Dorsinville's Caliban Without Prospero (1974) which conceives of the Québécois Caliban as partaking of two cultures.

ideology of representation and identity,"[8] it is worthwhile to explore in what way Prospero's "author-ity" is challenged by Caliban and to what extent both filmmakers here discussed expose a system of power that privileges certain representations over others. The question of power and of the endowment of authority is already inherent in the original *Tempest*, as it displays a series of conspiracies, of attempted usurpations of authority: Antonio's treachery. Sebastian's attempted murder, Caliban's rebellion. All these conspiracies are, as Barker and Hulme aptly argue, "differentially embedded there, figural traces of the text's anxiety concerning the very matters of domination and resistance" (1985: 198).

With Jarman and Greenaway, *The Tempest*, which had taken the whole world "by storm," inevitably swirls "back to the centre," i.e. Britain. Therefore Caliban in both films is European and white but retains a power-relationship with the master, content as he is with babbling against Prospero's hegemony. Except for his skin colour, Caliban thus at first seems like a reactionary throw-back to the incompetent yet articulate revolutionary of Shakespeare's play.

Although both films are postmodern works, Jarman and Greenaway have clearly different agendas. Whereas Jarman is interested in debunking Prospero and showing Caliban as an outsider who has rightfully revolted and refused Prospero's hegemony, Greenaway has elevated Prospero to his full role as God-like manipulator, concocting a bulimic amalgam of Greenaway-Gielgud-Shakespeare-Prospero as creator of all of the film's possible meanings. In this respect, the treatment of Caliban shows Jarman closer to the postcolonial and Greenaway closer to the postmodern. This is, for example, reflected in the context in which the films were produced.

Jarman's production was a hippy enterprise precariously conducted on a low budget (£150,000 – mostly funded by Don Boyd, a major independent British producer and occasional director), which Channel 4 bought in the end for only £12,000. The production is at the crossroads of gay discourse and the Punk movement of the 1970s, best embodied in the punk actress Toyah Wilcox who plays Miranda. Jarman's version of *The Tempest* has

---

[8] See, respectively, Craig Owens in Foster 1990: 57, and Marshall 1992: 10.

been said to be part of the same artistic tradition as the Shakespeare films of Orson Welles, most notably *Othello* (1955) (Collick 1989: 98). In fact, Welles' Shakespearean oeuvre has little in common with Jarman's *Tempest* or his other Shakespeare movie, *The Angelic Conversation* (1985), except that one could concede that both directors do embody very different types of independent movie-making on the periphery of Euro-American mainstream film production.

On the other hand, *Prospero's Books*, written and directed by Greenaway in 1993 was made with the participation of Dutch, French and Japanese producers. It is Greenaway's seventh feature film and, according to an interview with Greenaway, is in the cycle of his more complex endeavours: he claims that by chance he has alternated since *The Draughtsman's Contract* (1982) between more straightforward narratives and experimental productions (Ciment 1991: 38). *Prospero's Books* thus appropriately follows on Greenaway's most straightforward narrative to date, *The Cook, the Thief, His Wife and Her Lover* (1989). Greenaway has been particularly apt at securing financial backing in a British film production context where it is increasingly difficult to do so.

Although Greenaway was by no means working with a blockbuster budget, he was able to gleefully indulge in the deployment of artifice and special effects. He is also interested in seeing "how the cinema and television vocabularies can be put together" (Hacker and Price 1991: 221). On the other hand, Jarman is known to "hate television" (254) and has made use of a simpler and almost classical style, re-arranging Shakespeare's text so as to enable him to cultivate the Gothic. In true neo-Gothic fashion reminiscent of a Murdoch novel, Jarman's film is thus set within the quintessentially British confines of Stoneleigh Abbey in Warwickshire, in the haunted ruins of a fire-gutted manor house. This crumbling castle hovers over the prickly sand dunes of another location, i.e. the blue-tinted, chilly sea coast of Northumbria. Jarman used a blue filter in the exterior scenes "to give them the unreal texture of a dream and to avoid any associations with what he referred to as 'tropical island' realism" (Collick 1989: 102-03). In the powdery Georgian wing of the Abbey, filled with strange relics, curios, and panelled walls scrawled with alchemical symbols and caballistic spells, a younger, seductive Prospero with Beethoven features (Heathcote Williams) is busy hatching vengeance against his usurpers. He is a peevish master to Ariel, an anxious boiler-suited worker, and to Caliban (Jack Birkett), a grimy-toothed lecher, greedily sucking raw eggs and rubbing his crotch.

What strikes the spectator in Jarman's hobgoblin hall-of-images is that the staging of events (in Shakespeare criticism, Prospero is either a stage-director or the presentator of a huge masque) here takes place in Prospero's wide-screen cranium. This would seem to confirm the postmodern Prospero as a heliocentric arch-magician of the screen rivalling the Unmoved Mover of the Renaissance. Yet, the governing metaphor of control is quickly dismantled. Already, "an early script had the insane magician imprisoned in an asylum, recreating the performances of each of the characters while they visited him" (Collick 1989: 99), which ironically could serve as a description of Greenaway's film.

Jarman has always been "interested in challenges to authority, atmospheres of menace and the humour of absurdity" (Jackson 1980) and all of these concerns are ever-present in his *Tempest*, especially in the characterizations of Prospero and Caliban. Running counter to preferred (especially postmodern) readings of *The Tempest* that show Prospero as controlling all the events of the play, Jarman's Prospero is clearly overwhelmed to the point of being near-demented and out-of-control (shots of him sitting stubble-faced near a table cluttered with, among other things, half-empty wine bottles and glasses suggest that he may have taken to drink). Faced with the erosion of his magic, this Prospero is apprehensive and at his wit's end. Jarman here amplifies the paranoid and obsessive sides of Prospero's nature already sketched out in Shakespeare's original.

One of the main functions of the film's elaborate deployment of Gothicism is precisely to render Prospero's mindscape as unsettled and unstable. These Gothic techniques are similar to those of the horror film, German expressionism and *film noir*, usually used to create a sense of suspense, to render the absence of naturalism, and to forefront the unreal and the paranoid. This feeling of Gothic-inspired paranoia, for instance, is clear in the scene at the beginning of the film in which Prospero summons Ariel. After an ominous walk down a dark corridor filmed frontally with a hand-held camera, Prospero enters his cell and calls out for Ariel. Slow, pulsing bass beats and the tinkling of windswept chandeliers are interjected between his calls, as well as cut-away shots to a glass tipping over, a doorknob slowly turning and an insect running across the page of a book under a magnifying glass. Accompanied by a clap of thunder, Ariel suddenly appears behind Prospero's back, whispering his lines. Many of these elements are "classical" in their Gothicism (e.g. the doorknob, the chandelier, the whisper) and readily communicate not only suspense but a dreamlike mood and ambience while going to the core of Prospero's ontological insecurity.

Facing this estranged and tyrannical Prospero, Caliban has been conceived as a wronged victim of Prospero's reign of terror. His neurotic authoritarianism comes to the fore in an early scene, in which Prospero delights in crushing Caliban's hand under his foot. In his portrayal of Caliban, Jarman does not deal with the race issue and avoids choosing a non-white Caliban. Jarman said to Martin Sutton in an interview that "it was possible to make Caliban black, but I rejected it because I thought it would load the whole film in one way, make it more specific rather than general" (Sutton 1980). Caliban nevertheless has the bald head and bloodshot eyes of David Suchet's contemporaneous stage Caliban (Stratford-upon-Avon 1978) who was a composite version of the Black, Third World native. The emphasis in Jarman's film is therefore on the class issue and on the master-servant relationship in the context of the postmodern allegory of control.

In his revisitation of Victorian England, Jarman gives Caliban the trimmings of an Edwardian butler. In a way, as P. Barker observed in a film review, Caliban "becomes a real servant rather than a monster" (Barker 1980). He along with Stephano and Trinculo via their language, gesture and costume comprise "a heady concoction of menace, petulance and camp" (Sutton 1980), a statement that Jarman made about Caliban but which could be applied to the burlesque underclass trio of Caliban, Stephano and Trinculo. Stephano wears a cook's uniform and Trinculo a sailor's outfit. The butler, cook, and sailor represent lower-class male occupations and, as such, hint at the exploited classes of British society. Caliban has appropriately been described by reviewers as "a bald North Country prole" (French 1980) or as "a backstairs rascal [...] delighting in his own poetry as well as in his grossness, pathetic in his memories of usurped glory and necromantic origins as Sycorax's child" (Robinson 1980).

Caliban's physicality is yet another sign of his class positioning. On various occasions, he slobbers eggs, farts, spits, rubs his armpits and his crotch, and he is the only one who eats in the film. These frequent Rabelaisian associations with the body and especially bodily fluids is apparent in the scene in which a bare-chested Miranda is scrubbing herself in a tin tub and Caliban bursts into the room, sticking out his tongue, laughing out loud, showing his behind and pretending to fart. Collick has compared Caliban in that scene to "a character from a *Carry On* film" (Collick 1989: 105). Although Caliban is acting in a lewd and lecherous manner, his interest in Miranda is not sexual but lies in using his body and its gaping orifices to provoke and shock her.

If sexuality is lacking in Caliban's dealings with Miranda, Caliban's physicality takes on homoerotic overtones once he joins company with Stephano and Trinculo, who are constantly roughhousing about, willfully pushing, grabbing and slapping each other. Sexuality is an issue that Jarman has repeatedly dealt with; he increasingly became a virulent and militant campaigner against Heterosoc[9] and for gay freedom and used his films as a medium to express his concerns. For instance, *Caravaggio* concentrates on the artist's position as a homosexual during the Renaissance. "In *The Angelic Conversation*, he wanted to restore the feminine element sometimes lacking in gay films, and so made a beautifully poetic film conjuring up the romantic feelings between two young men on a summer afternoon. It was even accused of 'coming close to a homosexual version of heterosexual kitsh' – an unfair comment more appropriate for *Sebastiane*" (Hacker and Price 1991: 236).

In terms of gays in Shakespeare, apart from the Sonnets controversy (the Sonnets, incidentally, are central to *The Angelic Conversation*),[10] critics have "spotted" homosexual characters in Shakespeare's plays, such as Antonio in *The Merchant of Venice* and his namesakes in *Twelfth Night* and

---

[9]"Heterosoc" is "heterosexual society." See Jarman 1993.

[10] Sonnets 27, 29, 30, 43, 53, 55, 56, 57, 61, 90, 94, 104, 126, 148.

in *The Tempest* (Shepherd 1988: 96). The possibility for androgyny is ever-present in Shakespeare, if only for the fact that the Elizabethan stage provided an arena where cross-dressing, transvestism and changing gender definitions could be displayed and where anxieties about women's roles being played by men could be expressed. However, Jarman (and Greenaway, for that matter) have created a homoerotic aura about the Stephano/Trinculo pair, and if they are not overtly homosexual, they are at least overtly campy (which for many will amount to the same thing).

In Jarman's film, camp is Stephano's and Trinculo's very essence, from the shrill delivery of their lines to their constant laughter and frivolity, to their awe and fetishistic fascination with the "frippery" they come across, to Stephano's mock description of his imagined wedding to Miranda. The film's camp is brought to its climax during the nuptials of Ferdinand and Miranda. Unlike the original fertility masque which was later included by Shakespeare on the occasion of James I's daughter's marriage to the Elector Palatine, gay discourse is once again foregrounded by having the sailors hug each other by the waist while swirling in a traditional hornpipe dance. The nuptials, indubitably a part of "the theatre of light" that clashes with the overall Gothic treatment, are rounded off with the perennial Elizabeth Welch, crooning "Stormy Weather" under confetti showers. Here Jarman's camp draws on the consciously artificial techniques of the Elizabethan masque and imitates the Hollywood musical revue. The film thus hinges on two countercultural discourses: "the underground cinema that developed from Pop Art and which was used to parody and interrogate the clichés and methods of Hollywood [and] [...] the transgressive and bohemian world of demi-monde gay culture" (Collick 1989: 106).

Although Caliban remains serious and intent on overthrowing Prospero throughout, his association with Stephano and Trinculo gives a further ideological twist to his underclass status. Despite his jocularity and campy characterization that would seem to preclude any seriousness in the treatment, it remains that Caliban is obsessively on Prospero's mind (and vice versa). In comparison with his presence on the stage in Shakespeare's original, Jarman shows his endearment for Caliban by giving him quite a considerable amount of screen time. Caliban appears in approximately 25 minutes of this 96 minute-long film and his off-screen laughter is often heard long after he exits or even before he enters a scene. Eight minutes of the 25 either comprise scenes which have been added to Shakespeare's text, showing Caliban sweeping the stairs, sucking on a raw egg, or harrassing Miranda; or place Caliban in scenes where he is absent in Shakespeare such as during the amorous meeting between Ferdinand and Miranda, or when Caliban is grinding a circus organ while Prospero is humiliating Ferdinand, or again when he is nibbling on nuts during Ferdinand's monologue (I.ii.487-94). Jarman brings Ferdinand and Caliban to the same level as household woodchoppers, when in fact their log-bearing activities served different functions in Shakespeare. Whereas it was part of Caliban's thraldom, it corresponded, in the case of Ferdinand, to the *ascesis* or trial period before the marriage consummation.

Caliban is also given certain prerogatives and a degree of autonomy denied to him in the play. He is allowed to be the first to give his own version of the colonization of the island. It is during that scene, after the hand-crushing incident, that Caliban, in one of the rare point-of-view shots in the film, defiantly looks upon Prospero as he rises. This increased subjectivity might entail that Caliban is part of a questioning which involves what Linda Hutcheon has called in another context "an energizing rethinking of the margins and the edges, of what does not fit in the humanly constructed notion of centre" (1992: 42). Caliban's positioning may therefore be integrated in a postmodernism of resistance.

Whereas Jarman rearranges Shakespeare's text in order to contemporize it, Greenaway's main concern is with sources and origins, fossilizing *The Tempest*-as-Bardscript in the cloven pine of the baroque, with an excess of ornaments and repetitive allusions. Therefore, Prospero-the-playwright (played by John Gielgud) becomes some sort of da Vinci-like humanist who is mounting a pageant that is being cast, written, directed and shown under our very eyes. According to Greenaway's amply detailed "footnotes" in interviews and the "book" of *Prospero's Books*, Prospero's poor cell becomes a portable Renaissance study modelled after the platform writing-room of Da Messina's St Jerome in a Piranesi palace and a bath-house where he first conceives the storm with its besodden victims while ruminatively glaring at a tiny galleon model in his cupped hand (Geenaway 1991: 50). In his library, a facsimile copy of Michelangelo's Laurenziana library, he regularly consults twenty-four books, the twenty-fifth being *The Tempest*, which is being dreamed up. Around this master-enquirer hover four embodiments of Ariel at different stages of his life, the youngest one being a curly-haired *manneken pis* with "exhibitionist impudence" (Greenaway 1991: 49).

Greenaway's film is clearly bulimic because of the general philosophy of display, the cultivation *ad libidum* of the huge masque or fresco, because of the sheer surplus or cornucopia of allusions that obscure the ultimate goal of the film, but also because of the excessive extra-cinematic information that Greenaway provides in interviews. His catch phrase to describe *Prospero's Books* is "You are what you read" and it is surely necessary to have read his interviews in order to grasp the postmodern pleasures of anachronism such as Gericault's "Raft of the *Medusa*," which is suitably Renaissanc-ed for the purpose (Greenaway 1991: 54); and to detect the pictorial allusions to Greek mythology and the numerous Biblical as well as allegorical references to water – "Mr. and Mrs. Noah with their ark [...] Moses in the bulrushes [...] Leda and the swan [...] Icarus falling into the sea" (Rodgers 1992: 16).[11]

Water being the source of Greenaway's obsessions, Caliban is presented as a naked choreographic creature (Michael Clark) swimming gracefully in the murky dark waters of the Palace's sewer system. Rather than the eighteenth-century drunken beast (already Caliban was a lecherous drunk in the 1667 Dryden-Davenant adaptation, *The Enchanted Isle*), the nineteenth-century Noble Savage and missing link or the mid-twentieth-century Third World victim of European imperialism, Greenaway has chosen an aquatic Caliban. Already in *The Tempest*, Caliban had been recurrently described as a fish, whether "debosh'd" (III.ii.25) or "plain" (V.i.266), complete with "fins like arms" (II.ii.33). And on the stage and later illustrations, Caliban has indeed been portrayed with scales, fins and other aquatic attributes, before his later apish counterpart became endowed in the nineteenth century with shaggy hair, animal skins, bushy brown fur, or given the head of a puppy (Vaughan 1985: 394).

---

[11] Greenaway's fascination with water can be observed in the short subject *Making a Splash* (1984) in *Twenty-Six Bathrooms* (1985), and *Drowning by Numbers* (1988). See also Masson 1991: 37.

The conception of Caliban as a tortoise-like amphibian may have originally come from Darwinist theories, more precisely, Daniel Wilson's *Caliban: The Missing Link* (1873) where he is portrayed as a being evolved from some aquatic species (Vaughan 1985: 399). The Caliban in Beerbohm Tree's 1904 production wears fur and seaweed and a necklace of shells and coral; and "when this Caliban hears the island's music, he dances and tries to sing" (Vaughan 1985: 400). This sea-creature may be the ancestor of Greenaway's dancing sewer rat.

Greenaway's conception of Caliban, which he wanted to be a monstrous, deformed, threatening creature (Ciment 1991: 44) stands in sharp contrast to the extremely fluid and kinetic being swimming effortlessly at the confluence of six sewers. Yet we know that Greenaway could easily have portrayed Caliban as a monstrosity, since he is known to create vile creatures, making use of grotesque bodies and images, as in e.g. *Belly of an Architect* (1986), *Drowning by Numbers* (1988), and *The Cook, the Thief, His Wife and Her Lover* (1989). As a "freckled whelp," Caliban's body is appropriately tattooed with marks. Yet, he is very far from resembling an oppressed African as in post-colonial discourse, the only African in Greenaway's film being Claribel's husband in Tunis. Caliban's traditional bestiality is here somewhat abated by his aquatic grace, which is Greenaway's way of rendering Caliban's poetic prowess in the original play. Caliban's grace in Greenaway's film is certainly not an inherited feature from his dam Sycorax nor can it be guessed at birth. Sycorax is seen delivering some sort of creature resembling a piglet amidst pus, maggots, and a buzz of flies, Greenaway's shot of Caliban's birth is reminiscent of Peter Brook's 1968 experimental rendition at London's Round House where Sycorax is portrayed as an enormous woman who "gives a horrendous yell, and Caliban, with black sweater over his head, emerges from between her legs: Evil is born" (Croyden 1968-69: 125-8). Prospero acts as a midwife to the pregnant Sycorax. He is the ultimate deliverer: he delivers Ariel from the cloven pine; and he "delivers" all the lines of the voiceless characters in the play.

Prospero's retort to Ferdinand and Miranda during the Masque – "No tongue! all eyes! be silent" – has here been explored to the limits of the absurd to the extent that Prospero takes away Caliban's voice, point of view and lines and that he himself even plans the conspiracy of Caliban through the Book of Travellers' Tales. Caliban's subversive potential in terms of class, race or sexuality, which was truly palpable in Jarman's sympathetic rendering has here been sublimated into an art form: dance. Caliban is presented as an abstraction, an Id of sorts,[12] a mere presence to contrast with Miranda's, Ferdinand's and Ariel's purity and their higher training in the civilized arts. Caliban has no class, no race, no sexuality. Yet he is dappled with the superficial features of different marginal figures. As a pseudo-colonized, his body is mottled with a few tattoos to show his allegiance to "the wretched of the earth." His association with Stephano and Trinculo, who retain their campy nature, along with the fact that he is a naked male dancer hint at – just enough but not too much – homoeroticism. He has however none of the monstrous sexual and copulatory potency for which he has been traditionally reputed and which enabled Leslie Fiedler to label him "the first nonwhite rapist in White man's literature" (1972: 234). Greenaway flirts with these options but rather settles for a non-descript version of Caliban that creates a sense of the nightmarish and the subversive without being truly horrifying or threatening.

This can be seen if we compare Jarman's and Greenaway's use of fluids. Although Caliban's birth scene is grotesque and horrific in the tradition of Greenaway's previous explicit renderings of bodily functions, after this scene there are no further associations between Caliban and viscosity. Whereas Jarman sticks to uncomfortable and unstable fluids such as saliva, wine, and eggyolk, Greenaway allows such sliminess to dissolve and be cleansed by pure waters: dew, torrential rain, fountains, baths. Even the sewer water in which Caliban thrives seems limpid on the screen, although Greenaway describes the water as being littered with kitchen debris (1991: 94). Unlike the much more externalized Caliban of Jarman's film, Greenaway's Caliban does not libidinously revel in viscous fluids nor does he project these fluids as weapons (in the form of spit, for instance) against

---

[12] Caliban as the Monster of the Id is featured along with Prospero as Dr. Morbius, and Ariel as Robby the Robot in Fred McLeod Wilcox's 1956 sci-fi film, *The Forbidden Planet*, in which the Planet Altair 4 – a spatialization of the original island – is eventually destroyed by the Monster of the Id which is its collective subconscious.

his enemies. Greenaway's Caliban is resolutely passive and restrained. However, when Prospero nonchalantly hurls his twenty-four books into the sea, Caliban in a last gesture is seen surfacing and rescuing the last two books, *Shakespeare's Thirty-Six Plays* and the as yet unfinished *Tempest*. That Caliban salvages the books is further evidence of Greenaway's underestimation of Caliban's rebellious potential. This ambiguous rescue-operation makes Caliban a complicit player in the very story that oppresses him. In this aquatic *mise-en-abyme*, Prospero does not truly "drown [his] book[s]" (V.iii.57), for *The Tempest* always already contains the books that Prospero needed to write *The Tempest*.

***

Both Jarman and Greenaway return to the founding myths of Englishness and are therefore concerned with England's role in the world during the Renaissance. Greenaway spends a lot of time congratulating and explaining himself, most of the time taking his hat off to European high culture during the Renaissance, which he considers a period of pure Enlightenment. Greenaway also takes care to mention only European rewritings of *The Tempest* such as W.H. Auden's *The Sea and the Mirror* (1945) but none of the post-colonial ones, which is in keeping with his lack of interest in the "Caribbean island." Even when describing the African scenes, Greenaway emphasizes the "high culture" aspect of African civilization. The flashback to Claribel's wedding shows Claribel and her husband being attended by a myriad of bustling servants with shiny, muscular bodies, wearing feathers and gold arm bands. They are surrounded by chalices and Moorish arches and the accompanying soundtrack features the beating of African drums. The natives, Greenaway notes, "as befits (Prospero's) European imagination [...] have the look both of classical figures and of John White's American Indians" (1991: 65), who have indeed been classicized to suit European taste, both aesthetic and sexual.

Jarman is also a "Renaissance man" in his own way with a keen interest in Renaissance and Enlightenment culture. However, what motivates Jarman is how the Renaissance or Victorian England can help us reassess priorities in our own culture. It is not the first time that Jarman has the Elizabethan period directly mirror contemporary times, as in his previous film *Jubilee*

(1978) which, in typical postmodern fashion, revisits Queen Elizabeth (Jenny Runacre) 400 years before, as she is escorted through time by her own magus, John Dee, into the contemporary devastation of 1970s Punk London.

Neither Jarman, despite his obvious ideological leanings, nor Greenaway have made "popular" films. Both films aim at informed publics, possibly because of the directors' highly personal visions and strong authorial presences. This is seen in the way in which Greenaway clearly identifies with Prospero, and in the way in which he has set up an entire inter- and extra-textual network of associations between Greenaway-Shakespeare-Gielgud-Prospero. In the condensation of these four terms, Prospero is seen as Shakespeare writing his play; as Gielgud, the venerable Shakespearean actor (Greenaway 1991: 60) taking leave of the theatre, and as the alter-ego of the movie-maker (Bénoliel 1991). Greenaway's vision is consistent with his Eurocentrism, centering on the Mediterranean and European frame of reference rather than the Atlantic one, and with the poststructuralist notion of author-ity and the God-like fathering of the text or script. Jarman as an author has denied his authority and made the production of his film a collective endeavour. Sarah Radclyffe, Jarman's producer, reports that during the shooting the cast and crew "all got kicked out of [their] hotel and had to move into the location, Stoneleigh Abbey, where [they] all got snowed in. The whole cast helped build the set. [They] never had call sheets. There was no production manager [...]" (Hacker and Price 1991: 233).

Taking their inspiration from the same Shakespearean source, Jarman and Greenaway have bifurcated in their interpretations of Prospero's authority and of Caliban. Both directors reflect divergent dimensions of postmodernism. Greenaway is symptomatic of a _fin-de-siècle_ formalism which foregrounds the cult of the individual,[13] the death of ideology and

---

[13] Notable is the cult-like attention that Greenaway receives on the Continent and in France, in particular, where the release of his films is treated as an important cinematic event. Greenaway is praised for bringing "Art" to cinema and a small, elitist "Greenaway industry" has cropped up, which includes the many interviews he grants, the publication of his scripts (which, before _Prospero's Books_, were published by a Parisian editor (DIS VOIR), the exhibition of his paintings, and the

art as an end in and of itself. By contrast, Jarman embodies an oppositional type of postmodernism in its collective spirit, "rebelling against anything which can be construed as authoritative, or even just established, and which also yearns for certain traditional values" (Hacker and Price 1991: 232). Jarman confronts the moral crises of our times whereas Greenaway, "rapt" as he is in "secret studies" (I.ii.77), neglects the affairs of this century and seeks refuge in his Books. As a result, Caliban is abstracted and essentialized by Greenaway but is enriched and empowered by the late Jarman.

References

Barker, Francis and Peter Hulme. 1985. "Nymphs and Reapers Heavily Vanish. The Discursive Con-texts of *The Tempest*." In Drakakis 1985: 191-205.

Barker, P. 1980. "The Bard Weathers the Storm." *Evening News*, 8/5/1980.

Bénoliel, Bernard. 1991. "Peter Greenaway. L'Illusion comique." *La revue du Cinéma* 475: 62-69.

Ciment, Michel. 1991. "Une conflagration de l'art. Entretien avec Peter Greenaway." *Positif* 368: 38-46.

Collick, John. 1989. *Shakespeare, Cinema and Society*. Manchester & New York: Manchester UP.

Croyden, Margaret. 1968-69. "Peter Brook's *Tempest*." *The Drama Review* 3: 125-28.

Drakakis, John, ed. 1985. *Alternative Shakespeares*. London/New York: Routledge.

Fernández Retamar, Roberto. 1989. *Caliban and Other Essays*. Translated by Edward Baker. Foreword by Fredric Jameson. Minneapolis: U of Minnesota P.

Foster, Hal, ed. 1990. *Postmodern Culture*. London: Pluto Press.

success of the composer of his films' music (Michael Nyman), who also receives a lot of attention and gives concerts on the Continent.

French, P. 1980. "Such Camp as Dreams are Made On." *The Observer*, 4/5/1980.

Greenaway, Peter. 1991. *Prospero's Books. A Film of Shakespeare's "The Tempest."* London: Chatto & Windus.

Hacker, Jonathan and David Price. 1991. *Take 10. Contemporary British Directors*. Oxford: Oxford UP.

Hantman, Jeffrey L. 1992. "Caliban's Own Voice. American Indian Views of the Other in Colonial Virginia." *New Literary History* 23 (1): 69-81.

Hutcheon, Linda. 1992. *A Poetics of Postmodernism. History, Theory, Fiction*. London: Routledge.

Jackson, Paul. 1980. "What Derek Did with £ 150,000." *Western Mail*, 30/10/1980.

Jarman, Derek. 1993. *At Your Own Risk. A Saint's Testament*. London: Vintage.

MacCabe, Colin. 1992. "A Post-National European Cinema. A Consideration of Derek Jarman's *The Tempest* and *Edward II*." In Petrie Duncan, ed. *Screening Europe: Image and Identity in Contemporary European Cinema*. London: British Film Institute, 9-18.

Marshall, B.K. 1992. *Teaching the Postmodern. Fiction and Theory*. London: Routledge.

Masson, Alain. 1991. "This Insubstantial Pageant – Prospero's Books." *Positif* 368: 36-37.

Robinson, David. 1980. "A Tempest Full of Magic and Surprises." *The Times*, 2/5/1980.

Rodgers, Marlene. 1991-'92. "Prospero's Books – Word and Spectacle. An Interview with Peter Greenaway." *Film Quarterly* 45 (2): 11-19.

Shepherd, Simon. 1988. "Shakespeare's Private Drawer. Shakespeare and Homosexuality." In Graham Holderness, ed. *The Shakespeare Myth*. Manchester: Manchester UP, 96-117.

Skura, Meredith Anne. 1989. "Discourse and the Individual. The Case of Colonialism in *The Tempest*." *Shakespeare Quarterly* 40: 4-69.

Stoll, Karl-Heinz. 1984. "Caliban's Caribbean Career." *Komparatische Hefte* 9: 7-21.

Sutton, Martin. 1980. "Interview with Derek Jarman." *Time Out*, 2/5/1980.

Vaughan, Alden T. 1988. "Shakespeare's Indian. The Americanization of Caliban." *Shakespeare Quarterly* 39: 137-53.

— and Virginia Mason Vaughan. 1991. *Shakespeare's Caliban. A Cultural History*. Cambridge: Cambridge UP.

Vaughan, Virginia. 1985. "'Into Something Rich and Strange.' Caliban's Theatrical Metamorphoses." *Shakespeare Quarterly* 36 (4): 390-405.

Zabus, Chantal. 1994. "Prospero's Progeny Curses Back. Postmodern, Postcolonial and Postpatriarchal Rewritings of *The Tempest*." In Theo D'haen and Hans Bertens, eds. *Liminal Postmodernisms*. Amsterdam/Altanta: Rodopi, 115-138.

Banville's Caliban as a Prestidigitator

Hedwig Schwall

As I say, merely a hypothesis

(Banville, *Ghosts*)

Within all great art there is a wild animal: tamed...

(Wittgenstein, *Culture and Value*)

Ghosts (1993) is the second novel of a trilogy that started with *The Book of Evidence* (1990). In the latter book the protagonist, Freddie Montgomery, kills a maid while he is stealing the portrait of a woman. *Ghosts* relates his ten years' emprisonment and how he tries to endure his subsequent life sentence of exile on an island by writing about paintings. In the third novel, *Athena* (1996), Freddie leaves the island with the purpose of authenticating a few paintings on behalf of a couple of crooked art dealers. All three novels deal with the problem of the status of images. Here, we are only interested in the middle part of the trilogy, since this is inspired by *The Tempest*.[1]

---

[1] Banville's main work consists of two trilogies, which are linked by one novel, *Mefisto*. In this book we find the figure constellation of *Ghosts* prefigured: a "devil

In his interpretation of *The Tempest*, Banville concentrates on the Caliban-figure, Freddie Montgomery. Freddie can be associated with Shakespeare's Caliban because of his brutish qualities and his cannibalistic dreams, which start a few days before he commits the murder related in *The Book of Evidence*. Yet our Caliban also shows Ariel-like features, as his *imagination* is very strong, and must help him chase away those *nightmares*. Also, he has an Ariel-like ability to make people do his will, "to treat a fool [...] as if I esteemed him the soul of probity, to string him along in his poses and his fibs, that is a peculiar pleasure" (BE 13), thus showing Freddie/Caliban as a prestidigitator. Banville's incarnation of Caliban is thus a rather complex one, and this is also shown on another level: Freddie is not only the protagonist of *Ghosts*, but also its only – and unreliable – narrator, who offers us his autobiography. In this last capacity, and since he is rather narcissistic, Freddie/Caliban offers us as many partial incarnations of his own personality as there are figures on the novel's scene; but he likewise shows how a "dark other" is at work in all these other figures.

As will be clear from this brief presentation, Banville's Caliban-figure is very close to poststructuralist paradigms of thought. More in particular, the ideas expressed in *Ghosts* can be related to Lacan's and Derrida's views on identity and writing. Although Banville never clearly mentioned their influence, a reading of his work in a Lacanian and Derridean perspective helps us to better understand the complexity of his particular Caliban. We will therefore briefly summarize their theories in so far as they elucidate this strange version of Shakespeare's *Tempest*. However, due to its complexity, the story of *Ghosts* should be presented first in some detail.

Ghosts, *Lacan and Derrida: an Introduction*

The island Freddie Montgomery settles on after leaving prison is inhabited by the famous professor Kreutznaer, an art critic. The Professor used to be very influential in art circles, but has now, for some reason unclear to Freddie, withdrawn from the circle of art dealers on the mainland. When

---

guardian" strives to control a "low-natured" protagonist. The analogy is reinforced by the fact that Mefisto/Felix addresses the protagonist as "Caliban" (*Mefisto*, 142).

Freddie arrives, Kreutznaer is stuck in his work, a monograph on one Vaublin. Freddie will help out till the work is done. In fact, he believes the work will have a liberating effect on him. After finishing the monograph, in which he will *revive* figures from forgotten paintings, he thinks he will have made up for the murder he committed and will be free to go back to the mainland to once again lead a normal life. Upon his arrival on the island, Freddie meets Licht, the Professor's other servant. Licht used to help the Professor with the typing of his manuscript and other menial tasks. Now, Freddie will take his share in those chores, especially those of logbearing and gardening.

The whole narrative, however, only really starts at the moment when a shipwrecked party strands on the island. The status of these figures remains uncertain, as a curious relation obtains between the newly-arrived castaways and the figures on the painting that must form the cornerstone of Kreutznaer's and Freddie's work on Vaublin: the latter represent the former. This coincidence leads the reader to assume that all these characters operate in one continuum. What remains unclear to the end is whether this belongs to reality or to Freddie's imagination. All we have to go on is Freddie's account.

The uncertainty just alluded to results from the fact that Freddie wants his narrative to fulfil two purposes at once. On the one hand, he wants to finish the monograph on Vaublin which Kreutznaer started. On the other hand, he also feels the urge to write his autobiography in order to rid himself of the horrifying dreams that haunt him. Both writings get imperceptibly mixed. With this double enterprise, then, Freddie has high hopes: his work on art, and his analysis of his own human nature, must help him to atone for his crime. Art made him kill, now it must help him to bring his victim to some kind of life again. Freddie calls this exercise in sublimation "a kind of necromancy." In other words, his writing is therapeutic rather than realistic.

Three ways offer themselves in which to relate Lacan's theories to Banville's novel. First of all, to Lacan a human being is not an entity but a fragmented subject. He is split into the Other (his unconscious), which, together with the "others" (figures in his real life and in his dreams) constantly models and remodels the I. Likewise, Freddie Montgomery is not a unified subject: his qualities are dispersed over all figures and he in turn assimilates the other figures' qualities. Second, since our "self" is only constituted in our interactions, every human being is incomplete. Humans cannot know themselves, cannot find ultimate meaning, but only a signifier that promises truthfulness. In *Ghosts*, Freddie suffers from a double lack in the sense that he has murdered and must now try to live with that death on his conscience. Third, *Ghosts* is most of all a story about the workings of language, thereby underscoring a main point in Lacan's theories: the human being is "a speaking animal." Freddie is an eloquent writer, who wants to recreate Vaublin's figures by describing them in such a vivid way that they assume "life" in the eyes of the readers of his monograph. Professor Kreutznaer on the other hand, though very good at imitating, cannot speak (nor write) about Vaublin: he actually forged the supposed masterpiece, yet this very fact also makes him tongue-tied when it comes to "saying" something about it. Thus, Freddie represents Lacan's view on language as always creating, as performative, whereas his predecessors – like the professor – saw it primarily as a descriptive tool.

As for the Derridean elements in *Ghosts*, which partly overlap with Lacan's ideas, we can be brief. Derrida's most famous essays start from the assumption that there is no well-delineated firm first Signifier: in order to "function," i.e. to "mean" something, one signifier always needs a second one, a supplement. Thus Derrida replaced the notion of primordiality and its ensuing concept of causality by that of the supplement to interact with the so-called "first" signifier, in order to bring about the effect of meaning. Thus he showed that there are no evidences of any clearly delineated origin. As Banville makes Freddie suppose in *Ghosts*: "What we seek, are those evidences of origin, will and action that make up what we think of as identity. We shall not find them" (228). Derrida also points out that fact is always "contaminated" by fiction, since facts can only be conveyed by a representation in language. As man cannot retrace the ultimate origin or truth of some event, nor its ultimate meaning, in every tale there will always remain a certain "undecidability."

These "poststructuralist" views make Banville's *Ghosts* into more than just another adaptation of *The Tempest*. If the novel reminds us of Shakespeare's drama because of its themes (the power of art versus nature), its form (of romance, needed for such implausible projects as the revival of dead persons), its cast (boss and two servants with party of shipwrecked) and even its setting (an island filled with strange sounds), the differences are significant too, as has been indicated above. In the next three parts of my essay I will trace these differences in more detail. First, I will explain what it means to say that Banville's characters are no complete entities in themselves. Second, I will discuss the importance of language and imagination in *Ghosts*, and particularly the idea that Art is ambiguous. Third, I will demonstrate how the causal relationships inherent in the Renaissance idea of "good magic" in Banville's novel are complicated into a net of simultaneities and doubles, which leaves the reader in the end not with the happy feeling of restored harmony, but with the puzzling undecidabilities of an open end.

The Cast

The "Names of the Actors"

> *"I was myself no unitary thing," the narrator confesses: "I was like nothing so much as a pack of cards, shuffling into other and yet other versions of myself." (26-27)*

Freddie is both an I-protagonist and an I-narrator; so, he can project his own troubles, the psychic difficulties he has with his life and his art work into his writing. Thus we find that his Calibanesque characteristics contaminate his own characters. First, there is Licht, who represents Caliban's typical qualities. Second, there is Freddie who reveals the complexity of Caliban's character, and who combines the roles of Caliban, Ariel, Prospero and Ferdinand. Third, there are the castaways, of whom we will only discuss the two most important ones, Felix and Flora. The former incarnates, like Antonio, negative forces, the latter the lifegiving influence of Miranda: together, they symbolize respectively Evil and Good at work in the Caliban-character.

Two further remarks need to be made about the figures. First, a word about the painting, in which both groups figure, the islanders and the castaways, and which is the central piece of Freddie's monograph on Vaublin. To picture this artist, Banville borrows the life story and works from the eighteenth-century French painter Watteau, who usually represents figures from the Commedia dell'Arte in pastoral landscapes. The pastoral, of course, is a major influence also on *The Tempest*. But since Freddie's narrative works with simultaneities and doubles, the origin of Vaublin's most important painting, "Le Monde d'Or" is obfuscated by three complications. First, the description Freddie gives fuses three of Watteau's really existing pictures in one: "Le Monde d'Or," "L'Embarquement pour Cythère" and "Pierrot, dit Gilles." Second, Vaublin's painting of "The Golden World," it is inferred, was counterfeited by the champion art critic, Kreutznaer: so the painting has two "authors." And third, this pictorial work is translated by Freddie into a literary account, in which he adds his own version of the island, *the tempest*uous sky, the wrecked ship and its passengers. So, all the characters of his story are in the painting – except Kreutznaer, who made the copy Freddie works from. Thus, "Le Monde d'Or" functions as a "mise en abyme" of the whole story; or as the "sogetto," the thin plot from which the improvising actors of the Commedia dell'Arte had to take their clues.

My second remark about the cast concerns the names: all have a paradoxical ring to them – an indication of the novel's idea that man is a paradoxical being. Licht (German for "light") is enveloped in darkness; Freddie has a popular name though he leads an aristocratic lifestyle; Kreutznaer, in his Prospero-position as the head of the household is all but prosperous; Felix (Latin for "happy") is spiteful, and Flora (Latin for "flower") is deflowered.

The Outer Appearance of Caliban in Licht

Prospero's first servant, Licht, has all exterior qualities of Caliban: He was born on the island from a witch; and though he owns the house in which the three of them live, Kreutznaer bosses him around without ever deigning to ask his advice (215). Licht has outspoken animal features: he has something of a fish, with his "blubby lips" (112), but he also has a rabbity look (93, 129). It is also implied that he stinks (93). "Poor Licht," then, fits Prospero's observation of Caliban as being "disproportion'd in his manners As in his shape" (V.i.290-91). He is subject to uncontrolled nervous movements: "a hand twitching in his pocket and one leg jigging. Never still, never still" (205). He is mostly speechless (15), and at other occasions he speaks awkwardly, either "blurting out" things, or he is "saying things under his breath" (214). Nurture doesn't stick with him, nor can he cultivate other things. According to Kermode, Caliban is Nature without nurture, he has no power over the created world and over himself (1993: xxiv). Licht, as "a most poor credulous monster," is always sending off "for things advertised in the newspapers" (217). He "cleaves to the principle of the perfectability of man" (sic!, 217) but he never pushes on: he is merely "Always busy, always in motion, frantically treading the rungs of his cage-wheel" (217). These descriptions make me agree with Vaughan and Vaughan, when they see modern Caliban as a symbol of the masses, "who presumably thirst for an inspiring word from the humanist poet (a modern Prospero), but instead hear only the empty verbiage of press, radio and television."[2] Yet, Banville's Prospero will never provide the inspiring word: as a forger of paintings, he himself is decidedly short on authenticity. I again agree with Vaughan and Vaughan when they find modern Caliban's "entrapped feeling reflecting society's malaise."[3] As Licht is always at the mercy of circumstances, Freddie pictures him "nodding and twitching like a marionette" (41): he is in other people' s hands. Further, Licht also shares Caliban's sad fate in love: "That was him all over, always on the look-out for something to love that would love him in return and never finding it" (19). Yet, in his relation to Flora, he is more subdued than Shakespeare's Caliban. Licht never thinks of raping the Miranda-figure, but at times he stands motionless before her room, with little hope for entrance (144).

---

[2] After Magnus Jan Krynski and Robert A. Maguire in Vaughan and Vaughan (1993: 262). As J. Smith points out, the frustration of the Caliban-figure is due to the baulking of his expectations (in Bloom 1992: 128).

[3] Commenting on Alexander Reid's "Twelve variations on Caliban" [1947] quoted in Vaughan and Vaughan 1993: 259.

As all the novel's characters are to be found in the painting "Le Monde d'Or" Licht is there too, in the form of "an anthropomorphic donkey" (96) which has Licht's eyes (64). Though we expect that the Caliban-figure is situated in the (only) animal figure of the painting, the fact that Caliban's aspects are dispersed over all figures is shown in the fact that the donkey's eye is "gazing out at us... – at us, the laughing animal, the mad animal, the inexplicable animal" (230-31). So the ones who are looked at, all the figures in the painting, also belong to the animalesque pole, as is shown in the thrice-stressed animal aspect. This feature is then especially prominent in Freddie.

The Complex Caliban in Freddie

Freddie considers himself a "forked beast" (126), an animal metaphor which is very often repeated: "Bunter, you are a beast" (132); the party of the shipwrecked see him as "Tarzan the ape-man" (122); he moves about like a "softly padding animal [...] half fierce and half afraid" (217). As befits a popular interpretation of the Caliban-figure, cannibalistic metaphors creep into his description of his drinking a cup of tea: "I love bone china, [...] I want to take the whole thing, cup and saucer and all, into my mouth and crack it lingeringly between my teeth, like meringue" (54). His reminiscences of the murder become very strong when he is alone with Flora, the most beautiful and vulnerable girl of the shipwrecked group:

> How brittle she seemed, how easily breakable. This is what the poor giant in the old tales never gets to tell, that what is most precious to him in his victims is their fragility, the way they crack so tenderly between his teeth,...He will never know what he yearns to know, how it feels to be little like them, gay and gaily vicious and full of fears and impossible plans. The human world is what he eats. It does not nourish him. (238)

Freddie refers to himself as a "wodewose": he is "the wildman of the woods," (66), "the ogre himself" (67). Yet, he is amphibian, as his element is not only the earth – as the gardener of the household, he finds himself rooted in earth: "my ankles crossed and feet in the clay (which is their true medium, after all)" (100) – but also air and fire (31), which indicates that this Caliban has also Ariel-elements in him. Though he has "a bullish weight," he can try to "float away" (181, 182) in order to forget his terrible past. In the moments when he feels hopeful that he will be able to overcome his remorse, bring his victim girl back to life, and so win his full freedom back, the Ariel-imagery dominates, and he feels "with [...] wet wings, an astonishment standing up in the world, straining drunkenly for flight" (195). As a result, Freddie does not call out to Setebos, but to "Hyperborean Apollo" (203), the god of art. While Licht remains the "marionette with twitching fingers" (41), Freddie is the real "twitcher," handling the figures of his tale: he is the puppeteer, and a prestidigitator at that. Though he vacillates between being good and bad, he has poetry in his speech, which makes him at least the literary master of all events. But Freddie also plays the Ferdinand-role: he has been educated at the best institutions (Berkeley), but on his arrival at the island he has to provide wood for the household; meanwhile, he observes Flora, the Miranda-figure, to whom he will be courteous.

Of course, Freddie figures in "The Golden World." As the narrator, he has a special position: he is dressed like Pierrot, the sad but leading figure in the Commedia dell'Arte. He is foregrounded, standing on a dais, while the other figures behind him are urging the donkey on (symbol of the text, going its own ways?)[4] Yet, the picture's protagonist stands apart from the others. "He is isolated from the rest of the figures, [...] suspended between their world and ours, a man alone. Has he dropped from the sky or risen from the underworld?" (225) Thus, the Freddie-Caliban character occupies an intermediate position; he is indeed linked with both diabolic and angelic forces, as we will see presently.

---

[4] Chapter III of *Ghosts* is entirely devoted to a detailed description of what figures in Freddie's tale as "The Golden World." This description however corresponds strikingly to an existing painting by Watteau: "Pierrot, dit Gilles." Things become even more interesting when we remember that Freddie, in the previous novel of the trilogy, called himself "Gilles the Terrible." This picture of Watteau's helps to visualize the narrator's position.

The Shipwrecked Party: an Allegorical Version of Caliban's
Good and Evil Forces

I will only discuss Felix and Flora here – the devil and the angel, so to
speak: together, they form a mini-demonology. Both figures represent a
Caliban- and Ariel-version in "pure" form: allegorical figures offer more
clear-cut distinctions than "real" characters. Still, Flora in particular
presents a dazzling array of qualities.

Felix is linked with devil-worshippers who once terrorized the island
(138). He is the prince of darkness, who incites people to do bad actions
(60). Above all, he is "der Geist der stets verneint": he tries to destroy the
good in people and brings out the dark side in every individual. While
Felix constantly works his evil upon people, Flora counteracts him in
every way. First, Felix takes away all hope, and brings to nought all
endeavours of people that try to redeem themselves, so as to leave them
only their culpability; while Flora restores their hope. Felix reminds
people of their shame and isolates them, like Kreutznaer; he also steals or
contaminates their good memories, by distorting scenes which people
cherish as scenes of innocence. Thus, he perverts Freddie's belief in the
existence of paradise – which the latter thought he had found in "The
Golden World" at the art gallery of Whitewater – by alluding to the fact
that the picture was forged by Kreutznaer. Flora counters Felix in lifting
people's burdens; she reminds them of the times when they were
innocent, in childhood. By her welcoming attitude she somewhat restores
people's self-confidence, thus for instance diminishing the distrust Freddie
has towards "the beast" in himself. In the end, Freddie's brutish Caliban-
qualities are soothed and metamorphosed into a chivalric attitude towards
Flora. Felix sows eternal doubt, by enacting the principle of never-ending
mutability (115). Flora convinces Freddie that he can be liberated from his
ghostly existence between the human world and that of nightmare, and
that he can enter the realm of humanity again: "And somehow by being
herself like this she made the things around her be there too. In her, and in
what she spoke [...] the world [...] was realised" (147). Instead of Felix'
derision, Flora offers compassion and encouragement: she is the ultimate
help the narrator needs to undo his crime, by bringing his victim back to
life by way of the arts. Finally, we find Felix as the death-dealer, while
Flora is the source of new life. This needs some further explanation.

As *Ghosts'* version of Antonio, Felix illustrates the radical perversion of virtue, as prescribed in the Machiavellian codex. Though Freddie thought for a moment that he had chased his worse self from the island, he ends his "autobiography" in a pessimistic mood: there is "No: no riddance (of him)" (244-45). Apparently, Felix incorporates the evil that is in all mankind. In brief, Felix is opposed to life; he is the one who makes people kill. Hence he is represented in Freddie's picture of "The Golden World" as the "smirking Harlequin mounted on the donkey" who "seems to know the answers" to the mysteries of being (228), and Freddie wonders: "is it he who has lent Pierrot his club?" In other words, maybe the Felix-figure who is riding the donkey-like Caliban has incited the other Caliban, Freddie, to commit the murder.

Flora, however, seems to offer a way out of Freddie's predicament. She dreams that she is in "The Golden World," where Harlequin chases her (Felix raped her), but she finds refuge in the figure of Pierrot, who turns out to be a hollow puppet. In offering the ex-murderer of a woman the chance to rescue another woman, Flora helps Freddie to live with his remorse. But she goes further: she helps him in his creative endeavour, to bring the woman he killed back to life.

> Still the dream persists, suppressed but always there, that somehow by some miraculous effort of the heart what was done could be undone. What form would such atonement take that would turn back time and bring the dead to life? None. None possible, not in the real world. And yet in my imaginings I can clearly see this new cleansed creature streaming up out of myself like a proselyte rising drenched from the baptismal river amid glad cries. (68-69)

For this task, the narrator "would need help... And so he waits for [...] the soundless falling into step beside him that will announce the presence of the ghost that somehow he must conjure" (87). In this "conjuring," Flora will be a vital help. Thus, she counteracts Felix once more in that she gives life, by bringing out Freddie's better self, who wants to "make proper restitution."

Though allegorical figures are usually clear-cut, Banville's postmodern ways make him represent them in a nuanced way. Though Flora's name contains echoes from a Neoplatonic cosmos, she is not simply angelic and spiritual. Freddie is happy to see her not only as "Venus," or "Our Lady of the Enigmas": she is also "just a girl," with "a speck of sleep in the canthus of her eye" (147).

Finally, it is important to notice that *Ghosts* presents us with a plot wherein the shipwrecked are not rescued by the islanders, but vice versa. We will come back to this point when we discuss the relations between the author and his text.

The Theatre of Language

In his "commedia erudita," Freddie is wildly imaginative. After all, this ex-murderer has something of Ariel. We will now see how this imagination functions in the interaction of three oppositional poles: that of art and nature; that of self and other, of truth and significance; and that of conscience and the unconscious.

Art and Nature

Whereas Art (but ultimately forgiveness) is the rescuing factor in *The Tempest*, Freddie is three times cheated by art. The danger lurking in products of sublimation is strikingly illustrated at the story's start, when fascination with the portrait of a lady grips the narrator so strongly that it makes him steal it and kill a living woman as a result. So it is art that corrupted Freddie's originally sedate "nature"; it metamorphoses the dazed admirer into a murderous, drunken Caliban.

Later, Freddie is tricked a second time by art, when his boss makes him work from a fake. Yet, Freddie has learned to live with lies, and he forgives Kreutznaer (as he is a patented liar himself). Like Shakespeare, the narrator refuses to make clear-cut differences between "unspoiled" nature and art: he admits that a bad work can produce a good reaction (the forgery launches Freddie on his work of atonement), and vice versa: a good work of art may produce a bad deed (the murder). Both pure art and pure nature, then, are dangerous: only their mixture is beneficent to man. Since the narrator knows what happens when he lets himself go, he is aware of the need of artful behaviour to protect him from all too spontaneous reactions. Thus, Freddie too satirizes that "primitivistic view that a natural society, without the civilized accretions of law, custom, and other artificial restraints, would be a happy one," which Shakespeare's contemporary Montaigne already doubted (Kermode 1994: xxxiv). But nature is also necessary, to revitalize art. So Freddie needs the shipwrecked people: "Company, [...] the brute warmth of the presence of others to tell us we were alive after all, despite appearances" (39). They are the ones that "gave the tale its substance"; they "are the human moment" (222).

And yet in the end Freddie is deluded a third time. Through his writings, he seems to have struck the right balance between art and life in the "artful" nature of his creative work. He even believes he has found a maxime, an ontology to go by, which says that man is fundamentally theatrical, constantly remaking himself: "to act is to be, to rehearse is to become" (199). But even this paradox is not a truth: Felix, *der Geist der stets verneint*, suggests that even this statement cannot convince, as it gives Freddie "the feel of [...]a delusion" (199). So there is no truth whatsoever to go by. Yet, Flora will show him a way to exist. Thanks to his overriding conviction that Flora can help him, Freddie's therapeutic writing seems to work. The calibanesque narrator originally suffers from a speech deficiency, a "babble" that "would come pouring out, a hopeless glossolalia" (27). Flora eventually leads him to a zenith of reality, which he finds he can also convey: "She was simply there, an incarnation of herself, no longer a nexus of adjectives but pure and present noun" (147). It is thanks to Flora that Freddie's art can become a way of life, and one that is beneficent.

Thus, the art-nature interaction shows the human subject as an actor and a speaking being, who can take up several positions in between both poles. Whereas Felix, and in his wake Kreutznaer are artificial, faking, copying, Freddie tries his hand at the artistic, the hard work of creating lives, inventing. Thereby, Felix and Flora allegorically represent black versus white magic (Felix is named in connection with Licht's Sycoraxlike mother). Yet, both

exemplary positions always interact (hence the need for tolerance
and forgiveness): Freddie's invention is inspired by Kreutznaer's
fake, while in the subplot the "good" Flora has been overcome,
deflowered by Felix.

Self and Other, Truth and Significance

As we saw in the introduction, Lacanian figures have no "centre" in a self.
The actor Freddie, who pictures himself as "a pack of cards, shuffling into
other and yet other versions of myself" (26-7), seeks not ultimate
"meaning," nor truth in life: "Truth... is a much overrated quantity" (190):
"versions of it is all I can manage" (101).

He always feels "lacking" something: in experiences which have a strong
impact on him, the narrator is either without speech or without
knowledge. So, paradoxically, the subject is never entirely present at the
times when he is confronted with "pure existence" (always situated at the
border between life and death). This observation in his own life is
underscored by Freddie's interpretation of Vaublin's art, where he sees
how, paradoxically, only the trying and *failing* self can reach his aim in
art: "It is a world where nothing is lost, where all is accounted for while
yet the mystery of things is preserved [...] in the failing evening of the
self..." (231). His own narrative is also the product of a non-unified self, as
we see in the inconsistenties which picture Flora now as a being,
"assembled gradually" (94), now as "all of a piece" (147). Yet she is so
vividly present that "in what she spoke... the world... was realised" (147),
and the narrator with it. The self is nothing, but, as Lacan indicated, he
exists fully in the interaction with another "speaking being." And Freddie
is indeed granted that which Lacan calls "full speech" ("parole pleine"),
which happens when people's unconscious relate to each other. This
happens in "transference," through the language of the Other, i.c. in a
conversation between Freddie and Flora. This kind of "full speech" is so
powerful, that it can even liberate the narrator from the cell of his own
(narcissistic) imagination. It is a kind of speech which does not concentrate
on the conveyance of facts, but of atmosphere and seemingly unimportant
details, the "impurities" that constitute the human being through the

overtones his unconscious sends up. Though seemingly nothing, this heart-strengthening talk makes all the difference to Freddie:

> Easy. Go easy. What happened, after all, except that she began to talk? Yet it has changed everything, transfigured everything, I don't know how... How eloquent at these times the sounds that humble things make... And then without warning she began to talk. Oh, I don't know what about, I hardly listened to the sense of it; something about a dream, or a memory, of being a child... (145-47)

It is not the "self," but the Other which finally makes Freddie "real," liberating him from the limits of his subjective consciousness. It is Flora, incarnation of that unconscious, which makes him "present" to himself:

> I felt everyone and everything shiver and shift, falling into vividest forms, detaching themselves from me and my conception of them and changing themselves instead into what they were, no longer figment, [...] no longer a part of my imagining. And I, was I there amongst them, at last? (147)[5]

This brings me to my second point: in such a "fluid" world, it is not truth or meaning, no heart-revealing talk but *significance* that makes a thing or person be real, have "presence." Significance is what makes the narrator "live." It exists in situations, loaded with a certain amount of electricity, energy; it slumbers in things such as Vaublin's pictures, "waiting to be brought to some kind of life" (82). Significance is "the ravelled complexity of things," that which fascinates, what is on the point of being understood, but not quite yet. It is not knowledge, but the promise of it; it is "what holds it all together and yet apart, this sense of expectancy, like a spring tensed in mid-air and sustained by its own force" (40). So, Freddie feels

---

[5] "Them" are the figures in the painting which have their double in Freddie's life, as they arrive as a group of shipwrecked people. With their calamity, they bring in nature and spontaneity, those qualities the murderer feared and repressed, and which the art critic lacked.

ghosts around him, "yearning to speak" (38), Presences, lives who "speak to me... of matters I do not fully understand" (101). As Lacan would say, it is not the signified that liberates us but the (penultimate) signifier.

Conscious and Unconscious

In order to understand Freddie more fully, we must take a look at the theatre in which the actors of the company of his intrapsychic system are rehearsing Freddie's life and improvising the images that will be sent up to his imagination.

When we consider Freddie's "situation of discourse," we discern three factors at work in the drama of his artistic work: the Super-Ego who is the addressee of the whole narrative; the Ego who directs the play, and the Id, who often puts a word in sideways. That Id is, according to Freud, to be divided in beneficent and malicious influences. In his belief that the beneficent Id is the stronger one, Freddie seems to side with psychoanalysts like Georg Groddeck, one of Freud's colleagues. With his mastery of literary techniques, Freddie hopes to improve his internal household, but he learns how this depends upon a good interaction between Ego and Id, which must be presented to the Super-Ego. So he tries to call up his good Id in the forms of Flora, but he also needs to face Felix, Id's worse aspect.

As I go through the labyrinth of Freddie's psychic system, I will follow the red thread Freud offers us. First there is the Super-Ego, Freddie's conscience and the addressee of his story: "to whom was I offering these implausible farragos...?" "I would have liked to see the face of my oneiric accusers," who are presented with the "bloodstained pageants" of his nightmares as well as with his endeavours to create new life in his writings (28). Freddie fears the internal authority of his Super-Ego more than the public institutions. Hence, his writing must make the players obey him, and at the same time convince the public (the readers of his monograph/autobiography) that all is real, that he can make up for what he did wrong in another world.

Second, there is Freddie's Ego which, thanks to his strong narcissism, is quite powerful. Hence, the narrator is self-conscious about his status. He sees himself as a "little god," since the author is a "life- and death-dealer": he can stop the figures, "the human element," any time: "That would be a laugh, for me to die and leave them there, trapped, the tide halted, the boat stuck fast forever... all of creation cowering before us, the death-dealers" (126). In this sense, this Ariel-figure does not lose his Caliban-aspect of the "poor, dumb destroyer" (126).

As a director of figures, the Ego alternates between three attitudes. He represses his "dark other," obliterating Felix but foregrounding Flora, Freddie's benevolent Id. The narrator can also hesitate as to the way he will stage himself, as when he vacillates over the number of shipwrecked he will need to represent his "Id." Further, he cautiously tries to acknowledge his past, using the whole arsenal of methods Freud discovered in his *Traumdeutung*. One recognizes Freud's four devices to mention the unmentionable indirectly: the narrator condensates his wishes in Flora, substitutes his own heart-rending feelings of remorse for those of all characters, whereby he displaces the facts of his own life and of his own struggles with art into those of Vaublin. Finally, secondary revision is visible everywhere, as the narrator tries to rationalize the chaotic structure of his story.[6]

This "rationalization" is complemented by an overtly strong performative use of language: "Vaublin shall live!" (245). His "necromantic" writing is part and parcel of the expiation of his crime, and magic is always performative. Yet, apart from the overt rhetorical elements, the "Id" slips in as well, as the I is also an improviser. As a result, the unconscious rhetoric of Freddie's worse Id, his Caliban-aspect, establishes itself, especially in metaphors that link Freddie's present life with the moment of his murder. When he stoops over a suitcase to stuff his shirts in, he sees himself "like a ravisher over his splayed victim" (186). In his quality of

---

[6] This chaos, of course, is due to the fact that Freddie's "life" depends on this story, on this endeavour to create life. And life is always chaotic: "A life! with all its ragged complexities, its false starts and sudden closures, the summer solitudes and winter woes, the inexplicable exaltations in April weather, the meals to be eaten, the sleeps to be slept..." (86). The novel's (hardly visible) structure reflects Freddie's view on life, a chain of unconnected scenes of what happens to the shipwrecked, who are "dispers'd in troops about the isle."

improviser, Freddie resembles the Pierrot-figure from the Commedia dell'Arte. In line with what is usual in that art, Freddie borrows his "skeleton" plot from "The Golden World." Even in the style and imagery of his narrative, Freddie sticks to the species of the Commedia dell'Arte that was known as pastoral tragicomedy, in which erudite allusions are mixed in. Thus, *Ghosts* can be read, like *The Tempest*, as an erudite joke.

The dark scene of Freddie's Id is laid out as if by Freud himself. The centre of his being, the narrator remarks, is emptiness: it is a "black vacuum the self keeps rushing into yet can never fill" (236). As a result, Freddie is a desiring being: Lacan's "desire of desire" is clearly expressed in Freddie's Id that will never know what he yearns to know": though "the human world is what he eats, it does not nourish him" (238). Yet, this black hole, the "primary repression" in Freud's terms, is filled with images: Freddie recognizes "a handful of emblematic fragments from the deep past that seem mysteriously to constitute something of the very stuff of which I am made" (39). These images betray their "origin" in the primary system in that they have a special tendency to form inconsistenties rather than logical configurations. Thus, the "ogre himself" often feels vulnerable, as "in a little skiff [...] out over depthless waters" (66-67); he is "a childish man, a mannish child" (226), both the "beast" and "the shepherd, guarding them against the prowling wolf" (92). Throughout the story, the narrator's imagination proves his "unreliability" in all kinds of inconsistencies, resulting from the fact that Ego and Id alternately stir and soothe each other, multiply and order, ignore and summon, imprison and liberate, create and receive, lie and correct. "To lie is to create," says the narrator – thus proving his unreliability.

The theatre of Freddie's writing shows us man in a Lacanian view: the subject is fragmented, without a firm "self" at the centre from which to deduce a -certain "essence" and character. Such a subject depends on interaction with the elements of its own psyche and with others, and that interaction always happens through language.

Paradigmatic Shifts between The Tempest *and* Ghosts*: Undecidabilities Concerning the Notions of the Author, the Text and its Reception*

> *What we seek, are those evidences of origin, will and action that make up what we think of as identity. We shall not find them.*

> (Banville, *Ghosts*)

In each of the works of art mentioned in *Ghosts*, more than one author is involved; moreover, the work itself "works" too. In *The Tempest*, the author's position and that of the reader is relatively clear. To Ferdinand's remark, during the performance of the masque, that "This is a most majestic vision, and Harmonious charmingly. May I be bold To think these spirits?" (IV.i.118-20), Prospero answers: "Spirits, which by mine Art I have from their confines call'd to enact My present fancies" (IV.i.120-23). In *Ghosts* however, both the confines and the Art are not simply at the author's disposal. His position, as we can expect by now, is mirrored several times: Vaublin inspired Kreutznaer, whose fake sets Freddie working, who in his turn makes a narrative out of that counterfeited Vaublin. Thus, "those evidences of origin" are lost. Further, each of these authors has a crime on his conscience, so the "confines" of their art are heavily influenced by the "Id" that typified the calibanesque narrator Freddie. Thus, the "evidences of will" are crossed. Third, none of the authors feels he is the only creator of his works: all feel accompanied by a double. When Vaublin "steps to the canvas, another, heavier arm seems to lift alongside his" (128). Kreutznaer's basic experience is that of "Incongruity...the grotesqueries of the always-slipping mask" (43). And Freddie notices "how strangely matters arrange themselves at times, as if after all there were someone, another still, whose task it is to set them out just so" (40). Thus, "the evidences of action" cannot be traced back.

Moreover, the author does not manage his writing entirely himself, the words themselves fulfil an important part of that task, as becomes clear from Freddie's observation of Vaublin's "The Golden World":

> Evidently there is an allegory here, and symbols seem to
> abound, yet the scene carries a weight of unaccountable
> significance that is disproportionate to any possible
> programme or hidden discourse. It is first of all a master-
> piece of pure composition, of the architectonic
> arrangement of [...] presence and absence and yet we
> cannot prevent ourselves asking what it is that gives the
> scene its air of mystery and profound and at the same
> time playful significance. (227)

The ideal correspondences of romance along with its simple codes have
become untenable in *Ghosts*. The chivalric hero has "a dewlapped neck,"
while the angel, Flora, walks in a faintly urinous smell. The events don't
take place in one single, unified pastoral landscape, but figures walk in and
out of pictures. The frames do not hold, the anarchy of possible worlds is
loosed upon this tale. So the castaways step back and forth over the
painting's frame and into the world of the narrator (55). Moreover, the old
chivalric code, especially the respect for chastity, is not upheld in this
story. Flora, the rescuing angel, is no virgin, and though the narrator
sticks to the knight's attitude towards her, it is not certain that he has
known her only through conversation. In romance, it was a condition of
the magus to be chaste, in order to have his white magic "work." In
Ghosts, Freddie's behaviour remains as ambiguous as the outcome of his
therapeutic writing. As a result, he has not, like most of *The Tempest*'s
figures, found himself after "no man was his own" (V.1.210-3) throughout
the turbulence organised by Prospero. Freddie found a woman who
rescued him and whom he rescued, but at the end of the story, he is still
not "his own," simply because in Banville's story, there is no "self" to
regain after the tempestuous invasion by the shipwrecked. Through these
shifts, grown from a poststructuralist paradigm, *Ghosts* loosens all those
schematizations of alienation and restitution scholars tried out to "tame"
The Tempest.

As for us, the readers, Freddie's ghosts don't make our job easy. We find
ourselves at a loss when we try to decide whether the shipwrecked party
actually belonged to the brute reality related, or whether they are just
ghosts invented by the narrator. The problem thus raised is artfully
forestalled by the author of the Vaublin "monograph": "The question has

frequently been asked if the figures ranged behind Pierrot are the products of the artist's imagination or portraits of real people" (230). It is not reflection that will sort this out: with Coleridge, we might say the whole story is but an appeal to the reader's imagination, to his abilities to mirror the author's position once more. Thus, *Ghosts* is not a "postcolonial" interpretation of Shakespeare's famous play, nor does it concentrate on a "Third World" in the political sense. Rather, the "third world" it is set in is that of the imagination.

References

Banville, John. 1993a. *Mefisto* [1986]. London: Minerva Paperback.

—. 1993b. *The Book of Evidence* [1990]. London: Minerva Paperback.

—. 1993c. *Ghosts* [1993]. London: Minerva Paperback.

Bloom, Harold, ed. 1992. *Caliban (Major Literary Characters)*. New York: Chelsea House.

Kermode, Frank, ed. 1994. *The Arden Edition of the Works of William Shakespeare. The Tempest* [1954]. London: Routledge.

Vaughan, Alden T. and Virginia Mason Vaughan. 1993. *Shakespeare's Caliban. A Cultural History* [1991]. Cambridge: Cambridge UP Paperback.

The Tempest, Now and Twenty Years After

Rachel Ingalls's *Mrs Caliban* and Tad Williams's *Caliban's Hour*

Theo D'haen

Vaughan and Vaughan, in their otherwise very able and pertinent *Shakespeare's Caliban. A Cultural History*, give short shrift to Rachel Ingalls's 1982 *Mrs Caliban* (after Vaughan and Vaughan we will call it a novel, though actually it is rather a novella). In the introductory paragraph to their first chapter, "Caliban's debut," Vaughan and Vaughan are out to show the range of "bizarre characters, inspired by Shakespeare's Caliban" (3) in contemporary culture, and hence to "attest to the monster's integral place in our cultural heritage" (3). Ingalls's protagonist they see as an extreme example of such a bizarre character: "a six-foot seven-inch human amphibian of insatiable sexual appetite and simultaneously a fetus; both are figments of the heroine's starved libido" (3). Doubtless, Dorothy, Ingalls's heroine, can do with some sexual gratification from Larry, the Caliban-like character from *Mrs Caliban*. And yes, there are indications in the text that Larry fills the role of the "baby" that Dorothy is "guaranteed" (2) to make up for the unborn child that she so tragically lost shortly after the accidental death of her infant son many years earlier. Still, to therefore simply reduce this character to "[a] figment[s] of the heroine's starved libido," and therefore of her imagination, is to beg the question as to the function of such a refiguration. In what follows, I will try to answer this question by looking at Ingalls's text as a rewrite of *The Tempest*, and thereby as expressive of a certain attitude toward (specifally Western) modernity, the age Shakespeare's play can be taken to be emblematic of. In order to flesh out my interpretation of *Mrs Caliban*, I will also address another recent rewriting of *The Tempest*, viz. Tad Williams's 1994 *Caliban's Hour*, a text I see as imaginatively articulating a similar attitude toward modernity.

I

In "(Post)Modernity and Caribbean Discourse," a piece shortly to appear in Volume III of *A History of Literature in the Caribbean*, edited by A. James Arnold under the auspices of the International Comparative Literature Association, I tried to relate various modernist and postmodern rewrites of *The Tempest* to the issue of modernity. Taking my cue from New Historicist or Cultural Studies scholars such as Brown (1985), Barker and Hulme (1985), Hawkes (1985), Hulme (1986), Eagleton (1986), and Greenblatt (1988), to name only some of the more obvious contenders, I construed *The Tempest* as deeply enmeshed in the emerging discourses of capitalism, colonialism, and imperialism rather than, as earlier and traditional Shakespeare criticism has tended to do, as primarily concerned with the issues of authority, sovereignty, and usurpation within a strictly European and Europeanist Renaissance context. Simon Gikandi, in *Writing in Limbo: Modernism and Caribbean Literature* (1992), posits that "entry into the European terrain of the modern has often demanded that the colonized peoples be denied their subjectivity, language, and history" (1992: 2). The following well-known passage from Act I, Scene II, ll. 334-67 (Kermode 1988: 31-33) of *The Tempest* can be read as famously backing Gikandi's claim:

> CALIBAN: This island's mine, by Sycorax my mother
> Which thou tak'st from me. When thou cam'st first,
> Thou strok'st me, and made much of me; wouldst give me
> Water with berries in 't; and teach me how
> To name the bigger light, and how the less,

That burn by day and night: and then I lov'd thee,
And show'd thee all the qualities o'th'isle,
The fresh springs, brine-pits, barren place and fertile:
Curse'd be that I did so! All the charms
Of Sycorax, toads, beetles, bats, light on you!
For I am all the subjects that you have,
Which first was mine own king: and here you sty me
In this hard rock, whiles you do keep from me
The rest o'th'island.

PROSPERO: Thou most lying slave,
Whom stripes may move, not kindness! I have us'd thee,
Filth as thou art, with human care; and lodg'd thee
In mine own cell, till thou didst seek to violate
The honour of my child.

CALIBAN: O ho, O ho! would't had been done!
Thou didst prevent me; I had peopled else
This island with Calibans.

MIRANDA: Abhorred slave,
Which any print of goodness wilt not take,
Being capable of all ill! I pitied thee,
Took pains to make thee speak, taught thee each hour
One thing or other: when thou didst not, savage,
Know thine own meaning, but wouldst gabble like
A thing most brutish, I endow'd thy purposes
With words that made them known. But thy vile race,
Though thou didst learn, had that in't which good natures
Could not abide to be with; therefore wast thou
Deservedly confin'd into this rock,
Who hadst deserv'd more than a prison.

CALIBAN: You taught me language; and my profit on't
Is, I know how to curse. The red plague rid you
For learning me your language!

This passage is crucial because it is the only instance in the play where Caliban tries to gainsay Prospero's version of things, and this version is immediately "overwritten" by Prospero, abetted by Miranda. The legitimation for Prospero's assertion of authority is provided by the enormity of the crime Caliban is here charged with: the attempted rape of Miranda. In turn, the credibility of this alleged intention ascribed to Caliban rests in the Nurture/Nature distinction also being made in this passage. Together, as Robert Young has demonstrated in *Colonial Desire: Hybridity in Theory, Culture, and Race* (1995), the tenets of the innate sexual promiscuity and the permanent un-educability of the "dark races" over the next few centuries built into the cornerstones of the fullfledged racial theories underpinning European colonialism and imperialism in their nineteenth-century heyday. The crime Caliban is here accused of, then, is not so much an isolated instance of individual misbehavior as a continued and fundamental threat to the system of modernity itself. However, if we turn things around, we can read Prospero's accusation of Caliban not as the description of something that actually happened within the imaginative realm of the play's pre-history, but rather as the projection of a basic fear gnawing at the root of modernity: miscegenation as a threat that risks halting and even reversing the direction of history as perceived by modernity, in which the racial superiority of the white man was the safeguard of as well as the corollary to modernity. At the same time, Prospero's accusation implicitly exonerates Miranda as possibly willing accessory to Caliban's crime, and thus also re-asserts Prospero's patriarchal authority over his daughter, who, as some of the more recent critics I mentioned have argued, stands in a similar position of "subjectness" to him as Caliban, and this nothwithstanding all other possible differences. After all, Miranda's purity is the necessary condition to her marriage to Ferdinand, heir to the throne of Naples. As such, it is also part of Prospero's ticket to his re-instatement as Duke of Milan, and the guarantee of the final and continuing restoration of the legal order. With regard to Prospero's and Miranda's respective "voices" in the discourse of modernity, it is useful to remember that in the specific passage under consideration there is considerable editorial uncertainty as to whether the lines here attributed to Miranda should properly not also be given to Prospero, which would effectively enhance the latter's authority as the sole "speaker" of modernity: the fully and exclusively empowered Western male. Summarizing things, I interpreted Shakespeare's play as imaginatively filling out the discourse of modernity as "the usurpation of native suzerainty, the commodification of native labor, the de-territorialization of native language and the re-territorialization of the native's use of the colonizer's language as 'bad' English, the appropriation and erasure or distortion of native history, the vilification of native science and knowledge as black magic, the disfranchisement of native identity, and the 'thingification' of women in terms of exchange rather than intrinsic value."

Modernity's instrument in *The Tempest* is Prospero, and traditional Shakespeare criticism's easy acceptance of Prospero's patriarchal authority to act as he does with regard to the isle, Caliban, and Miranda is convincing testimony as to the West's age-long naturalization of the discourse of modernity, and to its until recently largely unchallenged hegemony. However, when the discourse of modernity started to be seriously interrogated from the era of modernism on – as various critics, among them Edward Said in *Culture and Imperialism* (1993), have argued, it is not to be wondered at that *The Tempest*, given its iconic status as a "master text" of European modernity, became a prime subject for such interrogation. In imaginative literature, this took the form of rewrites of Shakespeare's play. In my discussion, in "(Post)Modernity and Caribbean Discourse," of some twentieth-century rewrites of *The Tempest*, I distinguish between modernist, postmodern, counter-modernist, and counter-postmodern versions. Basically, I see the latter two as postcolonial "counter-discourses," in the sense given to the term in Ashcroft, Griffiths and Tiffin (1989), emanating from the periphery of modernity, to the two former currents, springing from the "center" of modernity, and traditionally credited with a global reach. Of course, it is this global pretension, particularly with regard to the use of the term "postmodernism," that most recently and vehemently has been challenged by spokesmen for postcolonialism.

Perhaps the most concise way of outlining the difference between the "central" and the "counter-"variants of modernism and postmodernism is to argue that the latter try to recover that "subjectivity, language, and history" that modernity has denied to the West's "Others," and that the former voice the (male) West's "Self's" increasing despair as to the same things. This is the grid against which, in "(Post)Modernity and Caribbean Discourse," I read T.S. Eliot's *The Waste Land* and W.H. Auden's *The Sea and the Mirror* as "central" modernist rewrites, and Aimé Césaire's *Une Tempête* as a counter-modernist rewrite of *The Tempest*. In particular, though, I discussed Paule Marshall's 1983 *Praisesong for the Widow*, Gloria Naylor's 1988 *Mama Day*, and Marina Warner's 1992 *Indigo* as counter-postmodern rewrites of the same text. Though I did not do so, I might have discussed John Fowles's 1963 *The Collector* and 1966 *The Magus* as examples of postmodern rewrites. In the context of the present collection, I am interested in looking at Rachel Ingalls's *Mrs Caliban* and Tad Williams's *Caliban's Hour* as two more instances of central postmodern rewrites of *The Tempest*, concentrating, as their respective titles suggest – and at variance, for instance, with Fowles's texts, upon the character of Caliban. Moreover, I have chosen to juxtapose these two specific texts because, although at first sight they seem like poles apart – the one, *Mrs Caliban*, with a contemporary setting, and told in a typical contemporary American short-story idiom with science-fiction overtones; the other, *Caliban's Hour*, a historical novel set close to the time of action of Shakespeare's original – in my opinion they express a similar attitude toward the modernity *The Tempest* is iconic of. Both *Mrs Caliban* and *Caliban's Hour* focus upon a number of issues that are also central to *The Tempest*, and specifically upon the issues of sexuality, language, and Nature vs. Nurture. In both cases *The Tempest*'s valorization of "true" or "correct" language, sexual purity, and Nurture over Nature, as typical of Western modernity is reversed. Yet, as distinct from counter-postmodern rewrites such as those by Marshall, Naylor, and Warner mentioned earlier, Ingalls's and Williams's rewrites do not, in the words of Stephen Slemon, express "oppositional truth-claims" (1991: 5) predicating the entry of the West's "Others" into modernity as full participants, as sharers rather than as "subjects." Though clearly rewrites of a "canonical 'master text'" (Slemon 1991: 5) of Western modernity, then, they equally clearly also stop short of rewriting modernity itself, and this at variance with their counter-postmodern counterparts.

II

Mrs Caliban ingeniously transposes Shakespeare's play to a contemporary American setting. At first sight Mrs Ingalls's text, except for the give-away reference in its title, seems to have little to do with *The Tempest*. Yet, once we start seeing parallels, we soon realize that the enchanted isle of *The Tempest* here is re-created as the (most probably Los Angeles) suburban home of Dorothy, one-time television studio extra and at present housewife. The role of Ariel is played by the radio, which starts addressing personal messages to Dorothy at odd hours of the day, and also by television, which prompts various characters' actions, but particularly those of "Caliban," a sea-creature recently captured somewhere off the coast of South America and transported to the United States for the purpose of scientific research. At the same time, radio and television also assume the guise of "His Master's Voice," Prospero's, in that they relate the antecedents of the sea-creature before its unexpected arrival in Dorothy's kitchen. Like Prospero in *The Tempest*, they also provide the only link with the "outside" world. Minor characters from *The Tempest*, like Stephano and Trinculo, are re-incarnated as Kelsoe and Wachter, the guardians of the sea-creature at the "Jefferson Institute for Oceonographic Research." Even such a minor action from *The Tempest* like the chess game between Miranda and Ferdinand has a parallel in *Mrs Caliban* in the game of checkers between Dorothy and Fred. Yet, for all the parallels obtaining, and as already indicated in my previous paragraph, *Mrs Caliban* is also very different from *The Tempest*.

To begin with, there is the sexual aspect so one-sidedly stressed by Vaughan and Vaughan. Of course, non-Western man's voracious sexual appetite is a stock-in-trade of Western modernity's racially prejudiced worldview, and *The Tempest* makes much of this. However, instead of condemning such sexuality *Mrs Caliban* welcomes it, not only in the novel's "Caliban" but also in its "Miranda," Dorothy. Indeed, when *Mrs Caliban*'s "Caliban," more prosaically named "Larry," escapes from the research institute he is held at, and blunders into Dorothy's kitchen, he is hid by her, and very quickly becomes her lover. That this relationship, physically but also emotionally, constitutes a form of therapy for both Larry and Dorothy is never in doubt. In fact, both Larry and Dorothy are damaged by the repressive practices of the society they find themselves the victims of, the one as an "alien" creature, the other as a woman. In this novel, then, as in the original *Tempest*, Caliban and Miranda - or Larry and Dorothy, occupy closely related positions. *The Tempest* forces these two characters apart in the interests of modernity. *Mrs Caliban*, though intimating that true happiness for these creatures lies in a natural alliance against their oppressor, at the same time also makes the point that such an alliance, at least in the long run, is doomed. From the very beginning of their relationship Dorothy has vague plans to take Larry back to his own country of origin. Things come to a head, however, when Larry, on an outing from the enchanted isle that Dorothy's house is for him, kills a number of youths that gang up on him, and discovery becomes imminent. One of the youths involved is the son of Estelle, Dorothy's closest friend. Sensing that a break-up is inevitable, Dorothy drives Larry to a particular garden which they have been in the habit of visiting regularly after dark. There, they stumble upon Dorothy's husband, Fred, making love to Estelle's teenage daughter Sandra. Confused, Dorothy, with Larry, takes the highway to the ocean. Fred wrecks his car, killing himself and Sandra, trying to overtake Dorothy. Afraid that Larry, who is in the car with her, will be found out, Dorothy tells him to take to the ocean. They'll meet again later on, at the beach. Years go by, but Larry never shows.

The relationship between Dorothy and Larry, however, is also doomed in another way. As I mentioned before, Dorothy is "guaranteed" another "baby" for the one she lost many years ago. This promise is made to her via the radio, in one of the mysterious personal messages she receives, and which all assure her that everything will be "allright." As I also already indicated, in a certain sense Larry himself can be taken as that other "baby" mentioned, both in the immediate sense of an infant, and in the more metaphorical sense of "lover." But Larry, as an obviously very active and potent lover could presumably also literally father a new "baby" upon Dorothy. All of these "promises" turn out to be false: Larry disappears, and from the final pages of the novel it is very clear that Dorothy spends the rest of her life childless, and alone. Finally, then, nothing is "allright" for Dorothy.

On one level, the failure of all these promises points to the role of language in *Mrs Caliban*. In *The Tempest* the language of truth is spoken by the voice of authority, Prospero, and the noise, music, and magic Ariel lets loose upon the play's other characters is backed by that authority. Caliban, on the contrary, is branded a liar. In *Mrs Caliban*, all this is reversed. Larry speaks the truth, and radio and television messages prove notoriously unreliable, while still highly "authoritative." One way in which *Mrs Caliban* makes this point is via the various names assigned to, and the various descriptions of, its particular Caliban-figuration. In the official messages we are allowed to overhear early in the novel there is talk of "Acquarius the Monsterman [...] a giant lizard-like animal" (4), and "the monsterman" (5). As these are the very same messages Dorothy hears, not surprisingly her first impression when "Caliban" walks into the door is of "a gigantic six-foot-seven-inch frog-like creature" (14). Upon closer inspection, though, she finds that

> His eyes were huge and dark, seeming much larger than the eyes of a human being, and extremely deep. His head was quite like the head of a frog, but rounder, and the mouth was smaller and more centred in the face, like a human mouth. Only the nose was very flat, almost not there, and the forehead bulged up in two creases. The hands and feet were webbed, but not very far up, in fact only just noticeably, and as for the rest of the body, he was exactly like a man – a well-built large man – except that he was a dark spotted green-brown in colour and had no hair anywhere. And his ears were unusually small, set low down and rounded. (15)

In fact, the longer Dorothy knows Larry, the more human he seems. The same point is made in another way when Larry turns out to speak English quite well, although Dorothy finds that he "pronounced all the syllables of 'vegetable,' but she had met one or two ordinary Americans who said the word that way" (16). Of course, the fact that this "Caliban" should be called the homely "Larry" only underscores his final "ordinariness." While the wavering over this particular Caliban's name and precise description, then, accurately reflect the historical uncertainties as to the character's representation on the stage, it at the same time also illustrates the Foucauldian point that whatever is seen as "Calibanesque" is as much a matter of definition, that is to say of language, as of fact. The ultimate "humanity" of Larry is confirmed at the close of the novel. Dorothy goes to visit her late husband's grave. When asked for his name by another grieving widow, she answers: "His name was actually Frederick. But I called him Larry" (89). Here, the identification between this novel's "Ferdinand/Fred," and "Caliban/Larry" is complete.

The irony of it all, though, is that Larry's ultimate elevation to manhood, at least in the eyes and language of Dorothy, does not really make him any "better." Initially, Larry shows up *The Tempest*'s wisdom about the "savage's" imperviousness to the effects of Nurture as mere prejudice: it is Larry's "Natural" kindness and intelligence that actually make him into a model of everything that Nurture should teach a human being to become. It is precisely the "Nurture" that Larry receives at the hands of the Research Institute guardians – the two men torture him and submit him to sexual degradations – and watching television, that teach him to behave in a fully "human" way, that is to say "unnaturally" as compared to the spontaneity, tolerance, and good humor that he displays originally. The one thing that "Nurture" in *The Tempest* most explicitly is meant to prevent Miranda, and Caliban, from doing is to have "unnatural" sex. Sex with Larry is what is most "natural" to Dorothy in *Mrs Caliban* , and this in stark contrast with all the degraded and "unnatural" sex, or starvation from sex, that is going on around her. Larry therefore becomes "human" also in this respect when towards the end of the novel he insists on watching a human couple make love, and thereby becomes a voyeur, sharing in the sexual degradation of humankind. As he also insists on Dorothy watching with him, and as the people they are watching turn out to be Fred and Sandra, this is also what sets off the final climax of the novel leading to Fred's and Sandra's deaths and Larry's disappearance. Even in their ultimate removal from Dorothy's life, then, Fred and Larry do indeed become "one" or interchangeable at the end of *Mrs Caliban*.

In *Mrs Caliban* the Western modernity that *The Tempest* so triumphantly rings in has grounded to a sterile standstill. Prospero, the voice of authority and truth, and Ariel, his faithful amanuensis, have been replaced by the modern mass media. On the one hand these feed humanity an interminable stream of half-truths at best. On the other hand they are at the mercy of each individual listener's or viewer's whim as to whether he or she actually turns them on or not. Fred and Dorothy, middle-aged Ferdinand and Miranda, legitimate heirs to modernity's brave new world, have succumbed to the dullness and grayness of mechanical modern life. The death of their infant son, Dorothy's subsequent miscarriage, and the couple's final lack of sexual interest in each other – though especially Fred's lack of interest in Dorothy – spell doom to the continuation of this world. The arrival of Larry at first seems to hold out the possibility of a second chance, of re-engendering modernity while at the same time putting right some of the wrongs committed in its name. In the end, though, the sterility of Western modernity proves too strong. Larry is lured into conformity with Western modernity, even while this modernity continues to exclude him and his likes. This is also where the specific setting, as well as some other features of *Mrs Caliban* begin to make sense.

The American setting of *Mrs Caliban*, of course, tallies with what we know of the genealogy of *The Tempest*. Beyond this, though, "America," in the guise of the United States, is certainly the most shining example of Western modernity, and within the United States Southern California, and especially Hollywood, the American Dream's Dream Factory, fulfil the same role. In fact, the United States is itself a direct product of that modernity, and specifically of its eigtheenth-century avatar, the Enlightenment ideas of the *philosophes*, translated into the *Declaration of Independence* and the American *Constitution*. Pride of place, of course, in the *Declaration of Independence* takes the profession of belief in the equality of all men. It is a supreme irony, therefore, as well as a terrible judgement on what modernity has come to in "America," that the Research Institution from which Larry escapes, and where he is so rudely introduced to the inequality inherent in American life, should be named after the American *philosophe* who framed the *Declaration of Independence*: Thomas Jefferson. And it is only logical that the only other person from whom Larry should experience any such thing as sympathy or mercy is Mr Mendoza, Dorothy's Mexican gardener. Mr Mendoza too is both co-opted and excluded by Western, in this case American, modernity. Perpetually on sufferance, he is unable to make any real difference. And yet, Mr Mendoza has older claims to the land he is working on than the Anglos that now own it: his people were there before, in practice and in law; after all, Southern California *was* part of Mexico for much longer than it has been part of the United States!

The picture *Mrs Caliban* finally leaves us with is that of Dorothy/Miranda at the beach, waiting for Larry to return, and for yet another chance. "But he never came." (90) Ingalls seems to imply that modernity is a dead end street, and there is no regeneration possible. If we decide in the end to go along with Vaughan and Vaughan's reading, and to look upon this novel's Caliban as a mere figment of the "dotty" heroine's imagination or starved libido, this would neatly bring us back to the "central" postmodern paradigm in which textuality is all. To recycle some terms first used by John Barth, *Mrs Caliban* then truly becomes an instance of the West's "literature of exhaustion," without hope for "replenishment."

III

If Rachel Ingalls's *Mrs Caliban* is concerned with the tail end of modernity, Tad Williams's *Caliban's Hour* takes us right back to the period of the original *Tempest*, i.e., to the dawn of modernity itself. On a stormy night, twenty years after the events chronicled in Shakespeare's play, Caliban comes to visit Miranda in Naples. Miranda is now the mother of four, with two daughters married off already, and a male heir to the throne as well as Giulietta, the third daughter, still at home. Ferdinand is more often away on vague official visits – it is intimated that actually he is pursuing amorous interests away from Miranda – than he is at home. Caliban makes his way into Miranda's bedroom, and tells her that he has come to kill her. Originally he had meant to kill Prospero, and had travelled to Milan to do so. However, on arriving there he found that Prospero had already died. So now his vengeance can only fall upon Miranda. But before killing Miranda Caliban is going to do what Prospero, or Prospero and Miranda, had prevented him from doing in *The Tempest*: he is going to tell his own tale.

Once again, as with *Mrs Caliban*, we find that *Caliban's Hour* reverses the tale of *The Tempest*. In Caliban's own tale he is not the lecherous savage Prospero makes him out to be. Instead, he genuinely loves Miranda, and when it looks as if it will come to a sexual encounter between the two this is just as much Miranda's doing as it is his. Only later will Miranda obliquely accuse Caliban in order to save her own reputation with her father. He is not innately depraved and impervious to Nurture. Instead, he is innately good and "naturally" innocent. He does not speak "bad" English, but shows himself to be as quick and astute a student of language as of other things. He does not balk at the menial tasks imposed upon him by Prospero, but voluntarily and willingly takes these tasks upon himself, moved in this by love for Miranda, and admiration for Prospero. Or at least, Caliban does so initially. He does change his attitude, but only after Prospero himself has relegated Caliban to the position of a slave, and after he has so severely beaten him, following the sexual episode with Miranda, as to indeed make him into the "deformed slave" from the roll call of characters from the First Folio. Before this, Caliban, who has been taught by Prospero to call the latter by his name, had hoped to be able to call him "Father," as he had hoped to be called "Son" himself sometime. Instead, henceforth he has to call Prospero "Master." Indeed, though Caliban in *Caliban's Hour* is consistently referred to as "the villain," this is only done so ironically, with a nod to the terminology usually applied to him by the human race, and therefore to show how wrong and prejudiced this terminology is. The real villain of this piece is rather Prospero, who here is shown to be a master of black magic – rather than white, as in *The Tempest*, and who is also reputed to be a "warlock" by some of the minor characters in the book – and we note that the customary color scheme of Western imperialism, and of *The Tempest* is here turned upside down. A similar irony applies when Caliban is likened to the "devil" by some of the humans in *Caliban's Hour*. A much more likely devil – at variance with Shakespeare's "airy spirit" – is Ariel. In fact, the episode in which Caliban and Miranda almost engage in sexual contact uncannily echoes the Biblical scene of Man's banishment from the Garden of Eden, with Ariel in the role of the snake. The only difference is that here Ariel interrupts the love game, thus spoiling the chances for a "natural" union between Caliban and Miranda.

Crucial in *Caliban's Hour*, as in *The Tempest*, is the role of Miranda. In Caliban's tale she is made out to be a faithful instrument in the hands of her father, and later in those of Ferdinand, the heir to the patriarchal tradition of Prospero. By telling Miranda his tale, then, Caliban, as the icon of Western modernity's colonized man, is flinging the injustices perpetrated against him in the name of civilization in the very face of that civilization. By doing so, Caliban is also turning the instrument that most contributed to his enslavement against its original owners: language. Yet,

Caliban's feelings toward this same language are deeply ambiguous, as this description of the effect of language upon himself reveals:

> You two [Prospero and Miranda] took my innocence from me. You stole my island, but not merely the physical fact of it. With your words, your names, your ideas, even your very presence, you took the place I had lived all my life and set it somewhere beyond my reach. During the two decades of miserable, solitary exile after you sailed away, the island never again felt like the home it had been. Everything now had a name, and each name was an artefact of Prosper and Miranda. Every place was somewhere we had experienced together, and contained some ghost of your father or you. Even the way I thought about my childhood home was irretrievably changed. You *stole* it from me – damn you, damn you, damn you! You took the only things I possessed – my island, my heart, my life – and sailed away.
> And perhaps cruellest of all, you infected me with speech, then uncaringly left me to live out my life in empty, lonely silence. (169)

Caliban here reveals the same kind of bondage Larry, and Mr Mendoza from *Mrs Caliban* are in: while demoted by Western modernity to less than full citizenship even in their own "country of origin," they still are irrevocably allured by, and enmeshed in that very same modernity. Instrumental in the bond thus created, at least for Caliban, is language. On a more general plane, it is perhaps not too farfetched to read Caliban's words here as a description of what the language of the colonizer means to the colonized, even – or perhaps especially – after the former's departure.

In the telling of his own tale to Miranda, then, it seems as if Caliban fulfils that act of "writing back" to the centre that Ashcroft, Griffiths and Tiffin (1989) see as so essential to post-colonial literature. In *Caliban's Hour* it seems as if Caliban indeed recovers that "subjectivity, language, and history" Gikandi saw Western modernity as robbing its colonized of. Yet, the novel does not end on this triumphant note. At the very moment when Caliban moves to exact the vengeance he announced he would carry out at the very beginning, and prepares to kill Miranda, he is interrupted by Giulietta. Unknown even to her mother, she has been hiding behind a wall-hanging all through Caliban's tale. Moved by his words, she now offers to accompany him to his island, if he lets her mother go. Caliban agrees to the deal, swearing to "treat [Giulietta] with exactly the same respect and kindness and love which [he] showed [Miranda]" (178). He asks Miranda to consider whether, after having heard his tale, she still agrees with her father's initial judgment that Caliban is a "brute" and a "beast" (179), and hence considers herself "guiltless in anything [she] has done to him" (179). If not, he asks her to "give us until the candle burns down to escape" (179). After he has exited, with Giulietta, Miranda "stood a long time watching the curtains billow/around the broken window. At last, the candle failed and the room was dark again" (179-80). Implicitly, then, she belatedly recognizes Caliban as what her daughter has already explicitly named him earlier, i.e. "no monster, but a man" (174).

The same language that sealed Caliban's bondage, then, in *Mrs Caliban* also seems to offer him, and with him modernity, a second chance. Caliban's return to his island with Giulietta would theoretically enable him to do what he claimed he wished he had done in *The Tempest*: "people[...] th[e] island with Calibans," fathered now not upon Miranda, but upon her daughter Giulietta. Perhaps it is not too exaggerated to even hear some echoes here of *Romeo and Juliet*, and to interpret *Caliban's Hour* as a rewrite also of that Shakespeare play, translating the tragic ending to a family "vendetta" pictured by Shakespeare into the happy union of distinct races, and thus enlarging the frame from a provincial Italian town living – and dying – by late medieval rules to the entire globe entering upon modernity. *Caliban's Hour* would then hold a "second chance" for these Shakespeare characters too. However, as with *Mrs Caliban*, this second chance is stillborn. To begin with, if Caliban lives up to his promise to treat Giulietta the same way he had treated Miranda twenty years earlier, this precludes sexual contact, and hence the generation of offspring. Thus, the prospective re-engendering of modernity here projected is annulled from the very outset. Second, after Caliban and Giulietta's departure, life in Naples will presumably go on as before. Of course, there will be the initial shock of Giulietta's abduction, but as the girl herself already indicates at the beginning of the novel, she is in fact expendable. Her parents have two older daughters that have already been married off, strenghtening family connections, and there is a male heir to the throne. In other words: even if temporarily checked, the modernity Ferdinand, as heir to Prospero's male authority, and Miranda, as obedient helpmate to Ferdinand, as before to her father, represent, in the end will not be thrown off course. Ultimately, Miranda's acquiescence to Caliban's request to let him escape will not have amounted to anything more than the assuaging of her own temporarily aroused guilt. To her own defence and solace she can further adduce that Giulietta after all wanted to get out in the world and have her own "life," as the girl calls what her mother had on the island with Prospero, Ariel and Caliban. Finally, should Caliban's return to the island, with Giulietta, prove successful, and their life there harmonious; — should Giulietta in the end even come to love Caliban to the point where sexual union between them would mean no disrespect, and a dynasty of Calibans proceed to rule the island, even then a true recovery of the prelapsarian state of grace and innocence lamented by Caliban in the passage quoted earlier would prove impossible - as Caliban himself fully well knows. In the end, then, the return to the island for Caliban equals at best withdrawal into a reservation. For Miranda, letting her daughter go with Caliban equals vicariously deluding herself into thinking that youth can be recaptured, and life lived over. Either "solution," looking back upon the dawn of modernity, amounts to ineffectual nostalgia, thus creating the effect Fredric Jameson (1991: 20) sees as one of the features characteristic of the intertextuality of "postmodernism" - what I call "central" postmodernism - *Caliban's Hour* partakes of.

IV

Both *Mrs Caliban* and *Caliban's Hour* refigure Caliban as a "man," and reject Western modernity's figuration of him as a "monster." Valorizing precisely that element in Caliban's make-up negatively appraised by modernity - Nature - they reconstitute him as the truly and radically *human* "Other," and at the same time as the repressed "Self," of Western modernity's mechanized and disembodied civilized male. In both novels the occasion for the re-affirmation of this "Other Self" comes about through intervention of that other "Other" to Western modernity's patriarchal authority: woman. Unlike with counter-postmodern rewrites of *The Tempest*, though, this does not lead to Slemon's "positive production of oppositional truth-claims in these texts" (1991: 5). Showing Western modernity as rotten at the core from its very beginning, as in *Caliban's Hour*, or as little better than dead and putrifying at the end of the twentieth century, as in *Mrs Caliban*, these novels, in true "central" postmodern fashion, *de-construct* the discourse of modernity as the West's privilege, but fail to *re-construct* it as a more democratic horizon.

References

Adam, Ian and Helen Tiffin, eds. 1991. *Past the Last Post. Theorizing Post-Colonialism and Post-Modernism*. London: Harvester/Wheatsheaf.

Arnold, A. James, ed. 1994. *A History of Literature in the Caribbean*, 3 Vols., Vol. I. Amsterdam/Philadelphia: John Benjamins.

Ashcroft, Bill, Griffiths, Gareth, and Helen Tiffin. 1989. *The Empire Writes Back. Theory and Practice in Post-Colonial Literatures*. New Accents. London/New York: Routledge.

Auden, W. H. 1976. *Collected Poems*. Ed. Edward Mendelson. London: Faber and Faber.

Barker, Francis and Peter Hulme. 1985. "Nymphs and Reapers Heavily Vanish. The Discursive Con-texts of *The Tempest.*" In Drakakis 1985: 191-205.

Barth, John. 1984. *The Friday Book. Essays and Other Nonfiction*. New York: The Putnam Publishing Group.

Brown, Paul. 1985. "'This Thing of Darkness I Acknowledge Mine.' *The Tempest* and the Discourse of Colonialism." In Dollimore and Sinfield 1985: 48-71.

Césaire, Aimé. 1969. *Une Tempête*. Paris: Seuil.

Dollimore, Jonathan and Alan Sinfield, eds. 1985. *Political Shakespeare: New Essays In Cultural Materialism*. Ithaca and London: Cornell UP.

D'haen, Theo and Hans Bertens, eds. 1994. *Liminal Postmodernisms. The Postmodern, The (Post-) Colonial, and the (Post-)Feminist*. Postmodern Studies 8. Amsterdam/Atlanta GA: Rodopi.

D'haen, Theo. "(Post)Modernity and Caribbean Discourse." Forthcoming in A. James Arnold, ed. *A History of Literature In the Caribbean*, Vol. III. Amsterdam/Philadelphia: John Benjamins.

Drakakis, John, ed. 1985. *Alternative Shakespeares*. London/New York: Routledge.

Eagleton, Terry. 1986. *William Shakespeare*. London: Blackwell.

Gikandi, Simon. 1992. *Writing In Limbo. Modernism and Caribbean Literature*. Ithaca: Cornell UP.

Greenblatt, Stephen. 1988. *Shakespearean Negotiations*. Oxford: Oxford UP.

Hawkes, Terence. 1985. "Swisser-Swatter. Making an English Man of Letters." In Drakakis 1985: 26-46.

Hulme, Peter. 1986. *Colonial Encounters. Europe and the Native Caribbean 1492-1797*. London: Methuen.

Ingalls, Rachel. 1993. *Mrs Caliban and Other Stories*. London/Boston: Faber and Faber – according to my information the title story, novella, or novel was first published in 1982. Vaughan and Vaughan list first date of book publication as 1983.

Jameson, Fredric. 1991. *Postmodernism, Or, The Cultural Logic of Late Capitalism*. Durham: Duke UP.

Kermode, Frank, ed. 1988. *The Arden Edition of the Works of William Shakespeare. The Tempest* [1954]. London/New York: Routledge.

Marshall, Paule. 1983. *Praisesong for the Widow*. New York: Plume.

Naylor, Gloria. 1988. *Mama Day*. London: Hutchinson.

Nixon, Rob. 1987. "Caribbean and African Appropriations of *The Tempest*." *Critical Inquiry* 13: 916-44.

Rushdie, Salman. 1991. *Imaginary Homelands*. London: Granta Books.

Said, Edward. 1993. *Culture and Imperialism*. London: Chatto and Windus.

Slemon, Stephen. 1991. "Modernism's Last Post." In Adam and Tiffin 1991: 1-11.

Vaughan, Alden T. and Virginia Mason Vaughan. 1993. *Shakespeare's Caliban. A Cultural History* [1991], Cambridge: Cambridge UP.

Warner, Marina. 1992. *Indigo*. London: Vintage.

Williams, Tad. 1994. *Caliban's Hour*. London: Legend (Random House UK).

Young, Robert. 1995. *Colonial Desire. Hybridity In Theory, Culture and Race*. London: Routledge.

Zabus, Chantal. 1994. "Prospero's Progeny Curses Back. Postmodern, Postcolonial and Postpatriarchal Rewritings of *The Tempest*." In D'haen and Bertens 1994: 115-38.

THE TEMPEST TRANSPOSED

or CALIBAN ON THE MOORS

C.C. BARFOOT

The lord who lived on top the crag
in the exposed tumult of the north
set forth. Some said to beat the bounds
of his domain to keep intruders
out of its sheltering clefts and vales.
Others that he went to show respect
to aboriginal masters long
pressed to the edges of the sea
where they waited to be shipped abroad.
Whatever was true, Earnshaw (his
ancestral name) was gone but shortly.

When he returned, heavy with fatigue,
Catherine, his daughter, soon inquired
about the gift he had promised
– a whip or magic wand with which
to command her father's realm
when he was gone. Alas, through
accident or design her father
had forgot his daughter's wish,

and instead brought home a dirty,
black-haired child, which set on its feet
could only stare about, repeating
gibberish none could understand –

"As wicked dew as e'er my mother brush'd
With raven's feather from my unwholesome fen
Drop on you both! a south-west blow on ye
And blister you all o'er!" –

over and over again he said,
and other curses too he had,
for this is how folk understood
the creature's babbling prattle,
one "Sycorax," particularly
seemed to epitomize the monster's
deformed roots and nature:
"Sycorax, Sycorax, Sycorax,"
harshly he would sound in the rough
unequal sounds of nature,
"All the charms of Sycorax, toads,
beetles, bats, light on you!" The
maledictions on his lips
expressed the dark scowl in his heart:
with infections, diseases, bites
pricks, he inflicted himself
and smelt like a fish.

                        But, strange to tell,
Cathy grew fond of him, which is to say,
the untamed girl, who freely roamed
the moors about her father's dwelling,
with its narrow openings to light
and dark, its corners of sharpening
shadows and chill winds, Catherine
who sought the freedom of the heath
and enjoyed the fierce rough heat of bare
rocks; this Catherine, tumbling

towards womanhood, found in Heathcliff –
named in honour of the landscape –
a companion to challenge
and to comfort her.

                  She sensed his burly
figure would follow her father
when he succumbed to his anger
that drove him to wreckage and revenge,
and help to hold the wild domain
with grit and ardour. Times there were
she thought that Heathcliff made her whole,
even consumed her. Confiding
once to Ariel, she said "My love
for Heathcliff resembles the eternal
rocks beneath – a source of little
visible delight, but necessary. Nelly,"
(the name she gave her garrulous maid
to drag her down to earth) "I *am*
Heathcliff – he's always, always in my mind
– not as a pleasure, any more than I am
always a pleasure to myself – but as
my own being ...." Indeed, so strong she felt
she never thought it would be possible
ever to live without him. Hence
the name she reserved for one who
threatened to devour her, "Caliban."

But part of her still answered
to that fond name her father used,
Miranda, "Daddy's little wonder child";
and then she understood that embracing
Heathcliff, surrendering herself
to Caliban, she was breaching
an injunction of the lord,
her father. She dreamed she heard him
tell her of his past, of his doubtful
friends and certain enemies who

had called him "Prospero" in mockery
of his exile; that truly once
he had ruled a paradise,
which through neglect he'd surrendered
to the devil, his brother. One
day he hoped to regain this lost
land, which might be done were his daughter
to make a worthy match to lift
father and daughter from off these
bleak heights and once more land them
amongst the comforts he had known.
So day and night Earnshaw studied
the workings of chance and fortune,
endeavouring to snatch the secrets
of the elements and providence
out of the air, for which he employed
Joseph; a wild natural,
forever raving and raging
with admonitions and prophecies.

Therefore had Miranda realized
her father would not welcome
Heathcliff as her mate; indeed would be
enraged were he to discover
her fantasies. The Baron himself
had taken on the education
of her Caliban, chiefly to ease
the pain his gibberish caused.
The Baron, discovered in the brat
he had saved from the streets,
or transportation as a slave,
an aboriginal of the place
– "Sycorax" he came to realize
was the rascal's cry for his mother –
and though they too had been invaders,
he felt sufficient pang of conscience
to recognize the claim; should he

ever return to his own land,
he might be ready to return
the Heights to Heathcliff, even though
he knew that Ariel stood in thrall
of Heathcliff, just as Jane, her
cousin Eyre, was soon to be plunged
and joined with the burnt-out shell
and gulf of Rochester. But
teaching Heathcliff the colonial
tongue enlarged the ruler's pain
since now the cur was all the better
able to curse.

          Earnshaw grew impatient
with mysteries still held from him;
hence he planned to command Lockwood
from the easy south, a cultivated
squire, whose name signalled
exclusion from the cerebral
delights, whom, the Baron trusted
to provoke both Joseph and Ariel
into revelations of the
spiritual air and mystic ground
of the estate. He trusted such relief
would come before he was forced to break
his rod and bury in his coffin
the great book where he had scribbled
the first steps of his partial knowledge.

But, before summoning Lockwood
Baron Earnshaw made one last bid
to lure into his grasp the tools
of his first fall. The trap he set
was conjured up in a sheltered
corner of his estate, a splendid house
carpeted with crimson, and crimson-covered
chairs and tables, a pure white ceiling
bordered by gold, a shower of glass-drops

hanging in silver chains from the centre,
and shimmering with little soft tapers.
This mirage, Thrushcroft Grange, at a word
could be evoked and banished, and yet
sufficient to entice tired travellers
caught in the storms around the Heights
and seeking refuge in the vale.

The day of vengeance duly came,
when Prospero's former friends and family
who had pushed him with his babe
to the glowering north, much off course,
were on their way home from the wedding
of the King's fair daughter Claribel
to the King of Tunis. A violent
thunderstorm split the party, travelling
in different coaches. The younger
ones found their way to the Grange,
where, Catherine and Heathcliff
having run down from the Heights
at the first crack of thunder,
lurked in the park. Drawn by the lights
of the drawing-room, and planted
on a flower-pot, Cathy and Caliban
stared through the window.
The youngsters within, already scared
by their mishaps, hoped it was their elders:
the young girl stopped screaming and the boy
standing on the hearth stopped crying too.
But then they saw the startling face
of Heathcliff staring in, and took such fright
they set the bulldog on them. Heathcliff
ran away, but Cathy's ankle was seized
by the dog, and wounded, she was carried
into the house. And that is how
Cathy met Edgar, her fairy-tale
Ferdinand as she called him, bringing to mind

another Edgar of an even bleaker
family tale her father told her,
of madness and blindness in times gone by.
When first he saw her, Ferdinand blushed,
one minute lamenting the king
his father's death in the floods
of the moors, the next gazing
upon this wondrous maiden,
his goddess. Miranda, too,
thought him divine, for never had she
beheld a youth more noble.

                         Heathcliff
rambling in the night, fell on his face
to avoid discovery by Trinculo,
one of missing servants, even more scared
than Heathcliff, speculating what
sort of corpse this might be with the fishy
smell. Shaken by another lightning
flash and roll of thunder, Trinculo
threw himself under Heathcliff's cloak,
transmogrified to a monster with two heads.
Against another figure lurching
drunkenly out of the thunder,
bawling a song, cried Heathcliff
in deep fright, "Do not torment me:–
O!" The servant, Stephano, drunk
on liquor salvaged from the wreck,
was amazed to discover the monster
with four legs. Six tipsy legs
began in darkness first to reel
and then to sprawl, sensing murkily
that when restored from their drunken slumbers,
even years hence, they'd have strength
to bring their masters down.

                         Heathcliff
returned from outer darkness

when Cathy was wed; after torment
and excessive lamentation, she was dead.
Here the comedy of the moors,
the tale of exile that should traject
a course from retribution to mercy
and pardon, the form of true Romance,
late, last, but never swerving,
always serving, Romance, is obstructed
by further manipulations
of marriage, cruelty, murder, and revenge.
Near twenty years of terror passed
in two hours traffic of the stage,
time disjointed, foreshortened, disrupted
by narrative craft. Prospero's
dream of retribution is melted
into thin air, disturbed with infirmity,
rounded in a sleep, and transferred to Caliban.
Heathcliff haunted, as even bumbling
Lockwood, lately come, perceives,
seizing an ice-cold hand at the window
– "Let me in – let me in," rubbing the wrist
on the broken pane till the blood
ran down and soaked the bedclothes.

Earnshaw and his misbegotten
relatives, the godly ranting
Joseph, the goodly Gonzalo,
the unrepenting Antonio,
Alonso and Sebastian
all weary of August, are harvested,
foison plenty in these old myths
of island and moor, of exiled
dukes, and of slaves in their nightmares
fulfilling the justified vengeances
of kings: "this thing of darkness I
acknowledge mine."

The new young
succeed to learn to read aright
the lessons of their tribal wrongs.
While others swear that Caliban *walks*
consumed with Cathy and wonder
"under t' Nab," others cling
to the fantasy of a benign sky,
moths fluttering among the heath
and harebells; the soft wind
breathing through the grass;
calm seas, auspicious gales, all crimes
pardoned, by indulgence set free.
Not only Lockwood left wondering
how any could imagine unquiet slumbers,
for the sleepers in the quiet earth;
but still we return to confusions
of old crimes, calculated malice,
chance injustices, blundering revenge,
and consoling conclusions of happiness
ever after in stories told long ago.

Notes on Contributors

James Arnold (1939) is Professor of French at the University of Virginia. He authored a critical study of the French-Caribbean writer Aimé Césaire, *Modernism and Negritude. The Poetry and Poetics of Aimé Césaire*, and edited the same writer's *Lyric and Dramatic Poetry, 1946-1982*. Most recently, he has edited *Monsters, Tricksters, and Sacred Cows. Animal Tales and American Identities*, as well as a three-volume *History of Literature in the Caribbean* under the aegis of the International Comparative Literature Association. He is founding editor of *CARAF* books and serves as editor of *New World Studies*, two series published by the University Press of Virginia. He is on the advisory board of the *New West Indian Guide*.

Barbara Baert (1967) prepares a Ph.D. dissertation on the iconography of the Cross-Legend in the Middle Ages at the Catholic University of Leuven, Belgium. She has published on the cult of mountains, trees and the Wood of the Cross. She became a Laureate of the Royal Academy of Belgium, Division of Fine Arts, with a study on the fifteenth-century illustrated incunable "Het Boec van den Houte" (The Book of the Wood of the Cross).

Cedric C. Barfoot (1937), English Department, Leiden University, published *The Thread of Connection. Aspects of Fate in the Novels of Jane Austen and Others* (1982); has most recently edited *In Black and Gold. Contiguous Traditions in Post-War British and Irish Poetry* (1994), and *Ritual Remembering. History, Myth and Politics in Anglo-Irish Drama* (1995).

Dirk Delabastita (1960) teaches English and General Literature at the University of Namur, Belgium. He published a book on the translation of Shakespeare's wordplay (*There's a Double Tongue*, 1993) and co-edited a volume on Shakespeare translations in the romantic age (*European Shakespeares*, 1993, with Lieven D'hulst). He has edited two volumes on the theme of wordplay and translation, one of these a special issue of *The*

Translator (1996), the other *Traductio. Essays on punning and translation* (1997).

Maarten van Delden (1958) is Assistant Professor of Spanish and Portuguese and Comparative Literature at New York University. He has recently completed a book on Carlos Fuentes (to be published with Vanderbilt University Press in 1997) and is editor of a special issue of *Annals of Scholarship on Latin American Intellectuals*. He is currently at work on a study of the cultural and political debate in Mexico in the 1960s and 70s.

Theo D'haen (1950) is Professor of English and American Literature at Leiden University, The Netherlands. He has published widely on modern European languages and literatures.

Kevin Dwyer (1960) holds a Ph.D. in Film Studies from the University of Warwick, U.K. His dissertation was entitled "On a Celluloid Platter. An Analysis of the Representations and Functions of Food in the Cinema".

Paul Franssen (1955) lectures in British Literature at the English Department of the University of Utrecht, The Netherlands. His 1987 dissertation was concerned with the Mystic Winepress in English Poetry, 1500-1700. He has published recently on Sterne, Marvell, Shakespeare, Herbert and Donne, and is currently co-editing a volume on "The Author as Character".

Koenraad Geldof (1963) teaches French literature of the twentieth-century and French literary theory at the Catholic University of Leuven. His publications include *La voix et l'événement* (1993) and *Analytiques du sens* (1996). He is co-editor of a book on Michel de Certeau (*Sluipwegen van het denken*, 1996).

Ortwin de Graef (1963) is Research Associate with the Belgian National Fund for Scientific Research and teaches 19th-century British literature and literary theory at the Catholic University of Leuven. He is the author of two books on Paul de Man (*Serenity in Crisis*, 1993, and *Titanic Light*, 1995) and of essays on, among others, Edgar Allan Poe, Ernst Jünger, William Wordsworth, Matthew Arnold, Jacques Derrida, Alfred Tennyson, Charles Taylor, Jon Elster and Henry Rollins.

Nadia Lie (1964) teaches Romance Literatures at the Catholic University of Leuven. She co-edited *Literatura y Poder* (1995) and published a book on the cultural discourse of the Cuban Revolution (*Transición y Transacción*, 1996).

Bart Philipsen (1961) studied in Leuven and Freiburg i. Br. (Germany). He holds a position of researcher with the Belgian National Fund for Scientific Research and teaches German Literature at the Catholic University of Leuven. He published a book on Hölderlin (*Die List der Einfalt*, 1995) and is currently preparing a study on Tragedy and (Post-) Modernity (Sophocles, Hölderlin, Brecht, Müller).

Jürgen Pieters (1969) prepares a doctoral dissertation on the work of Stephen Greenblatt at the University of Ghent, Belgium. He has a position as researcher with the Belgian National Fund for Scientific Research. Publications include essays on I.A. Richards and S.T. Coleridge, and a review-essay of Edward Said's *Culture and Imperialism*.

Hedwig Schwall (1956) teaches German Languages and Literatures in Brussels and at the Catholic University of Leuven. She did a Ph.D. on "Theatricality in W.B. Yeats," and is currently doing research on psychoanalytic methods - mainly those of Freud and Lacan - with which to analyse literature. Publications include articles on Yeats, Heaney, Rilke, Hofmannsthal and German Expressionism. She also published a study on Rilke and Cézanne.

Herman Servotte (1929) was professor of English Literature in the Catholic University of Leuven from 1962 until his retirement in 1994. He has always been interested in contemporary poetry and fiction, especially if they have something to do with theology, and in the theory of literature. His latest publications include *Stem en visioen* (1992), a series of essays about the disappearance of God, an annotated translation (W.H. Auden, *De zee en de spiegel*, 1993), and *According to John* (1994), a literary reading of the fourth gospel.

Kristine Vanden Berghe (1965) teaches Romance Languages in Antwerp and at the Catholic University of Leuven. She obtained an M.A. degree in Latin American Literature at the U.N.A.M. in Mexico City, and a Ph.D. at the Catholic University of Leuven with a dissertation about the

Brazilian review *Cadernos Brasileiros* (to be published as *Intelectuales y anticomunismo*). Her current research interests include the sociology of intellectuals in Latin America, and Latin American literature in general.

Georgi Verbeeck (1961) studied History and Philosophy at the Catholic University of Leuven. He was a Research Fellow at the Institut für Europäische Geschichte in Mainz and the Russian and East European Center of the University of Illinois at Urbana-Champaign. He published a book on the historiography of fascism in the former German Democratic Republic (*Geschiedschrijving en politieke cultuur*, 1992) and currently works as a Senior Research Fellow of the Belgian National Fund for Scientific Research at the History Department of the University of Leuven.

Tim Youngs (1961) is Senior Lecturer in English at The Nottingham Trent University. He is the author of *Travellers in Africa. British Travelogues 1850-1900* (1994), and the editor of *Writing and Race*, to be published in 1997. He currently works on a study of travels in late nineteenth-century fiction.

Chantal Zabus (1955) is Professor of English and American Studies at the Université catholique de Louvain at Louvain-la-Neuve, Belgium. Her publications include *The African Palimpsest* (1991) and she currently works on a book on Postcolonial, Postmodern and Postpatriarchal Rewritings of *The Tempest*.

Index

Vaughan, A.T. & V. Mason
  Vaughan, i, 4, 22, 24, 26, 27,
  29, 30, 32, 42, 43, 44, 50, 53,
  55, 56, 59, 112, 130, 131, 135,
  142, 146, 161, 176, 182, 185,
  192, 198, 217, 218, 222, 229,
  250, 254, 266, 270, 273, 289,
  297, 311, 313, 319, 324, 330
Venmans, P., 245
Verbeeck, G., ii, 174, 180, 182
Vinci, L. da, 281
Viollis, A., 107
Volkov, S., 170, 183
Voltaire, 106

Wanckel, C.O., 59
Warner, M., 318, 331
Watteau, 296, 299
Wedgwood, J., 139
Welch, E., 280
Welles, O., 276
Wells, S., 26, 37, 42, 50, 54, 59
Wenzel, G., 164, 183
Whatley, J., 72, 79
White, H., 59
White, J., 56, 58, 285
Whitsun, 47
Wilberforce, B.S., 123
Wilcox, T., 211, 275, 284
Wilde, O., 176
Williams, H., 276
Williams, P., 247, 258, 270
Williams, Raymond, 64
Williams, Rosalind., 226, 229
Williams, T., i, 313-324, 331
Wilson, D., 4, 18, 21, 131, 282
Wittgenstein, L., 291

Wittkower, R., 59
Woolford, J., 129, 142
Wordsworth, W., 113-120, 122,
  124, 137, 138, 140, 141, 143

Yeats, W.B., 204
Young, R., 316, 331

Zabus, Ch., ii, 289, 331
Zainer, G., 48
Zizek, S., 69, 79
Zum Felde, A., 156, 161
Zweig, A., i, 163-183

LIBRARY, UNIVERSITY COLLEGE CHESTER